NOVELL'S

Dictionary of Networking

NOVELL'S

Dictionary of Networking

KEVIN SHAFER

Novell.
PRESS

Novell Press, San Jose

Novell's Dictionary of Networking
Published by
Novell Press
2180 Fortune Drive
San Jose, CA 95131

Library of Congress Catalog Card No.: 97-74810

ISBN: 0-7645-4528-0

Printed in the United States of America

10 9 8 7 6 5 4 3 2 1

2E/QW/RQ/ZX/FC

Distributed in the United States by IDG Books Worldwide, Inc.

Distributed by Macmillan Canada for Canada; by Transworld Publishers Limited in the United Kingdom; by IDG Norge Books for Norway; by IDG Sweden Books for Sweden; by Woodslane Pty. Ltd. for Australia; by Woodslane Enterprises Ltd. for New Zealand; by Longman Singapore Publishers Ltd. for Singapore, Malaysia, Thailand, and Indonesia; by Simron Pty. Ltd. for South Africa; by Toppan Company Ltd. for Japan; by Distribuidora Cuspide for Argentina; by Livraria Cultura for Brazil; by Ediciencia S.A. for Ecuador; by Addison-Wesley Publishing Company for Korea; by Ediciones ZETA S.C.R. Ltda. for Peru; by WS Computer Publishing Corporation, Inc., for the Philippines; by Unalis Corporation for Taiwan; by Contemporanea de Ediciones for Venezuela; by Computer Book & Magazine Store for Puerto Rico; by Express Computer Distributors for the Caribbean and West Indies. Authorized Sales Agent: Anthony Rudkin Associates for the Middle East and North Africa.

For general information on IDG Books Worldwide's books in the U.S., please call our Consumer Customer Service department at 800-762-2974. For reseller information, including discounts and premium sales, please call our Reseller Customer Service department at 800-434-3422.

For information on where to purchase IDG Books Worldwide's books outside the U.S., please contact our International Sales department at 415-655-3200 or fax 415-655-3295.

For information on foreign language translations, please contact our Foreign & Subsidiary Rights department at 415-655-3021 or fax 415-655-3281.

For sales inquiries and special prices for bulk quantities, please contact our Sales department at 415-655-3200 or write to the address above.

For information on using IDG Books Worldwide's books in the classroom or for ordering examination copies, please contact our Educational Sales department at 800-434-2086 or fax 817-251-8174.

For press review copies, author interviews, or other publicity information, please contact our Public Relations department at 415-655-3000 or fax 415-655-3299.

For authorization to photocopy items for corporate, personal, or educational use, please contact Copyright Clearance Center, 222 Rosewood Drive, Danvers, MA 01923, or fax 508-750-4470.

For general information on Novell Press books in the U.S., including information on discounts and premiums, contact IDG Books at 800-434-3422 or 415-655-3200. For information on where to purchase Novell Press books outside the U.S., contact IDG Books International at 415-655-3021 or fax 415-655-3295.

John Kilcullen, *CEO, IDG Books Worldwide, Inc.*
Steven Berkowitz, *President, IDG Books Worldwide, Inc.*
Brenda McLaughlin, *Senior Vice President & Group Publisher, IDG Books Worldwide, Inc.*
The IDG Books Worldwide logo is a trademark under exclusive license to IDG Books Worldwide, Inc., from International Data Group, Inc.

KC Sue, *Publisher, Novell Press, Inc.*
Novell Press and the Novell Press logo are trademarks of Novell, Inc.

Welcome to Novell Press

Novell Press, the world's leading provider of networking books, is the premier source for the most timely and useful information in the networking industry. Novell Press books cover fundamental networking issues as they emerge—from today's Novell and third-party products, to the concepts and strategies that will guide the industry's future. The result is a broad spectrum of titles for the benefit of those involved in networking at any level: end user, department administrator, developer, systems manager, or network architect.

Novell Press books are written by experts with the full participation of Novell's technical, managerial, and marketing staff. The books are exhaustively reviewed by Novell's own technicians and are published only on the basis of final released software, never on prereleased versions.

Novell Press at IDG is an exciting partnership between two companies at the forefront of the information and communications revolution. The Press is implementing an ambitious publishing program to develop new networking titles centered on the current version of IntranetWare, GroupWise and Novell's ManageWise products. Select Novell Press books are translated into 14 languages and are available at bookstores around the world.

KC Sue, Publisher, Novell Press, Inc.

Novell Press

Publisher
KC Sue

Events and Publicity
Lois Dudley

Acquisitions Editor
Jim Sumser

Development Editor
Ron Hull

Technical Editor
Ken Neff

Copy Editor
Marcia Baker

Production Coordinator
Tom Debolski

Graphics and Production Specialists
Renée Dunn
Stephanie Hollier
Kurt Krames

Quality Control Specialist
Mick Arellano

Proofreader
Sharon Duffy

Cover Photographer
©Daryl Solomon/Photonica

About the Author

Kevin Shafer of Pleasant Hill, California, has been a reporter and columnist for a midwestern newspaper, a technical editor for the Department of Defense, a managing editor/senior editor for Osborne/McGraw-Hill, and, most recently, a freelance development editor and copy editor for IDG Books Worldwide.

To Dori and Alicia

Preface

Ironic as this may seem, communication in the realm of computer network communications can seem like a foreign language, consisting of a scrambled potpourri of terms and concepts intermingled with abbreviations and acronyms. The result can often lead to an alphabet soup simmered into a stew of seemingly nonsensical vernacular that only the most technically oriented can discern.

Computer dictionaries and glossaries abound on bookstore shelves and on a plethora of Web sites across the Internet. Most of these, however, are too general to be an effective resource for anyone venturing into the world of networking. While many of these references address computing in the most general of terms, *Novell's Dictionary of Networking* concentrates on the terms and concepts bandied about in networking circles, even as it still provides information about the general genre of computing.

About This Book

This valuable reference source is designed as a concise, handy tool for computer users of all levels of experience, whether you are the administrator of a network encompassing the world or simply the head of a household with computer access to the Internet. This book clarifies the concepts, identifies the technology, and untangles the World Wide Web.

Throughout this book, you will find information to expand your knowledge and understanding of the world of network computing. The following topics provide a brief overview of what you will find in this book:

- Acronyms and abbreviations
- Connectivity tools and equipment
- Electrical and electronic terms and concepts
- Electronic mail (e-mail)
- File systems and system architectures
- Hardware cables, cards, connectors, memory, and more
- Industry standards
- Macintosh products
- Measurement systems
- NetWare and IntranetWare file attributes
- NetWare and IntranetWare file-access and directory-access rights

- Novell Directory Services (NDS) objects and properties
- Novell products
- Operating systems such as DOS, OS/2, UNIX, and Windows
- OSI Reference Model
- Protocols and interfaces
- Security
- Systems Network Architecture (SNA) communication architecture
- Software applications
- Storage media
- Varieties of networks, including ARCnet, ATM, Banyan VINES, DECnet, Token Ring, and others
- World Wide Web (WWW)

Novell's Dictionary of Networking is a valuable resource because it saves time by compiling a rich collection of information all in one source, with thousands of entries encompassing a complete cross section of network computing.

How This Book Is Organized

Entries appear in alphabetical order throughout this book. A concise explanation follows each entry. To supplement its comprehensive coverage, *Novell's Dictionary of Networking* is designed to be an appropriate resource for users of all experience levels:

- Spelled-out headings for terms include any acronyms in parentheses.
- Because nouns used as adjectives often pile up rapidly in technical terminology, this reference uses punctuation that is more compatible with "Standard English" than is customary in the industry—notably hyphenation to link important pairs of words. Although old hands may find the results a little odd (for example, *File-Allocation Table* or *network-control program*), new users may find the meaning more immediately clear and the learning curve a little flatter.
- Network veterans to whom such strings as *Systems Network Architecture message vector data segment* are utterly transparent will be pleased to find the traditional order of the words remains intact for every term.

For an even more extensive coverage of networking concepts and terminology, see *Novell's Encyclopedia of Networking*, also from Novell Press.

Acknowledgments

This book would not have been possible without the dedicated efforts of many people. Thanks to Dan Blacharski, whose valuable talents, expertise, and input kept the project on schedule. At IDG Books Worldwide, special thanks to Jim Sumser, acquisitions editor, for granting the opportunity to tackle this huge project; to Ron Hull, development editor, kudos for keeping track of this complex process; and to Marcia Baker, senior copy editor, congratulations for adding the professional polish to what must have seemed like a never-ending manuscript. Thanks also go to the folks at Novell, including Ken Neff for his technical review of the material, as well as Lois Dudley, KC Sue, and Robin Wheatley for their continuing support.

Contents

Symbols
and Numbers

* (asterisk)

Used as a wildcard character in most operating systems. The asterisk represents one or more characters in a filename or extension, and may be used in searching or in file operations.

@ ("at" sign)

A symbol typically used in spreadsheet formulas and e-mail addresses. When used in an e-mail address, it follows the username, as in user@company.com.

\ (backslash)

A character used in some operating systems (such as DOS and NetWare) to separate directory and/or path names in a path statement. When used in some programming languages, the backslash is used to indicate that the character following it is an "escape" code.

// (double slash)

A character used to separate the transport protocol from an Internet address (for example, http://www.novell.com).

μ (mu)

Used to abbreviate the prefix "micro," meaning 2^{20}, or one-millionth.

. and .. (period and double period)

Characters used in some operating systems to refer to the current and parent directories in a hierarchical directory system.

? (question mark)

A character used in some operating systems as a wildcard character that represents a single character in a file or directory name.

/ (slash)

A character used in some operating systems (such as UNIX) to separate directory and/or path names in a path statement. In other operating systems (such as DOS or NetWare), the slash is used to separate command line switches.

1Base5

An Institute of Electrical and Electronic Engineers (IEEE) 802.3 specification for an Ethernet network operating at 1Mbps. A 1Base5 network uses unshielded twisted-pair (UTP) cabling, uses a physical bus and attaches nodes to a common cable.

4B/5B encoding

A data translation scheme that precedes signal encoding in Fiber Distributed Data Interface (FDDI) networks. Under this construct, each group of four bits is represented as a 5-bit symbol, which is then associated with a bit pattern. The bit pattern is then encoded using the Non-Return to Zero Inverted (NRZI) method, making further electrical encoding more efficient.

5B/6B encoding

A data translation scheme that precedes signal encoding in 100BaseVG networks. Under this construct, each group of 5 bits is represented as a 6-bit symbol, which is then associated with a bit pattern. The bit pattern is then encoded using the nonreturn to zero (NRZ) method, making further electrical encoding more efficient.

8B/10B encoding

A data translation scheme that is based on 4B/5B encoding and is used to re-code 8-bit patterns into 10-bit symbols.

9-track tape

A tape storage format using nine parallel tracks on half-inch magnetic tape. Eight of the tracks are used for data; the ninth is used for parity information.

10Base2

An Institute of Electrical and Electronic Engineers (IEEE) 802.3 specification for Ethernet networks using thin coaxial cable. This specification is often used for small local area networks (LANs), and offers a throughput of up to 10 megabits per second (Mbps). 10Base2 can support a cable segment as long as 300 meters (about 1,000 feet).

Synonym: *ThinNet*

10Base5

An Institute of Electrical and Electronic Engineers (IEEE) 802.3 specification for Ethernet networks using thick coaxial cable. This specification can accommodate a larger local area network (LAN) diameter than 10Base2 and offers a throughput of up to 10 megabits per second (Mbps). 10Base5 can support a cable segment as long as 1,000 meters (about 3,300 feet).

Synonym: *ThickNet*

10BaseF

An Institute of Electrical and Electronic Engineers (IEEE 802.3) specification for Ethernet networks using fiber-optic cable. This specification offers a throughput of up to 10Mbps and is divided into the following three subcategories:

- *10BaseFP (fiber passive)*. Used for desktop connections.
- *10BaseFL (fiber link)*. Used for intermediate hubs and workgroups.
- *10BaseFB (fiber backbone)*. Used for links between buildings.

10BaseT

An Institute of Electrical and Electronic Engineers (IEEE) 802.3 specification for Ethernet networks using unshielded twisted-pair (UTP) wiring. This method of wiring provides the network with 10Mbps of bandwidth and typically uses a star topology.

10Basex

A generic designation used to refer to the various types of baseband Ethernet networks.

10Broad36

An Institute of Electrical and Electronic Engineers (IEEE) 802.3 specification for broadband Ethernet networks using 75-ohm coaxial cable and a bus or tree topology. 10Broad36 networks offer throughput of up to 10 megabits per second (Mbps), and can support cable segments as long as 1,800 meters (about 5,900 feet).

10-tape rotation method

A method of tape rotation that uses 10 tape sets, with each tape set being used for equal time slots over a period of 40 weeks.

100BaseFX

A specification of 100BaseT (Fast Ethernet) that supports two-strand fiber-optic cable.

100BaseT

An Institute of Electrical and Electronic Engineers (IEEE) 802.3 specification for a 100Mbps Ethernet networks that retains Carrier Sense Multiple Access/Collision Detection (CSMA/CD), supports CAT-3 or CAT-4 cables, and restricts the length of the network to about 10 percent of that for an ordinary Ethernet network.

Synonym: *Fast Ethernet*

100BaseT4

A specification of 100BaseT (Fast Ethernet) that supports CAT-3 , CAT-4, or CAT-5 unshielded twisted-pair (UTP) cabling. 100BaseT4 requires four pairs of wires.

100BaseTX

A specification of 100BaseT (Fast Ethernet) that supports CAT-5 unshielded twisted-pair (UTP) and shielded twisted-pair (STP) cabling. 100BaseTX requires two pairs of wires.

100BaseVG

An Institute of Electrical and Electronic Engineers (IEEE) 802.12 specification that supports 100Mbps transmission over CAT-3 Unshielded Twisted Pair (UTP) cabling. 100Base VG supports a demand priority scheme to give priority to data packets over the network and guarantees all stations equal access to the network.

100BaseVG/AnyLAN

Hewlett-Packard's proprietary extension of the 100BaseVG standard, which is represented by the Institute of Electrical and Electronic Engineers (IEEE) 802.12 specification. Although similar to Ethernet, it cannot be truly called Ethernet because it does not use the Carrier Sense Multiple Access/Collision Detection (CSMA/CD) protocol. This architecture supports 100Mbps transmission over CAT-3 unshielded twisted-pair (UTP) cabling.

100BaseX

A generic term used to refer to the various types of Fast Ethernet networks.

802.x

The entire set of Institute of Electrical and Electronic Engineers (IEEE) 802 standards. Some of the most common include the following:

- *802.1.* Defines general local area network (LAN) architecture, internetworking, and network management at the hardware level.

- *802.2.* Defines the Logical Link Control (LLC) Layer for a Carrier Sense Multiple Access/Collision Detection (CSMA/CD) bus network.

- *802.3.* Defines the Media Access Control (MAC) Layer for a Carrier Sense Multiple Access/Collision Detection (CSMA/CD) bus network.

- *802.4.* Defines the Media Access Control (MAC) Layer for a token-passing bus network.

- *802.5.* Defines the Media Access Control (MAC) Layer for a token-passing ring network.

- *802.6.* Defines a metropolitan area network (MAN) based on a 30-mile long fiber-optic ring.

- *802.7.* A Technical Advisory Group (TAG) report on broadband networks.

- *802.8.* A Technical Advisory Group (TAG) report on fiber-optic networks.

- *802.9.* Defines integration of voice and data.

- *802.11.* A working group concerned with establishing wireless network standards.

3270

A family of IBM workstations and printers used with IBM mainframes. These devices rely on either Synchronous Data Link Control (SDLC) or Binary Synchronous Control (BSC) to communicate with the mainframe host. In Systems Network Architecture (SNA) terms, the 3270 devices are defined as Logical Unit (LU) Types 2 (3270 workstations) and Type 3 (3270 printers).

80 × 86

A family of Intel microprocessors found in early personal computers. Some of the most common include the following:

- ▸ *8086.* The main chip used in the original IBM PC and XT machines.
- ▸ *80286.* The 16-bit successor to the 8086 chip. The 80286 chip was used in the IBM AT machine and will run at speeds of 6MHz to 16MHz. Computers running the 80286 chip were limited to memory segments of 64K and could not access more than 1MB of memory.
- ▸ *80386DX.* The third-generation 32-bit microprocessor. The chip can run at clock speeds of up to 33MHz. Computers based on the 80386 chip overcame many of the limitations of the 80286 and could address as much as 4GB of physical memory and 64TB of virtual memory.
- ▸ *80386SX.* A low-end 80386 microprocessor whose external data bus was only 16 bits instead of 32 bits.
- ▸ *80486DX.* The successor to the 80386 microprocessor. With 1,185,000 transistors and clock speeds of up to 50MHz, it could process as many as 41 million instructions per second.
- ▸ *80486DX2.* A high-performance overdrive microprocessor for use with systems using 20MHz bus structures.
- ▸ *80486SL.* A low-end version of the 80486 microprocessor. The 80486SL included features for power management and was often used in portable computers.
- ▸ *80486SX.* A 80486 microprocessor with no math coprocessor.

80 × 87

A family of Intel coprocessors found in early personal computers. Some of the most common include the following:

- ▸ *80387.* A floating point coprocessor designed to be used with the 80386 computers.
- ▸ *80487.* A floating-point coprocessor designed to be used with the 80486SX microprocessor. The 80486 microprocessor includes an integrated coprocessor, making the 80487 unnecessary.
- ▸ *80387SX.* A floating point coprocessor designed to be used with the 80386SX computers.

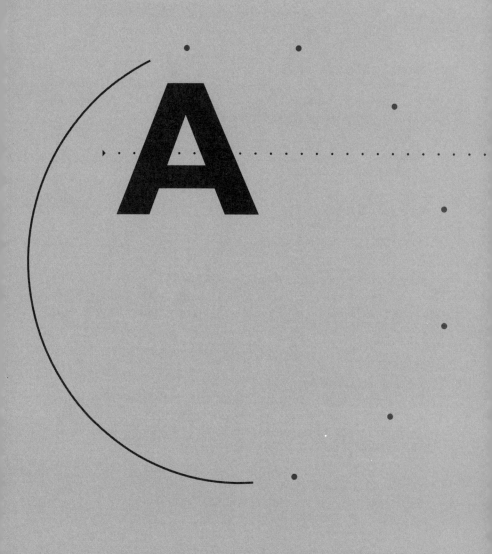

abandon

To cancel or revoke a task. Dialog boxes will often give the user a choice of either accepting or abandoning input or configuration changes.

abnormal end (abend)

An operating system message issued when a serious problem is detected, such as a hardware or software failure. An abend will typically stop the computer from proceeding with the program.

abort

To cease a task in progress.

Abstract Syntax

A machine-independent set of language constructs and rules used to describe objects, protocols, and other items.

Abstract Syntax Notation One (ASN.1)

A machine-independent, abstract syntax developed as part of the OSI Reference Model. ASN.1 is used to describe data structures and functions as a common syntax for sending data between two end systems that use different encoding systems.

Accelerated mode

A file open mode that appeared in Btrieve prior to the release of Version 6.x, which improved response time when updating files. Performance improvements to the Normal open mode in NetWare Btrieve Version 6.x made the old Accelerated mode obsolete.

accelerator board

An add-in board used to replace the main processor with one of higher performance.

Acceptable Use Policy (AUP)

A statement or set of rules that limit how a network or computer service is used.

access

To retrieve data from a storage device, or to log in to a computer system.

access control

A process that limits access to objects, files, or directories. The control is typically achieved through passwords, the granting of privileges, or the setting of attributes. The operating system uses access control to determine how users, groups of users, or resources can interact with the operating system, files, directories, and network resources. The level of access control is typically assigned by the network administrator.

Also used to denote a field in a Token Ring token or data frame.

access control list (ACL)

A list of available services and information, about which users and devices may access those services. In Novell Directory Services (NDS), ACL is an object property that contains a list of information about which users or devices can access a particular object. A user must have the appropriate property right to modify an ACL for an object.

Access Control right

One of the NetWare trustee rights that grants a user access to a file or directory. A NetWare or IntranetWare user with Access Control rights can change the trustee assignments and Inherited Rights Filter (IRF) of a directory or file.

access method

A technique for moving data between main storage and an I/O device. In a Systems Network Architecture (SNA) environment, the access method is the software used to control the network's information flow. This term also denotes a method — such as Token Ring or Carrier Sense Multiple Access/Collision Detection (CSMA/CD) — that regulates how, and in what order, a network's nodes may access its transmission media.

access network

A smaller network attached to a backbone network trunk by a gateway or router.

access protocol

A set of rules used by workstations to avoid collisions when transmitting data over the network.

access rate (AR)

A physical rate in a Frame Relay network that indicates the access of the user channel in bits per second (bps).

access rights

Properties that specify the use of, or access to, particular objects, files, or directories. Access rights may also limit what each user can do with any given resource. A resource may be configured with default access rights, although these rights can be overridden by additional access rights granted to a specified user. Access rights are system-dependent, with each different operating environment using its own nomenclature to denote different access rights. Table A.1 lists the access rights available in IntranetWare, as well as the classification of the rights.

TABLE A.1	*IntranetWare Access Rights*		

RIGHT	DIRECTORY	FILE	OBJECT	PROPERTY
Access Control	X	X		
Add Self				X
Browse			X	
Compare				X
Create	X	X	X	
Delete			X	
Delete Self				X
Erase	X	X		
File Scan	X	X		

RIGHT	DIRECTORY	FILE	OBJECT	PROPERTY
Modify	X	X		
Read Property				X
Read	X	X		X
Rename Object				
Rename			X	
Supervisor	X	X	X	X
Write	X	X		X

Synonyms: *access privileges; trustee rights*

access server

A central computer used for granting access to remote users who connect to the network via modem and for providing users with access to network resources, as if they were directly attached to the network.

access time

The time period actually required to request and receive data from a hard drive. Access time is determined as the product of seek time plus drive latency. A lower access time denotes better performance.

account

A specification that enables a user to access a workgroup or network. Each user who requires access has an account, which is used to log in to the network and to be recognized as a valid participant. User accounts can be configured by the network administrator to grant the holder specific access privileges. A temporary account can be configured to expire at a given date and time. The account can also be used by the administrator to track resource usage.

account management (AM) domain

A subdivision of accounts managed by a single entity.

account policy

A set of rules used to define which rights are granted to various users on the network.

account restrictions

Limitations on a user's account that can be configured by the network administrator to set an expiration date and limit access. Restrictions may also require users to enter a password upon login.

account server

A central computer used to control access to a network.

accounting

Tracking and reporting on network resources. The network administrator can allocate charges for network services throughout multiple departments and can assign each user an account balance of available services and resources. The administrator can further assign account balances to each user, which would set a limit on the amount of services accessible by each user. Most network operating systems have a built-in accounting utility or can use a third-party add-on package.

Accounting Management

A System Management Function Area (SMFA) in the OSI Network Management Model that refers to the administration of network usage, costs, and resource availability.

ACK

A control character (ASCII code 06) indicating a packet has been received error-free.

across-the-wire migration

A way to upgrade to a higher version of the NetWare operating system, using the NetWare Migration Utility. In this type of migration, data files are sent over the network to a destination server.

active
A term used to indicate when hardware is doing signal processing of any type.

active hub
A network device used to amplify transmission signals and connect additional nodes to the network.

active link
A device used to connect two network cable segments. Both cable segments must be connected to high-impedance Network Interface Cards (NICs).

Active Monitor (AM)
The first station on a Token Ring network to be started. The Active Monitor detects and addresses error conditions in the background and is responsible for passing and maintaining the token. The performance of the AM is constantly monitored by a standby monitor to guarantee the integrity of the token passing process.

active star topology
A network topology where the central node cleans and boosts a signal.

active termination
The capability of a Small Computer Systems Interface (SCSI) device to apply or remove terminations.

adapter
A hardware device that connects the computer to a peripheral device. Adapters mitigate the differences between the widths of the data buses between the personal computer and the peripheral.

adapter cable
A cable used in Token Ring networks to connect the network interface cards to the Multi-Station Access Unit (MSAU).

adaptive routing

A method used to reroute messages dynamically through the network using the best available path.

Add Self right

A NetWare property right that gives a trustee the privilege of adding itself as a value of that property. Used only for properties containing object names as values.

add-on board

A circuit board that can be added to a personal computer to give the computer additional capabilities.

address

A type of identifier, which can be assigned to network stations and devices or to locations in memory or disk storage. Each device must have a separate address to receive and reply to messages.

Address and Control Field compression

A way to minimize unnecessary network overhead by eliminating the All Stations Address and the Unnumbered Information fields from High-Level Data Link Control (HDLC) framing on a per-link basis.

address book

A feature of communications programs that enables the storage and arrangement of electronic mail (e-mail) addresses for future reference.

address bus

The electrical signal lines where memory locations are specified. Each signal line carries one bit.

Address Field

A frame field that specifies the virtual circuit (VC) numbering or data link connection identifier, flow control, and frame discard eligibility. Various local area network (LAN) topologies may use different sized address fields.

address mask

Part of the Internet Protocol addressing schema. The address is a group of bits, the values of which identify a subnetwork. The address mask simplifies the process of referring to members of a given subnet.

Synonym: *subnet mask*

address resolution

The process of mapping one type of address to another.

address resolution cache

An area of memory that contains the entries used to convert Internet Protocol (IP) addresses to physical addresses.

Address Resolution Protocol (ARP)

A method used to determine the physical address of a target host. ARP is a part of the Internet Protocol (IP) and AppleTalk protocol and enables a host that knows only the logical (IP) address of a target host to find the physical (Media Access Control, or MAC) address of the same target host. ARP can only be used on networks capable of hardware broadcasts.

Address Translation Table

A table containing Internet Protocol (IP) addresses and their equivalent physical addresses.

addressing

A method of assigning numbers for identification purposes. The addressing of each node on a network segment is defined by the Media Access Control (MAC) protocols. Node addressing is implemented via hardware.

addressing space

The amount of total random access memory (RAM) available to the operating system in a NetWare server.

adjacency

A record kept by a NetWare Link Services Protocol (NLSP) router concerning its connections to adjacent devices.

adjacent channel
The frequency band just before or just after the current channel.

Admin
A Novell Directory Services (NDS) user with special privileges. These privileges usually include supervisorial rights, which grant the user the ability to manage a NDS Directory tree and to create or delete Directory objects.

ADMIN object
A User object created in the process of installing the first NetWare 4 server in a Novell Directory Services (NDS) tree, which has the privilege of creating and managing other objects. By default, ADMIN has a trustee assignment to the root object. Because the trustee assignment includes the Supervisor object right, ADMIN can create and manage any object in the tree. Additional objects can later be given the Supervisor object right, as well, to decentralize control of the network.

administration
Tasks done by the network supervisor or administrator. The supervisor has access rights to all volumes, directories, and files. These tasks may include configuration management, hardware and software maintenance, and performance monitoring.

administrative distance
A rating that measures the trustworthiness of a routing information source.

Administrative Domain (AD)
The nodes, routers, and connectors managed by a single administrator.

administrator
An individual responsible for maintenance and administration of a network. The administrator's tasks usually include setting up the server, creating user accounts, establishing security, and maintaining the server. In NetWare 4.*x*, the default account for the administrator is ADMIN. In NetWare 2.*x* and NetWare 3.*x*, the administrator used the SUPERVISOR account.

Advanced Communications Function (ACF)

A family of IBM software, running under Systems Network Architecture (SNA). The ACF programs include *ACF/NCP (Network Control Program)*, which controls communications between network devices and a host machine; *ACF/TCAM (Telecommunications Access Method)*, which is a Virtual Telecommunications Access Method (VTAM) application that provides message handling functions; *ACF/VTAM*, which controls communications between a terminal and a host machine; and *ACF/VTAME (Virtual Telecommunications Access Method-Entry)*, a program that has been replaced by ACF/VTAM.

Advanced Data Communications Control Procedures (ADCCP)

An American National Standards Institute (ANSI) standard communications protocol that is a bit-oriented, symmetrical protocol based on IBM's Synchronous Data Link Control (SDLC).

Advanced Function Printing (AFP)

An IBM Systems Application Architecture (SAA) term referring to the capability to print both text and images.

Advanced Interactive Executive (AIX)

IBM's UNIX operating system.

Advanced Peer-to-Peer Networking (APPN)

A network architecture defined by IBM's Systems Application Architecture (SAA) that facilitates peer communications between microcomputers, without involving a mainframe computer or other Systems Network Architecture (SNA) device. Unlike SNA, APPN supports dynamic packet routing.

Advanced Program-to-Program Communications (APPC)

Part of the Systems Network Architecture (SNA) protocol involving Logical Unit (LU) 6.2 that enables programs to communicate over the network and facilitates communication between multiple processes in an SNA network, without involving a common host system or using terminal emulation.

Advanced Research Projects Agency (ARPA)
The government agency that funded the initial development of the Internet. The agency is now called Defense Advanced Research Projects Agency (DARPA).

Advanced Research Projects Agency Network (ARPAnet)
The first large, packet-switched, wide area network (WAN) developed in the 1970s with funding from the ARPAnet was officially decommissioned in 1991. The ARPAnet eventually became the Internet.

Adverse Channel Enhancement (ACE)
A method of adjusting a modem to compensate for noisy communications lines.

advertising
A process used by devices on a network to inform other devices of their existence. Under NetWare, advertising is accomplished via the Service Advertising Protocol (SAP).

AFP Server object
A leaf object in Novell Directory Services (NDS) that represents an AFP-based server functioning as a node on the NetWare network. The AFP Server may also function as a NetWare router to Macintosh computers or as an AppleTalk server to Macintosh computers.

agent
The part of a client-server system that automatically prepares and exchanges information or executes a task on behalf of a client or server application.

aging
The process of systematically removing older items or table entries.

alarm
A warning signal used to inform a network administrator of an event. The signal, which may be audible or visible, is typically used to warn the

administrator when an error or critical situation occurs on the network. Alarms can indicate the severity or type of related event and may trigger an automatic response from a network management software package.

Alarm Indication Signal (AIS)
A signal that indicates the presence of an alarm on the network. The AIS is used in broadband Integrated Services Digital Networks (ISDNs) and in the OSI Network Management Model.

alert
An alarm sent by an agent to the administrator, indicating a problem or other critical event has occurred.

algorithm
A mathematical process used to solve a specific problem. The algorithm consists of a set of well-defined rules or processes.

alias
An object that points to another object, which is usually named in an easily recognizable manner. Aliases are meant to simplify access to files and objects by establishing easy-to-recall nicknames for a file or object that may have an otherwise difficult-to-recall name.

Alias object
A Novell Directory Services (NDS) leaf object that points to the original location of an object in a Directory tree.

alignment error
A networking error that results from a packet having extra bits. This type of error may be caused by a faulty component or cable.

All Properties
A property right option that grants a trustee specific rights to all properties at once, as opposed to assigning rights individually.

allocation unit

A NetWare term that denotes an area used to store information from files and tables. An allocation unit may be a block or buffer. A block stores data on disk; a buffer stores data temporarily in random access memory (RAM).

alpha testing

The first step in testing a new hardware or software product. This stage precedes beta testing and is usually performed in-house.

alphanumeric

A character set containing only letters and numbers, and no special characters.

alt newsgroup

An Internet newsgroup that discusses "alternative" topics, often controversial, usually outside the mainstream (such as sexually explicit subjects).

alternate collating sequence

A sorting sequence that differs from the standard American Standard Code for Information Interchange (ASCII) sequence. This sequence is used to specify the order the Btrieve record management system uses to sort keys.

Alternate Mark Inversion (AMI)

A signal-encoding method in which a positive, negative, or zero voltage is used. A zero voltage usually represents one value and a nonzero voltage represents another.

alternate routing

The use of an alternative communications path if the primary path is unavailable.

ambiguous filename

A filename containing a wildcard character of ? or *. If a character or characters in a filename is replaced with a wildcard character, the resulting ambiguous filename may reference more than one file.

American National Standards Institute (ANSI)

The standards organization responsible for several data communications and terminal standards. ANSI is the U.S. representative of Consultative Committee for International Telegraphy and Telephony (CCITT) and the International Standards Organization (ISO).

American Standard Code for Information Interchange (ASCII)

A 7-bit code employed as a U.S. standard for interchanging data between communications devices. The standard ASCII character set has values between 0 and 127, each of which is assigned to letters, numbers, and other characters. The first 32 characters are used as control codes. An additional 128 characters make up the extended ASCII character set. These additional characters, however, may not be the same in all computers, and the characters may not display the same in all programs.

American Wire Gauge (AWG)

A classification system for copper wire. The values presented are based on the diameter (or gauge) of the wire, with lower gauge numbers corresponding to the thickest wires.

amplifier

A device used to boost an analog signal.

amplitude

The magnitude of a signal, expressed in volts or amperes.

amplitude modulation (AM)

A technique that conveys information through the amplitude of the carrier signal.

analog

A term meaning proportion or ratio, which also refers to a method of representing values by continuously varying a physical property (such as voltage in a circuit). Electronic devices that use this method are called *analog devices;* they can represent an almost infinite number of values. By contrast, a *digital device* (which maps values onto discrete numbers) can represent a finite range of values based on its capabilities of resolution.

analog communication
A telecommunications system (such as the voice-based telephone system) that uses analog signals to represent information.

Analog Intensity Modulation (AIM)
A communications modulation method that uses light instead of electrical signals. The intensity of the light source varies as a function of the transmitted signal.

analog signal
A continuous, sinusoidal communication often used in the context of transmission methods developed to transmit voice rather than high-speed digital signals.

Analog-to-Digital Converter (ADC)
A device used to convert analog signals to digital signals.

anchor
A starting point for a hypertext link that a user clicks to advance to a link location.

Anonymous FTP
An Application Layer (Layer 7 of the OSI Reference Model) protocol of the Transmission Control Protocol/Internet Protocol (TCP/IP) suite that enables a user to retrieve publicly available files from other networks.

anonymous remailer
A server used to facilitate privacy, by maintaining an internal list of anonymous IDs that correspond to valid electronic mail (e-mail) addresses. An anonymous remailer typically provides this service free of charge, enabling

users to send an e-mail to an individual or a newsgroup without the recipient becoming aware of the sender's name or e-mail address.

answer mode

A modem setting that allows the modem to answer an incoming call automatically. The answer mode is determined by the AT command ATS0=n, where n is the number of rings the modem waits before answering the call.

anti-virus program

A type of computer program used to detect and/or remove computer viruses. These programs seek out suspicious activity, such as unnecessary disk access, or look for patterns that indicate the presence of specific viruses.

Apple Desktop Bus (ADB)

A serial communications link used to connect low-speed input devices to a Macintosh SE, II, IIx, IIcx, and SE/30 computer. Up to 16 devices can be daisy-chained to a single Apple Desktop Bus.

AppleShare

A network solution from Apple Computer that requires a Macintosh computer to function as network server. AppleShare is made up of both server and workstation software, and uses the AppleTalk Filing Protocol (ATFP).

applet

A small Java application that can be embedded in a Hypertext Markup Language (HTML) document or any small application included with an operating system (such as the Windows Notepad).

AppleTalk

A suite of proprietary, Carrier Sense Multiple Access/Collision Detect (CSMA/CD) based protocols and products from Apple Computer that allows hardware and software on an AppleTalk network to communicate. AppleTalk also facilitates the routing of data and supports file and print services. As a layered environment, AppleTalk covers all the same networking services specified in the OSI Reference Model.

AppleTalk Phase 2

The most recent version of the AppleTalk protocols. This set of protocols offers more efficient routing algorithms, supports networks with thousands of nodes, provides multiple zones on a network, accommodates Token Ring topologies, and provides cabling for an improved performance in a multiprotocol environment.

AppleTalk printer

A printer connected to an AppleTalk network. The AppleTalk printer specified on the configuration line can be queried by AppleTalk Print Services (ATPS). AppleTalk Print Services can then use that printer's font list, even if the queue is serviced by a separate printer.

AppleTalk protocols

A set of rules that specify how the nodes on an AppleTalk network communicate. These protocols control the entire AppleTalk network, including both hardware and software. Table A.2 lists the protocols found in the AppleTalk Protocol Suite.

T A B L E A.2	*AppleTalk Protocol Suite*
APPLETALK PROTOCOL	**DESCRIPTION**
AppleTalk Address Resolution Protocol (AARP)	Maps AppleTalk addresses to physical addresses. Exists on the Network Layer of the OSI Reference Model.
AppleTalk Data Stream Protocol (ADSP)	Establishes full-duplex, byte-stream service between sockets. This is a symmetric, connection-oriented protocol. Through ADSP, two processors can open a virtual data pipe for reading and writing information for one another. Exists on the Session Layer of the OSI Reference Model.
AppleTalk Echo Protocol (AEP)	Determines whether two nodes are connected and available. Exists on the Transport Layer of the OSI Reference Model.
Apple Talk Filing Protocol (ATFP)	Allows workstations to share files and applications located on an AppleShare file server.

APPLETALK PROTOCOL	DESCRIPTION
AppleTalk Remote Access Protocol (ARAP)	Enables access to a network from a remote site using a serial line. Exists on the Data Link Layer of the OSI Reference Model.
AppleTalk Secure Data Stream Protocol (ASDSP)	Similar to AppleTalk Data Stream Protocol (ADSP), but offers more security against unauthorized usage. Operates on the Session Layer of the OSI Reference Model.
AppleTalk Session Protocol (ASP)	An extension of the AppleTalk Transaction Protocol (ATP), allows two processes to exchange transactions and commands.
AppleTalk Transaction Protocol (ATP)	Provides lossless packet delivery from a source socket to a destination socket. Exists on the Transport Layer of the OSI Reference Model.
AppleTalk Update-based Routing Protocol (AURP)	Functions similarly to the Routing Table Maintenance Protocol (RTMP), but only sends updates when a change occurs. Exists on the Transport Layer of the OSI Reference Model.
Datagram Delivery Protocol (DDP)	Establishes a best-effort, socket-to-socket delivery service for sending datagrams across an AppleTalk internetwork. Operates at the Network Layer of the OSI Reference Model and prepares data packets for sending on through the network medium.
EtherTalk Link Access Protocol (ELAP)	Used for EtherTalk—exists at the Data-Link Layer of the OSI Reference Model.
FDDITalk Link Access Protocol (FLAP)	Used for Fiber Distributed Data Interface—exists at the Data Link Layer of the OSI Reference Model.

(continued)

T A B L E A.2	AppleTalk Protocol Suite (continued)
APPLETALK PROTOCOL	**DESCRIPTION**
LocalTalk Link Access Protocol (LLAP)	Used for LocalTalk, and exists at the Data Link Layer of the OSI Reference Model.
Name Binding Protocol (NBP)	Converts entity names into their corresponding Internet addresses. Exists on the Transport Layer of the OSI Reference Model.
Printer Access Protocol (PAP)	Creates a path from the user or application to a printer. Exists on the Session Layer of the OSI Reference Model.
Routing Table Maintenance Protocol (RTMP)	Moves packets between networks. Exists on the Transport Layer of the OSI Reference Model.
TokenTalk Link Access Protocol (TLAP)	Used for TokenTalk. Exists on the Data Link Layer of the OSI Reference Model.
Zone Information Protocol (ZIP)	Helps to locate nodes. Exists on the Data Link Layer of the OSI Reference Model.

AppleTalk router

A router that can receive and forward AppleTalk packets on the network. The AppleTalk router can connect the AppleTalk network into an internetwork, so all nodes on each network can access any service or node on any of the connected networks.

AppleTalk stack

The suite of AppleTalk Phase 2 protocols in the AppleTalk module. The AppleTalk stack works with NetWare for Macintosh and enables Macintosh users to use NetWare file and print services.

AppleTalk Zone

A logical grouping of AppleTalk devices. AppleTalk zones are defined by the network administrator.

application

A software program that makes calls to an operating system and manipulates data. An application enables a user to perform a specific task, such as word processing. A standalone application runs from a hard disk or floppy disk in a nonnetworked computer. A network application, on the other hand, can be shared by many users and can access network resources. Applications may also be integrated into complementary suites.

application binary interface (ABI)

A specification that outlines the interface between the operating system and a particular hardware platform. In particular, ABI refers to the calls made between applications and the operating system.

Application Context (AC)

A term used in the OSI Reference Model referring to all the application service elements (ASEs) necessary to use an application in a given context.

Application Entity (AE)

Under the OSI Reference Model, a process or function that runs all or part of an application. An AE is made up of one or more application service elements (ASEs).

application interface

A set of software-based routines or conventions enabling programmers to use a given interface as part of an application. Generally, the application interface is used to simplify access to system or networking services.

Application Layer (OSI model)

The seventh layer in the OSI model. The Application Layer furnishes users with access to the network and sends a stream of bytes to the Transport Layer (the fourth layer) on the source machine. It includes such utilities as file transfer and virtual terminal services.

Application object

A leaf object of Novell Directory Services (NDS) that represents a network application in a NetWare Directory tree. The use of Application objects will make network management more efficient and simplify common tasks (such as assigning rights or supporting applications).

Application Process (AP)

A program that makes use of Application Layer services under the OSI Reference Model. The AP receives the requested services from the application service elements (ASEs).

application program

A program that processes transactions.

Synonym: *transaction program*

Application Program Interface (API)

A set of abstractions that provide easy access to operating system services and protocols. The application program uses the API to request low-level services from the operating system, usually for data communication, data retrieval, or access to system resources. In GUI-based operating systems, the API will also provide access to the various components of the interface.

Application Protocol Data Unit (APDU)

Under the OSI Reference Model, a data packet that serves as the exchange unit in the Application layer.

application server

A server in a client-server network that runs applications shared by client workstations. The application server shares the data processing burden with its clients. A file server, on the other hand, requires the client to run the application and process the data.

Application Service Element (ASE)

One of several elements in the OSI Reference Model providing services at the Application layer. These services are requested by an application process or application entity through a set of predefined Application Program

Interfaces (APIs). The two types of ASEs are common application service elements (CASE) and specific application service elements (SASE). CASEs are more generic and offer services that can be used by several different types of applications. An SASE provides services for a specific application or type of application.

application subsystem
A set of programs that logs errors, manages incoming communications, loads transaction programs, and provides other services.

Application-Specific Integrated Circuit (ASIC)
A special-purpose chip containing logic designed for a specific application or device, which is built from a library of standard circuit cells.
Synonym: *gate arrays*

applique
A mounting plate that contains network connector hardware and translates communication signals from a network interface into expected signals from a chosen communications standard.

AppNotes
A technical journal published by Novell that offers technical information about designing and administering NetWare computing systems.
Synonym: *Novell Application Notes*

arbitration
A set of rules used when conflicting demands occur for a computer resource.

architecture
A network communications system's logical and physical structure made up of protocols, formats, operation sequences, and other specifications. Also used to denote the hardware structure of a particular type of computer.

archive

To transfer files to long-term or redundant storage, such as optical disks or magnetic tape. The archive is used to create a backup copy of data that can be used in case the original is damaged.

archive bit

A DOS file attribute that can be set to indicate if a particular file or directory has been modified since the last backup.

Archive Needed (A) attribute

A file attribute set by the NetWare operating system to indicate a file has been changed since the last backup.

archive server

The central computer responsible for the archiving process.

archive site

A node on the Internet that provides access to files.

area

The domain of connected Internetwork Packet Exchange (IPX) networks that all share a common area address in a NetWare Link Services Protocol (NLSP) network. All users in one routing area have Network Layer (of the OSI Reference Model) access to the same services.

Synonym: *routing area*

area address

A 32-bit number and 32-bit mask that define a NetWare Link Services Protocol (NLSP) routing area.

area boundary router (ABR)

A router that attaches an Open Shortest Path First (OSPF) area to the background area. The area boundary router has at least one interface in a routing area and one in the backbone area.

area mask
A 32-bit hexadecimal number that indicates how the area network number identifies the routing area and the network within the routing area in a NetWare Link Services Protocol (NLSP) network.

ARJ
A DOS file-compression format used to compress multidisk files, which designates the compressed file with an .ARJ filename suffix. The program for creating this compression was developed by Robert Jung of ARJ Software.

AS/400
An IBM minicomputer introduced in 1988 to replace the System/36 and System/38 series.

ascending
A logical ordering of database records. Used as an attribute to instruct Btrieve to collate an index in low-to-high order.

ASCIIbetical sorting
A sort based on the ASCII strategy of numbers and symbols preceding letters, and uppercase letters preceding lowercase letters.

asserted circuit
A circuit that has been closed and has a voltage value. An asserted circuit is usually used to represent a 1.

assigned number
A numerical value used to denote a particular protocol, application, or organization, but not an address. Assigned numbers are assigned by the Internet Assigned Numbers Authority (IANA).

associated file
A data file connected with a particular job entry.

Association Control Service Element (ACSE)

An OSI Reference Model service that establishes a relationship between two applications. The ACSE facilitates cooperation and exchange of information between the applications.

Asymmetric Digital Subscriber Line (ADSL)

A high-speed telecommunications method used to move data over regular telephone lines, sometimes used as an alternative to Integrated Services Digital Network (ISDN) lines.

asynchronous

A type of data transmission where characters or blocks of characters may begin at any time, but each character or character block must have an equal time duration. Asynchronous transfer methods place start and stop bits to indicate the beginning and end of each character, as opposed to constant timing.

Asynchronous Balanced Mode (ABM)

An operating mode specified in the High-Level Data Link Control (HDLC) protocol of the International Standards Organization (ISO). ABM gives equal status to each node in a point-to-point link. Each node, therefore, functions as both sender and receiver.

Asynchronous Communications Server (ACS)

A dedicated PC or expansion board that gives other nodes on the network access to serial ports and modems.

Asynchronous Modem Eliminator (AME)

A serial cable and connector with a modified pin configuration, which allows two computers to communicate directly without the use of a physical modem.
Synonym: *null modem*

Asynchronous Response Mode (ARM)

A communications mode specified in the High-Level Data Link Control (HDLC) protocol of the International Standards Organization (ISO). An ARM configuration has a secondary (or *slave*) node that can initiate communications with a primary (*master*) node without first having to gain the permission of the master node.

Asynchronous Time Division Multiplexing (ATDM)

A variation on the Time Division Multiplexing (TDM) method of sending information in which time slots are allocated as needed, rather than being preassigned to specific transmitters.

Asynchronous Transfer Mode (ATM)

A connection-oriented, packet-switched networking architecture based on broadband ISDN technology. ATM can provide very high bandwidth, dividing data into 53-byte cells (48 bytes of data and a 5-byte header). ATM has three physical-layer specifications: OC-3 (155Mbps), OC-12 (622Mbps), and OC-48 (2.488Gbps). OC-3 is more common for typical WAN implementations; OC-48 is still largely experimental, though, combining 16 OC-3 switches can effectively create an OC-48 backbone. Although designed to run over large distances and often used as a backbone technology, ATM can also run to desktop units that require extremely high bandwidth to run high-end desktop applications. The 25Mbps variation of ATM is best suited for desktop connections; its Quality of Service (QoS) guarantees make it usable for many different types of traffic, including voice, data, and video. An existing network running NetWare, Windows, DECnet, TCP/IP, MacTCP, or AppleTalk can connect to an ATM network and run applications without modification, through a technique known as *LAN Emulation* (LANE).

ATM can run on fiber-optic cable or CAT-5 UTP cable and is deployed using a star topology. ATM offers four QoS levels, each of which can be assigned to particular types of traffic. These four levels are:

► *Class A: Constant Bit Rate (CBR)*. This is a "reserved bandwidth" service suited for applications intolerant of cell loss.

► *Class B: Variable Bit Rate-Real Time (VBR-RT)*. VBR is also a "reserved bandwidth" service but, instead of generating a constant bit rate, it establishes a peak rate, sustainable rate, and maximum burst size.

► *Class C: Variable Bit Rate-Non Real Time (VBR-NRT)*. This level is similar to Class B, but is applied to applications that can tolerate a slight delay, such as video playback or transaction processing.

▶ *Class D.* This class consists of unspecified bit rate (UBR) and available bit rate (ABR). UBR is a nonreserved, "best effort" service; the network does not allocate resources for a UBR connection. Both UBR and ABR can be applied to traffic that can tolerate more delays or cell loss.

The ATM Forum is the standards body responsible for establishing and promoting ATM standards.

asynchronous transmission

A method of transmission under which each character is individually synchronized. The time gap between characters is not a fixed duration. Instead, start bits and stop bits are applied to coordinate data flow.

AT Command Set

A command set developed by Hayes Microcomputer Products to operate its line of modems. The AT command, which is short for attention, precedes most modem commands. The AT command set is supported by most modem manufacturers and has become a de facto standard. Table A.3 shows the standard AT command set.

T A B L E A . 3	AT Command Set
COMMAND	**DESCRIPTION**
+++	Escape code from Online Command state
AT	Attention command that precedes the command line
A/	Repeat the preceding command
A	Answer the call immediately
DT	Dial Touch Tone mode
DP	Dial Pulse mode
E	Command echo disabled
E1	Command echo enabled
H	Hang up (on hook)
H1	Off hook
I	Output product code to computer
L	Speaker volume (L0, L1, L2, L3)

COMMAND	DESCRIPTION
M0	Speaker off
M1	Speaker on until Carrier Detect (CD)
M2	Speaker always on
M3	Speaker on from dial to Carrier Detect (CD)
O	Return to online communications
O1	Return to online communications and retrain
Q	Send Result Code messages
Q1	Do not send Result Code messages
Sr?	Read and display contents of register (r)
Sr=n	Set register (r) to value (n) (for example, ATS0=1 equals answer phone on first ring)
V	Result Code messages sent in numeric format
V1	Result Code messages sent in English word format
X	Extended Status mode
Y	Long space disconnect
Z	Reset and reinitialize modem

at-least-once transaction

An AppleTalk Protocol transaction method that guarantees a request will be executed at least one time.

ATM Adaptation Layer (AAL)

A method of adapting the highest-layer protocols of the OSI Reference Model for transport over an Asynchronous Transfer Mode (ATM) network. An ATM cell itself consists of 53 bytes (48 bytes of payload and a 5-byte header). The AAL determines the format of the cell's payload.

AAL is divided into the following two sublayers:

▶ *Convergence (CS)*. The CS Sublayer performs message identification and time/clock recovery services. To support data transport over ATM, the CS is subdivided into the Common Part Convergence Sublayer (CPCS) and a Service-Specific Convergence Sublayer (SSCS). AAL service data units are transported between AAL *service access points* (SAPs) throughout the ATM network.

▶ *Segmentation and Reassembly (SAR).* The SAR Sublayer divides higher-layer information into 48-byte segments for transport by the ATM cells. When the cell is received, SAR reassembles the segmented ATM cells into larger data units, which can then be delivered to the higher layers.

Five AALs have been defined, one for each class of service available in the ATM network, as follows:

▶ *AAL-1 (ATM Adaptation Layer Type 1).* This layer is responsible for AAL functions in support of Constant Bit Rate (CBR), time-dependent traffic.

▶ *AAL-2 (ATM Adaptation Layer Type 2).* This layer is undefined.

▶ *AAL-3/4 (ATM Adaptation Layer Type 3/4).* This layer is responsible for AAL functions in support of Variable Bit Rate (VBR), delay-tolerant data traffic that requires support for sequencing or error detection.

▶ *AAL-5 (ATM Adaptation Layer Type 5).* This layer is responsible for AAL functions in support of Variable Bit Rate (VBR), delay-tolerant, connection-oriented traffic that requires little support for sequencing or error detection.

ATM Data Service Unit (ADSU)
A Data Service Unit (DSU) used to access an Asynchronous Transfer Mode (ATM) network through a High Speed Serial Interface (HSSI).

attach
To create a connection between a workstation and a network server. The server assigns each workstation a connection number, and then attaches each workstation to its LOGIN directory.

Attached Resource Computer Network (ARCnet)
Developed in the 1970s by Datapoint Corporation, a proprietary, token-bus architecture widely licensed by third-party vendors. ARCnet is widely used in smaller installations and has a bandwidth of 2.5Mbps. It supports coaxial, twisted pair, and fiber-optic cable. Although ARCnet typically uses a bus

topology, it can also be deployed in a star configuration. ARCnet's advantage over Ethernet is components are inexpensive and it is simple to configure. It is less efficient, however, and is not suited to internetworking. A later implementation of ARCnet, called ARCnet Plus, offers a throughput of 20Mbps and support for larger data frames.

attachment
A connection to a device or peripheral. This term can also denote a separate file included with an electronic mail (e-mail) message.

Attachment Unit Interface (AUI)
A universal connector to Ethernet cables.

attack scanner
A software package that probes UNIX networks to discover security problems by posing as an intruder trying to steal data or force entry into the network.

Attention Dial Pulse (ATDP)
A command in the AT command set used to dial a number using a rotary (pulse) telephone.

Attention Dial Tone (ATDT)
A command in the AT command set used to dial a number using a Touch Tone telephone.

attention message
An AppleTalk Data Stream Protocol (ADSP) message that enables two transport clients to signal one another outside the regular data flow. The attention message is made up of a 2-byte attention code and as much as 570 bytes of data.
Synonym: *expedited transport service data unit*

attenuation

A reduction in signal strength caused by both electrical losses in the dielectric medium and the length of the conductor (the distance the signal must travel). Attenuation is expressed in *decibels per kilometer* (dB/km) and depends on a number of factors, including wire composition, wire size, and the effective range of the signal frequency.

attenuation factor

A value used to express the amount of attenuation (signal loss) over a given distance.

attribute

A way to describe access to (and properties of) files and directories. For example, attributes of NetWare files include Read, Write, Create, Delete, and Execute Only. Directory attributes may include Read, Write, Create, Execute, and Hidden. Attributes are applied to files and directories only, and not to objects. An attribute cannot be overridden, but may be changed by a user who has the appropriate right. Table A.4 lists attributes for IntranetWare and their classifications.

T A B L E   A.4   *IntranetWare Attributes*

ATTRIBUTE	DIRECTORY	FILE
Archive Needed (A)		X
Can't Compress (Cc)		X
Compressed (Co)		X
Copy Inhibit (Ci)		X
Delete Inhibit (Di)	X	X
Don't Compress (Dc)	X	X
Don't Migrate (Dm)	X	X
Don't Suballocate (Ds)		X
Execute Only (X)		X
Hidden (H)	X	X

ATTRIBUTE	DIRECTORY	FILE
Immediate Compress (Ic)	X	X
Indexed (I)		X
Migrate (M)		X
Normal (N)	X	X
Purge (P) X	X	
Read Only (Ro)		X
Read Write (Rw)		X
Rename Inhibit (Ri)	X	X
Shareable (Sh)		X
System (Sy)	X	X
Transactional (T)		X

Synonym: *flag*

Attribute Registration Authority (ARA)
The organization responsible for allocating unique attribute values in the X.400 Message Handling System (MHS).

attribute type
A set of letters used to distinguish the type of object name in the NetWare bindery and Novell Directory Services (NDS).

audio frequency range
A range of frequencies audible to the human ear. This range goes from 20Hz to 20KHz, although humans can typically produce sounds ranging only between 100Hz to 3,000Hz.

Audio Interchange File Format (AIFF)
A file format used to store and exchange sounds in sound files found on the Internet.

audit filter

A feature used to select or exclude specific events or time periods from an audit report.

audit trail

A running record of transactions generated automatically by several programs and operating systems. The audit trail can be used to track data and to determine the origin of any changes made to it.

auditing

A process of reviewing network transactions to ensure accuracy and security. An auditor can track network events and activities, but may not open or modify the network files unless specifically granted that right by the supervisor. File or directory events that may be audited include the following:

- Creation, modification, or deletion of a directory or file
- Salvaging, moving, or renaming of a directory or file
- Creation or deletion of a service queue

Server events that may be audited include the following:

- Occurrence of a server failure
- Creation or deletion of Bindery objects
- Mounting or dismounting of volumes
- Modification of security rights

Novell Directory Services (NDS) events that may be audited include the following:

- Adding or deleting objects
- Moving or renaming objects
- Adding or removing security equivalence
- Tracking User object logins and logouts

Auditing File object

A leaf object that allows the management of auditing file logs as objects in the Novell Directory Services (NDS) tree.

auditor

An independent individual with no bias, assigned to verify a network's integrity.

authentication

A way to verify an object is authorized to send messages or requests to Novell Directory Services (NDS). In NetWare 4.*x* authentication guarantees a given message does, indeed, originate at the workstation where the data was created. Along with login restrictions and access control rights, this feature functions to provide security on the network. From the end user's perspective, authentication consists of a request for a password and user ID upon login; subsequent operations are authenticated transparently. Although passwords and user IDs are the simplest and most common types of authentication, establishing a login-time restriction can sometimes provide additional security. This technique periodically forces the end user to log out, log in again, and reenter the password. Several other authentication mechanisms have been developed, including digital signatures.

authentication database

A list of valid remote system IDs and related Data Terminal Equipment (DTE) addresses. Each entry in the authentication database indicates a partner that is allowed to communicate with a given interface.

Authentication Information (AI)

The information used to determine whether a network user is authorized to access the system.

authentication system

A server that checks the validity of every user and every request on the network. Most of this is accomplished automatically.

authoring

The process of creating and formatting a document or World Wide Web (WWW) page, normally by using one of the available programs designed for that purpose.

Authority and Format Identifier (AFI)
Under the OSI Reference Model, the part of an address used for the Network-Layer Service Access Point (NSAP). The AFI specifies the administrator responsible for allocating the Initial Domain Identifier (IDI) values.

Auto Answer (AA)
A modem feature that responds and connects automatically to an incoming call.

auto endcap
A setting that specifies captured data should be closed and sent to the printer after exiting an application.

auto-answer
A modem feature for answering incoming calls automatically.

autoauthentication
A client-server utility that enables users to access unrestricted resources on the network without a password. If the user attempts to access a restricted resource, however, the utility will request a password.

autobaud
The automatic determination and matching of telecommunications transmission speeds.

autodial
A modem feature for opening a telephone line and placing a call.

AUTOEXEC.BAT
An automatically executing batch file that runs when DOS or OS/2 is booted. AUTOEXEC.BAT may load programs, utilities, or files, issue DOS commands, and trigger a login script.

AUTOEXEC.NCF
A NetWare server's executable batch file used to load modules and set the NetWare operating system configuration. The file holds the server name and

internal network number, loads local area network (LAN) drivers and network board settings, and binds protocols to installed drivers. It may also load NetWare Loadable Modules (NLMs) and make bindery-context settings. Executable server commands can be included in AUTOEXEC.NCF.

autologin
A network utility that imposes controls over user login attempts.

Automatic Alternate Routing (AAR)
A process by which network traffic is routed automatically to maximize throughput. AAR can also be used to minimize distance and balance channel usage.

automatic call distributor
A telecommunications device that automatically switches incoming calls to the next available telephone line.

automatic call reconnect
A telecommunications feature that reroutes automatic calls away from a failed trunk line.

Automatic Client Upgrade (ACU)
An IntranetWare feature that allows automatic upgrading of many existing NetWare workstations to Novell's 32-bit client software.

automatic dial-up
The automatic placement of a telephone call by an individual workstation or network node to a larger network without user intervention.

automatic flow control
A method of controlling data flow over a virtual circuit. Enabled by setting window and packet size, automatic flow control can be negotiated in each direction on a per-call basis.

automatic forwarding
An electronic mail (e-mail) feature that automatically retransmits incoming messages to another e-mail address.

automatic mailing list
A mailing list maintained by a computer.

Automatic Number Identification (ANI)
A feature that includes the sender's identification number in the transmission. ANI enables the recipient of a phone call to see who is calling before answering the phone.
Synonym: *caller ID*

Automatic Repeat Request (ARQ)
A communications control code that indicates a transmission error has occurred and requests a retransmission.

automatic rollback
A feature of the Transaction Tracking System (TTS) that returns a database to its original state. If a network running under TTS fails when a transaction is in process, the data in the database rolls back to its most recent coherent state.

automount
A graphical network utility used to simplify the process of finding a server, file system, or volume.

autonomous confederation
A group of Autonomous Systems (ASs) that trust the reachability or routing information for their network more than they trust reachability or routing information received from other ASs or other confederations.

autonomous switching
A process whereby packets are switched independently, without interrupting the system processor. The result of autonomous switching is faster packet processing.

Autonomous System (AS)
A set of routers and networks under a single administrative control, but part of a larger network (for example, the Internet). The autonomous system

is the largest unit in an internetwork topology. The routers communicate using an interior gateway protocol (IGP), such as Open Shortest Path First (OSPF).

Synonym: *routing domain*

auto-partition algorithm
An algorithm used by a repeater to disconnect a segment automatically from a network if the segment ceases to function properly.

A/UX
Apple Computer's implementation of UNIX. A/UX contains some Macintosh-specific features and is based on UNIX System V Release 2 with Berkeley extensions.

AUX
The logical name for an auxiliary device under DOS.

availability
The period of time a network device or program is ready for use. A device is considered available even if it is currently in use. Availability is determined by the ratio of mean time before failure (MTBF) and mean time to repair (MTTR).

Available Bit Rate (ABR)
A layer-service category for Asynchronous Transfer Mode (ATM). In ABR, ATM layer-transfer characteristics provided by the network may change after a connection is established. When those characteristics change, a flow-control mechanism is specified that supports several types of feedback to control the source rate of transmission.

Avalanche Photodiode (APD)
A detector component in a fiber-optic receiver. The APD converts light into electrical energy, emitting an "avalanche" of multiple electrons for each incoming photon.

avatar
A visual representation of a user in a shared virtual-reality network.

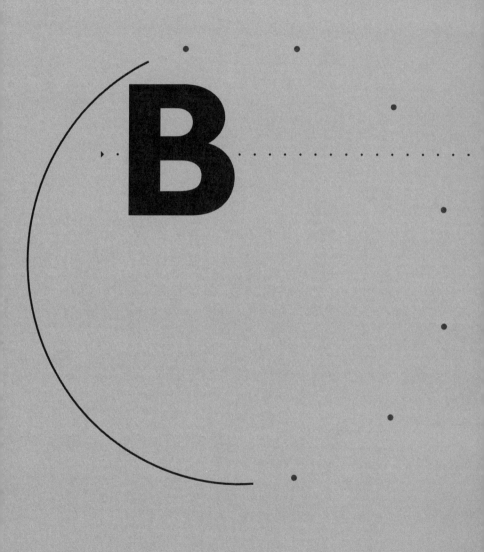

B channel

The bearer channel in an Integrated Services Digital Network (ISDN) system that can carry voice or data at the rate of 64Kbps in either direction.

back channel

A channel that sends control information in a direction opposite to the primary channel, so information can be delivered even when the primary channel may be malfunctioning.

Synonym: *backward channel* or *reverse channel*

back pressure

A propagation of congested information upstream through an internetwork.

backbone

The routing structure of an internetwork, made up of the central connection path to which other subnetworks or network segments with lower data-transfer rates can be attached. Using a backbone in an internetwork is an efficient way to reduce network traffic.

backbone bridge topology

A method for using bridges to connect multiple networks. Under this topology, each pair of networks is directly connected with a bridge, thereby enabling any one network to communicate directly with any other network.

backbone cable

The cable used to form the main trunk of a network. Individual nodes and peripherals can be attached directly to the backbone cable. The four main types of backbone cable are unshielded twisted-pair (UTP), shielded twisted-pair (STP), coaxial, and optical fiber.

backbone network

A type of central connection path to which other subnetworks (or network segments with lower data rates) can be attached. In this type of network, all systems may be configured to enjoy connectivity to each other, as well as to the backbone itself.

backdoor route

A route used by a border router to send data to a particular nonlocal network specified by the Interior Gateway Protocol (IGP).

back-end network

A network used to connect mainframes, minicomputers, and peripherals. A back-end network typically requires high bandwidth and often employs optical fiber as the transmission medium.

background

A process running transparently to the end user, while the user is engaged in other activities. A background process is allocated a lower level of priority than a foreground process and it cannot accept user input.

Background Explicit Congestion Notification (BECN)

A notification set by a Frame Relay network indicating the network is congested in the frame's reverse packet forwarding direction.

background noise

An unwanted signal on a line, channel, or circuit, typically caused by electrical or magnetic interference.

backing out

A process in NetWare's Transaction Tracking System (TTS) for abandoning an incomplete database transaction. The backing-out process prevents related data from being corrupted by the incomplete transaction.

backlink

A path returning to a starting point for a hypertext link a user has clicked to advance to a link location.

backoff

A retransmission delay enforced by the contention of Media Access Control (MAC) protocols when a node that wants to transmit senses a carrier on the physical medium.

backplane

A circuit board with slots into which other circuit boards are inserted.

backplate

A metal bracket at one end of a circuit board, normally flush with the casing, which provides cutouts for connectors or switches. Personal computers usually have blank backplates over expansion slots that are removed when a board is plugged into the slot.

backscattering

Light in a fiber-optic transmission that is reflected back in the direction from which it came.

backup

A duplicate of files, directories, or volumes copied to a storage device (such as a floppy disk, cartridge tape, or hard drive). If the original is destroyed or corrupted, the backup can be retrieved and restored. Method and frequency of backup depend on the age of the data, how many duplicate copies are desired, and the number of backup sessions the administrator is willing to restore. Files that change infrequently do not require backing up as often. A *full* backup makes a copy of all data; a *differential* or *incremental* backup only backs up the added data or the data that has changed since the last backup. Backup is often done in a rotation method that distributes current and older files over multiple storage devices.

backup engine

A module that runs on a host server and contains the interfaces needed to back up and restore data. The backup engine reads and translates user requests, determines session type, and activates the appropriate modules to back up and restore files.

backup host

A NetWare server on which a backup program is run. Normally a backup host has a storage device and a storage-device controller.

backup program

An application used to make archives or to back up copies of data files. Operating systems typically have some limited backup functions, although more full-featured backup programs are available separately.

backup server

A server system used to carry out shutdowns and backups at regular intervals. Although it needn't be a dedicated machine, a backup server runs the backup software. The software notifies all nodes on the network of the impending backup, allows them to end their sessions, and then begins the backup.

backward compatibility

Denotes a software program's capability of working with previous versions. For example, Bindery Emulation gives NetWare 4.*x* networks backward compatibility with earlier versions of NetWare.

Backward Error Correction (BEC)

An error correction method in which the error is detected by the recipient, who subsequently requests a retransmission.

backward learning

An information-gathering process often used in algorithms that assume a symmetrical network and infer information about the network on the basis of this assumption.

bad-block table

A table kept on the hard disk that lists faulty sectors in a storage device. The operating system refers to this table to ensure no data is written to faulty sectors.

bad sector

A portion of a hard disk or floppy disk that cannot be used to store data, usually because of physical damage. Operating systems will locate and mark bad sectors to prevent them from being used.

bad-block revectoring

A data-protection process in which data written to a faulty area of a storage device is retrieved from memory and rewritten to a different area of the device. To prevent subsequent writes to the faulty area, its location is then recorded in a bad-block table.

balanced configuration

A point-to-point configuration in a High-Level Data Link Control (HDLC) network that contains two combined nodes.

balun

A hardware device used to adjust impedances for connecting different cable types. The term *balun* is derived from *balanced/un*balanced, because the device is often used to connect twisted-pair cable (balanced) to coaxial (unbalanced) cable. A balun typically has different connectors at each end, allowing the use of twisted-pair wiring with coaxial cable.

bandwidth

The highest signaling rate possible for a given type of connection. Bandwidth is typically expressed in bits per second (bps) for digital circuits. For analog circuits, bandwidth is expressed in hertz (Hz), and is the equivalent of the highest possible frequency minus the lowest possible frequency. A higher bandwidth offers greater data-transmission capabilities.

bandwidth-on-demand

The capability of an individual virtual circuit to exceed the Committed Information Rate (CIR) to provide additional bandwidth required by an application.

Synonym: *dynamic allocation of bandwidth*

bandwidth reservation

The reservation of call bandwidth for high-bandwidth or high-priority calls in circuit-switched lines.

bang path

An Internet term used to denote a path between two nodes. A bang path is used in a UNIX-to-UNIX Copy Program (UUCP) for electronic mail (e-mail) or Because It's Time Network (BITNET) communications. The path is made up of multiple domain or machine names, separated by exclamation points.

barrel connector

A connector used to link two pieces of identical cable in a straight run.

base address

The starting location for a block of contiguous memory (such as a buffer area, video memory, or the memory area allocated to an I/O port).

base schema

A set of defined object classes in Novell Directory Services (NDS).

baseband

A network technology using a single carrier frequency requiring all stations attached to a network to participate in every transmission that takes place. A baseband connection sends signals without modulation over twisted-pair, coaxial, or fiber-optic cable. Multiple signals can be sent over the same baseband connection by multiplexing.

baseline

A reference metric used in performance analysis. Baseline measurements in a networking context indicate performance levels under what is considered to be a normal load.

Basic Encoding Rules (BER)

In Abstract Syntax Notation One (ASN.1), a rule for encoding data elements that is used to specify any ASN.1 element as a byte string. The string includes a Type, Length, and Value field. The Type field indicates an object's class, the Length field indicates the number of bytes used to encode the value, and the Value field indicates the information associated with the ASN.1 object.

Basic Information Unit (BIU)
A Systems Network Architecture (SNA) packet of information created when the Transmission Control Layer adds a request/response header to a request/response unit, and is then the resulting packet to the Path Control Layer.

Basic Input/Output System (BIOS)
A set of firmware-based programs that allows a computer's central processing unit (CPU) to communicate with printers and other peripherals. Each time the computer starts up, these services load automatically.

Basic Link Unit (BLU)
A packet of information that exists at the Data Link Layer in a Systems Network Architecture (SNA) network. The BLU is contained in an Synchronous Data Link Control (SDLC) frame.

Basic Message Handling Service (MHS)
A scaled-down version of the Global Message Handling System (MHS) included with NetWare 3.12.

basic mode
A mode of operation in a Fiber Distributed Data Interface (FDDI) II network. Under basic mode, only data can be transmitted using packet switching.

Basic Rate Access (BRA)
Access to an Integrated Services Digital Network (ISDN) Basic Rate Interface (BRI).

Basic Rate Interface (BRI)
An interface between a user and an Integrated Services Digital Network (ISDN) switch. The BRI interface contains two 64Kbps B channels and one 16Kbps D channel. The two B channels handle voice and data; the D channel holds information about the call and the customer.
Synonyms: *2B+D*; *Basic Rate ISDN*

Basic Telecommunications Access Method (BTAM)

A mostly obsolete method for communicating between IBM mainframes and terminals. BTAM does not support Systems Network Architecture (SNA) and it has been replaced by ACF/VTAM as the preferred method of remote communications with IBM mainframes.

Basic Transmission Unit (BTU)

A Systems Network Architecture (SNA) term denoting an aggregate block of one or more path information units (PIUs) with the same destination. Multiple PIUs can have a single destination and can be combined into a single packet, even when they are not part of the same message.

batch file

An American Standard Code for Information Interchange (ASCII) file containing a sequence of commands. To execute all the commands contained in a batch file in the order specified, a user enters the name of the batch file at the command line.

batch-processing server

A server that carries out tasks specified by batch files. The batch-processing server makes it possible to offload time-consuming tasks to an idle workstation. Batch-processing services are typically furnished by third-party software programs. The server does not require a dedicated machine.

baud

A unit referring to the data transmission speed of a modem or other serial device.

baud rate

In serial communications, a measurement of signal modulation rate used to indicate the speed at which a signal changes (that is, the number of *state changes per second* on an asynchronous communications channel). A serial port is limited by the baud rate. Baud rate is sometimes incorrectly used to denote *bit rate*, but the two rates are not identical.

Bay Area Regional Research Network (BARRNet)

A San Francisco Bay Area network whose backbone is composed of the University of California, Berkeley; the University of California, Davis; the University of California, San Francisco; the University of California, Santa Cruz; Stanford University; the Lawrence Livermore National Laboratory; and the NASA Ames Research Center.

Bc (committed burst)

The highest number of data bits a network can transfer under normal conditions over a given period of time.

Be (excess burst)

Maximum number of uncommitted data bits the network attempts to deliver over a specified period of time.

beaconing

A signaling process used by nodes of a Token Ring network to indicate a *hard* (serious) *error* has occurred on the network, either at the node itself or at the nodes Nearest Active Upstream Neighbor (NAUN). Beaconing prevents communications from taking place until the error condition has been corrected.

Because It's Time Network (BITNET)

A computer network used to connect more than 1,000 educational institutions in North America and Europe, which provides users at those institutions with easy access to files from remote locations. BITNET uses the Remote Spooling Communications Subsystem (RSCS) and Network Job Entry (NJE) protocols common to IBM mainframes. Consequently, BITNET users must use a gateway to communicate with other networks (such as the Internet).

bel

A value proportional to the logarithm of the ratio that measures the relative intensity of two levels for an acoustic, electrical, or optical signal. A decibel is one-tenth of a bel.

Bell communications standard

A set of standards for data transmission developed by AT&T in the 1980s, which have since become a de facto standard for modem manufacturers.

Bellcore

An organization responsible for research and development for the following Regional Bell Operating Companies (RBOCs): Ameritech, Bell Atlantic, BellSouth, Nynex, Pacific Telesis, SBC Communications, and US West.

Bellman-Ford Algorithm

An algorithm that detects routes through an internetwork by using vectors instead of link states.

Synonym: *old ARPAnet algorithm*

Bell Operating Company (BOC)

One of several local telephone companies that formerly existed in each of seven regions of the United States. A court-ordered deregulation of the telephone industry eliminated BOCs.

benchmark program

An initiative designed to establish a consistent performance metric, against which multiple hardware or software products can be compared.

Berkeley Internet Name Domain (BIND)

A domain name system (DNS) server developed at the University of California, Berkeley. BIND is commonly used on Internet machines.

Berkeley Software Distribution UNIX (BSD UNIX)

A UNIX operating system variant developed at the University of California, Berkeley. BSD UNIX offers some enhancements to the original implementation of UNIX designed by AT&T, including virtual memory, networking, and interprocess communications.

Bernoulli drive

A high-capacity, removable cartridge drive.

best-effort delivery

A type of delivery system in networks that do not incorporate a sophisticated acknowledgment system to guarantee the reliable delivery of information.

beta site

A location where a hardware or software product undergoes pre-release live testing to examine its features and detect flaws before commercial release.

beta software

A software product that has been released to a selection of end users for live testing before the product is released commercially.

beta testing

A process whereby a new hardware or software product is field tested before it is released commercially.

big-endian

A term describing the order in which a word's individual bytes are stored. A big-endian system stores high-order bytes at the lower addresses. Mainframe processors, some RISC machines, and minicomputers use the big-endian system.

Bilateral Closed User Group (BCUG)

A facility offering more access control than the standard Closed User Group (CUG). The BCUG limits a CUG relationship to a pair of Data Terminal Equipment (DTE) units, where access between the DTEs is unlimited, but access to DTEs outside the given pair is not allowed.

binary

A numbering system that uses only zeroes and ones.

Binary Coded Decimal (BCD)

An encoding mechanism under which each digit is encoded as a 4-bit sequence.

binary file
A file containing binary information. The data contained in the file is machine-readable, as opposed to human-readable.

binary-capable
Describes a channel that allows a printer to receive all 8-bit characters. A binary-capable channel can accommodate both American Standard Code for Information Interchange (ASCII) and binary (that is, PostScript) print jobs.

binary transfer
Transmission of a file using a link configured to expect any type of data or bit pattern.

bind session
An Advanced Program-to-Program Communications (APPC) process used to establish a session between two logical units (LUs).

bindery
A nonhierarchical network database maintained by the network operating system on each server. Older versions of NetWare use this bindery mechanism to define network entities, including users, print queues, and workgroups. The bindery contains three types of components: objects (users, devices, and other physical or logical entities), properties (attributes such as full name or login restrictions), and a property data set (values to be stored in the object's property list).

bindery context
A NetWare container object that indicates where bindery services are set. *Bindery emulation*, used by Novell Directory Services (NDS) to provide backward compatibility with the older NetWare bindery model, requires a bindery context to be set for each NetWare 4.*x* server.

bindery emulation
A NetWare 4.*x* feature that enables bindery-based utilities and users to work with Novell Directory Services (NDS) on the same network. Under bindery emulation, NDS emulates the flat structure of the bindery to represent all objects within an Organizational container object. The objects within the

container object can then be accessed by NDS objects and by bindery-based clients and servers. As a result, bindery-based programs can access information from NDS. Bindery emulation applies only to leaf objects within the Organizational container object.

Bindery object

A leaf object representing an object placed in the Directory tree by an upgrade utility, which further cannot be identified by Novell Directory Services (NDS). Bindery-based clients need to use older NetWare utilities to gain access to these objects via bindery emulation. The Bindery object is placed for the purpose of backward-compatibility with bindery-based utilities.

Bindery Queue object

A Novell Directory Services (NDS) leaf object that represents a queue placed in a Directory tree by an upgrade utility, which further cannot be identified by Novell Directory Services (NDS). The Bindery Queue object is placed for the purpose of backward-compatibility with bindery-based utilities.

Bindery services

A NetWare 4.x feature that enables bindery-based utilities and clients to coexist with Novell Directory Services (NDS) on the same network. Bindery services emulate a flat database for holding network objects, as opposed to the hierarchical database as is used in NDS.

binding

A process that assigns a communications protocol to network boards and local area network (LAN) drivers (for example, Internet Packet Exchange/Sequenced Packet Exchange to an NE2000 Ethernet adapter). Every board must have a minimum of one communications protocol bound to the LAN driver for that board. It is possible to bind the same protocol stack to multiple LAN drivers on the server.

binhex

A contraction for "binary hexadecimal" that describes the process of converting nontext files into an American Standard Code for Information

Interchange (ASCII) text format. The conversion is often necessary because Internet electronic mail (e-mail) cannot be transmitted in a format other than ASCII.

bionet newsgroup
A type of newsgroup that discusses topics of interest to biologists.

BIOS Extensions
A set of firmware-based services that supplement those furnished by the standard Basic Input/Output System (BIOS).

biphase coding
A bipolar coding scheme in which clocking information is embedded into the synchronous data stream and then recovered without the need for separate clocking leads.

bipolar
An electrical circuit with both positive and negative polarity.

Bipolar with 8 Zero Substitution (B8ZS)
A signal-encoding scheme that represents a 1 alternatively as positive and negative voltage, with 0 representing zero voltage. Under the B8ZS encoding scheme, at least 1 out of every 8 bits must be set to a 1.

Bisynchronous Communication (BSC)
A protocol used in mainframe networks under which both sending and receiving devices must be synchronized before transmission begins. Under the bisynchronous model, data is collected into a frame (which contains a header and trailer recognized by the two computers) for synchronization purposes.

bit
The smallest unit of data in a computer. A bit is a type of virtual electronic switch, which is given a value of 0 to indicate an *off* condition, or a value of 1 to indicate an *on* condition. Eight bits equal one byte.

bit-array operations

Commands used by NetWare to manipulate bit arrays. NetWare Loadable Modules (NLMs) use bit array operations to scan bit arrays and to set or clear bits.

Bit Error Rate (BER)

The number of erroneous bits per million. The BER depends on the type and length of transmission, and the media involved in the data transfer.

Bit Error Rate Transfer (BERT)

A hardware device used for checking a transmission's bit error rate. The BERT sends a predefined signal, and then compares it with the received signal. A BERT may be used for troubleshooting a network's wiring.

bit interval

The amount of time a digital signal is left at one voltage level. The bit interval usually indicates the value of a single bit, although multiple bits can be encoded into one voltage level, which makes it possible to send multiple bits within a single bit interval.

bit rate

The rate at which bits are transmitted over a communications link. The bit rate is usually represented in bits per second (bps). A higher bit rate indicates a shorter bit interval. Bit rate is sometimes incorrectly used to mean *baud rate*.

bit stuffing

A technique for ensuring that a specific bit pattern does not appear as part of data in a transmission. Bit stuffing involves inserting additional bits, which are removed when the transmission is processed.

bitmap

A binary file in which each bit (or set of bits) corresponds to part of a graphical object, such as a font or an image.

bitmap/sequence field
A single-byte field in the AppleTalk Transaction Protocol (ATP) header. The field holds a transaction bitmap, which is used for a Transmission Request (TReq) packet, or a sequence number, which is used for a Transmission Response (TResp) packet.

BITFTP
A popular server to which users can send an electronic mail message to request that a file be mailed by way of electronic mail.

bit-oriented protocol
A communications protocol that transmits data as a stream of bits instead of bytes.

Bitronics
A specification developed by Hewlett-Packard Company to allow bidirectional parallel printing on a Centronics-type interface.

bits per second (bps)
A rate that shows the number of bits of information transmitted per second. This metric is similar, but not identical, to *baud rate*.

biz newsgroup
A type of newsgroup that discusses topics of interest to business and commercial entities.

black hole
In the context of internetwork routing, an area in which packets enter, but do not emerge because of adverse conditions or poor system configuration.

black tab folder
A folder that appears with a black band on the tab, indicating the particular user accessing the folder has the appropriate Access Control rights for modifying that folder's security parameters.

blackout

A complete loss of electrical power that may be the result of broken power lines or natural disasters.

block

A set of continuous bits or bytes that make up a piece of information. The block is the smallest amount of disk space that can be allocated at any one time on a NetWare volume. Block size depends on the volume size and is set automatically during installation. A NetWare block is usually 4K (although it can be set to 8K, 16K, 32K, or 64K); DOS blocks are usually a multiple of 2K. A disk allocation block that stores network data; a directory entry block that stores directory information. The term also denotes a capability of preventing a certain right from being exercised.

Block Check Character (BCC)

A character placed at the end of a block for the purpose of error detection. Each of the BCC's bits is a parity bit for a column of bits in the block.

Block Error Rate (BLER)

A communications error rate based on the proportion of blocks containing errors.

Block Error Rate Tester (BLERT)

A hardware device that determines a transmission's block error rate (BLER).

block parity

An error-detection method used in serial transmissions in which a value is calculated for each bit place value in a block of bytes. Block parity is always set to even.

Synonym: *longitudinal redundancy checking*

block suballocation

A procedure that allows the last part of several files to share a single disk block. The procedure is meant to make better use of disk space and divides a partially used disk block into 512-byte suballocation blocks. These suballocation blocks are then used to hold fragments of other files.

Blocked Asynchronous/Synchronous Transmission (BLAST)

A protocol that specifies data transmission in blocks containing a fixed number of bits. The BLAST protocol simplifies framing and may be used to multiplex transmissions.

blocking functions

Subroutines that can cause an application to give up control of the central processing unit (CPU). A function in blocking mode waits for a specific event to occur before returning control to the application.

Synonym: *synchronous functions*

Blue Book Ethernet

Ethernet version 2.0 (or Ethernet II), as distinguished from the Ethernet variant defined in the Institute of Electrical and Electronic Engineers (IEEE) 802.3 standard.

BNC connector

A connecting device with a half-turn locking shell for coaxial cable. The BNC connector is used with thin Ethernet and RG-62 cabling.

Bolt, Beranek, and Newman

The Massachusetts-based company responsible for development and maintenance of the Advanced Research Projects Agency Network (ARPAnet) and Internet core gateway system.

bookmark

An Internet browser device that marks a specific menu or directory and provides the user with easy access to the marked menu or directory.

bookshelf

An icon representing a set of related books.

Boolean

A logic system that incorporates True or False values combined with AND, OR, and NOT operators. Search engines on the Internet often employ the

Boolean logic system by enabling users to specify search strings that include the Boolean operators to expand the scope of a search.

boot

The process of starting up a computer. The boot process loads the operating system kernel into the random access memory (RAM), executes and loads programs, and configures the operating environment.

boot disk

An external disk used to load and start the operating system.

boot files

A set of files that start the operating system and its driver, set environment variables, or execute other system tasks. DOS boot files include AUTOEXEC.BAT and CONFIG.SYS. NetWare server boot files include AUTOEXEC.NCF and STARTUP.NCF.

boot **PROM**

A nonvolatile type of programmable read-only memory (PROM) that can be transmitted over a network and contains information for initializing a computer system at startup.

boot **ROM**

A read-only memory (ROM) chip used to start up a diskless workstation and connect it to the network.

boot sector

In IBM-compatible PCs, a record contained in a storage device (such as a disk) that provides the computer's built-in operating system with basic information about the disk and the version of DOS in use. The boot sector facilitates placing DOS in the computer's memory.

bootstrap program

A program that provides the end user with a prompt at startup, offering an opportunity to select which disk-image file to boot.

Bootstrap Protocol (BOOTP)

A protocol used by a host computer to obtain its Internet Protocol (IP) address. The host obtains this information by broadcasting a BOOTP request on the local network. The server then receives the request, and replies with a packet that contains the host's address.

border gateway

An Autonomous System (AS) router that communicates with other AS routers.

Border Gateway Protocol (BGP)

A routing protocol designed to replace the External Gateway Protocol (EGP). BGP that interconnects organizational networks and evaluates each possible route for the best available option.

bot

A shortened version of the term *robot*, describing a program that responds to network requests by using a specified set of actions or responses.

bounce

Occurs when a message moves back and forth between servers indefinitely because of an error condition or is returned to the sender when undeliverable.

boundary function

A capability of subarea nodes in Systems Network Architecture (SNA) networks that provides protocol support for attached peripheral nodes.

braid shield

A braid or mesh conductor that surrounds the insulation and foil shield in coaxial cable. The braid protects the carrier wire from interference.

branch

A container object and all the objects it contains. In a Novell Directory Services (NDS) Directory tree, the branch can contain other container objects.
Synonym: *subtree*

breakout box

A device connected to a multicore cable for testing signals in a transmission. The breakout box features Light Emitting Diodes (LEDs) to indicate when a signal is being transmitted.

bridge

A hardware device used to connect two or more physical networks or network segments. A bridge forwards frames between the connecting networks on the basis of information contained in the data-link header. Operating at the Data-Link Layer (Layer 2) of the OSI Reference Model, bridges are transparent to Network-Layer (Layer 3) protocols. (A bridge differs from a *router*, which forwards packets between different network topologies and determines the best path between the two. A router operates at the Network Layer of the OSI Reference Model.) The bridge also functions as a filter, discarding packets intended for the originating network and sending on packets intended for the destination network.

A bridge is protocol-independent and can, therefore, handle packets from multiple higher-level protocols. It can operate at the Media Access Control (MAC) sublayer or the Logical Link Control (LLC) sublayer of the Data-Link Layer. A MAC Layer bridge can connect only networks using the same architecture; an LLC bridge can connect networks using different architectures.

Bridge Protocol Data Unit (BPDU)

A hello packet in a spanning-tree protocol.

broadband

A transmission technology that multiplexes several independent network carriers onto a single cable. Broadband networking permits multiple networks to coexist on a single cable.

broadband network

A network employing broadband technology to transmit multiple streams of information over long distances over the same cable. The network is divided into multiple channels that can be used concurrently by different networks, using a frequency-division multiplexing technique. Each channel is protected from the others by *guard channels*, small bands of unused frequency placed in between the data channels.

B

broadband transmission
An analog communication technique that uses several communications channels simultaneously. Data in a broadband transmission is modulated into *frequency bands* (*channels*). A *guard band* is a band of unused frequency inserted between these data channels to provide a buffer against interference.

broadcast
A transmission method in which all nodes on the network receive a copy of a frame or packet.

Broadcast and Unknown Server (BUS)
An Asynchronous Transfer Mode (ATM) server that handles data sent to a LAN Emulation client, as well as all multicast traffic (and initial unicast frames) sent by a LAN Emulation client.

Broadcast Integrated Service Digital Network (BISDN)
A high-speed communications standard for wide area networks (WANs) that can accommodate high-bandwidth applications (such as video or graphics).

broadcast storm
A condition in which one workstation triggers several other workstations to transmit large numbers of frames simultaneously. A broadcast storm can result from loops occurring on a bridged network and can cause network congestion.

broadcast-oriented cable
Cable designed to carry video signals sent from one location in the network. Broadcast-oriented cable is designed for one-way communication.

brouter
A hardware device that combines the functions of a bridge and router, routing some protocols and bridging others. A brouter can operate at either the Data-Link Layer (Layer 2) or the Network Layer (Layer 3) of the OSI Reference Model.

brownout

A short-term decrease in voltage level that may occur when a piece of heavy machinery is started. A brownout may cause a computer to crash unless a device such as an uninterruptible power supply (UPS) is in use.

Browse right

An object right that grants the right to see an object in the Directory tree. Upon installation, if every trustee is granted the Browse right at the Directory tree [Root], all users have unlimited access. The Browse right can be removed from the [Root] object if desired.

Synonym: *Browse object right*

browser

A window in the NetWare Administrator utility that shows objects in the Directory tree; or part of the DOS menu utility that enables users to move around the Directory tree; or an Internet utility (such as Netscape Navigator or Microsoft Internet Explorer) that enables users to view pages on the World Wide Web (WWW).

browsing

A way to find objects in a Novell Directory Services (NDS) Directory tree. To find a desired object, a user can browse the Directory tree in either direction to view different parts of the Directory.

BSD Socket Layer

A layer in BSD UNIX that represents the Application Program Interface (API) between user applications and the networking subsystem of the operating system kernel.

Btrieve

A key-indexed, record-management system used for file handling. A function call can be issued from most standard programming languages to invoke Btrieve. The Btrieve program stores data in Btrieve files, which can be recognized by several existing database programs. More than one user or application can access a Btrieve data file at the same time, and Btrieve maintains the file integrity during this concurrent access. The program is available in both client-based and server-based implementations. In addition to record management, Btrieve also includes communications facilities, requesters, utilities, data-protection functions, and support for Novell Directory Services (NDS).

buffer
An area of a computer's random access memory (RAM) that temporarily holds data until its disposition. A buffer can be used to mitigate differences in data-flow rates.

buffer (fiber-optic cable)
A layer that surrounds the cladding in fiber-optic cabling.

buffered repeater
A device for cleaning and boosting signals before sending them. A buffered repeater holds a message temporarily if a transmission is already on the network.

bug
A logical or programming error that exists in hardware or software. A software bug can be repaired by altering the program; a hardware bug requires new physical circuits.

bug fix
A release of hardware or software that corrects known bugs. The bug fix generally does not introduce new features, but is released merely to correct flaws.

built-in command
An operating system command that resides in memory.

Bulletin Board System (BBS)
A computer or group of computers equipped with modems, used to permit access by other computers dialing in from remote locations. BBSs enable users to send messages, get technical support, or access files. Special interest groups often use BBSs to disseminate information and to provide services to members.

bundled software
Software applications sold with hardware (or with other applications) for a single price.

Burned-In Address (BIA)
A hardware address for a Network Interface Card (NIC), typically assigned by the manufacturer, that is different for each card.

burst
Several units of data sent in a single high-speed transmission.

burst mode
A method of transmitting data across a network. In burst mode, data is collected and sent as a unit in a single high-speed transmission.
Synonym: *packet burst*

burst speed
The highest speed at which a device can function without interruption. The burst speed is usually achieved only for short periods of time.

bus
A path for electrical signals between a central processing unit (CPU) and attached peripherals. Buses are defined by their bit values, speed, and control mechanisms. Also denotes a physical network topology in which all messages are broadcast over a central cable.

Bus Interface Board (BIB)
An expansion board that functions as an interface between the computer and the network medium.

Bus Interface Unit (BIU)
A network interface card that functions as an interface between a computer node and the network.

bus mastering

A bus-access method that allows a hardware device to take control of the bus and sends data directly to it, without assistance from the central processing unit (CPU). Bus mastering can significantly improve throughput; various architectures support it: Microchannel Architecture (MCA), Extended Industry Standard Architecture (EISA), VESA local (V), and Peripheral Component Interconnect (PCI). Industry Standard Architecture (ISA) machines, however, do not support bus mastering.

bus network topology

A type of network topology in which all workstations and servers are connected to a central cable. Ethernet networks are often designed with a bus topology.

bypass

A telephony connection that uses an interexchange carrier without going through a local exchange carrier.

bypass printing

A method of printing that runs the print job directly from a client workstation to the printer. Bypass printing circumvents the print queue and can be prevented by configuring the AppleTalk Print Services (ATPS) NetWare Loadable Module (NLM) and AppleTalk Extended Remote Printer (ATXRP) NLM to hide printers.

byte

A unit of data consisting of eight bits. A byte is the amount of storage that represents a single character.
Synonym: *octet*

byte reversal

A data-storage format used by IBM personal computers. Byte reversal stores numeric 16-bit and 32-bit values with the least-significant bytes stored in lower-numbered addresses. Larger IBM computer systems (such as minicomputers and mainframes) use the opposite method.

Byte-Control Protocol (BCP)
A character-oriented protocol, as opposed to a bit-oriented protocol.

byte-oriented protocol
A communications protocol used to transmit data as a series of bytes, or individual characters. Many asynchronous protocols used with modems are byte-oriented.

Byzantine failure
A situation in which a network node fails, but does not disappear from the network, and continues to operate, but functions improperly.

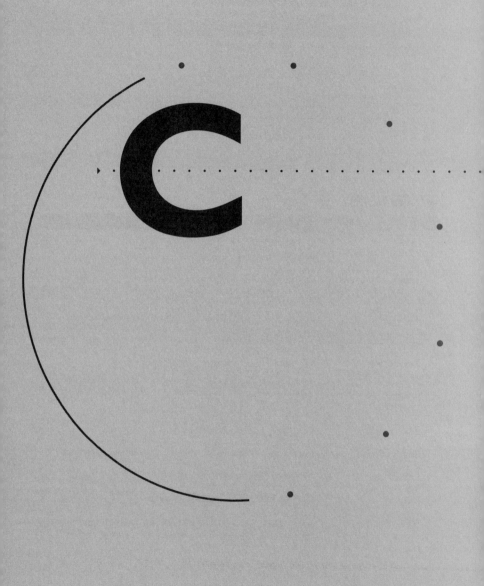

C2

A level of enhanced operating system security defined by the National Computer Security Center.

cable

A linear physical medium used to transmit information between nodes in a network. The five main types of cable used in networking are coaxial, shielded twisted-pair (STP), unshielded twisted-pair (UTP), IBM, and fiber-optic. Cable components include a conductor medium to carry the signal, insulation, and an outer sheath. Table C.1 lists common cable types.

TABLE C.1	Cable Types
CABLE TYPE	**USE**
1394	Connects multiple digital devices (such as video and audio hardware)
adapter	Connects Token Ring Network Interface Card (NIC) to hub or Multistation Access Unit (MAU)
backbone	Serves as primary cable for connecting networks
broadcast-oriented	Carries video signals
Category x	Connects telecommunications devices
CATV	Carries cable television signals
coaxial	Carries data transmissions
data-grade	Carries data transmissions
distribution	Serves as intermediate cable for connecting networks
drop	Connects NIC to a transceiver
feeder	Carries both voice and data signals
fiber-optic	Connects Fiber Distributed Data Interface networks, long-haul networks, network segments (nodes), mainframe computers to peripherals, and high-speed, high-performance workstations

CABLE TYPE	USE
horizontal	Connects wiring closet to wall outlet in work area
IBM	Connects Token Ring networks, 10BaseT Ethernet networks, ARCnet networks, Integrated Services Digital Network (ISDN) lines, and some IBM 3270 networks
patch	Connects two hubs or MAUs
plenum	Serves as a fireproof connection through a conduit in a wall, floor, or ceiling
quad shield	A variation of coaxial cable used where heavy electrical interference can occur
quadrax	A variation of coaxial cable that is a hybrid of triaxial and twinaxial cable with the same uses as coaxial cable
ribbon	Connects internal disk drives or tape drives
riser	Serves as vertical connector (for example, between floors in a building)
shielded twisted-pair	Connects IBM Token Ring networks and ARCnet networks
thick coax	Connects thick Ethernet networks and cable television
thin coaxial	Connects thin Ethernet and ARCnet networks
transceiver	Connects a NIC to a transceiver in an Ethernet network
triaxial	A variation of coaxial cable that adds grounding and improves protection
twinaxial	A variation of coaxial cable that connects IBM and AppleTalk networks
twisted-pair	Connects IBM Token Ring networks, ARCnet networks, 10BaseT networks, and telephone lines
IBM Type 1	Connects Token Ring networks

(continued)

TABLE C.I	Cable Types (continued)
CABLE TYPE	**USE**
IBM Type 2	Transmits voice and data
IBM Type 3	Connects 16 megabits per second (Mbps) networks
IBM Type 5	Connects MAUs in a Token Ring network
IBM Type 6	Serves as a short-distance patch
IBM Type 8	Serves as a flat cable placed beneath a carpet
IBM Type 9	Serves as a connector between floors
unshielded twisted-pair	Connects 10BaseT networks, ARCnet networks, and telephone lines
voice-grade cable	Transmits voice signals

cable modem

An interface box or computer adapter board that enables cable television to serve as a data link.

Cable Retransmission Facility (CRF)

The starting point in a broadband network. End stations can transmit control and error information, but not data, to the CRF.

Cable Signal Fault Signature (CSFS)

A unique signal used for testing a line's electrical activity when using time domain reflectometry. The CSFS may assist a technician in pinpointing the source of a problem.

cable standards

Standards that establish a minimum level of functionality for a cable. Most of these standards have been established by the National Electric Code (NEC) and from Underwriters Laboratories; others have also been specified by the Electronics Industry Association/Telecommunications Industries Association (EIA/TIA), Electrical Testing Laboratory, and Manufacturing Automation Protocol.

cable tester

An instrument that tests for such cable properties as attenuation, resistance, and characteristic impedance.

cabling system

A specific physical layout of network cable. This portion of a network's physical structure gives the network a characteristic shape (*topology*).

cache

A portion of random access memory (RAM) that can be accessed quickly. The cache is often used to store frequently used blocks of data as a way to minimize the time the central processing unit (CPU) must spend accessing it. Because RAM can be accessed faster than a hard drive, storing frequently used data in RAM improves a system's performance. When a processor references a memory address, the cache first checks to see whether the address holds the desired data. If so, the information is sent directly to the processor.

cache buffer

A block of server memory where files are stored temporarily for quick access. The size of the cache buffer depends on the default block size, which in turn depends on the size of the volume. Because reading data from memory is faster than reading it from disk, the cache buffer facilitates faster access to the data it holds.

cache controller

A specialized coprocessor that manages the cache memory. In some newer processors, cache management is incorporated directly into the main processor.

cache hit

An event that occurs when a block of disk memory is used for a file.

cache memory

Available random access memory (RAM) that can be used by NetWare to improve server access time. Cache memory allocates RAM for the hash table, File Allocation Table (FAT), Turbo FAT, suballocation tables, directory cache, temporary storage for files, and other functions.

The two types of cache memory are as follows:

▸ *Directory cache.* This is the area holding the directory entries when the FAT and Directory Entry Table (DET) are written into the server's memory.

▸ *File cache.* When a workstation makes a read request to the server, the server executes a hash algorithm to calculate the file's address from a hash table. After the directory entry is located, the server sends the file to the workstation—either directly from server memory or after retrieval from disk.

caddy
A flat, plastic container used to load a compact disc into some CD-ROM drives.

call
A request issued by a network node to establish communications with another node.

call authentication
A method used to protect against unauthorized access into a system from a remote location. The authentication often is accomplished through the use of the Password Authentication Protocol (PAP) or through Challenge Handshake Authentication Protocol (CHAP).

call control
A set of actions that can establish, maintain, or disconnect a wide area network (WAN) connection. Call control exists within the Call Support Layer.

Call Control Agent
A software module that works with the Call Support Layer. The Call Control Agent includes wide area network (WAN) media-specific connection management logic.

call packet

A block of data that holds addressing information and other data needed to establish a switched virtual circuit that complies with the X.25 specification of the Consultative Committee for International Telegraphy and Telephony (CCITT).

call priority

A priority assigned to each origination port in a circuit-switched system. The order of call priorities defines the order in which cells are reconnected.

Call Request packet

A control packet sent to a Directory Table Entry (DTE) to request initiation of a virtual call.

call setup time

The time needed to establish a connection between two nodes on a network.

Call Support Layer

A software module that provides a general interface for controlling wide area network (WAN) calls.

callback modem

A type of modem that does not answer incoming calls. The caller, instead, enters a code and hangs up, and then the modem returns the call if the code matches an authorized number.

caller ID

A telecommunications feature that includes a sender's identification number in the transmission, so the recipient can see who is calling before the call is answered.

Synonym: *automatic number identification*

Calling Line Identification (CLID)

A feature of the Integrated Services Digital Network (ISDN) that includes the sender's identification number as part of the transmission, so the recipient knows who is calling before answering the call.

Campus Area Network (CAN)

A network that connects local area networks (LANs) from many locations, such as several floors of a building or several buildings. These locations can be physically separated over a great distance. A campus area network does not require remote communications devices such as modems or telephones, which makes it different from a wide area network (WAN).

Campus-Wide Information System (CWIS)

An online collection of information (such as an events calendar, course listing, and job openings) concerning a particular school or campus.

Canadian Standards Association

A Canadian agency responsible for certifying that products comply with Canadian national safety standards.

cancelbot

A contraction for "cancel robot," a system that automatically sends out messages requesting the removal of newsgroup messages.

canonicalize

To expand an abbreviated Novell Directory Services (NDS) name to its canonical form, which includes the full naming path and a type specification for each naming component.

Can't Compress (Cc) attribute

A NetWare file attribute that produces a status flag to indicate a file cannot be compressed because doing so would not yield significant space savings.

capacitance

The capability of a nonconductive material to store electricity and resist voltage changes. Capacitance is measured in microfarads or picofarads. Cable with lower capacitance is considered superior.

capacitor

An electrical component designed to hold a charge. Capacitors are available in several sizes and, typically, clean incoming power by absorbing surges and interference.

capacity threshold

A predetermined percentage of a server's hard disk that shows how much of the disk can be used before files must be migrated to a backup storage device.

card

A printed circuit board or adapter plugged into a computer to add a specialized function or support for a peripheral device.

carriage return

A control character for a hard return, as represented by American Standard Code for Information Interchange (ASCII) code 13, which signals the display cursor or print head to return to the first position of the line.

carrier

An analog signal of fixed amplitude and frequency that, with a data-carrying signal, forms an output signal used for transmitting data.

carrier band

A communications system that uses the entire bandwidth for one transmission. The signal is modulated before transmission.

Carrier Detect (CD)

A signal sent from a modem to a personal computer to indicate the modem is available for operation.

carrier frequency

The rate at which a carrier signal repeats, measured in hertz (Hz). The carrier frequency is modulated by superimposing a second signal that represents the information being transmitted.

Carrier On

A signal used in Carrier Sense Multiple Access (CSMA) media-access mechanisms to indicate the network is in use. If a node detects the Carrier On signal, it waits a random period of time before attempting to transmit.

carrier pulse

A signal consisting of rapid constant pulses that form the pulse modulation.

Carrier Sense Multiple Access/Collision Avoidance (CSMA/CA)

A media-access method that functions at the Media Access Control (MAC) Sublayer of the OSI Reference Model and is used in Apple LocalTalk networks. Under the CSMA/CA process, before a node transmits on the network, it first listens for activity. If activity is detected, the node waits a random period of time before attempting again. CSMA/CA is *contentious;* the first node that tries to gain access to an unused network is the one allowed to transmit. CSMA/CA has no methods for assigning priority to data. In the event of a collision, LocalTalk passes the problem on to a higher-level protocol. Collision avoidance is less sophisticated than collision detection and is, therefore, less expensive to build into a chip set.

Carrier Sense Multiple Access/Collision Detection (CSMA/CD)

A media-access protocol for dealing with the effects of packet collision. CSMA/CD is used in Ethernet and 802.3 networks, and functions on the Media Access Control (MAC) Sublayer of the OSI Reference Model. In the CSMA/CD model, a node first attempts to detect whether traffic exists on the network. If there is activity, the node waits a random period of time before attempting to transmit. If no activity exists, the node transmits. If two nodes transmit at precisely the same moment, a collision occurs. In the event of a collision, CSMA/CD discards the packets, causes the nodes to cancel their transmissions, and waits a random period of time before attempting to retransmit. CSMA/CD is *contentious;* the first node that tries to gain access to an unused network is allowed to transmit. CSMA/CD has no methods for assigning priority to data.

carrier signal

An electrical signal that forms the basis of a transmission. The carrier signal does not send any information, although it does have defined properties. The carrier signal is modified (or *modulated*) to transmit information.

carrier wire

A conductive wire that serves as a medium for an electrical signal.

Carrier-Switched Multiplexer (CS-MUX)

A component used in a Fiber Distributed Data Interface (FDDI) network to pass time-dependent data to the architecture's Media Access Control (MAC) Layer.

cartridge

A hardware peripheral device, such as a PostScript cartridge, which attaches to a primary hardware device, such as a printer.

cascaded bridge topology

A method of using bridges to connect several networks. In this topology, a middle network serves as an access point between two other networks; the two end networks must go through the middle network to communicate. The advantage of a cascaded bridge topology is it eliminates the need for one bridge; no direct connection exists between the two end networks.

cascaded star

A network topology that connects multiple hubs in a succession of levels to allow more connections than would be possible in a single level.

cascading

A method of addressing one Interrupt Request Channel (IRQ) to another IRQ. Cascading is used to avoid losing access to an IRQ in the first bank.

case-insensitive

A characteristic applied to information sorting. In a case-insensitive sort, the values of uppercase letters are equal to the values of lowercase letters.

case-sensitive

A characteristic applied to information sorting. In a case-sensitive sort, the values of uppercase letters are distinct and different from the values of lowercase letters.

Category *x* cable

A set of cabling standards (sometimes abbreviated CAT 1-5) established by the Electronics Industry Association/Telecommunications Industry Association (EIA/TIA).The categories are as follows:

► *Category 1*. Unshielded twisted-pair (UTP) telephone cable.

► *Category 2*. UTP cable for use at speeds of up to 4 megabits per second (Mbps).

► *Category 3*. UTP cable for use at speeds of up to 10Mbps. 10BaseT networks require a minimum of Category 3 cabling.

► *Category 4*. The lowest grade of UTP cabling acceptable for a 16Mbps Token Ring network.

► *Category 5*. UTP cable for use at speeds of up to 100Mbps.

catenet

A network (such as the Internet) that connects hosts to a diverse set of networks, which are themselves connected with routers.

CD-ROM drive

A hardware peripheral for reading compact discs. A CD-ROM drive may be connected to an individual workstation or to a network. If connected to the network, the compact discs can be shared between multiple users.

CD-ROM Extended Architecture (CD-ROM/XA)

An extension to the CD-ROM format developed by Microsoft, Phillips, and Sony. CD-ROM/XA facilitates storage of audio and visual information on a compact disc, thereby enabling users to play audio while viewing visual data at the same time.

CD-ROM File System (CDFS)
A specialized file structure used to store information on a compact disc. The file allocation table (FAT) is inadequate for use on a CD-ROM because of the high number of files that may be contained on the CD-ROM.

cell
A fixed-length data packet.

cell (ATM)
The individual unit of data used in transmitting information in an Asynchronous Transfer Mode (ATM) network. An ATM cell contains a uniform 53 bytes: 48 bytes are used for data and 5 bytes are used for header information.

Cell Loss Priority (CLP)
In an Asynchronous Transfer Mode (ATM) network, a bit value that specifies whether a particular cell can be discarded if necessary. ATM's traffic policing function uses a buffering technique, known as a *leaky bucket*, where traffic flows (or leaks) out of a buffer (or bucket) at a constant rate, regardless of how fast it flows into the bucket. If the buffer starts to overflow, the ATM switch polices the buffer by examining the CLP bit that exists in the header of every ATM cell. This bit identifies cells that can be discarded, if necessary.

cell relay
A type of packet transmission used in a Broadcast Integrated Service Digital Network (BISDN).

cell-switched network
A type of network that offers the advantages of both circuit-switching and packet-switching. A cell-switched network offers guaranteed bandwidth, as well as the efficiency inherent in a packet-switched network.

cellular communications
A wireless communications technology. In the cellular model, the communications area is divided into smaller geographical areas, or cells, and transmissions are passed between cells until they reach their final destinations. Every cell has an antenna to pick up signals from the adjacent cells or callers.

Cellular Digital Packet Data (CDPD)

A cellular communications method for sending data that transmits over any cellular channel currently not in use, in an attempt to achieve a greater level of efficiency.

cellular network

A type of wireless network that operates in the 825 to 890 megahertz (MHz) range. A cellular network uses individual stations, or cells, to pass signals from the sender, between stations, and, eventually, to the recipient. A cellular data network competes with cellular voice channels for bandwidth.

cellular radio

A telecommunications technology that uses radio transmissions to access a telephone network through a series of cells (transmission areas).

Central Office (CO)

The nearest telephone switching station that provides switching services, dial tone services, private lines, and Centrex. Telephone customers are directly connected to a CO, which, in turn, connects them to the rest of the telecommunications system.

central processing

A network configuration where a single server processes tasks for several workstations. All the workstations in this configuration can communicate with the server, and all share the computing power of the central processor. Because the workstations share the server's processing power, central processing networks with more workstations operate slower than networks with fewer workstations.

central processing unit (CPU)

The part of a computer that processes data. This term typically refers to the computer's chassis and all its attached components.

centralized network

A type of network where a single machine controls network activity. A mainframe-based network is usually centralized.

Centrex (Central Exchange)

Services offered to a company by the local telephone company. All switching takes place in the telephone company's central office as opposed to the customer's site.

Centronics parallel interface

A 36-pin interface used for connecting a personal computer to a peripheral device. The Centronics parallel interface uses eight parallel data lines and additional lines for status and control information.

Certificate Authority (CA)

The issuer of a chunk of information used by certain network protocols to secure a network connection. The information (often embedded in a text file) enhances network security levels.

Certified Novell Administrator (CNA)

A certificate program in which users responsible for daily network operations take classes and pass tests to achieve the CNA designation.

Synonym: *Certified NetWare Administrator*

Certified Novell Instructor (CNI)

A certification program in which users take classes and pass tests to achieve the CNI designation. CNIs are certified to teach Novell courses.

Synonym: *Certified NetWare Instructor*

Certified Novell Technician (CNT)

A certification program in which users take classes and pass tests to achieve the CNT designation.

Synonym: *Certified NetWare Technician*

chaining

The act of grouping together Systems Network Architecture (SNA) Request/Response Units (RUs) to aid in error recovery.

Challenge Handshake Authentication Protocol (CHAP)

An inbound call-protection method that allows a receiving node to initiate a challenge sequence, which is then modified by the caller before the call can take place.

change-direction protocol

A data flow control protocol in a Systems Network Architecture (SNA) network used when the logical unit (LU) stops sending requests and sends a signal indicating it has done so to the receiving LU. The LU then prepares to receive requests.

channel

A logical or physical path for transmitting electromagnetic signals. The path may include a host bus adapter, cables, and storage devices. A *communications channel* is used to transmit data or voice. A *disk channel* includes the components that connect a hard drive to an operating environment.
Synonyms: *line; link*

channel attachment

The direct connection of data channels (or Input/Output channels) to a computer.

channel bank

A device that multiplexes several low-speed signals into one high-speed signal.

channel operator (chan-op)

A person who starts an Internet Relay Chat (IRC) session and controls such parameters as public accessibility and who can participate.

channel service unit (CSU)

A digital signal processor that performs transmit-and-receive filtering, signal shaping, longitudinal balance, voltage isolation, equalization, and remote loopback testing for digital transmission. The CSU functions as a buffer between customer premises equipment (CPE) and the public carrier wide area network (WAN), preventing a faulty CPE from affecting the public carrier's system. The CSU takes data from a Digital Data Service (DDS) line and hands it off to a Data Service Unit (DSU), which then interfaces with computer equipment. A CSU may be combined with a DSU to form a single Integrated Service Unit (ISU).

CHAOSnet protocol

A network protocol used primarily in the artificial intelligence community. CHAOSnet was developed at the Massachusetts Institute of Technology (MIT).

character

A group of eight binary digits that function together as a single unit. This group represents a single letter or symbol in an encoding scheme, such as American Standard Code for Information Interchange (ASCII) or Extended Binary-Coded Decimal Interchange Code (EBCDIC).

Synonyms: *byte; octet*

character code

A code that represents an alphanumeric character in a character set, such as American Standard Code for Information Interchange (ASCII) or Extended Binary-Coded Decimal Interchange Code (EBCDIC).

character length

The number of bits that form a character. The standard American Standard Code for Information Interchange (ASCII) character set requires a character length of 7 bits for transmissions.

Character Manipulation Services

A set of American National Standards Institute (ANSI) functions for testing alphanumeric characters. These services can convert alphanumeric characters between uppercase and lowercase, or to convert multibyte characters into wide-character codes.

character mode

A video adapter mode used in personal computers. A personal computer in character mode displays characters onscreen from the built-in character set, but does not show graphics or a mouse pointer.

Synonym: *text mode*

character set
A group of letters, numbers, or symbols, such as American Standard Code for Information Interchange (ASCII) or Extended Binary-Coded Decimal Interchange Code (EBCDIC), which is used by a computer.

character string
An array of any number of adjacent characters followed by a NULL character, which marks the end of the string.

character-based interface
An operating system or application that uses only text characters for the user interface.

Character-Oriented Windows Interface (COW)
A Systems Application Architecture (SAA) compatible interface used in the OS/2 operating system.

characters per second (cps)
The number of characters transmitted every second during a data transfer.

chat
A real-time online conversation with other network users.

chat room
An Internet site where real-time online conversations with other network users take place.

chatter
An error condition in which a flawed network board may cause the Packet Receive Buffer count to climb quickly.

CHDIR command
A DOS command for changing directories. The CHDIR command changes the current drive directory and displays the current directory path.

CheaperNet
A 10Base-2 thin coaxial cable network.

checkbox
A Graphical User Interface (GUI) box used to select options. When a checkbox option has been selected, an *x* appears in the box.

checksum
A calculation that keeps a running total of the bits of a transmitted message as a means of detecting errors in transmission. This value is transmitted with the message; the recipient will then recalculate the checksum and compare it to the received value.

child
A data set with no subordinates or the lowest level of a directory structure.

child document
A file or document called up by a World Wide Web (WWW) browser to fill a frame under the direction of a layout document (called the *parent document*).

child VLM
A NetWare Virtual Loadable Module (VLM) that handles a specific implementation of a logical group of functions.

chip creep
The loss of a solid electrical connection between an integrated circuit and its socket. Chip creep can result from frequent temperature changes.

chmod
A UNIX command that sets who can read, write, or execute a file, as well as other technical parameters.

choke packet
A packet that tells a transmitter congestion exists on the network and the transmitter should reduce its sending rate.

Chooser

A Chooser Desk Accessory (DA) utility that enables Macintosh users to access network devices, including file servers and printers.

chromatic dispersion

The dispersion of a light signal in a fiber-optic transmission. Chromatic dispersion is the result of the different propagation speeds of the light at different wavelengths.

chunk

An arbitrary portion of a record or piece of data, usually specified by offset and length.

Cipher Block Chaining (CBC)

An operating mode used by the Data Encryption Standard.

Cipher Feedback (CFB)

An operating mode used by the Data Encryption Standard.

ciphertext

Text that has been encrypted to make it impossible to read without the key to the encryption scheme.

circuit

A closed path that carries an electrical current.

circuit board

A flat board on which electrical components are mounted and interconnected to form a circuit. The board is constructed of an insulating material, such as epoxy or phenolic resin. Interconnection between the components usually is made with patterns of copper foil that may appear on one or both sides of the board.

circuit switching

A technique for establishing a nonsharable, temporary connection between two end devices.

circuit-switched network

A type of connection-oriented network in which a temporary dedicated circuit is established between two nodes. The circuit provides a guaranteed level of bandwidth for the connection and is disabled when the transmission is completed.

cladding

The material surrounding the fiber core in a fiber-optic cable. Cladding has a lower refraction index than the core; light that hits the cladding will reflect back to the core and can continue on its path.

clamping time

The amount of time a surge protector requires to deal with a voltage spike or surge, and then to return the voltage to an acceptable level.

Class A Certification

A Federal Communications Commission (FCC) certification for industrial, commercial, or office equipment. The Class A commercial certification is not as restrictive as the Class B certification.

Class A network address

An Internet address class used for networks with as many as 16.8 million nodes. This class has 128 addresses available.

Class B Certification

A Federal Communications Commission (FCC) certification for computer equipment intended for home use. The Class B certification is more restrictive than the commercial Class A certification.

Class B network address

An Internet address class used for networks with up to 65,536 nodes. This class has 16,384 addresses available.

Class C network address

An Internet address class used for networks with up to 255 nodes. This class has 2 million addresses available.

Class D network address

An Internet address class used for multicast networks. This class has 268.4 million addresses available.

Classless Interdomain Routing (CIDR)

A routing strategy that enables organizations or corporations with more than 256 nodes—but fewer than 65,536 nodes—on a network to use a special Class C Internet address. This strategy allows the assignment of consecutive Class C addresses to these organizations and corporations so that routers view the cluster as a "supernetwork," rather than viewing the entire organizational or corporate network as a separate network (which would require a Class B address).

Clear Request packet

A control packet sent to Data Terminal Equipment (DTE) to request a virtual call be terminated.

Clear to Send (CTS)

A control signal generated by data communications hardware to indicate readiness to transmit data. The CTS signal is usually sent in response to a Request To Send (RTS) signal issued by a node requesting to transmit data over the network.

Clearing Center (CC)

A message-switching element of Electronic Data Interchange (EDI). The Clearing Center transmits documents to their destinations.

Clearinghouse Protocol

A protocol in the Xerox Network Systems (XNS) protocol suite used in the Presentation Layer (Layer 6) of the OSI Reference Model.

clear-text User Authentication Module (UAM)

A type of authentication that does not use password encryption. The network interprets each user's password as entered and is, therefore, more vulnerable to detection.

client

A workstation in a network capable of gaining access to network services. In other contexts, the term can be used to refer to a software (such as network-connectivity software or the Btrieve engine) that runs on a given workstation, as opposed to the workstation itself.

client application

In Object Linking and Embedding (OLE), the application that starts the server application for the purpose of manipulating linked or embedded information.

Client 16

Workstation-connectivity software that provides 16-bit DOS or Windows 3.x access to NetWare 2.2, NetWare 3.12, and NetWare 4.11 servers that have Open Data-link Interface (ODI) drivers, Virtual Loadable Modules (VLMs), and the NET.CFG file.

Client 32

Workstation-connectivity software that provides 32-bit access to NetWare 2.2, NetWare 3.12, and NetWare 4.11 servers from Windows 95, Windows 3.1, or DOS. Client 32 provides a graphical utility to log in from Windows or the capability to access network files and printers through Windows 95 dialog boxes, such as Network Neighborhood or Windows Explorer.

client type

Refers to the operating system the client machine runs. For example, under NetWare, client types can include DOS, Macintosh, OS/2, UNIX, and Windows.

client-based application

An application executed from the client machine (or workstation) in a network.

client-server model

A type of network configuration that distributes intelligence from the server to the individual workstations on the network. In this model, the client requests services from the servers, which receive the requests and return data or results. The server is typically a more powerful computer, with the client being a desktop machine. Processing can occur on the client, the server, on both client and server (as *distributed processing*) on many machines. A client-server application can be divided into a *front end* (which runs on the client) and a *back end* (which runs on the server). The front end includes an interface that enables end users to make requests and issue commands to be carried out at the back end.

client-server network

A network that dedicates at least one personal computer to function as a server. The server runs the network operating system, controls communication, and manages shared resources. The clients, on the other hand, are individual user workstations that share those resources while connected to the network.

client-server operating system

An operating system that runs on a server in a client-server network. This operating system is responsible for coordinating how clients access the resources of the server. NetWare 3.x and NetWare 4.x are client-server operating systems.

clock

An electronic circuit that generates periodic pulses used to synchronize information flow through a computer's internal communications channels.

clock doubling

A technique used by some processors to process data internally at double the speed used when communicating with other system components.

clock speed

A measurement of processing efficiency, expressed in megahertz (MHz).

clocking

A method of time-synchronizing a system's communication data.

clone
A hardware device that uses the same physical architecture (structure) as another.

closed architecture
A hardware design that does not enable user-supplied or third-party additions.

Closed User Group (CUG)
A facility for configuring virtual private networks within a larger public network. A CUG enables an administrator to collect many Data Terminal Equipment (DTE) devices into one logical group. That group's ability to receive or make outgoing calls can then be restricted.

cluster
A group of I/O devices in a Systems Network Architecture (SNA) network that share a communications path to the host machine. A *cluster controller* manages the communications between the cluster and the host.

cluster controller
An IBM-compatible device for attaching 3270-class terminals. The cluster controller can be channel-attached to a host system or may communicate with the host via Synchronous Data Link Control (SDLC).

CMOS RAM
Memory that stores the date, time, and other system configuration information when the computer system is shut down.

CNE
A certification program in which users take classes and pass tests to achieve the CNE designation. CNEs are certified to provide support for NetWare and IntranetWare networks, including system design, installation, and maintenance.
Synonym: *Certified NetWare Engineer*

CNE Professional Association (CNEPA)

An association of CNEs that offers benefits to members, including technical workshops, subscriptions, and admission to network-related events.

coax booster

A hardware device that strengthens the signal carried over a coaxial cable. Use of a coax booster makes it possible to run cable over a greater distance with a minimum of signal loss.

coaxial cable

A type of cable that uses a central solid wire surrounded by insulation. A braided-wire conductor sheath surrounds the insulation and a plastic jacket surrounds the sheath. Coaxial cable can accommodate high bandwidth and is resistant to interference. Variations of coaxial cable include quad-shield, quadrax, thick coaxial, thin coaxial, triaxial, and twinaxial.

Code Division Multiple Access (CDMA)

A transmission method that uses codes to fit up to ten times as much data into a channel. Every signal is given a different code; the receiver decodes only signals with appropriate codes. CDMA uses a *soft-handoff* mechanism to avoid lost bits: Both cells transmit transitional bits at the same time on the same frequency, thereby increasing the chance that one of the transmissions will be within range of the receiver. CDMA is not compatible with time-division multiple access (TDMA).

Code-Excited Linear Predictive Coding (CELP)

A variant of the Linear Predictive Coding (LPC) voice encoding algorithm capable of generating digital voice output at 4,800 bits per second (bps).

code page

A table that stores a character set in support of a language script. Some operating systems support many code pages and enable users to switch from one to another. A single-byte code page stores up to 256 codes to represent lowercase and uppercase letters, numbers, and symbols. Differences between code pages may result in unreadable text. The 850 common code page has been established to remedy this incompatibility between character sets; it can handle most character sets of the Roman script. The Unicode code page goes even further, supporting 64,000 characters in the Roman, Chinese, and other character sets.

code-page switching
An operating system mechanism that enables users to switch between character sets employed by different languages.

code/decode (codec)
A device or method that converts analog signals to digital signals. Codecs are used in digital telephone systems to transmit voice over digital lines.

coding
A general term used to denote a representation made using a predefined syntax or language.

cold boot
The process of starting up a computer, which begins after the power is switched on.

collapsed backbone
A local area network (LAN) architecture in which the backplane of a device acts as a network backbone by routing traffic between nodes and other hubs in a multiple-LAN environment.

collapsed directory
A directory in which the subdirectories are not displayed.

collision
A conflict between two network packets that results when two devices transmit data at the same time. Depending on the type of network, the originating stations may attempt to retransmit after a collision.

collision detection and avoidance
The act of detecting and/or avoiding a collision of two data packets. In an Ethernet network, a collision occurs when signals from two nodes are transmitted on to the network at the same time. In such a case, the packets are discarded and must be retransmitted.

com (commercial)
A suffix attached to an Internet address of a site maintained by a commercial organization or individual.
Synonyms: *com domain; com hierarchy*

COM port
An asynchronous serial communications port on an IBM PC-compatible computer.

combiner
A fiber-optic coupler device that combines many incoming signals into one outgoing signal.

command
A short program used for a specific task.

command button
An icon in a graphical utility for carrying out a specific action.

command file
A user-defined file containing a sequence of commands. A command file can execute a frequently used command or a sequence of commands.

command format
Instructions showing how to type a command at the keyboard.
Synonym: *syntax*

command history buffer
A portion of memory that saves command strings entered from the keyboard. This buffer enables previously entered commands to be retrieved by using the up arrow and down arrow keys. The commands can be edited, and then re-executed.

command line
A command, followed by additional information, given to the computer one at a time. The command line ends when the Enter key is pressed.

command-line interface (CLI)

An interface between a user who is typing commands and a computer program or operating system receiving instructions from the user.

command-line switch

A parameter that changes the default mode of a command. A command-line switch is commonly made up of one or more letters that follow the slash character (/) in a command. In UNIX, the command-line switch is a character following a hyphen in a command.

Synonym: *command line argument*

command-line utility (CLU)

A utility accessed through a single-word command.

command processor

Part of an operating system that displays a command prompt onscreen. The command processor interprets and executes any valid command issued by the user, retrieves requested files, and displays error messages.

Synonym: *command interpreter*

command prompt

A screen symbol indicating the operating system is ready to receive input.

CommExec object

An object in NetWare for Systems Application Architecture (SAA) that provides management capabilities and rights privileges for the [Root] level of the Novell Directory Services (NDS) Directory tree.

committed burst (Bc)

The highest number of data bits a network can transfer under typical conditions, over a given period of time.

Commitment, Concurrency, and Recovery Service Element (CCRSE)

An Application Layer (Layer 7) service specified in the OSI Reference Model that implements distributed transactions among many applications.

committed burst size
The highest number of data bits a network can transfer under normal conditions, over a given period of time.

Committed Information Rate (CIR)
A Frame Relay network term indicating the rate of information, measured in bits per second (bps), at which the network transfers data on a virtual circuit under normal conditions. If network activity exceeds the CIR, the Frame Relay controller marks packets to indicate whether they can be discarded.

Common Applications Environment (CAE)
Standards for the operating system, networking protocols, languages, and data management that enable applications to be ported across platforms from different manufacturers.

Common Authentication Technology (CAT)
A specification for distributed authentication that supports public-key and private-key encryption strategies on the Internet. Both client and server use a common interface that provides the authentication services. The interface connects to either Distributed Authentication Security Service (DASS) for public-key encryption, or Kerberos for private-key encryption.

common carrier
A private company that provides communications services to the public.

Common Channel Interoffice Signaling (CCIS)
A telephone communications transmission method that uses different channels for voice and control signals. A faster, packet-switched mechanism transmits control signals, making it possible to include additional information (such as caller ID or billing information) in the control channel.

Common Channel Signaling (CCS)
A telephone transmission method that uses different channels for voice and control signals. The control signals are sent using a fast, packet-switched technique, making it possible to include additional data (such as caller ID or billing information) in the control channel.

Common Channel Signaling 7 (CCS 7)

An implementation of the Signaling System 7 (SS7) specified by the Consultative Committee for International Telegraphy and Telephony (CCITT). CCS 7 is an Integrated Services Digital Network (ISDN)-based transmission method that makes special services (such as call-forwarding) available anywhere on a network.

Common Gateway Interface (CGI)

A platform-independent interface used by a Hypertext Transfer Protocol (HTTP)-based information server to run external programs. A CGI program receives client requests and responds with the requested information. In NetWare, the CGI is the feature that enables the NetWare Web Server to modify Web pages before they are sent to a browser.

Common Hardware Reference Platform (CHRP)

An open hardware architecture (originally designed by IBM) that ensures compatibility among compliant systems built by different manufacturers.

Common Mail Calls (CMC)

An Application Program Interface (API) that enables message-handling agents to communicate with post offices in a manner independent of hardware platforms, operating systems, electronic mail (e-mail) systems, and messaging protocols.

Synonym: *common messaging calls*

Common Management Information Machine (CMIPM)

In the OSI Network Management Model, an application that can accept operations from a Common Management Information Service Element (CMISE) user and initiate the appropriate actions for responding with valid Common Management Information Protocol (CMIP) packets.

Common Management Information Protocol (CMIP)

The OSI management information protocol for network monitoring and control information. CMIP includes specifications for accounting management, configuration management, fault management, performance management, and security management.

Common Management Information Protocol Data Unit (CMIPDU)

A packet conforming to the Common Management Information Protocol (CMIP). The packet's contents depend on the CMISE request.

Common Management Information Service (CMIS)

The specification used in the OSI Network Management Model for network monitoring and control.

Common Management Information Service Element (CMISE)

An entity that furnishes network management and control services under the OSI Network Management Model. The seven types of CMISEs are Action, Cancel Get, Create, Delete, Event Report, Get, and Set. The system-management functions use these services to carry out specific tasks.

Common Management Information Services and Protocol over TCP/IP (CMOT)

An initiative that attempted to implement two services of the Open Systems Interconnection (OSI) framework—Common Management Information Service (CMIS) and Common Management Information Protocol (CMIP)—over the TCP/IP suite. CMOT was never implemented because of widespread usage of Simple Network Management Protocol (SNMP) and the complexities of porting the OSI model to TCP/IP.

Common Name (CN)

The naming attribute that denotes leaf objects in Novell Directory Services (NDS). For a User object, the Common Name is the user's login name.

Common Object Model (COM)

An object-oriented, open architecture that enables client-server applications that run on different platforms to communicate transparently with one another. COM was developed jointly by Microsoft Corp. and Digital Equipment Corp. as a way of enabling networks using Microsoft's Object Linking and Embedding (OLE) technology to communicate with networks using Digital's ObjectBroker technology.

Common Object Request Broker Architecture (CORBA)

A multiplatform architecture, developed by the Object Management Group, that enables object-oriented applications to communicate and exchange data, regardless of their hardware platforms. CORBA employs Object Request Brokers (ORBs) to establish communications between objects and to invoke methods on behalf of objects. A standard Interface Definition Language (the CORBA IDL) defines an object's interface.

Common Programming Interface for Communications (CPIC)

A set of Application Programming Interfaces (APIs) for program-to-program communications used in IBM's Systems Application Architecture (SAA).

Common User Access (CUA)

In IBM Systems Application Architecture (SAA), a common set of specifications for user interfaces, providing a consistent look and feel for all applications and platforms.

Communicating Application Specification (CAS)

A proposed interface standard for fax/modems, developed by Intel and Digital Communications Associates, that competes with the *Class x* hierarchy developed by the Electronic Industries Association (EIA).

communication

The process of transferring data from one device to another in a computer system.

communication protocol

A set of rules used by a program or operating system to communicate between endpoints. A communication protocol facilitates the packaging, transmission, and delivery of information. Communication protocols may be workstation-based or server-based.

communication protocol stack
A protocol that defines the rules for sending and receiving information by a network device. The stack furnishes routing and connection services by adding information to any packet that passes through it.

communication server
A type of server that provides access to modems and telephone lines. The communication server can be a dedicated machine or it can reside on a workstation. It runs applications necessary to establish connections, prepare files, and send or receive data. A communication server can also provide terminal emulation services for mainframe access.

communication services
A basic network service that facilitates connections between two or more nodes.

communications buffers
The area in a file server's memory that temporarily holds data packets arriving from workstations.
Synonym: *packet-receive buffers*

communications channel
A pathway that employs a specific set of signals and methods for transferring data between a workstation and printer.

communications controller
A machine attached to the host computer in a Systems Network Architecture (SNA) network that processes communications destined for the host.
Synonym: *front-end processor*

Communications Decency Act (CDA)
Legislation enacted in 1996 to forbid obscenity and indecency on the Internet. Its constitutionality was challenged in 1997.

communications line
A physical connection (such as cable or circuit) that links one or more devices to another device.

communications/modem server
A network server with one or more modems that can be shared by users on the network.

communications parameters
A group of settings that must be set before computers can communicate. Communications parameters include baud rate, number of data bits, number of stop bits, and parity.

communications program
A personal computer program that enables a user to call and communicate with other computers.

community
A logical group of Simple Network Management Protocol (SNMP) and Network Management System (NMS) devices located in the same administrative domain.

Community Antenna Television, or Cable Television (CATV)
A broadband transmission facility using 75-ohm coaxial cable. The cable can carry many television channels, using guard channels to keep them separated.

comp newsgroup
A type of newsgroup that discusses topics of interest to computer users.

compact disc (CD)
A nonmagnetic optical disc that stores digital information. A single CD can store 650MB of information or more. Data is stored on the CD as a series of alternating microscopic pits and smooth regions, each with different reflective properties. A laser beam pointed at the disc detects these properties and converts them into digital information.

Compact Disc Read-Only Memory (CD-ROM)

An optical storage device that can store up to 650MB of data. Often CD-ROMs store large multimedia applications, encyclopedias, or large reference works, and libraries of fonts or clip art. A CD-ROM uses a constant linear velocity encoding scheme to store data in one spiral track, which is divided into segments of equal length.

Compact Disc-Interactive (CDI)

A standard compact disc format for data, text, audio, still video images, and animated graphics.

companding

A Pulse Code Modulation (PCM) process in which an analog signal sample value is logically rounded to scale-step decimal values on a nonlinear scale, the decimal values are then coded into a binary equivalent. The process is reversed at the receiving terminal. The term *companding* is a contraction of *compressing* and *expanding*.

Compare right

A NetWare and IntranetWare property right that indicates the holder has the right to compare another value to a value of the given property to see whether they are equal. The Compare right can be applied to an operation to yield a value of *True* or *False*, but not the actual value of the property.

compatibility

The shared capability of two or more devices or programs to work together. Compatibility may be built into some products; with other products, it must be achieved through additional drivers or filters.

compatible

A term that describes a computer whose architecture is compatible with that of the IBM PC. This term also describes a peripheral device, data file, or application program that can either work with or understand the same commands, formats, or languages as another.

Synonym: *clone*

Complementary Metal Oxide Semiconductor (CMOS)
A battery-powered memory chip that holds system configuration parameters when the computer is shut down. The CMOS chip is usually located on the system board.

complete name
In Novell Directory Services (NDS), a NetWare object's common name, followed by a period, the name of the container object, another period, and so on, through all succeeding container objects down to the root of the Directory tree.

Complete Sequence Number PDU (CSNP)
A Protocol Data Unit (PDU) sent by a designated router to an Open Shortest Path First (OSPF) network to maintain database synchronization.

Complex Instruction Set Computing (CISC)
A processor-design strategy that gives the processor a large number of powerful assembly-language instructions. These instructions may be complex and may slow down overall processing.

complex network
A network with different platforms (including Macintosh, DOS, OS/2, UNIX, Windows, and other platforms), typically in a wide area network (WAN) configuration.

component
An element of hardware or software combined with other elements to form complete systems, functions, or programs.

compress
To enable a storage medium to hold more online data by removing redundant information.

Compressed (Co) attribute
A NetWare file attribute that indicates a file has been compressed by generating a status-flag attribute.

Compressed Internet Packet Exchange (CIPX) protocol

A variant of the Novell Internet Packet Exchange (IPX) protocol that uses a compressed header of between 1 and 7 octets (provided only the IPX header is compressed); a 30-octet header is normally characteristic of IPX packets. CIPX compression can speed up transmissions over slow wide area network (WAN) lines.

Compressed Serial Line Interface Protocol (CSLIP)

A variant of the Serial Line Interface Protocol (SLIP) that uses the Van Jacobsen compression strategy to compress packet headers. CSLIP is used to transmit Internet Protocol (IP) packets over serial line connections.

compression

The process of compacting information. Because compressed files take up less space, more files can be placed on a storage medium. Files must be decompressed before use.

computation bound

A state under which the processor's speed limits the speed of a program's execution.

Computer Emergency Response Team (CERT)

An Internet group formed by the Defense Advanced Research Projects Agency (DARPA) to respond to security problems on the Internet.

Computer object

A Novell Directory Services (NDS) leaf object representing a computer on the network. The Computer object's properties can hold information, such as the physical computer's serial number or the name of the person to whom the computer is assigned.

Computer Science Network (CSNET)

An internetwork consisting of universities, research institutions, and commercial concerns. CSNET merged with Because It's Time Network (BITNET) to form the Corporation for Research and Educational Networking (CREN).

Computer-Based Messaging System (CBMS)
An older term that denotes a Message Handling System (MHS) or electronic mail (e-mail) system.

Computer-Telephone Integration (CTI)
A technology that integrates telephone services into a computer to achieve greater productivity.

Computer-to-PBX Interface (CPI)
An interface used by a computer to communicate with a private branch exchange (PBX).

concentrator
A hardware device with a single bus and many connections. A concentrator can send many input channels out to fewer output channels and can store the input data until an output channel becomes available. When employed as a hub, a concentrator is a termination point for the cables connected to nodes in the network, and forms the basic topology of the network. Concentrators may also connect different network elements with different cabling schemes or architectures. A concentrator may also include a processor, network monitoring features, and many boards (each functioning as one hub).
Synonyms: *hub; wiring center*

concurrent
A condition under which two or more programs are accessing the processor at the same time. Processes that run concurrently must share system resources.

conditional search
A search that locates information in a database or file on the basis of a given set of criteria.

conditioned analog line
Analog line formed by adding devices to improve the electrical signal.

conductor
A material that can carry an electrical current.

conference

A logical meeting place where computer users interact over the network.

Conférence Européene des Postes et Télécommunications (CEPT)

An association of 26 European organizations that recommends communications standards to the Consultative Committee for International Telegraphy and Telephony (CCIT).

CONFIG.SYS

A configuration file executed by the DOS operating system upon start up. Located in the root directory of the default boot disk, the CONFIG.SYS file contains the basic commands that set up the system for operation. Some applications or hardware peripherals require an explicit statement they must add to the CONFIG.SYS file to function.

configuration (hardware)

The way network hardware is used and connected. Hardware may include servers, workstations, printers, cables, network boards, routers, and other devices.

configuration (router)

Settings and parameters established to configure a NetWare server as a router. Accomplished with the INETCFG utility, these settings can configure AppleTalk or TCP/IP packet routing across network segments. Router-configuration settings can also configure Internetwork Packet Exchange/Sequenced Packet Exchange (IPX/SPX) parameters, load and bind protocols to network boards, enable Network Link Services Protocol (NLSP), and display recent console messages.

configuration (server)

Settings and parameters that specify how the network server is used. In NetWare, the server configuration parameters are selected through the INSTALL NetWare Loadable Module (NLM). Configuration includes loading and binding the drivers for disks, CD-ROMs, and local area networks (LANs).

In addition, the server configuration assigns an IPX internal or external network number, partitions the hard disk, creates and mounts NetWare volumes, modifies volume segments, enables file compression, or install Novell Directory Services (NDS).

configuration (software)

Settings and parameters that specify how network software is used. Software configuration may include a specification on how the software is installed, as well as preference options, default settings, and a set of configuration files.

configuration file

A file containing commands that set up the computing environment and execute automatically upon start up.

Configuration Management

Of the five OSI Network Management Model domains, the one that manages networked applications and user access. Configuration Management encompasses several tasks, including identifying objects on the network and determining information about those objects. The process of configuration management may also include the storage and reporting of this information, modifying the parameters of the objects' settings, and managing relationships between objects. According to the OSI Network Management Model, any object has four operational states: Active, Busy, Disabled, and Enabled.

configuration services

Network services in a control point and in the physical unit. Configuration services activate, deactivate, and maintain the status of physical units, links, and link stations.

configured router

A router configured on the network, instead of from a seed router.

confirmation

An application's acknowledgment data has been received.

Conformance Testing Service (CTS)

A series of programs that test how well a product implements a particular protocol as per specifications set by the International Standards Organization (ISO).

congestion

A state in which excessive traffic is occurring on the network. In a congested network, individual packets may arrive late at their destinations and performance may be adversely affected.

congestion control

The use of mechanisms designed to limit excessive traffic, usually by providing network switches with a way to signal the router to slow a transmission.

connect

To establish an authenticated connection to a server.

connect time

The amount of time a node has been connected to a server.

connection

The state that exists when two devices on a network are communicating.

Connection Management (CMT)

A process in the Fiber Distributed Data Interface (FDDI) that handles the transition of a ring through its various states.

Connection Mode Network Service (CMNS)

A service that extends local X.25 switching to such networks as Ethernet, Fiber Distributed Data Interface (FDDI), and Token Ring.

connection number

A number assigned to the workstations, printers, or applications attached to a NetWare server. The connection numbers may be different each time the device is attached. A connection number may also be used to assign a process.

connection services
A set of services used that obtain information about a workstation or other device currently using the services of the file server.

connectionless
In the Internet Protocol (IP), a type of datagram delivery that transmits all packets independently of other packets. Communication takes place without having first established a direct connection. In a connectionless networking scheme, each packet contains addressing information.

Connectionless Broadband Data Service (CBDS)
A wide area network (WAN) technology based on high-speed, packet-switched datagram delivery.
Synonym: *Switched Multimegabit Data Service*

Connectionless Mode Network Service (CLNS)
In the OSI Reference Model, a service on the Network Layer (Layer 3) where data transmission can occur without a fixed connection between source and destination. In this model, packets are independent, may reach their destinations through multiple paths, and may arrive out of order. Consequently, each packet carries the destination address. Most local area networks (LANs) operate in connectionless mode.

Connectionless Network Protocol (CLNP)
An Open Systems Interconnection (OSI) protocol that provides the OSI Connectionless Network Service. In the OSI model, CLNP is the functional equivalent of the NetWare Internet Packet Exchange (IPX) protocol and the Internet Protocol (IP). CLNP datagrams include destination information along with each unit of data; a direct connection is unnecessary.

connectionless service
A network service that transmits data packets without first arranging a predetermined path between the source and destination. Each packet of a transmission may take a different route to reach its destination; no guaranteed delivery or priority services are available. A connectionless service is defined in the Network Layer (Layer 3) and Transport Layer (Layer 4) of the OSI Reference Model.

Connectionless Transport Protocol (CLTP)

A protocol that provides transport data with end-to-end addressing and error correction. CLTP does not guarantee delivery or offer flow control. In the OSI Reference Model, CLTP is the functional equivalent of the User Datagram Protocol (UDP) datagram service.

Connectionless Transport Service (CLTS)

In the OSI Reference Model, a best-effort transport service on the Transport Layer (Layer 4), CLTS uses end-to-end addressing and error checking; it does not guarantee delivery.

connection-oriented

A term describing data transfer without the existence of a virtual circuit.

Connection-Oriented Convergence Function (COCF)

A function of the Distributed Queue Dual-Bus (DQDB) network architecture that prepares data going into or out of a connection-oriented service. The service establishes a fixed connection, sends the data, and then breaks the connection.

Connection-Oriented Network Protocol (CONP)

A protocol in the OSI Reference Model that provides connection-oriented operations to upper-level protocols.

Connection-Oriented Network Service (CONS)

A network service where transmissions of data occur after a predetermined path has been determined between source and destination. In a connection-oriented service, packets reach their destination in the order in which they were sent.

connectivity

The ability to connect computers, sometimes with many architectures, on a single network for the purpose of sharing resources.

connector

A device that provides a physical link between two components. Table C.2 lists common connector types and their uses.

TABLE C.2	Common Connector Types
CONNECTOR TYPE	**USE**
AUI (attachment unit interface)	Links a drop cable to a network interface card (NIC)
barrel	Links two segments of cable in a straight run
BNC (bayonet nut connector)	Links Ethernet thin coaxial cables or link twinaxial cable segments
D-4	Links fiber-optic cable
DIN	Links a keyboard to a personal computer or link components on a LocalTalk network
D-type	Links serial, parallel, and video components
elbow	Links two sections of cable in a corner to change the direction of a cable linkage
ESCON (Enterprise System Connection Architecture)	Links fiber-optic cable
F	Links cables in a broadband Ethernet network or a broadband token bus network
FC	Links fiber-optic cable
fiber-optic	Links two segments of the optical core of fiber-optic cable
IBM Data	Links components of a Token Ring network
ISO 8877	Links telephones to the wall or to modems
L-to-T	Links two frequency division multiplexing (FDM) groups into a single-time division multiplexing (TDM) group.
MIC	Links fiber-optic cable in a Fiber Distributed Data Interface (FDDI) network

(continued)

CONNECTOR TYPE	USE
N-Series	Links coaxial thick cable
RJ-*xx*	Links telephones to the wall or to modems
SC (subscriber connector)	Links fiber-optic cable connectors
SMA	Links fiber-optic cable
straight-tip	Links fiber-optic cable
T	Attaches a device to a section of cable
TNC (threaded nut connector)	Links Ethernet thin coaxial cables or links twinaxial cable segments

T A B L E   C.2 *Common Connector Types (continued)*

Conseil Européen pour la Récherche Nucléaire (CERN)

The original name for an organization now known as the European Laboratory for Particle Physics, located in Switzerland, where Tim Berners-Lee developed a system (part of what is now known as the World Wide Web) to enhance the availability of research to remote users.

console

The monitor and keyboard used to view and control server or host activity.

console operator

A user who has been given rights to manage the NetWare server.

constant angular velocity (CAV)

A fixed rotation speed. Hard disks employ a CAV-encoding scheme in which the disk rotates at a constant rate. Under a CAV scheme, sectors toward the center of the disk have a higher density. As the read/write heads move outward, data-transfer rates decrease because the heads must then cover a greater circumference to read the outer sectors.

Constant Bit Rate (CBR)

A type of Asynchronous Transfer Mode (ATM) connection under the *Class*

A Quality of Service (QoS) level. CBR is typically reserved for voice or video, or for other data that must be transmitted at a constant rate and is intolerant of loss. CBR is a *reserved bandwidth* service that generates a steady bit stream.

constant linear velocity (CLV)

A changing rotation speed. To ensure a constant data density, CD-ROM drives use a CLV-encoding scheme in which the disc rotates at a varying rate. Data on a CD is stored in a single, spiral track divided into equal segments. To read the data at a constant rate, the CD-ROM drive changes the speed of rotation as the read head approaches the center of the disc.

Consultative Committee for International Telegraphy and Telephony (CCITT)

A subgroup of the International Telecommunications Union (ITU) that defines data-communications standards. The CCITT is responsible for several communications, telecommunications, and networking standards, including documents that specify X.25, X.400, V.42 and V.42*bis*, and 1.*xxx* Integrated Digital Services Network (ISDN) standards.

Three main sets of standards exist:

▶ *CCITT Groups 1-4.* These are used for facsimile transmissions.

▶ *CCITT V Series.* These are used for modems, error detection, and correction mechanisms.

▶ *CCITT X Series.* These are used for local area networks (LANs).

Many standards appear in documents from both the CCITT and the International Standards Organization (ISO). Although the CCITT is now officially called the *International Telecommunications Union-Telecommunications Standardization Sector* (ITU-TS), it is still commonly referred to as the CCITT. The French name on which the CCITT acronym is based is Comité Consultatif International Téléphonique et Télégraphique.

container

A high-level object (also known as a *parent*) used to organize other objects in the Novell Directory Services (NDS) Directory tree. The three types of container objects are Country (C), Organization (O), and Organizational Unit (OU).

Container login script
A script that sets the environment for all users within a given container.

container object
In NetWare 4.x and IntranetWare, a high-level object capable of holding other objects. A container object is used to organize other objects logically in the Novell Directory Services (NDS) Directory tree. Table C.3 lists the four types of container objects and their uses.

TABLE C.3 *Container Objects*

OBJECT	USE
[Root]	A special object that appears at the top of the Novell Directory Services (NDS) Directory tree
Country (C)	Uses a two-letter designation to define where a company is located
Locality (L)	Not currently supported by NetWare utilities, can define a locality (L) or a state (S)
Organization (O)	Defines the name of a company
Organizational Unit (OU)	Defines the locations, departments, divisions, or workgroups of a company

contention
The state that occurs in some media-access methods where nodes compete to gain access to the network. In a contention-based access method, the first node to seek access is the one that gets the privilege of transmitting.

contention-loser polarity
A designation indicating that a logical unit (LU) is the contention loser for a session.

contention-winner polarity

A designation indicating a logical unit (LU) is the contention winner for a session. When a requesting LU indicates it should be the loser in the event of a contention, the responding LU automatically accepts the status of contention winner.

context

In NetWare 4.x or IntranetWare, the location of an object within its container in the Novell Directory Services (NDS) Directory tree. If an object is moved from one container object to another, it has changed contexts.

context switching

Switching between applications without ending the first application. Context switching enables users to work with many applications simultaneously. It differs from *multitasking* because only one program is active at a time.

context-sensitive help

Help information concerning a current item or task that can be accessed by an end user.

control character

A special formatting character often used in word processing programs. The character is generated by pressing the Control (Ctrl) key along with an additional key.

control code

A sequence of characters used for hardware control.
Synonyms: *setup string; escape sequence*

control information byte

The first byte in an AppleTalk Transaction Protocol (ATP) header. This byte holds the packet's function code, XO bit, EOM bit, and STS bit.

control packet

A link-control or network-control packet that establishes encapsulation format options, packet-size limitations, link setup, peer authentication, or protocol management in the OSI Reference Model Network Layer (Layer 3).

Control Unit Terminal (CUT)

An operating mode for terminals that allows one session per terminal.

Controlled Access Unit (CAU)

An intelligent access concentrator used in a Token Ring network. The CAU can establish connections for as many as 80 workstations by using pluggable lobe-attachment modules. It can determine whether a node is operational, monitor activity, and pass data to the LAN Manager program. The CAU can also connect and disconnect individual nodes.

Controlled Access Unit/Lobe Attachment Module (CAU/LAM)

A box, providing ports to which new nodes can be attached, that is plugged into the Controlled Access Unit (CAU) in a Token Ring network.

controller

In mainframe computers, a device that regulates the communications between a host computer and the terminals accessing it. In personal computers, a device responsible for accessing other devices.

controller address

A number used by the operating system to locate the controller on a disk channel. The address is usually set physically by moving jumpers on the disk controller board.

controller board

A hardware device that allows a computer to communicate with a peripheral device. The controller board manages input/output (I/O) and regulates the operation of the peripheral device.

conventional memory

Computer memory below 640K. The operating system and applications are typically loaded into conventional memory.

Synonym: *base memory; random access memory (RAM)*

convergence rate

The rate at which NetWare Link Services Protocol (NLSP) routing information converges on all NLSP routers on the Internet Packet Exchange (IPX) internetwork.

convergence time

The time necessary to propagate routing information throughout the network.

conversation

As a logical process, communication between two transaction programs in a Type 6.2 LU-LU session.

Conversational Monitor System (CMS)

A Systems Network Architecture (SNA) subsystem used for managing interactive sessions.

conversational transaction

Occurs when two or more applications communicate using the services of logical units (LUs).

convert

To change the format of a document or piece of data without changing the underlying content. A common example is converting a document created with one software program (say, a word processor) into a format recognizable by another software program (such as a spreadsheet).

cooperative multitasking

A type of multitasking in which all applications share system resources. A cooperative multitasking operating system maintains a list of active applications and an execution order. When one application is operating, others cannot run until the first application returns control to the operating system.

cooperative processing

A method that allows an application to execute its various tasks on different machines. Cooperative processing is sometimes used in client-server computing, for example, when the front-end of an application executes on the client and the back-end on the server.

Copper Distributed Data Interface (CDDI)

A network architecture that implements Fiber Distributed Data Interface (FDDI) specifications on electrical, instead of optical, cable.

coprocessor

A microprocessor chip that carries out a specific group of tasks for another processor. Coprocessors are often used for floating-point arithmetic, graphics, disk management, or input/output.

Copy Inhibit (Ci) attribute

A NetWare file attribute that prohibits users from copying the file.

core

The transparent central fiber in a fiber-optic cable, through which the light signal travels. The core is surrounded by cladding, which reflects light back into the core.

core gateway

A primary router on the Internet. Historically, a core gateway has been defined as one of a set of gateways or routers operated by the Internet Network Operations Center (INOC). As a central part of routing on the Internet, the core gateway system requires all groups to advertise paths to their networks from a core gateway.

corona wire

A thin wire in a laser printer that emits an electrical charge to attract toner to the paper.

Corporation for Open Systems (COS)
A group involved in testing and promoting products that support the OSI Reference Model.

Corporation for Open Systems Interconnection Networking in Europe (COSINE)
A European project to build a communication network consisting of scientific and industrial organizations.

Corporation for Research and Educational Networking (CREN)
A research organization concerned with the ongoing operation of the Internet.

cost
A metric applied to a circuit, which indicates the likelihood traffic will be routed over that circuit. Cost is defined in terms of hop count.

count to infinity
An artifact that can occur in distance-vector routing. A count to infinity condition occurs if a network becomes unreachable because routers are relying on incorrect information.

country code
A two-letter abbreviation used in the last part of an Internet address to signify the country (for locations outside the United States).

Country (C) object
A Novell Directory Services (NDS) optional container object that designates the country in which a given network resides. The Country object is necessary only for global networks that exist across several countries.

coupler
A device for transferring energy among many channels. In a fiber-optic network, a coupler routes an incoming signal to many outgoing paths or routes many incoming paths into a single outbound path. A coupler may have

one of several designs, including

▸ *Tee coupler.* Divides the incoming signal into two outgoing signals
▸ *Star coupler.* Divides the signal into more than two signals.

cracker

An individual who attempts to gain unauthorized access into a network or computer system.

crash

A condition that occurs when a program unexpectedly stops because of a hardware failure or a software error. The computer must usually be restarted to recover from a crash and unsaved work is usually lost.

Create right

A NetWare directory right or file right. An object Create right grants the user the right to create new objects in the Novell Directory Services (NDS) Directory tree. A File system Create right grants a user the right to create new files or subdirectories.

crimper

A small tool for crimping the end of a cable to attach the cable to a connector.

critical error

A program error that causes an application to stop until the error condition is corrected.

critical path

A chain of links needed to accomplish a given task. Outlining a critical path may be useful in spotting where bottlenecks may occur.

cross-connect device

A connection between a horizontal cable running from a machine to the cable running to the network hub. A cross-connect is the connection that exists between two punch-down blocks.

crosspost
Directing a single news article to more than one Usenet newsgroup by using a newsreader program.

cross-referenced
A condition where items or topics may have related details in another text and are so referenced.

crosstalk
Interference that exists when two wires are in physical proximity. *Far-end crosstalk* (FEXT) is interference in a wire at the receiving end of a signal sent on a different wire. *Near-end crosstalk* (NEXT) is the interference in a wire at the transmitting end of a signal sent over a different wire.

cross wye
A cable that switches from one wiring sequence to another, thereby changing the pin assignments of the incoming cable.

current context
The current position of an object in a Novell Directory Services (NDS) Directory tree.

current directory
The current position on the disk, used by the operating system to locate files. If the PROMPT PG command is added to the AUTOEXEC.BAT file, the command line displays the current directory.

current disk drive
The drive presently used by the operating system to locate files. The current disk drive letter is displayed in the system prompt.

custom backup
A way of storing files in which only selected portions of files are archived. In a custom backup, the *exclude* and *include* options indicate what subsets to backup or restore.

Custom Device Module (CDM)

The driver component in the NetWare Peripheral Architecture (NPA) that drives the storage devices attached to a host adapter bus.

Customer Information Control System (CICS)

A transaction processing subsystem used on IBM mainframes. CICS supports IBM's Systems Network Architecture (SNA).

Customer Information Control System for Virtual Storage (CICS/VS)

A host program that runs on the IBM System/370. This program can be used in a communications network.

Customer Premises Equipment (CPE)

Hardware leased or owned by the customer and used at the customer's location.

cut-off wavelength

In single-mode fiber optics, the shortest wavelength at which a signal takes a single path through the core.

cut-through switching

A type of Token Ring switching in which data is forwarded as soon as the first 20 to 30 bytes of a frame have been received. These first few bytes contain the Media Access Control (MAC) Layer destination address information, and must be received before data is transmitted. After the header has been read, a connection is established between the input and output ports, and transmission begins immediately.

Synonym: *on-the-fly switching*

Cyberspace

A term describing information resources available through computer networks. The term was coined by William Gibson in his novel *Neuromancer*.

cycle (FDDI II)

In a Fiber Distributed Data Interface (FDDI) II network in hybrid mode, a 12,500-bit protocol data unit (packet). Such a cycle provides the framework for the FDDI transmission. The cycle is repeated 8,000 times per second, generating a bandwidth of 100 megabits per second (Mbps) for the network. The cycle contains a *preamble* (which establishes synchronization), *cycle header* (which specifies how the cycle is used), *dedicated packet group* (used for packet control); and the *wideband channel* (used for the actual data transmission).

cycle (periodic analog signal)

A complete repetition of a periodic analog signal. A cycle is the movement of a signal from its peak to its low point and back to the peak.

cyclical redundancy check (CRC)

An error-checking value. Every Ethernet frame includes a CRC to guarantee data integrity.

cylinder

A group of concentric tracks on a hard disk that organizes data and *is numbered* according to the tracks they reference.

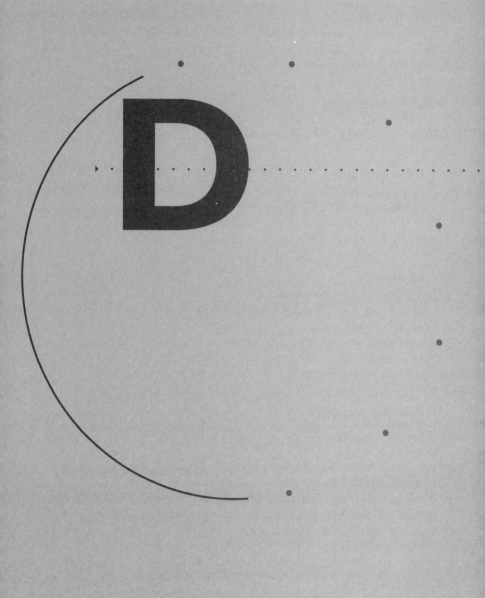

D channel

A signaling channel in an Integrated Services Digital Network (ISDN) connection. The D channel is used to control signals and to send information about the call being placed.

D-4 connector

A fiber-optic connector with a threaded coupling nut. The D-4 connector is used for single-mode or multimode fiber cable.

D4 framing

A method of identifying individual channels in a DS-1 channel. D4 framing combines twelve 193-bit frames into a single D4 superframe, such that each DS-1 channel comprises two D4 superframes. Every 193rd bit identifies the individual (DS-0) channels

daemon

A background process capable of initializing other processes with little or no input from the user. Daemons typically provide services (such as printing or server advertising) in the UNIX environment. Other daemon processes may perform some administrative functions or access the host file system. On an IBM-compatible personal computer, a daemon typically runs from the CONFIG.SYS file at system startup, and need not be executed again.

daily full backup

A backup strategy that backs up all data on the network at the end of every day; each day's data occupies a separate tape.

daisy chain

A series of components that are serially linked, as in bus-based networks. Devices may be daisy-chained if they are connected to a Small Computer System Interface (SCSI) adapter.
Synonym: *cascading*

dark fiber

A fiber-optic cable that is not carrying a signal, or fiber-optic cable through which no light is transmitted.

data

Any entity that conveys meaning. For example, computer data is stored as a series of electrical charges arranged in patterns that convey information.

Data Access Arrangement (DAA)

A telephony device used to protect the public telephone network against user equipment that does not meet Federal Communications Commission (FCC) standards.

Data Access Language (DAL)

An extension of the Structured Query Language (SQL) database language used in Macintosh-based client-server environments. DAL establishes a uniform level of access to any SQL-compliant database.

Data Access Manager (DAM)

A feature of the Macintosh System 7 operating system that accesses network databases by mediating between an application and the database it needs to access.

data bit

The number of bits that defines a character on a serial data transmission. In serial communications, information is sent in a stream of bits or a *frame*. Each frame is made up of start bits, data bits, a parity bit, and stop bits. Whether the data-bit parameter is set to seven or eight depends on the parity bit, which can be set to zero or one.

data bus

The internal bus used by devices and system components to communicate with the central processing unit (CPU). The first personal computers used an Industry Standard Architecture (ISA) bus, which ran at 4.77 megahertz (MHz). The ISA bus was later extended to form the Extended Industry Standard Architecture (EISA). Other bus architectures include the proprietary IBM MicroChannel bus, Video Electronics Standards Association (VESA) bus, and Peripheral Component Interconnect (PCI) bus.

Data Carrier Detect (DCD)

A telecommunications signal in an RS-232 connection asserted (or marked as True) if the modem detects a signal with a frequency that is appropriate for the modem being used.

data channel

A Systems Network Architecture (SNA) device that connects a processor and main storage with peripherals.

Data Circuit Terminating Equipment (DCE)

A device associated with a single network port responsible for establishing, maintaining, and terminating a connection with Data Terminal Equipment (DTE).

data communications

The transmission of information electronically over a physical medium. The sender of the information encodes and transmits the data, and the recipient receives and decodes it. The data may be transmitted in any one of several different methods, including point-to-point, switched, broadcast, multicast, store-and-forward, time division multiplexed, or frequency division multiplexed.

data-communications equipment (DCE)

Network equipment that maintains and terminates a data-communications session.

data compression

A way to compress information for transfer over a communications link to facilitate a faster transfer. Data compression, which typically involves the elimination of redundant information, requires both peers to support a common compression methodology. Compression may be based on patterns in bit sequences, patterns of occurrences of byte values, or commonly occurring words or phrases.

data connector (Type 1)

A connector used with Type 1 cable and used in Token Ring network wiring centers.

Data Definition Language (DDL)
A language that describes data and its relationships.

Data-Encryption Algorithm (DEA)
An algorithm that encrypts data for the Data-Encryption Standard (DES). This process divides a message into 64-bit blocks, each one of which is encrypted separately and one character at a time. Each character is scrambled 16 times during the encryption process, and the encryption method constantly changes.

Data-Encryption Key (DEK)
A value that encrypts data. The data-encryption algorithm uses the DEK to encode a message. The DEK can also be used to decrypt the message once it has been received. Some encryption methods use a different key for encrypting and decrypting.

Data Encryption Standard (DES)
A standard encryption methodology that scrambles data into unintelligible code for safe transmission over a public network. DES relies on a 64-bit key and a private-key encryption methodology to convert text into encrypted form. The messages are divided into 64-bit blocks, which are encrypted separately using the Data-Encryption Algorithm (DEA). In this private key strategy, only the sender and receiver know the key used to encrypt the data. The encryption algorithm is publicly known.

Data-Exchange Interface (DXI)
An interface between a router and a Data Service Unit (DSU) that performs segmentation and reassembly.

data file
A file that contains information as opposed to executable code.

Data-Flow Control layer (SNA model)
The fifth layer (Layer 5) of IBM's Systems Network Architecture (SNA) that defines the more general aspects of the connection. Methods used for recovering lost data execute in this layer and the rules for packet acknowledgment are also specified here.

data fork

Part of a Macintosh file that contains user-specified information. The data fork is one of two parts of a Macintosh file; the other part is the resource fork.

data link

The medium (generally fiber or wire) and components (transmission devices and receiving devices) required to establish communications between two network workstations.

Data-Link Connection Identifier (DLCI)

A 10-bit routing address used by the virtual circuit in a frame relay network. The DLCI is used at either the User-to-Network Interface (UNI) or the Network-Network Interface (NNI). With this identified, both user and network management platforms can identify a frame as originating from a particular Permanent Virtual Circuit (PVC).

Data-Link Control (DLC)

A protocol in IBM's Systems Network Architecture (SNA) used to manage the physical connection and to ensure messages reach their destinations.

Data-Link Control Layer

The second layer (Layer 2) of the seven-layer Systems Network Architecture (SNA) communications model that contains the link stations that schedule data transfer over a link between two nodes and executes an error-control mechanism for that link. Furthermore, the Data-Link Control Layer defines the protocols used to send data over the Physical Layer (Layer 1).

Data Link Layer (OSI model)

The second layer (Layer 2) in the seven-layer OSI Reference Model. The Data Link Layer packages and addresses data, and controls transmission flow over communication lines.

Data Link Services (DLS)

The services provided at the second (Data Link) layer of the OSI Reference Model.

data migration

The transfer of inactive or infrequently used data to less-expensive storage media. Under NetWare, data migration moves data from the NetWare volume to tape, optical disc, or another near-line or off-line media. Although the data is physically located on this alternative media, the operating system still sees it as residing on the volume. The process of data migration frees up hard disk space for more frequently accessed files, while still giving users a way to access less frequently used files.

Data Network Identification Code (DNIC)

A unique four-digit value assigned to public networks and public network services.

Data Over Voice (DOV)

A communications strategy for sending data over a voice channel at the same time a voice transmission is taking place.

data packet

A defined block that contains data and also typically includes administrative information (such as addresses) in the packet header or footer. The structure of data packets may be more specifically defined for different protocols.

Data-Personal Communications Services (Data-PCS)

A wireless communications service proposed by Apple Computer, which involved requesting the Federal Communications Commission (FCC) to set aside a 40 megahertz (MHz) bandwidth in the 140MHz range between 1.85 and 1.99 gigahertz (GHz). The bandwidth would be used for wireless communications sent via radio waves.

data processing (DP)

Processing typically done by minicomputers or mainframes in a data center.

data protection

A way to guarantee the safety of data on the network. NetWare offers data protection by keeping duplicate file directories and by redirecting data from bad blocks to more reliable blocks on the hard disk. Although duplexing or mirroring may be one part of a data-protection scheme, by itself, either of these techniques are still inadequate and should be used along with a regular backup scheme.

data rate

The speed at which data bits are sent and received. Data rate is usually measured in bits per second (bps). Usually, the data rate in bps is approximately equivalent to the baud rate divided by ten.

Data Service Unit/Channel Service Unit (DSU/CSU)

In a digital telecommunications network, two components of a Data Communications Equipment (DCE) device that provide access to digital services over a variety of lines. The DSU connects to the Data Terminal Equipment (DTE) through a synchronous serial interface, formats data for transmission, and controls data flow between the network and the CSU. The CSU terminates the long-distance connection at the user's end, processes digital signals, tests remote loopback, and functions as a buffer to prevent nonstandard customer-premises equipment from bringing down the public carrier's network.

data set

A term used by the telephone company to refer to a modem.

Data Set Ready (DSR)

A signal sent from a modem to indicate the modem is ready to function.

data sink

The recipient of a data transmission.

data source

The sender of a data transmission.

Data Stream Compatibility (DSC)

A minimal printing mode used in IBM's Systems Network Architecture (SNA).

data switch

A location or physical device that routes data to a destination. In a switching network, a data switch groups data together and routes it on the basis of network traffic or other predetermined criteria.

Data Switching Equipment (DSE)

Physical equipment used in a switching network.

Data Terminal Equipment (DTE)

A network-attached, customer premises, or end-user hardware device that operates in packet mode and connects with the data communications equipment (DCE) to establish data communications.

Data Terminal Ready (DTR)

A signal from a modem indicating a device is ready to send and receive data.

data transfer

Sending data between devices, such as from a storage device to a processor.

data transparency

A data-transmission strategy meant to guarantee data is not misinterpreted as control signals. Any bit or byte sequence that could potentially be interpreted as a flag or command is modified before transmission, and then restored to its original sequence upon receipt.

Data Under Voice (DUV)

A telecommunications strategy for sending voice and data over the same line.

data warehousing

A method of storing large amounts of historical transaction processing data in a central location for subsequent analysis and reporting. The data warehouse is usually accessed with a multidimensional database product capable of examining raw data, spotting business and marketing trends, and generating comparative reports. The warehouse uses metadata (or information about data) to allow this large amount of information to be turned into something more meaningful.

database

A set of one or more records or files compiled into a single type of structure or format. A database usually contains indexed files or records that pertain to a related subject or given application, and it allows single or multiple users to accept, store, and provide data. The records of a database can be accessed, edited, or retrieved by way of a query language, such as Structured Query Language (SQL). A *flat-file database* holds all information in a single file that contains individual records. A *relational database* organizes data as a set of tables, with rows representing records and columns representing individual fields. An *object-oriented database* organizes information into objects, each of which contains properties and specifies allowable operations.

database management system (DBMS)

A software application that controls data in a database. The DBMS organizes, stores, and retrieves data; as well as applying security and data integrity to the database. A DBMS typically includes features for reporting, importing, and exporting data from external applications and a data-manipulation language used to query the database.

database model

A method used by a database management system. The database model organizes the structure of the database.

database server

A database application that follows the client-server model. The application is divided into a *front-end* that runs on the user workstation and a *back-end* that runs on a server or host. The front-end interacts with the user, collects data, and displays data to the end-user. The back-end performs computing-intensive tasks (such as data analysis and manipulation).

Data-Compression Protocol

A set of rules and methodologies that compress data before transmission.

data-encoding scheme

A method used by a hard-disk controller to store information on a hard or floppy disk.

data-grade cable

Twisted-pair cable that can be used for data transmission. Data-grade cable encompasses Categories 2, 3, 4, and 5.

datagram

A type of packet containing information and address information routed through a packet-switching network. The information, or data, held by the datagram is referred to as the *payload*; the addressing information is usually contained in a header. Because datagrams hold address information, they do not need to arrive in consecutive order.

Datagram Delivery Protocol (DDP)

An AppleTalk protocol that establishes a best-effort, socket-to-socket delivery service for sending datagrams across an AppleTalk internetwork. DDP operates at the Network Layer (Layer 3) of the OSI Reference Model and prepares data packets for sending on through the network medium.

Dataphone Digital Service (DDS)

A four-wire, digital communications service from AT&T that operates at speeds ranging from 2,400 bits per second (bps) to 56 kilobits per second (Kbps) over a point-to-point connection. No modem is required, but a Data Service Unit/Channel Service Unit (DSU/CSU) is needed at the interface between the digital lines and the customer equipment.

dataset

A collection of data collected by a software agent, generally relative to a particular network function or device. NetWare further defines a dataset as manipulable by the SBACKUP utility. A dataset can contain different items or records, depending on the Target Service Agent (TSA) to which it is related.

DC-2000

A quarter-inch tape cartridge used in tape backup systems that can store up to 250MB of compressed data.

de facto standard

A standard that has come about through widespread usage, instead of through an official standards organization.

de jure standard
A standard that has come about through the formal processes of an official standards organization.

deadlock
A condition that occurs when multiple network nodes are waiting for messages from each other and cannot continue processing. Deadlock can also occur when multiple applications are attempting to lock the same files at the same time. Deadlock can be alleviated either by ending the transaction or by releasing the record locks.

debug screen
A troubleshooting screen accessible from an assembly or C program with a special key sequence. The screen is usually hidden unless the file server is at a breakpoint.

debugger
A program utility used by application developers to identify problems in program code.

DEC Alpha
A 64-bit Reduced Instruction Set Computing (RISC)-based computer system from Digital Equipment Corporation. The DEC Alpha was introduced in 1992, and uses a superscalar design that enables the processor to execute more than one instruction for each clock cycle. The Alpha can be used in symmetrical multiprocessing environments. The Alpha chip is deployed in both workstations and servers.

DEC Management Control Center (DECmcc)
The network management software used in Digital Equipment Corporation's DECnet networks.

decentralized network
A distributed network.

decibel (dB)
One-tenth of a bel. A decibel is a logarithmic unit of measurement that indicates a signal's intensity.

decimal
A base-ten numbering system that uses the numbers zero through nine.

D

DECnet
Digital Equipment Corporation's set of proprietary networking protocols. DECnet is used in Digital's VAX line of computers to exchange messages and data. The newest DECnet implementation, DECnet Phase V, merges itself with the standard OSI protocols in an attempt to establish interoperability with any other OSI-compliant network code. Phase IV, which was introduced in 1982, roughly corresponded to the OSI Reference Model. The eight layers of DECnet Phase IV were: Physical, Data Link, Routing, End-to-end Communications, Session Control, Network Application, Network Management, and User. DECnet Phase V was introduced to comply more rigorously to the seven-layer OSI Reference Model.

decryption
The act of unscrambling or decoding encrypted data.

dedicated circuit
A circuit that connects a user's location directly to a telephone company's point of presence.

dedicated line
A leased or private communications line. A dedicated line, as a permanent connection between two points, is always available.

dedicated router
A device whose sole function is to operate as a router. A dedicated router cannot function as a workstation or a server at the same time.

dedicated server
A network computer that functions solely as a server. The dedicated server performs tasks such as storing files, printing, and managing communications.

Dedicated Token Ring (DTR)

A Token Ring specification outlined in the Institute of Electrical and Electronic Engineers (IEEE) 802.5r specification that allows full-duplex connections and establishes a connection speed of up to 32 megabits per second (Mbps). By enabling full-duplex communications, the token-passing mechanism is bypassed and communication can take place between a device and a switch port at any time.

default

A preset option or value usually meant to accommodate the most common configuration used by the most users. Defaults can normally be changed by users to reflect a new value.

default directory

A standard directory created and used by an operating system or by an application.

default drive

The drive a workstation uses after initial startup or login. On a network, the default drive is assigned upon login and is identified by the drive prompt.

default login script

A script containing basic commands, such as drive mappings. This script is pre-coded into the LOGIN.EXE command and cannot be edited. Users may, however, choose to write an alternative login script, which would supersede the default login script.

default path

A path used by a router to send a packet when the packet does not contain any routing instructions, and the router does not have a predefined path. The default path usually sends the packet to another router that has more detailed routing information.

default route

An entry in a routing table that can redirect frames for which a next hop has not been explicitly listed in the table.

default value

A preset value used for a parameter or other type of setting. The default value is usually meant to accommodate the most common configuration used by the most users. Default values can ordinarily be changed by users to reflect a new value.

default zone

The zone to which a device belongs in an AppleTalk Phase 2 network until it has been assigned to a specific zone. If no default zone has been defined, the first zone name on the zone list becomes the default zone. Every zone list has a default zone.

Defense Advanced Research Projects Agency (DARPA)

The United States government agency that funded the Advanced Research Projects Agency Network (ARPAnet). ARPAnet was a network of government agencies and universities that later became the Internet. DARPA was originally termed Advanced Research Projects Agency (ARPA), and is part of the United States Department of Defense (DoD).

Defense Communications Agency (DCA)

A United States government organization responsible for Defense Data Networks (DDNs) such as MILnet.

Defense Data Network (DDN)

The network used that connects military installations. The DDN encompasses MILnet and Advanced Research Projects Agency Network (ARPAnet) and the Transmission Control Protocol/Internet Protocol (TCP/IP) protocols they employ.

Defense Data Network Network Information Center (DDN NIC)

The control center of the Defense Data Network (DDN). The DDN is a global network used by the United States Department of Defense, part of which is accessible through the Internet and part of which is classified. The DDN NIC provides information and services through the Internet. Its functions include assigning numbers to domains, assigning IP network addresses, and functioning as a repository for Requests for Comments concerning the Internet community.

deferral time

A specification of the Carrier Sense Multiple Access (CSMA) media-access method, which is the period of time a node waits before attempting to access the network after a packet collision. The deferral time depends on a random number and on the network's level of activity.

Defined Context Set (DCS)

A Consultative Committee for International Telegraphy and Telephony (CCITT) X.216 recommendation that establishes a context for the delivery and usage of services on the Presentation Layer (Layer 6) of the OSI Reference Model.

definition file

A file that contains linking information about a NetWare Loadable Module (NLM). The definition file may contain the names of the object files to link and the name of the executable to create. This file includes a set of keywords for directing the NetWare linker as it creates the executable.

defragmentation

Reorganizing and rewriting files so they occupy a large, contiguous area on a disk, instead of multiple smaller areas. Defragmentation consolidates the file fragments into a contiguous area and allows for faster access.

defragmenter

A software utility that rewrites files so they occupy a large, contiguous area on a disk instead of multiple smaller areas. A defragmenter can improve performance that has been lost because of fragmentation.

delay

The time required to send a byte of data from one system to another. Delay is usually measured in microseconds.

delay distortion

Signal distortion caused by the relative difference in speed of the various components of that signal.

delete

Removing a file from a disk or an item from a file. File deletion can be done through operating system commands or directly from some applications. When a file is deleted, it is not immediately removed from the disk, which allows for the possibility of recovering a deleted file if it was deleted accidentally.

Delete Inhibit (Di) attribute

A selectable NetWare file system attribute. This attribute prohibits users from erasing a particular directory or file, even if that user has the Erase right. A file that has been assigned the Delete Inhibit attribute cannot be deleted by any user, including the owner of the file or the system supervisor.

Delete right

An object right in Novell Directory Services (NDS) that provides a user with the privilege of deleting a particular object from the Directory tree. A container object cannot be deleted unless the objects within the container are deleted first. Furthermore, the Write right for existing object properties must also be granted before objects can be deleted.

Delete Self right

A property right in Novell Directory Services (NDS) that provides a trustee with the privilege of removing itself as a value of the property. The Delete Self right is used only for properties for which the User object can be listed as a value.

delimiter

A symbol or other character that indicates a command, command parameter, or data field has begun or ended. A delimiter is commonly represented as a comma (,), period (.), slash (/), backslash (\), hyphen (-), or colon (:).

delivery confirmation bit

A component of a user packet used to acknowledge receipt of a complete packet sequence. The delivery confirmation bit can be set to one to indicate an acknowledgment is sent from the recipient to the sender.

Synonym: *D-bit*

Demand Assigned Multiple Access (DAMA)

A way to allocate access to communications channels. Under a DAMA configuration, idle channels are combined in a pool. When a channel is requested, an idle channel is selected, given the requested bandwidth, and assigned to the requesting party.

demand paging

A type of virtual memory management that reads pages of information into memory from disk as they are needed by a program.

demand priority

The media-access method used in 100BaseVG, a 100 megabits per second (Mbps) networking implementation similar to Ethernet, but originally designed by Hewlett-Packard. The demand priority scheme differs from the Carrier Sense Multiple Access/Collision Detection (CSMA/CD) method used in IEEE 802.3 Ethernet, in that packet collisions are avoided by using the hub for controlling network access. Because network access centers around the hub, a 100BaseVG network must be deployed in a star topology. Demand priority avoids the possibility of standard priority packets constantly being left behind by keeping track of access requests. If standard priority packets are waiting too long for network access, the hub will automatically upgrade those packets to high priority.

demarcation point

The point where the customer premises equipment (CPE) begins and the telephone company's equipment begins.

demodulation

The process of recovering data from a previously modulated carrier frequency. Demodulation is accomplished by converting analog signals into digital signals.

demultiplexer

A hardware device that separates multiplexed material sent from a single input into discrete elements. The demultiplexer then sends these elements to multiple output paths.

de-ossification
The process of converting definitions that conform to the OSI network management model into definitions that conform to the IP network management model.

Department of Defense (DoD)
The United States governmental agency responsible for funding and development of communications protocols.

departmental LAN
A small or medium-sized local area network (LAN) of as many as 30 users. The nodes on the departmental LAN all share local resources.

Departmental Area Network (DAN)
A network that services a single department. This terminology usually applies only to government agencies.

dependent LU
A Logical Unit (LU) that has an active session to an LU within the Systems Network Architecture (SNA) host system.

designated router
A NetWare Link Services Protocol (NLSP) router responsible for exchanges of link state information between all other NLSP routers on the local area network (LAN). The designated router is the router with the highest priority. In Open Shortest Path First (OSPF) protocol networks, a router that generates a link state advertisement for a multiaccess network and reduces the number of adjacencies is required on a multiaccess network.

desk accessory
A small application that can be selected from the Apple operating system menu while within another application.

desktop
Generically, a workstation that resides on a user's desk. In the Apple Macintosh and Microsoft Windows environments, the term refers to the

interface that shows a graphical representation of files and programs located on the workstation.

desktop computer

A small, microprocessor-based computer system that usually sits on a desktop.

Synonyms: *microcomputer; personal computer*

desktop database

A database maintained by the server in an AppleTalk network. This database holds information that associates files with icons and documents with applications. Under the AppleTalk Filing Protocol (ATFP), every server must maintain a desktop database.

Desktop Management Interface (DMI)

A standard supported by several vendors used to automate the process of identifying a personal computer (both hardware and software) to the network. No user intervention is required. The DMI identifies information about any personal computer component, including manufacturer, component name, version, serial number, and installation date and time.

Destination Address (DA)

The address in a packet header that identifies the recipient of that packet.

Destination ID (DID)

The address of a destination node in an Attached Resource Computer Network (ARCnet) packet.

destination node

Under the OSI Reference Model, a node that represents the host computers at each end of a connection. In a packet-switching network, the destination node is the node attached to the Data Terminal Equipment (DTE).

destination server

The NetWare 4.*x* server to which data files, bindery files, and other data are migrated during an upgrade from a server running an earlier version of the operating system.

destructive test

A surface test that functions as a disk format, destroying data and making multiple passes over the disk surface to read and write test patterns.

Details dialog box

A dialog box from the NetWare Administrator utility that appears when the user double-clicks an object. It can also be found by selecting Details from the File menu after selecting an object. The dialog box shows the Novell Directory Services (NDS) properties of an object.

developer environment

A complete set of tools that enables a programmer to create a computer program. The developer environment includes a programming language and other components, such as a compiler, debugger, text editor, and code libraries.

device

Any hardware attached to a computer (such as a printer, mouse, or Network Interface Card).

device dependence

A requirement that a specific device be present before a program can function.

device driver

A software program (or firmware) that establishes an interface between the operating system and a peripheral device and controls the software routines that make the peripherals work.

device independence

The ability to produce similar results across multiple environments, without having to have specific hardware.

Device Independent Backup Interface (DIBI)

An interface meant to simplify the process of moving backed-up data from one environment to another on the same network.

device name
A name used by the operating system to identify a peripheral or other component.

device numbering
A way to identify devices that may entail three different numbering schemes: the physical address, device code, or the logical device number. The drive establishes the *physical address* when it reads the address set by jumpers (or by software-based configuration). The *device code* is determined by the driver ID, driver load instance, disk number, and controller number. The *logical device number* is determined by the order in which disk drivers are loaded.

Device object
A Novell Directory Services (NDS) subclass that represents a computer, peripheral, or other component on a Directory tree.

device sharing
A method of sharing a centrally located device, such as a printer or storage peripheral. Device sharing presents a more efficient way to use network resources.

diagnostic program
An application that tests computer hardware and peripherals to detect *hard faults* and *soft faults*. Most computers run a simple diagnostic program at startup.

dial backup
A configured backup serial line through a circuit-switched connection, used to protect wide area networks (WANs) from downtime. If the WAN link goes down, the serial line can still transmit data until the link is restored.

dial-back
A security mechanism meant to prevent unauthorized dial-up access to the network. Network-based software retains a list of authorized users and the numbers from which they may call. If a user needs access to the network, the server receives the user's call, receives the login information, and then

terminates the connection. Then the software refers to the dial-up table and calls the number back to re-establish the connection.

Dialed Number Identification Service (DNIS)
A character string that indicates the number dialed by the caller and specifies how the call should be handled by the Private Branch Exchange (PBX).

dialog box
A window in a graphical application that usually appears when the application requires some sort of additional input from the user before carrying out a task.

dial-on-demand routing
A routing process that provides on-demand network connections through the Public Switched Telephone Network (PSTN).

dial-up
Accessing a telephone circuit through manual or automatic dialing sequences.

dial-up access
A way to connect a remote workstation temporarily to a server over a standard telephone connection.

dial-up connection
A connection to the Public Data Network (PDN) often used by personal computer users to access data from remote hosts. A dial-up connection usually carries a slower rate than a leased line.

dial-up line
A nondedicated communications line that can be accessed through dial-up facilities. The public telephone network is composed of dial-up lines. A dial-up connection is temporary—established at the time of dial-up and destroyed when the call is terminated.

dial-up service
A type of account with an Internet service provider (ISP) that enables a personal computer to connect to the Internet using a modem and the public telephone network. Normally the user makes this connection by placing a phone call to a *system port connection point*, a pool of modems; the call may not be long distance and the line may be busy if all modems are in use.

dibit
A bit pair that is treated as a single unit.

dielectric
A nonconducting material used to form an insulating layer around conductive wire in either coaxial or twisted-pair cable. The dielectric material can be rubber or certain types of plastic.

differential backup
A backup that archives only new files or those modified since the last full backup. Files that require differential backup are marked with a *modify bit* to point them out to the backup utility.

differential encoding
A digital coding technique that denotes a binary value by a signal change rather than by a particular signal level.

differential Manchester encoding
A digital coding scheme that uses a transition in the middle of a bit time for clocking; the transition at the beginning of the bit time denotes a zero. Differential Manchester encoding is popular in Token Ring networks.

digerati
A term (probably derived from *literati*) that refers to people considered knowledgeable about the digital revolution.

digest
A compilation of messages posted to a mailing list over a period of time. A digest provides the receiver with one big message instead of numerous smaller messages.

digital
The representation of information by zeroes and ones. Data characters in a digital stream are discrete electrical pulses or signal levels.

Digital Access and Cross-Connect System (DACS)
In digital communications, a mechanism used to switch a 64 kilobit-per-second (Kbps) DS-0 channel from one T1 line to another.

Digital Audio Tape (DAT)
A storage medium often used for network backups. Using the Data/DAT logical recording format (which supports random data reads and writes), DAT permits data to be updated in place. Modified data need not be rewritten to a new location. DAT is often deployed on a small audiotape cassette, most commonly a 4-millimeter tape in a helical-scan drive.

digital cash
An electronic payment system found on the Internet that allows payments to be made without traditional cash transactions.

digital circuit
A line that transmits data in unmodulated square waves that represent values of zero or one.

digital communication
A method of telecommunications that uses digital signals in the form of binary values to represent information. A digital signal is encoded as a discrete value, represented as a zero or a one. The binary values are encoded as different voltage or current levels. Analog signals, by contrast, represent information as variations in a continuous waveform.

Digital Cross-Connect System (DCS)

In digital telephony, a switch that switches a digital channel from one device to another by cross-connecting the digital channels. The cross-connection takes place at the slowest rate common to the two lines involved.

Digital Data Communications Message Protocol (DDCMP)

A byte-oriented, link-layer synchronous protocol designed by Digital Equipment Corporation as the primary data-link component in DECnet.

Digital Data Service (DDS)

Leased lines that can accommodate a transmission rate of between 2.4 kilobits per second (Kbps) and 56Kbps.

digital ID

An element assigned by a certification authority and attached to an electronic message. A digital ID authenticates the message and sender through such information as the sender's name, address, organization, and public key, as well as by digital signature, serial number, and a limited validity period.

Digital-Intel-Xerox (DIX)

Refers to the three companies (Digital Equipment Corporation, Intel, and Xerox) whose early research led to the development of the Blue Book Ethernet standard.

Digital Multiplexed Interface (DMI)

A T1 interface between a Private Branch Exchange (PBX) and a computer.

Digital Network Architecture (DNA)

Digital Equipment Corporation's layered architecture used in DECnet.

Digital Service (DS)

A telecommunications service that uses digital signaling and is defined as a North American service using a five-level transmission hierarchy. A DS relies on Pulse Code Modulation (PCM) to encode analog signals in digital form. The five levels of digital services are DS-0 (64Kbps), DS-1 (1.544Mbps), DS-2 (6.312Mbps), DS-3 (44.736Mbps), and DS-4 (274.176Mbps).

Digital Service Unit (DSU)
A device that sits between a user's Data Terminal Equipment (DTE) and a common carrier's digital circuits. The DSU formats data for transmission on the public carrier's wide area network (WAN). The DSU is required to connect to carrier services, such as frame relay or Switched Multimegabit Data Service (SMDS)

Digital Signal Cross-Connect Between levels 1 and 3 (DSX1/3)
An interface that connects DS-1 and DS-3 signals.

Digital Signal Processor (DSP)
A device used to extract and process elements from a digital stream.

digital signature
A unique value assigned to a particular transaction. Designed to be impossible to forge, this security method verifies the identity of the sender and origin of the message.

Digital Simultaneous Voice and Data (DSVD)
A standard used in terminal adapters that enables a user to talk over a telephone line being used simultaneously to transmit data.

Digital Speech Interpolation (DSI)
A method of improving the efficiency of a communications channel. By sending transmissions during the quiet periods that normally occur in a voice conversation, DIS can double the number of voice signals a line can carry.

Digital Termination Service (DTS)
A service that allows the private network to access the carrier networks with digital microwave equipment.

Digital-to-Analog Converter (DAC)
A hardware device used to convert a digital signal to an analog signal.

Dijkstra's algorithm

An Open Shortest Path First (OSPF) routing algorithm that uses path length to determine a shortest-path spanning tree. Dijkstra's algorithm is commonly used in link-state routing algorithms.

dimmed command

A command displayed in light gray in the graphical user interface. A command is dimmed when it is not currently available.

DIN connector

A connector that complies with the German Deutsche Industrie Norm (DIN) standards body. Some Macintosh computers use a DIN connector as the serial port connector; some IBM computers use a DIN connector to connect the keyboard to the system unit.

Direct Broadcast Satellite (DBS)

A satellite that broadcasts signals directly to subscribers without having to go through a central station first.

direct connection

An immediate connection to the network. In wide area networking, a direct connection does not go through a local carrier.

direct-control switching

A network switching system that establishes the packet path directly through network signals, instead of through a central controller or hub.

Direct Current (DC)

Electrical power that travels only in one direction, often used in batteries and electronic components.

direct distance dialing (DDD)

Dialing a long-distance number without going through an operator.

direct inward dialing (DID)

A system in which an external caller dials a number in a Private Branch Exchange (PBX) directly, without first going through the switchboard.

direct link

A circuit that connects two stations directly, with no intervening nodes or stations.

Direct Memory Access (DMA)

A circuit used to facilitate data transfer between a device and system memory. A special processor called the *DMA controller chip* is required to manage DMA because the computer's central processing unit (CPU) is not involved in the transaction.

direct outward dialing (DOD)

A system in which an internal caller dials an outside number in a Private Branch Exchange (PBX) directly, without first going through the switchboard.

direct wave

In wireless communications, a wave that requires a direct line of sight between sender and recipient.

directed search

A search request sent to a node—known to contain a resource—to determine the continued existence of the resource, while determining routing information about the node.

directed transmission

In AppleTalk networks using LocalTalk, a transmission intended for one specific node. In infrared communications, a way of aiming a signal at a central reflective target.

directional coupler

A type of coupler that can send a split signal in only one direction.

directory

A disk structure that contains files. Generically, a directory is a way to organize and group files for easier access by placing them in a logical order and related subsections. A directory can contain many levels of subdirectories in a tree-like structure. The term can also refer to the Directory database in NetWare. The Novell directory organizes the Novell Directory Services (NDS) objects in a hierarchical tree structure called the *Directory tree*.

Directory Access Protocol (DAP)

An X.500 Directory Services (DS) protocol. The DAP establishes communications between a Directory User Agent (DUA) and a Directory System Agent (DSA).

directory attributes

A set of eight properties that can be assigned to NetWare Directories to establish File System Security. The directory attributes detail how users may manage a directory.

directory cache

Part of the server memory that holds frequently requested directory entries copied from the disk directory tables. The purpose of the cache is to facilitate faster access to a file's location.

directory caching

A feature of NetWare that improves performance by writing copies of the File Allocation Table (FAT) and Directory Entry Table (DET) into the network server's memory. This enables a file's location to be read directly from memory, instead of accessing it from a physical disk.

directory entry

A record containing the basic information about directories and files on a NetWare server. Directory entries may include names, owners, date and time of last update, and location on the hard disk. The directory entries are located in a directory table on the network hard disk.

Directory Entry Table (DET)

A table located on a network volume that contains information about files, directories, directory trustees, or other directory entries for the particular volume on which it is located.

directory hashing

A NetWare feature used to improve performance by indexing file locations on a disk to reduce the time needed to locate a file. Instead of conducting a sequential search, a directory hashing feature makes a calculation to predict a file's address.

directory ID

An AppleTalk feature that assigns a unique value to a directory when that directory is created.

Directory Information Base (DIB)

A database used to hold Directory Services information in the X.500 Directory Services model. The DIB can be partitioned and stored in separate locations. In this model, the DIB is accessed by Directory System Agents (DSAs) on behalf of Directory User Agents (DUAs).

Directory Information Tree (DIT)

The structure that holds the information for a Directory Information Base (DIB) in the X.500 Directory Services model. If a DIT is large, the information contained in it may be distributed to provide faster access. A DIT's objects can be used to represent intermediate categories or specific objects. The DIT does not contain the objects themselves; it holds information about the objects. The DIT supports both retrieval and modification, and any DIT operation may be configured to apply to one entry or a group of entries. End users can access the DIT's information through a Directory User Agent (DUA) or a Directory System Agent (DSA).

Directory Management Domain (DMD)

In the X.500 Directory Management Services scheme, a set of Directory System Agents (DSAs) managed by a single organization.

directory management request

A request that controls the physical distribution of the Novell Directory Services (NDS) database. Administrators use these requests to install new Directory partitions and to manage their replicas. Directory management requests include Add Partition, Add Replica, List Replicas, Remove Partition, Synchronize Replicas, Create a New Partition, and Merge Partition.

Directory Map object

A Directory Schema term and a leaf object in Novell Directory Services (NDS), referring to a directory on a volume. The Directory Map object specifies a path on a volume. It permits the drive to be mapped to a given application without requiring the actual path and volume where the application is physically located. A Directory Map is often used in login scripts to avoid having to map a drive to a specific directory path.

directory node

An addressable entity on a NetWare network, containing information about a directory. The directory node is a 128-byte entry contained in the server's Directory Entry Table (DET). The directory node includes the directory name, attributes, Inherited Rights Mask, creation date and time, creator's object ID, link to parent directory, and link to the trustee node.

Directory object

A set of properties stored in the Novell Directory Services (NDS) Directory database. The three types of directory objects are the *root object*, *container objects*, and *leaf objects*. A Directory object can represent a physical or a logical network resource. Although it represents the resource, the Directory object does not contain the actual resource, only information about how to use it.

directory path

A character string indicating the position of a file within the file system. The directory path lists the server name, the volume name, and the name of each directory that leads to the file system directory to which access is desired.

directory rights

Rights used to control the actions a NetWare trustee can take with a given directory. Directory rights are not assigned to Novell Directory Services (NDS) objects; they are part of the file system. A User object can be granted directory rights to a directory on a volume.

Directory root
An object in the NetWare Directory tree. The directory root establishes the highest point of access for different Country and Organization objects. It also permits trustee assignments to grant rights to the entire Directory tree.

Directory Schema
The set of rules defining how to create the Novell Directory Services (NDS) Directory tree and store information in the Directory database. The schema defines attribute information, inheritance, naming, and subordination. *Attribute information* concerns the different types of information that can be associated with an object. *Inheritance* specifies which objects can inherit the properties and rights of other objects, and *naming* determines the structure of the Directory tree. *Subordination* determines the location of objects in the Directory tree.

directory server
A software application that can access directory information and directory services for other nodes on the network.

Directory Service Area (DSA)
The calling area covered by a directory service.

Directory Services (DS)
A feature of NetWare 4.x, a global, distributed, replicated database that retains information about all resources in the network. The Directory Services feature centrally manages any size network through a hierarchical, treelike representation. Other directory services include the X.500 standard and the Domain Naming System (DNS).

Directory Services request
A request made to NetWare's Directory database by users or network supervisors. The three types of Directory Services requests are as follows: End users or administrators make *directory access requests* to create, modify, or retrieve objects. *Directory access control requests* set the access rights to

Directory objects. Administrators make *directory management requests* to enact management functions (such as partitioning) that pertain to the physical distribution of the Directory's database.

directory structure
A hierarchical structure that represents how NetWare directories are related to each other on a volume.

directory structure duplication
A feature of NetWare used to protect data from the effects of hardware failure. The feature copies the Directory Entry Table (DET) and File Allocation Table (FAT) to separate areas of the hard disk. If the primary copy is destroyed, the operating system accesses the secondary copy.

Directory synchronization
Maintaining multiple instances of a NetWare Directory and ensuring all are properly updated.

Directory System Agent (DSA)
Software used in the X.500 Directory Services model for accessing, using, and updating the Directory Information Base (DIB) or Directory Information Tree (DIT).

Directory System Protocol (DSP)
A protocol used by Directory System Agents (DSAs) to communicate with each other.

directory table
A table containing basic information about files, directories, directory trustees, and other entities contained on the volume. The directory table may occupy one or more blocks on the volume, with each block containing 4K of data. Each block can hold 128 directory entries, with each entry being 32 bytes long.

Directory tree
A hierarchical structure representing objects in a directory services database. The Directory tree shows container objects, which are used to

organize the network, and leaf objects, which represent individual resources. The X.500 specification developed by the Institute of Electronic and Electrical Engineers (IEEE) provides a standard method for organizing information in a directory tree pattern, so it is globally available. Novell Directory Services (NDS) is a directory service that complies with the X.500 specification.

Directory tree name
A name assigned during installation to each NetWare Directory tree. The Directory tree name can be up to 32 characters. Characters can be uppercase or lowercase letters, numbers, and hyphens, but may not contain a space or a trailing underscore.

Directory User Agent (DUA)
A program used in the X.500 Directory Services model for accessing directory services, which establishes an interface between an end user and a Directory System Agent (DSA), which retrieves the requested services.

directory verification
A feature of NetWare used to protect data from the effects of hardware failure. Directory verification occurs whenever the server is started up. During this verification, the operating system performs a consistency check to ensure that duplicate sets of Directory Entry Table (DET) and File Allocation Table (FAT) are identical.

dirty cache block
A temporary memory storage space that contains updated information not yet written to disk. These blocks are sent to the disk when a client-write operation completely fills a cache block or after an Aged Write default setting value has been reached.

dirty cache buffers
File blocks that exist in memory and are waiting to be written to disk.

disable
To turn off a function. A Graphical User Interface (GUI) will typically show disabled menu commands in gray to indicate they are unavailable.

Discard Eligibility (DE)

A frame relay network term. The DE bit is set by an end node to indicate certain frames can be discarded in the event of network congestion.

disk

A plate-like storage medium magnetically encoded. A disk may take the form of a *hard disk* (which is usually installed within a computer system), a *floppy disk* (which is removable and has less storage capacity), a *CD-ROM* (which cannot be written to or erased), or an *optical disc* (which can be erasable and writable).

disk-allocation block

A data-storage unit used by network volumes. Disk-allocation blocks may be 4K, 8K, 16K, 32K, or 64K in size, and may vary in size between volumes. One volume, however, can have only one block size. The disk-allocation block represents the smallest file size for that volume, unless suballocation is used.

Disk Array Subsystem (DAS)

The combination of cabling, circuitry, and the carriage required for using multiple hard disks.

disk cache

An area of random access memory (RAM) used to store frequently accessed data. A disk cache increases performance by relieving an application from having to reaccess data constantly from a physical disk. When an application requests information from the hard drive, the disk cache program will first check to see whether the information exists in the cache memory. If so, the information is loaded from the cache memory instead of from the hard disk.

disk controller

A hardware device used to control how data is written to and retrieved from an attached hard disk. The disk controller regulates the movement of the physical disk head as it reads data from the disk or writes data to it.

disk coprocessor board (DCB)

An intelligent board that functions as an interface between the host microprocessor and the disk controller. This board can increase performance by relieving the host microprocessor of data storage and retrieval tasks.

disk drive

A peripheral storage device that reads from and writes to magnetic or optical discs. The operating system assigns a unique name to each installed drive.

disk driver

A program that facilitates communication between the disk controller and the server's central processing unit (CPU), or between the operating system and hard disks.

disk duplexing

A data-protection scheme that duplicates data onto two hard disks, each one on a separate disk channel. If the first hard disk fails, the second one takes over automatically.

disk format

A way of preparing and structuring a disk so it can receive data from a particular operating system. Disk formatting is a function of the operating system. Usually, a disk formatted by one operating system cannot be read by a different operating system without a special translation utility.

disk interface board

An add-on board that functions as an interface between a host microprocessor and the disk controller.

disk mirroring

A procedure that involves duplicating data from a NetWare partition on one hard disk to the NetWare partition on another disk. Disk mirroring pairs multiple hard disks on the same channel. If the original disk fails, the secondary disk automatically takes over. Disk mirroring cannot protect against failures that occur along the channel between the disks and the NetWare server, because the duplicate disks exist on the same channel.

Disk Operating System (DOS)

A set of programs that manage computer resources and the applications that run on a computer. The operating system establishes a link between the physical computer and associated peripherals, files, and the applications being run on them. DOS is used on IBM-compatible computers. The more common DOS implementations include Microsoft's MS-DOS, Novell's Novell DOS, and IBM's PC DOS.

disk optimizer

A utility for rearranging files and directories for better performance. A defragmenter utility is a type of disk optimizer.

disk partition

A logical subdivision of a hard disk. One disk can have multiple partitions, with each partition having a unique name. In the NetWare operating system, a NetWare disk partition is created on each hard disk, and volumes are then created from the NetWare partitions.

disk striping

A data-storage strategy that combines partitions on multiple hard disks into a single volume. Because each partition is on a separate disk, multiple partitions can be read from or written to simultaneously.

disk striping with parity

A disk striping strategy that distributes parity information across multiple hard disk partitions. In the event of a failed partition, the information on the other partitions can reconstruct the missing data.

disk subsystem

An external unit that can be attached to a server and contains any combination of hard drives, tape drives, or optical drives. A disk subsystem gives the server additional storage capacity.

diskette

A disk that can be removed from a drive.
Synonym: *floppy disk*

diskless workstation

A networked computer with no local disk storage capacity. A diskless workstation boots from a network file server and also loads all of its programs from the file server.

dispersion

The broadening of a light signal as it travels through fiber in a fiber-optic connection. Dispersion is proportional to distance traveled and imposes a limit on bandwidth. In wireless communications, dispersion is the scattering of the wireless signal caused by atmospheric conditions. In an electrical transmission, dispersion is the signal distortion that occurs as the signal travels along the wire.

disruptive test

A network diagnostic test that requires ordinary network activity to cease before it can be run.

distance vector

An algorithm used to disseminate routing information to routers on the network. Routers employing this algorithm only retain the information necessary to reach the next router destination on the network.

distance vector algorithm

The class of routing algorithms that broadcast routing information periodically, instead of sending information only when a change occurs in a route. Routers use this algorithm to exchange information about accessible networks with neighboring routers.

distance vector protocol

The protocol used to derive best path information from the information contained in adjacent nodes. Some examples of distance vector protocols include Internet Protocol (IP), Routing Information Protocol (RIP), Internet Packet Exchange Routing Information Protocol (IPX RIP), and Routing Table Maintenance Protocol (RTMP).

distinguished name
The full name or path from an object to the [Root] of the Novell Directory Services (NDS) Directory tree.

distortion
An undesirable change in a signal that may be caused by attenuation, crosstalk, interference, or delay.

distortion delay
Fluctuating and nonuniform transmission speeds of the components of a communications signal through a transmission medium.

distributed applications
Applications that operate in a distributed computing environment, which may contain modules running on different computer systems.

distributed architecture
A processor configuration in which the processors are contained in multiple devices. Each processor can function independently or in cooperation with other elements.

Distributed Authentication Security Service (DASS)
A system for authenticating users logging into a network from unattended workstations. DASS relies on public key encryption to provide security.

distributed computing
A method of computing that distributes processing between multiple devices.

Distributed Computing Environment (DCE)
An open networking architecture designed by the Open Software Foundation (OSF). DCE provides all the elements needed to distribute applications and their functions across a network transparently. Under the DCE model, the network would appear to the end user as a single entity. This makes all the network's resources transparently available to every user.

Distributed Data Management (DDM)

A service of IBM's Systems Network Architecture (SNA) used to enable file sharing and remote file access in the network.

Distributed Data Processing (DDP)

A way of processing data where the work is distributed across multiple computers.

distributed database (DDB)

A database that provides services to all network applications and users over different platforms. The distributed database may be stored on different hard disks in different locations.

Distributed Database Management System (DDBMS)

The software used to reference a distributed database.

Distributed File System (DFS)

A file system in which files located on multiple machines appear to an end user as if they were all in a single location.

Distributed Foundation Wireless Media Access Control (DFWMAC)

A data-link-layer protocol for wireless local area networks (LANs).

Distributed Function Terminal (DFT)

A terminal mode in IBM's System Network Architecture (SNA) capable of supporting as many as five sessions, thereby enabling the user to access five applications through the same terminal.

distributed network

A type of network where processing is distributed to multiple computers instead of being carried out by a single computer. Processing may be shared between clients, file servers, print servers, or application servers. The distributed model promotes efficiency by dynamically assigning processing, depending on the existing workload and specific task.

Distributed Network Architecture (DNA)

A network architecture developed by Digital Equipment Corporation whereby processing and services are distributed across the network, instead of being located in a single host.

Distributed Office Applications Model (DOAM)

An Open Systems Interface (OSI) model used for several application-layer processes. The functions of DOAM include document filing and retrieval (DFR), document printing application (DPA), Message-Oriented Text Interchange System (MOTIS), and referenced data transfer (RDT).

Distributed Office Supported System (DISOSS)

An IBM mainframe-based software package that offers users a variety of document preparation and electronic mail (e-mail) features. The DISOSS system allows documents created by different products to be shared among different IBM systems; it is often used as a way to transmit documents between IBM systems and non-IBM systems.

distributed processing

A technique used to allow multiple networked computers to complete a task jointly. In a distributed processing model, different nodes are assigned responsibility for specialized tasks.

Distributed Queue Dual Bus (DQDB)

A network architecture defined in the Institute of Electronic and Electrical Engineers (IEEE) 802.6 Metropolitan Area Network (MAN) standard. DQDB is the main platform used for Synchronous Multimegabit Data Service (SMDS) access. The DQDB consists of the protocol syntax and the distributed queuing algorithm used for shared medium access control. Generally, DQDB requires fiber-optic cable and can support a transmission speed of up to 50 megabits per second (Mbps).

Distributed Relational Data Architecture (DRDA)

A distributed database architecture designed by IBM that forms the basis of the database management features offered by IBM's SystemView network management software.

distributed star topology

A physical topology with two or more hubs having workstations connected in a star arrangement around each one.

distributed system

Multiple, autonomous, linked computers that can (through proper software) give the appearance of being a single, integrated computer system. Unlike a centralized system (in which multiple personal computers are connected to a single host machine), a distributed system entails computers that may be parts of local area networks (LANs), wide area networks (WANs), or global area networks (GANs). The Internet and automated teller machine (ATM) networks are examples of distributed systems.

Distributed System Object Model (DSOM)

A system designed by IBM for sharing objects across a network. DSOM is compliant with the Common Object Request Broker Architecture (CORBA) model.

Distributed Systems Architecture (DSA)

An OSI-compliant architecture designed by Honeywell.

distributed transaction processing services

A set of services used to allow transaction programs to communicate with each other and to access remote resources. These services also facilitate synchronization and error recovery.

distribution cable

A cable used in a broadband network over intermediate distances or for establishing branches off a network backbone.

distribution frame

The location where wiring from multiple network components is concentrated.

Distribution List object

In NetWare, a Novell Directory Services (NDS) leaf object that represents a list of mail recipients. The Distribution List object enables an individual to avoid having to enter names of multiple recipients; simply entering the name of the Distribution List object disseminates the message to all members of the list.

diversity

A strategy used in microwave communications to protect against equipment failure. Frequency diversity allocates a separate frequency band that can be used if the primary band is unavailable because of noise or interference. Space diversity, on the other hand, sets up two receiving antennas in close proximity to each other, so if the primary antenna fails, the secondary one can be used.

Document Content Architecture (DCA)

A data-stream architecture defined by IBM, used in text documents, and consisting of three standard formats. The *Revisable Form Text* (RFT) format is used for text that can still be edited; the *Final Form Text* (FFT) standard is used for text that has already been formatted for a given output device and can no longer be edited; and the *Mixed Form Text* (MFT) format applies to documents that may contain graphics or other types of data in addition to text.

Document Interchange Architecture (DIA)

A set of services defined by IBM designed to make using documents throughout multiple IBM computing environments easier. The four services of DIA include Application Processing Services (APS), Document Distribution Services (DDS), Document Library Services (DLS), and File Transfer Service (FTS).

document management

Management of a large collection of electronic documents through a specific software program. Document management software may provide services for version control, check-in and check-out, text-string or phrase searching, and other features.

Document Transfer and Manipulation (DTAM)

Specifications for nontelephone and nontelegraph communications services (such as telex, fax transmissions, and telewriting) that define three service classes (bulk transfer, document manipulation, and bulk transfer and manipulation), primitive functional units for each service class, and related communications support functions.

documentation

A piece of reference material that accompanies computer software or hardware. Documentation may be printed or online, and may include tutorials, specifications, troubleshooting details, or other references.

domain

A logical group of network servers that appear to end users as a single network server. When used in the context of the Internet, domain refers to an element of the Domain Naming System (DNS) naming hierarchy. In NetWare, domain refers to the memory segment within NetWare used to separate NetWare Loadable Modules (NLMs) from the operating system.

Domain Control Database (DCDB) file

An IBM file associated with the LAN Manager and LAN Server applications.

Domain Naming System (DNS)

A distributed naming service that provides information about the Internet Protocol (IP) addresses and domain names of all computers on a network. The DNS server translates symbolic, easy to remember names into numeric IP addresses. Commonly used on the Internet, DNS domains may be based on geography or organization. The topmost domain is standardized and includes these domain names: com (commercial organization), edu (educational institution), gov (government agency), int (international organization), mil (United States military), net (networking organization), and org (nonprofit organization).

domain server

An Internet computer that translates between Internet domain names (such as xyz.abc.com) and Internet numerical addresses (such as 123.456.78.0).

Domain Specific Part (DSP)

Part of the address for the Network Service Access Point (NSAP) in the OSI Reference Model. The DSP is the address within the domain.

Don't Compress (Dc) attribute

A NetWare file system directory attribute used to prevent files from being compressed.

Don't Migrate (Dm) attribute

A NetWare file system directory attribute and file attribute used to prevent files from being migrated to secondary storage devices, such as a tape drive or optical disc.

Don't Suballocate (Ds) attribute

A NetWare file system attribute that prevents a file from being suballocated, even if suballocation has been enabled.

DOS boot record

A record used by the read-only memory (ROM)-Basic Input/Output System (BIOS) to determine from which device to boot. The boot record can reside on a floppy disk, local hard disk, or remote boot chip. ROM-BIOS runs a program from the boot record to determine the disk format and the location of system files and directories. ROM-BIOS is then able to load system files and the command processor.

DOS client

A workstation that boots with DOS and accesses the network through the NetWare DOS Requester software or a NetWare shell.

DOS device

A storage unit (such as a disk drive or tape backup unit) that is compatible with the DOS disk format.

DOS DIR scan

A DOS command used to view the contents of a directory.

DOS extender

A software program that allows DOS programs to be executed in protected mode and, therefore, use extended memory.

DOS menu utility

A utility where options are presented in a character-based menu.

DOS partition functions

A set of features used to allow access to files in the DOS partition of a NetWare server's disk. They are used primarily to install new software from the DOS partition to the NetWare partition. These functions adversely affect server performance and should be used only when necessary. If a file in the DOS partition is accessed frequently, therefore, that file should be moved into the NetWare partition.

DOS prompt

A screen prompt that indicates DOS is operational. The DOS prompt shows the current drive letter, a colon, and a greater-than symbol (>), but can be customized using the PROMPT command.

DOS Protected Mode Interface (DPMI)

A Microsoft interface specification that establishes a DOS extension, which allows DOS programs to run in protected mode and, therefore, use extended memory. Protected mode allows programs to run as DOS tasks on their own or under Windows 3.x. It provides these enhancements on 80286 and higher processors.

DOS Requester

The DOS client software written for the NetWare 2.x, NetWare 3.x, and NetWare 4.x operating systems, used to connect the workstation to network services. The DOS Requester replaces the NETX.COM shell from previous releases of NetWare. It mediates between applications, DOS, and NetWare, and consists of a Terminate-and-Stay-Resident (TSR) manager and multiple Virtual Loadable Modules (VLMs). DOS can call the DOS Requester to execute a network-based task that DOS would be incapable of executing by itself.

DOS setup routine

A routine used to set up the system configuration of a DOS client or NetWare server. This routine records the system's built-in hardware features and available system memory, and enables the user to set parameters such as the date and time, password, and keyboard speed.

DOS text utility
A DOS utility that provides instructions to the network. The command line and DOS menu utilities are both types of DOS text utilities.

DOS version
The version number and type of DOS being used. Different implementations of DOS (such as Novell DOS and MS DOS) are not compatible.

dot address
Four groups of numbers in an Internet Protocol (IP) address that are separated by periods (or dots) where each group represents the decimal equivalent of the corresponding 8 bits of the 32-bit IP address. A dot address (for example, 117.127.137.147) is also known as *dotted quad* or *dotted quad address*.

dot matrix printer
A type of printer that forms characters and images from patterns of dots.

dotted decimal
The notation system used to represent 4-byte Internet Protocol (IP) addresses.

double buffering
Using two buffers for input and output. Double buffering improves performance and increases throughput. In this type of system, one buffer is being processed while the other is still being filled.

down
To shut down a server or other network device.

Downgrading
The process of converting a message from the 1988 X.400 Message Handling System (MHS) to one that can be used by a system using the 1984 version of X.400.

downlink

A telecommunications link between a satellite and Earth station or stations.

downlink station

A group of communications equipment designed to receive and transmit signals to and from satellites.

download

The act of copying a file to a computer or peripheral device. Both host and recipient must use the same communications protocol for a download to take place.

downsizing

In networking, a technique that offloads applications from proprietary mainframe platforms to a network of smaller, less expensive microcomputers. A common downsizing strategy replaces or supplements mainframes with a client-server architecture.

Downstream Physical Unit (DSPU)

A device in a ring topology that lies in the direction in which packets are traveling.

downtime

The amount of time a server, network, or other device is inoperable. An unavailable machine is not necessarily down; it may simply be unavailable because of heavy activity.

Draft International Standard (DIS)

An early version of a proposed standard from a formal standards organization. The DIS is submitted to committee members for comment before the standard is formally ratified.

Draft Proposal (DP)

A preliminary version of a standard circulated by a formal standards organization or committee. Comments and criticisms are received and considered, and the proposal may be subsequently edited.

drag-and-drop function

A mouse pointer operation that enables a user to select an object and move it to a new location. Drag-and-drop is often used to simplify file operations.

drive

Refers to either a physical, logical, or virtual drive. A *physical drive* is a physical storage device (such as a disk drive or tape drive) to which data can be written or from which it can be read. A *logical drive* identifies a specific directory located on the physical drive. A *virtual drive* may take the form of a random access memory (RAM) disk and mimics a physical drive.

drive array

A group of hard drives used in a single Redundant Array of Inexpensive Disks (RAID) configuration.

drive letter

A letter used to show a specific disk drive is active.

drive mapping

A function whereby a pointer is established to point to a specific location in the file system. The pointer is represented as a letter assigned to a directory path on a volume. The path identifies the location of a directory and includes the volume, directory, and any subdirectories that lead to the desired directory. Drive mappings are created for the purpose of following these paths. NetWare can recognize four types of drive mappings: local drive mappings, network drive mappings, network search drive mappings, and Directory Map objects. *Local drive mappings* are paths to local media, such as a hard disk. *Network drive mappings* point to volumes or directories on the network. *Network search drive mappings* point to directories that contain specific files. *Directory Map objects* permit a drive to be mapped to an application without having to know the actual path to where the application is physically located. Furthermore, drive mappings can be either temporary or permanent. To make the mappings permanent, MAP commands must be placed in the login script or marked as permanent in the graphical login utility.

driver

An application that establishes an interface between the operating system and peripheral devices. Drivers can be created for almost any type of device, including printers, Small Computer System Interface (SCSI) devices, or Network Interface Cards (NICs). Specialized drivers support a single model of one device for one program, but more generic drivers are also created for use with multiple device models.

droid

A contraction for *software android* that refers to a program performing tasks on behalf of a user usually within preset parameters and without user intervention.

drop

An attachment to a horizontal cabling system, usually the point at which a computer is connected to the network transmission medium.

drop box

A folder in an AppleShare server used to grant write privileges.

drop-box folder

In NetWare, a folder for which a user has Create and File Scan rights. Users can copy files into the folder, but cannot see the folder's contents, delete files contained in the folder, or search the folder. A Macintosh folder marked with a belt around it is a drop-box folder.

drop cable

A four-pair Attachment Unit Interface (AUI) cable used to connect network interface cards. The drop cable is connected to the network cable by a clamp.

drop set

All the components required to connect a computer or peripheral to horizontal cabling. The drop set includes at least the cable and an adapter.

drop side

All the components required to connect a computer or peripheral to the patch panel or punch-down block that connects to the distribution frame.

dropout

The temporary loss of a transmission signal.

DS Login menu

A menu that can be accessed by clicking the tree icon in the Novell Directory Services (NDS) menu bar. The DS Login menu enables users to check their NDS status, log in to the Directory, change the NDS password, and log out of the directory. When a user logs in to Directory Services via the DS Login menu, the user is not connecting to any given server, but is instead logging directly into the Directory Services tree.

D-type connector

A type of connector that uses pins and sockets to establish contact. D-type connectors are commonly used for both serial and parallel ports on personal computers.

dual cable system

A networking configuration that connects a node to the network through more than one physical link. The value of this configuration is, if one link fails, the station is still able to communicate through the additional link.

dual homing

A Fiber Distributed Data Interface (FDDI) technique that uses redundant concentrators to improve reliability. Under this configuration, the server is attached to both concentrators, which are both connected to a dual-attached FDDI ring. Dual homing provides an alternative route to the FDDI network, in case the primary route is unavailable.

dual in-line package (DIP)

A type of switch that can have one of two settings. DIP switches provide an alternative to jumper settings that are used to configure components. DIP switches are common in dot matrix printers, modems, and other peripherals.

dual processing
A System Fault Tolerance (SFT) III configuration that assigns different parts of an operating system to separate processors. A server with dual processing capability has two central processing units (CPUs) installed.

Dual-Attachment Concentrator (DAC)
A concentrator used in a Fiber Distributed Data Interface (FDDI) to attach single-attachment stations or station clusters to the FDDI rings.

dual-attachment station (DAS)
In Fiber Distributed Data Interface (FDDI) networks, a station or node connected to both the primary and secondary rings. A station can be directly connected to the FDDI ring through a port on the DAS, with no concentrator required. A single-attachment station, on the other hand, must be attached to a concentrator.

Dual-Tone Multifrequency (DTMF)
A telephone technology used to create 16 separate tones from 8 frequencies. The 16 tones are used to provide a unique tone for each of the 12 base buttons on a Touch Tone telephone, plus 4 additional keys.

dumb terminal
A monitor and keyboard with limited capabilities, used mainly for displaying and editing data.

duplexing
A method of duplicating data to protect it. Disk duplexing involves copying one set of data onto two hard disks on two separate disk channels. Duplexing is preferable to mirroring, which copies data onto two hard disks on the same disk channel.

duty cycle
The proportion of a time period in an electrical signal when the signal is on and represented by a bit value of one.

dynamic

A term describing processes that change over time.

dynamic address resolution

The process of using an address resolution protocol to determine and store address information on demand.

dynamic addressing

An AppleTalk networking strategy under which network nodes automatically select unique addresses. Under this scheme, a node will continue to try new addresses until it finds one that is not in use.

dynamic configuration

A way to allocate resources according to current needs and resource availability. NetWare servers dynamically configure the following parameters: directory cache buffers, file locks, kernel processes, kernel semaphores, maximum number of open files, memory for NetWare Loadable Module (NLM) programs, router/server advertising, routing buffers, service processes, Transaction Tracking Service (TTS) transactions, and turbo FAT index tables.

Dynamic Data Exchange (DDE)

A technique used for application-to-application communications, available on the Microsoft Windows, Macintosh System 7, and OS/2 operating systems. Two DDE-compliant applications can exchange data and commands by DDE conversations or two-way connections that take place between the applications. A DDE conversation does not require any user intervention. DDE has been superseded by Object Linking and Embedding (OLE).

Dynamic Host Configuration Protocol (DHCP)

A protocol that dynamically assigns Internet Protocol (IP) addresses to Windows-based personal computers in a local area network (LAN). DHCP enables the administrator to assign a set of IP addresses. Then each client requests an IP address from the DHCP server, uses it only as long as necessary, and returns it to the address pool.

Dynamic Link Library (DLL)

A program library that holds related modules of compiled executable functions that can be called by other programs. The DLL model enables the developer to insert a pointer to the DLL, as opposed to inserting the full program code into an application. An application reads the functions in the DLL at runtime and several applications can use the same DLL. DLLs are used in Microsoft Windows and IBM's OS/2 operating systems.

dynamic link routine

A program that can be loaded on demand and terminated automatically. The dynamic link routine is a function of the OS/2 and Microsoft Windows 3.*x* operating systems.

dynamic memory

Memory used for random access memory (RAM) that continuously rewrites all stored information. All data is lost from dynamic memory when the system shuts down.

Dynamic Random

Access Memory (DRAM)

A type of chip memory that stores information in capacitors. The chip's charge must be renewed periodically. DRAM is slower, but less expensive, than static RAM (SRAM), and more widely used by personal computer manufacturers.

dynamic routing

The automatic rerouting of data transmissions to maximize throughput or to balance traffic. The automatic routing decisions are based on available data about current network traffic.

DynaText

A electronic document viewer provided in NetWare and IntranetWare that provides a Graphical User Interface (GUI) for reading online manuals on workstations throughout the network.

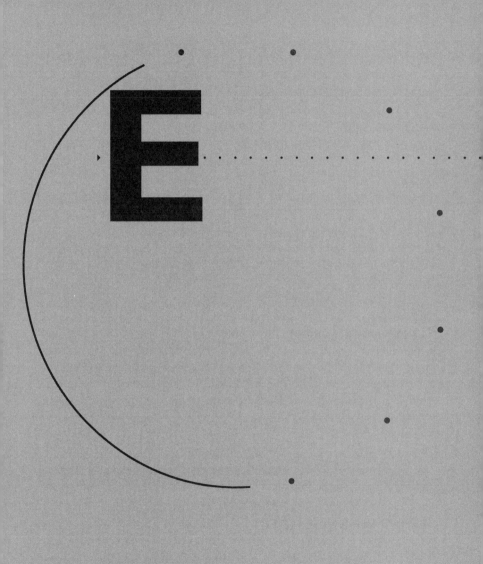

E
See exa-.

E channel
A 64 kilobits per second (Kbps) circuit-switching control channel in an Integrated Services Digital Network (ISDN).

E&M signaling
A standard signaling method often used in interoffice and toll trunk lines.

E.164
A Consultative Committee for International Telegraphy and Telephony (CCITT) recommendation for an evolution of telephone numbers in international telecommunications numbering. This specification especially affects Integrated Services Digital Network (ISDN), Broadcast Integrated Services Digital Network (BISDN), and Switched Multimegabit Data Service (SMDS) networks.

E1 carrier
A transport channel used to carry 30 voice channels, each one running at 64 kilobits per second (Kbps), for a total of 2,048 megabits per second (Mbps). It also holds two additional 64Kbps channels for signaling. E1 links can be multiplexed into single larger links. The E1 configuration is commonly used in Europe, Mexico, and South America, and is similar to the T carrier channels used in North America.

E3
A transmission rate (34 megabits per second) that is the highest rate generally available in the European digital infrastructure.

Early Token Release (ETR)
A control process used in Token Ring networks that allows multiple packets to travel in the ring at the same time. A standard Token Ring network only allows the single node that holds the token to transmit, so only one packet is traveling in the ring at any given time; the token can be passed only after the packet has been received. Under ETR, the token is released immediately after the sending node releases the packet into the ring.

e-cash (electronic cash)

An electronic payment system that offers many of the same benefits of traditional cash transactions.

echo

A type of distortion that occurs when a transmission is reflected back to the sender. An echo may occur if there is an electrical mismatch between the sender and recipient. Echo can also refer to a mechanism used to test network nodes, where each receiving station on the network sends a message back to the host.

echo cancellation

A mechanism used to control echoes on communications links. With echo cancellation, a modem checks for a delayed duplication of the original signal, and then adds a reversed version of the transmission to the channel on which the information was received. This removes the echo without adversely affecting the original transmission.

Echo/Echo Reply

A network management mechanism that determines whether network nodes are capable of receiving transmissions or whether the network connection is functioning properly. An echo signal is issued and the sender waits for an echo reply, which indicates the receiving node is operational.

echoplex

A verification mode in which keyboard codes are echoed back to a terminal screen when the appropriate signal is returned from the other end of the line to indicate the characters were received correctly.

edu (educational)

A suffix for an Internet address that indicates the host computer is run by an educational institution (probably a college or university) and the host computer probably is in the United States.

effective bandwidth

The portion of a communications channel's signal that is strongest.

Effective Isotropic Radiated Power (EIRP)

The relative strength of a signal received at the Earth station portion of a satellite communications system. This value is measured in decibels.

effective rights

The rights a Novell Directory Services (NDS) or bindery object can exercise to view or modify a given directory, file, or object. Every time an object attempts a task relating to a directory, file, or other object, the NetWare operating system calculates the seeking object's effective rights. If an object has no explicitly stated effective rights, at least it has the rights granted to [Public] or to the group EVERYONE.

effective throughput

The practical number of data bits that can be sent over a given period of time.

EGP peer

An Exterior Gateway Protocol (EGP) peer. When an EGP peer uses an Interior Gateway Protocol (IGP) distance vector algorithm to disseminate information about routing, continuous changes may make the algorithm unstable.

elbow connector

A connector with a right angle used to connect wires in a corner.

electrical signal

An electrical current sent as a waveform. Communications can take place over an electrical signal by superimposing a modulating signal over a fixed carrier signal. Information can be represented by changing or modulating the superimposed signal in different ways relative to the fixed signal.

electromagnetic interference (EMI)

A type of interference that may emanate from motors or other power supplies in close proximity to a computer. Electromagnetic interference may cause computer errors.

Electronic Cookbook (ECB)

An operating mode used in the Data Encryption Standard (DES).

electronic data interchange (EDI)

A way to exchange electronically standardized business documents, such as bills of material, purchase orders, or invoices. An EDI network can be established using OSI standards or through one of several commercially available proprietary products. EDI may also take place over the Internet, although more security-conscious users often prefer to use a private, value-added network.

Electronic Frontier Foundation (EFF)

A public policy organization whose goals include preserving the public availability of electronic networks (such as the Internet).

Electronic Industries Association (EIA)

A standards organization that establishes standards for cabling.

Electronic Key Telephone System (EKTS)

A key telephone system using electrical switches.

electronic mail (e-mail)

A method used to send files and messages between workstations. One user can send a message to another user or group of users on the same system. E-mail systems can be implemented on a peer-to-peer network, client-server architecture, mainframe computer, dial-up service, or through the Internet.

Electronic Mail Association (EMA)

A trade group consisting of developers and vendors of electronic mail (e-mail) products.

Electronic Mailbox

A directory in an electronic mail (e-mail) software system used to store a user's messages.

Electronic Switched Network (ESN)

A telecommunications service used by private networks that establishes an automatic switching mechanism between Private Branch Exchanges (PBXs), so one PBX can call any other PBX in the network without a dedicated connection.

electronic switching

Making circuit connections electronically, as opposed to electromechanically.

Electro-Static Discharge (ESD)

Charges generated by static electricity. Electro-static discharge of as low as 30 volts may harm a computer component.

elevator seeking

A way to organize how data is read from a hard disk storage device by logically organizing disk operations as they arrive at the server for processing. This mechanism can improve disk channel performance by minimizing back-and-forth movements of the physical disk head. Elevator seeking accomplishes this efficiency by queuing disk-read and disk-write requests for a given drive. The operating system then prioritizes the requests on the basis of the drive's head position, and fulfills them according to the current position of the drive head.

elm

An electronic mail (e-mail) reader for systems operating in the UNIX environment.

embedded SCSI

A hard disk with a Small Computer System Interface (SCSI) and hard disk controller both built into the unit.

Emitter-Coupled Logic (ECL)
A logical scheme for high-speed digital circuitry.

emoticon
A group of symbols often used within electronic mail (e-mail) messages. Emoticons often convey an emotion, such as irony, joy, displeasure, or anger. Many emoticons must be viewed sideways to understand their meaning. For example, one of the most common emoticons, which indicates happiness, is written as : -).

emulation
Making one device or software program appear as though it were another device or software program.

emulation mode
A network control program function that enables the program to perform activities equivalent to those performed by a transmission control unit.

enable
To prepare a software program or hardware device for a task. An enabled menu command is typically shown in black type.

Encapsulated PostScript (EPS)
The file format used by the PostScript page description language, which is service-independent (so images can be transferred between different applications). Images can also be sized and output to different printers. An EPS file contains PostScript commands and an optional preview image stored in PICT or TIFF format. An EPS file can be printed only to a PostScript compatible printer.

encapsulation
A technique whereby one protocol is enveloped within a second protocol for transmission.

encapsulation bridging

A bridge that carries Ethernet frames from one router to another across different media (such as serial lines and Fiber Distributed Data Interface lines).

encode

Representing characters or values in an alternative format.

encoding (signal)

A set of rules used to represent characters or values in an alternative format. A common type of signal encoding represents different voltage levels as either a zero or a one. This simple mechanism forms the basis of binary transmissions. Numerous types of encoding schemes exist, including Alternate Mark Inversion (AMI), Bipolar with 8 Zero Substitution (B8ZS), Differential Manchester, Manchester, NonReturn to Zero (NRZ), and Return to Zero (RZ).

encryption

A process used to transform text into an unreadable form (known as *ciphertext*) that can then be decoded using a conversion algorithm and predefined bit value (known as a *key*). The simplest type of encryption simply uses a single key, and the recipient must know both the encryption algorithm and the key to decrypt the message. *Private-key encryption* uses a private key, which only the sender and recipient know, and a public encryption algorithm. *Public-key encryption*, on the other hand, uses two halves of a bit sequence, each one constituting a key. One key is placed in an accessible public-key library. The other key is only known to an individual.

end bracket

Part of a circuit board with slots used to plug in other boards.

End Delimiter (ED)

A field in a Token Ring token or data frame used to indicate the end of the token or frame.

End Frame Sequence (EFS)

The last field in a Token Ring packet.

end node

The computer or other hardware unit that exists at the origin and destination of network traffic. The end node does not relay traffic to other nodes.

End of Content (EOC)

A character used to indicate the end of a message or a page.

E

End Office (EO)

A Central Office in a telecommunications network where subscribers' lines terminate and are connected with other exchanges.

end system (ES)

Under the OSI Reference Model, the computer containing application processes that can communicate through all seven layers of the OSI model.
Synonym: *end node*

End System to Intermediate System (ES-IS)

The connection between an end system or user station, and an intermediate system or the routing element in an internetwork.

end-of-file (EOF)

A code placed after the last byte in a file. The EOF code indicates no more data follows after that point.

end-of-text (ETX)

A character used to indicate the end of a text file.

end-of-transmission (EOT)

A character used to indicate the end of a transmission.

End-to-End Routing

A routing strategy that predetermines a message's full route before the message is sent.

end user
Individuals who use an application on their own workstations.

Energy Services Network (ESnet)
An internetwork that spans across multiple nations of the world.

engine
The core of a database or other application.

Enhanced Erasable Programmable Read-Only Memory (EEPROM)
A type of read-only memory (ROM) that allows old data to be erased by writing over it.

Enhanced Expanded Memory Specification (EEMS)
A revised version of the Expanded Memory Specification (EMS) that allows DOS applications to use more than 640K of memory.

Enhanced Graphics Adapter (EGA)
An IBM video display standard that requires a digital RGB Enhanced Color Display and provides medium-level resolution for both text and graphics. The EGA standard has been superseded by video graphics array (VGA).

Enhanced Parallel Port (EPP)
A parallel port with a signal rate of up to 16 megabits per second (Mbps).

Enhanced Small Device Interface (ESDI)
A standard used to interface a bus controller with a hard drive. ESDI has, in most cases, been replaced by Small Computer System Interface (SCSI).

enterprise
An entire business group or organization, including remote offices.

Enterprise CNE (ECNE)

An individual with the CNE designation who has also been certified by Novell to support enterprise-wide networks. This certification has been superseded by the Master CNE.

enterprise computing

A method of connecting all a company's computing resources, including those in remote locations. The enterprise network may encompass several different computing platforms and operating systems.

Enterprise Information Base (EIB)

A database used in an enterprise network to hold management and performance information about the network. Data held in the EIB is often accessed by network management software.

Enterprise Management Architecture (EMA)

Digital Equipment Corporation's network management model designed to manage multivendor enterprise networks and to comply with the International Standards Organization (ISO) Common Management Information Protocol (CMIP) standard. EMA is implemented in Digital's DEC Management Control Center (DECmcc) product.

enterprise network

An internetwork that connects multiple sites and runs mission-critical applications.

Enterprise Network Services (ENS)

Banyan Systems' software product (based on its StreetTalk Directory Service) that supports Internetwork Packet Exchange/Sequenced Packet Exchange (IPX/SPX) and includes the StreetTalk Directory Assistance, Banyan Security Service, and Banyan Network Management applications. ENS can be used by StreetTalk users to track servers running operating systems other than VINES.

Enterprise System Connection Architecture (ESCON)
A fiber-optic communications channel, developed by IBM, which connects mainframes and peripheral devices and uses muiltimode fiber with a Light Emitting Diode (LED) as a light source.

entity
An abstract device (such as a program or a function) that implements services or functions used by other entities at higher layers and requests services or functions from other entities at lower layers.

entrance facilities
The spot where a building's wiring meets the external wiring.

entry box
A box in a DOS menu utility or Windows application into which text is entered.

Entry-Level System (ELS) NetWare
An early version of NetWare meant for smaller networks. ELS NetWare was discontinued in 1991 and has been superseded by Personal NetWare.

entry point
The point where a network node is connected to a network. When applied to software, entry point refers to the point where a program starts to execute.

entry state
A value in a routing table in an AppleTalk network. The entry state shows the status of a path.

envelope
Information added to a data packet to ensure it reaches its destination and arrives without error. The envelope is usually added in the form of a data packet header.

envelope delay distortion
The amount of delay between different frequencies in an electrical signal.

environment

Generically, this term refers to all the hardware and software resources available to a user. It can also refer to the specific operating system needed to execute a program.

environment variable

A variable used to define the current operating system environment. The name of the environment variable is case-sensitive.

environmental security

A method of protecting the entire data processing environment. Environmental security involves protecting against both accidental or deliberate harm that may threaten data in any way.

EOM (End of Message) bit

A bit in an AppleTalk Data Stream Protocol (ADSP) header that indicates the previous packet was the last one in a single message.

equalization

Balancing a circuit by reducing frequency and phase distortion.

Erase right

A NetWare and IntranetWare directory and file right that grants a user the right to delete a directory, subdirectory, or file. A user with the Erase right, however, cannot erase a file if the Delete Inhibit attribute is enabled.

Erlang

A metric that shows the current usage of a communications channel relative to its total capacity. One Erlang is equal to 36 CCS (hundreds of call seconds).

error

The difference between what is expected and what actually occurs. Computer operating systems report unexpected or illegal events by issuing error codes. In telecommunications, an error may be caused by noise or distortion.

error control

A method of ensuring that data transmissions from a source are received at the destination without any errors.

Error Correction Code (ECC)

A type of code used to detect or correct communications transmission errors.

error detection and correction

The process of determining whether a bit (or bits) has changed during a transmission and of correcting those errors. Numerous methods exist for both detection and correction. The cyclical redundancy check (CRC) is a common error-detection method, based on a factor of the original bit pattern. The sender computes a CRC value and adds it to the data packet; the recipient then computes a CRC value on the basis of the received data packet. If the two CRC values are equal, no error occurred in transmission.

Error-Free Second (EFS)

A second of transmission that contains no errors. The number of EFSs that occur over a given period of time may be used as an indicator of transmission quality.

error handling

The method used by a program to handle errors that occur when the program runs. Error handling accommodates unexpected events or incorrectly entered data, often by issuing a dialog box to request the user take appropriate action.

error log exit

A NetWare Advanced Program-to-Program Communications (APPC) DOS extension, used to log errors during a conversation.

error message

A message issued by the operating system to indicate the existence of an error.

error rate

The ratio between the number of incorrectly received bits and the total number of bits in a transmission.

Error-Correcting Protocol

One of many communications protocols used to detect and correct transmission errors.

escape sequence

A sequence of characters that begins with the Escape character and is followed by one or more additional characters. This sequence is meant to perform a specific task and is often used to control monitors or printers.

ESCON (Enterprise System Connection Architecture) connector

A fiber-optic connector used with multimode fiber in a channel that complies with IBM Enterprise System Connection Architecture (ESCON).

Establishment Controller

An IBM device used to support multiple devices for the purpose of communicating with a mainframe host computer.

Ethernet

A type of shared-media local area network (LAN), originally developed in 1974 by Bob Metcalfe, founder of 3Com. Ethernet uses a bus or star topology and is a packet-switching, contention-oriented network. Ethernet is based on the Carrier Sense Multiple Access/Collision Detection (CSMA/CD) media-access method. (CSMA/CD detects packet collisions and causes the transmitting nodes to retransmit automatically after a random period of time.)

The Institute of Electronic and Electrical Engineers (IEEE) Ethernet standard, 802.3, has since been significantly extended to include Fast Ethernet, Gigabit Ethernet, and IsoEthernet. The still common 10Base-T Ethernet standard was introduced in 1990, and allows Ethernet to operate over a standard twisted-pair telephone wire. This standard operates with a throughput of 10 megabits per second (Mbps). Xerox introduced the first Ethernet LAN in 1981; 3Com introduced the first Ethernet adapter card the following year.

Table E.1 compares features of major types of Ethernet.

ETHERNET TYPE	CONNECTORS	TOPOLOGY	CABLE TYPE
TABLE E.1 *Ethernet Features Comparison*			
Twisted-pair Ethernet (1Base5, 10BaseT)	RJ-45	Star	Unshielded twisted-pair (UTP)
Thick Ethernet (10Base 5)	N-Series barrel, elbow	Bus	Thick (3/8 inch) 50-ohm coaxial
Thin Ethernet (10Base2)	BNC (T-connector, barrel, elbow)	Bus	Thin (3/16 inch) 50-ohm coaxial
Fiber-Optic Ethernet (10BaseF, 10BaseFB, 10BaseFP, 10BaseFL)	F, FC	Star	Fiber-optic
Broadband Ethernet (10Broad36)	F	Star	75-ohm (CATV) coaxial
Fast Ethernet (100BaseVG, 100BaseT, 100Base T4, 100BaseTX, 100BaseFX)	RJ-45	Star	UTP

Ethernet Configuration Test Protocol (ECTP)
A protocol used to determine whether a network conforms to the Blue Book Ethernet standard.

Ethernet meltdown
When traffic on an Ethernet network reaches its maximum capacity.

Ethernet packet

A variable-length packet transmitted over an Ethernet network. The packet includes a synchronization preamble, destination address, source address, type code indicator, data field, and cyclical redundancy check (CRC).

EtherTalk

An AppleTalk-based Ethernet network that may be nonextended (EtherTalk 1.0, also known as Blue Book Ethernet) or extended (EtherTalk 2.0). EtherTalk works with the AppleShare network operating system and runs over coaxial cable at 10 megabits per second (Mbps).

E

EtherTalk Link Access Protocol (ELAP)

An AppleTalk link-access protocol used for EtherTalk that exists at the Data-Link Layer (Layer 2) of the OSI Reference Model.

EUnet

A UNIX-based network, located in Europe, designed to provide interconnection and electronic mail (e-mail) services. This network began as an extension of Usenet.

Euronet

A networking scheme originally proposed by countries belonging to the European Common Market.

European Academic and Research Network (EARN)

A European network used to provide file transfer and electronic mail (e-mail) services to universities and research institutions.

European Computer Manufacturers Association (ECMA)

A trade organization that provides standards organizations with technical committees.

European Electronic Mail Association (EEMA)

A European trade group made up of developers and vendors of electronic mail (e-mail) products.

European Telecommunications Standards Institute (ETSI)

A European standards organization that recommends telecommunications standards.

European Workshop for Open Systems (EWOS)

A regional workshop for implementers of the OSI Reference Model.

even parity

A parity setting where, if the sum of all the bits set to one is even, the parity bit is set to zero; if the sum of all the bits set to one is odd, the parity bit is set to one.

event

Either a response to the occurrence of a significant task on the network (such as the completion of a request for information) or a message that indicates operational irregularities in physical elements of a network.

Event Control Block (ECB)

An entity used to control events relating to the transmission and reception of Internetwork Packet Exchange/Sequenced Packet Exchange (IPX/SPX) packets and sessions.

event reporting

A network management function. Event reporting uses software agents to gather information on all objects being managed by that agent. The agent then generates a report and issues it to the network-management package.

exa-

A prefix used to indicate one quintillion, or 10^{18}. When applied to computing, it refers to the power of two closest to one quintillion.

exabyte (EB)

A unit of measure equaling one quadrillion bytes.

exactly-once transaction
An AppleTalk Transaction Protocol (ATP) transaction method that guarantees a request is only implemented one time.

excess burst size (Be)
The highest number of uncommitted data bits a network can attempt to send over a given period of time.

exchange
An area serviced by a central telecommunications office. An exchange services a sequential block of telephone numbers.

exchange carrier
A company that provides telecommunications services within a given exchange.

executable
A program that can be operated by the computer. An executable program in DOS usually has the filename extension .EXE or .COM.

executable code
A series of instructions contained in a program that can be operated by the computer.

Execute Only (X) attribute
A NetWare file attribute that prevents a file from being copied. This attribute cannot be removed; instead, the file must be copied over with an identical file that does not have the Execute Only attribute set.

expandability
The ability of a system to encompass additional hardware or software (such as more memory, larger disk drives, or new adapters).

expanded memory
A way of allowing a program to access up to 32MB of memory outside conventional memory. Early personal computers were restricted to 1MB (640K

for applications and 384K for system use). Expanded memory allows these personal computers to go beyond that level by swapping address blocks in which data can be swapped in and out as needed.

Expanded Memory Manager (EMM)
A device driver used to support the software portion of the Expanded Memory Specification. This driver creates a block of addresses, used to swap data into and out of as needed.

Expanded Memory Specification (EMS)
The standard method of accessing expanded memory. This specification allows programs running on Intel 8086 processors to access up to 32MB of expanded memory.

expansion
Increasing a microcomputer's capabilities by adding hardware that can perform a certain task that could not otherwise be done with the basic system.

expansion bus
A common pathway between hardware devices. A bus is used to connect a CPU to its main memory and to the memory residing in its peripheral devices' control units. It can, therefore, transfer data from the motherboard to plug-in peripherals. The expansion bus can be used to expand the basic personal computer system by use of adapter cards. Several different types of expansion buses exist, including Industry Standard Architecture (ISA), Extended Industry Standard Architecture (EISA), Micro Channel Architecture (MCA), Peripheral Component Interconnect (PCI), Video Electronics Standards Association (VESA), and Personal Computer Memory Card International Association (PCMCIA).

expansion chassis
A hardware structure that includes a power supply and a backplane.

expansion slot
A connector on the expansion bus that allows an adapter to gain access to the system bus.

expansion unit
An external housing unit that adds additional expansion slots to a portable computer.

expedited delivery
An option set by a given protocol layer to tell another protocol layer to handle specific data more rapidly.

Expedited Transport Service Data Unit (ETSDU)
An Attention message in an AppleTalk Data Stream Protocol (ADSP) network. The message enables two transport clients to send a signal to each other outside the regular flow of data.

expert parameter
The parameters used to provide precise control over Packet layer and Frame layer operations. Expert parameters can be used to configure the advanced settings of a specific wide area network (WAN) call destination or to configure Permanent Virtual Circuits (PVCs).

Explicit Congestion Notification (ECN)
A frame relay mechanism used to indicate when the network is congested. This mechanism uses two bit values to indicate the congested condition. *The Backward Explicit Congestion Notification (BECN)* bit value is included in Frame Relay headers traveling in the direction opposite the congestion, in an attempt to inform source nodes that a congested condition is occurring downline. *The Forward Explicit Congestion Notification (FECN)* bit value is included in Frame Relay headers traveling toward the congestion, in an attempt to inform destination nodes that a congested condition is occurring ahead.

explicit route
A route from a Systems Network Architecture (SNA) source subarea to a destination subarea, as specified by a list of subarea nodes and transmission groups that connect the two.

explicit trustee assignments

The Novell Directory Services (NDS) object rights granted exclusively to an object in the Directory tree. An explicit trustee assignment overrides any trustee assignments made higher up in the Directory tree.

explorer frame

A method used in Token Ring networks to determine the best route between a source and destination.

extant number

A sequential set of numbers referring to one page of the extended directory space.

extended addressing

An AppleTalk Phase 2 mechanism that assigns 8-bit node numbers and 16-bit network numbers to each workstation.

Extended AppleTalk network

An AppleTalk network that supports the AppleTalk Phase 2 extensions, including zone lists and network ranges.

Extended Binary-Coded Decimal Interchange Code (EBCDIC)

A character set that has 256 characters, with each character represented by an 8-bit pattern. The character set, defined by IBM, includes values for control functions and graphics. It is commonly used on IBM mainframes and minicomputers and differs from American Standard Code for Information Interchange (ASCII) in that placement of the letters of the alphabet is discontinuous. No direct match can be achieved when converting between ASCII and EBCDIC because each character set contains some unique characters.

Extended Data Out (EDO)

Dynamic random access memory (DRAM) that improves memory speed and performance by altering the timing and sequence of signals that activate the circuitry for accessing memory locations.

Extended Industry Standard Architecture (EISA)

A 32-bit bus standard compatible with Industry Standard Architecture (ISA). Developed to enable input/output (I/O) to keep pace with faster processors, EISA also enables multiple processors to share the same bus.

extended memory

The memory above 1MB on 80286, 80386, and 80486 personal computers. Some applications require extended memory to operate on those platforms.

extended memory manager

A software utility required for a personal computer to make use of extended memory.

Extended Memory Specification (XMS)

The standard used to enable personal computers to access extended memory. DOS and Windows include an extended memory device driver called HIMEM.SYS, which is used to gain access to extended memory.

extended network

An AppleTalk Phase 2 network on high-speed media that can support the Phase 2 addressing extensions of the network range and zones list.

Extended Superframe Format Framing (ESF)

A method used to frame a DS-1 channel that groups 24 frames into a single superframe, such that one DS-1 channel holds one superframe.

extensible MIB

A Management Information Base (MIB) in a Simple Network Management Protocol (SNMP) environment that can be defined by individual vendors to allow new variables.

extension mapping

A type of mapping used to attach Macintosh application information to a non-Macintosh file. Extension mapping enables a Macintosh user to access a non-Macintosh file and to open the specified application automatically.

Exterior Gateway Protocol (EGP)

A protocol used by gateways in an internetwork to exchange network reachability information between autonomous systems. EGP is used in the Internet core system and is part of the Transmission Control Protocol/Internet Protocol (TCP/IP) suite.

Synonym: *Exterior Routing Protocol (ERP)*

exterior router

An AppleTalk network router that routes packets to a non-AppleTalk protocol, from which packets may be transmitted by tunneling.

external command

A command not automatically loaded into memory because it is used less frequently than other commands.

External Data Representation (XDR)

A machine-independent syntax developed by Sun Microsystems as part of their Network File System (NFS) and used to describe data structures.

External Entity object

A leaf object representing a nonnative Novell Directory Services (NDS) object that has been imported into NDS or registered into NDS. NetWare Message Handling Service (MHS) uses External Entity objects to represent users from non-NDS environments and, thereby, creates a fully integrated address book.

extremely low-frequency emission (ELF)

Radiation emitted by a computer monitor or other electronic appliance. An ELF emission ranges from between 5 Hertz (Hz) and 2,000Hz, and the frequency of the emission declines as a function of the square of the distance from its source.

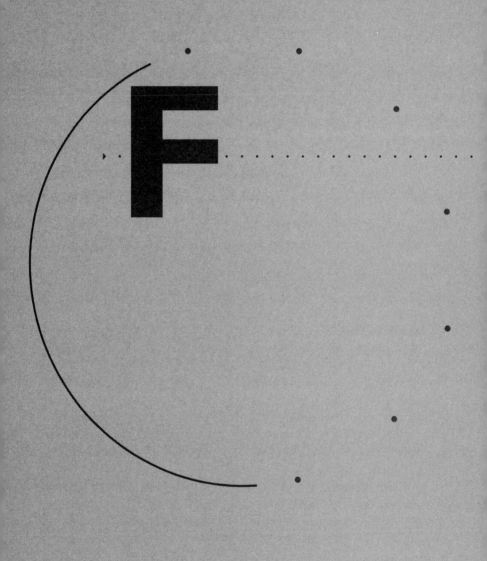

F connector
A connector used in broadband Ethernet networks and broadband token-bus networks.

facility
A transmission link between two stations in a telephone communications system. In an X.25 network, a facility is a packet field through which users request network services.

facility bypass
A telecommunications method of bypassing the telephone company's central office.

Facility Data Link (FDL)
Part of an Extended Superframe Format (ESF) that is a 4-kilobits-per-second (Kbps) communications link between a sender's station and the telephone company's monitors. The 4Kbps band is made by taking half the ESF's framing bits and using them to establish the link.

facsimile (fax)
An electronic reproduction of a document sent over a telephone line through a specialized hardware device or computer add-in board.

fading
The decrease of a wireless or electrical signal that may occur because of an obstruction blocking the transmitter or receiver's antenna, interference from other signals, or increased distance from the source of transmission.

fail-soft system
A system designed to cause the least amount of damage possible in the event of failure. A fail-soft system shuts down all nonessential functions and operates at a reduced capacity until the problem has been resolved.

fake root
A subdirectory that functions as a root directory. Under NetWare, the network administrator can map a drive to a fake root. This capability enables

the administrator to install an application in a subdirectory, even if it requires installation at the root, which is sometimes desirable for security reasons. The fake root function is also useful for applications that cannot be executed from a subdirectory.

fall time
The amount of time required for an electrical signal to move from 90 percent to 10 percent. This value is used to establish a maximum transmission speed.

fan switching
A process of using a route cache to expedite packet switching through a router.

fanout
A communications configuration in which more output lines exist than input lines.

Far End Block Error (FEBE)
An error reported to the sender by the receiver in a Broadcast Integrated Service Digital Network (BISDN) network. The error is determined by computing a checksum at the receiving end and comparing it with a checksum generated by the sender. If the two numbers do not match, an error is assumed and an FEBE is sent.

Far End Crosstalk (FEXT)
Interference in which a transmitted signal leaks from one wire into the transmitted signal of another.

Far End Receive Failure (FERF)
A signal sent upstream in a Broadcast Integrated Service Digital Network (BISDN) that indicates an error has occurred downstream.

Fast Ethernet
An extension of the Institute of Electronic and Electrical Engineers (IEEE) Ethernet standard that operates at 100Mbps. Fast Ethernet is structurally

similar to 10Mbps Ethernet, but achieves its tenfold increase by dividing the bit-timing (or the amount of time a bit requires for transmission) by 10. It uses the same packet format, supports twisted-pair copper wire, and uses the same error-detection methods. However, maximum cable lengths are shorter than a 10BaseT implementation. A Fast Ethernet network can include both 10Mbps and 100Mbps connections.

Fast Link Pulse (FLP)

One of a series of identical startup signals sent by an Ethernet device capable of supporting a transmission rate of 100 megabits per second (Mbps). These signals are used in a Fast Ethernet network.

Fast Local Internet Protocol (FLIP)

An Internet Protocol (IP) developed as an alternative to Transmission Control Protocol (TCP) to offer better security and network management capabilities for internetworks made up of large-scale distributed systems.

Fast Packet Switching (FPS)

A switching strategy that realizes higher throughput by simplifying the switching process. FPS uses fixed-size packets and simplified addresses. In addition, error checking and acknowledgment is left to higher-level protocols. FPS is used in certain frame and cell-relay implementations, such as Asynchronous Transfer Mode (ATM).

fast select

A facility used to expand the Call and Clear User fields beyond a 16-octet limit to 128 octets. Fast select is often used in point-of-sale (POS) and other transaction-oriented applications.

fast-connect circuit switching

The use of fast electronic switching devices to establish a circuit between two stations.

FastPath

A high-speed gateway between AppleTalk and Ethernet networks.

fatal error

An unrecoverable error that prevents a given system or application task from being accomplished.

fault

A physical or logical abnormal condition in a communications link.

fault management

One of five of the basic System Management Function Areas (SMFAs) found in the OSI Network Management. Fault management detects, diagnoses, and corrects network faults. Network management software applications can perform fault detection, by either requiring nodes to report faults or by polling all nodes on the network periodically. Correction can sometimes be corrected automatically by the system, although some faults may require manual intervention.

fault point

A location at which a fault can occur.

fault tolerance

A data-protection scheme that ensures the continued operation of the network. Fault tolerance may encompass several preventative measures, including duplicating data on multiple storage devices to protect it against hazardous events. Other types of fault tolerance may include running dual cabling systems or writing data to separate channels.

fax board

An add-in adapter used to convert electronic documents into fax format and transmit them over a telephone line.

fax modem

An internal computer modem that includes internal fax capabilities. A fax modem accepts electronic text or graphics files and converts them into fax format for transmission. A fax modem fits into a personal computer expansion slot and provides most of the same features as a freestanding fax machine.

fax server

A server that provides the network with fax transmission and reception services.

FC connector

A connector used for fiber-optic cable. An FC connector has a threaded coupling nut and a ceramic ferrule for holding the fiber.

FCC certification

Approval granted by the Federal Communications Commission (FCC) that indicates a particular computer meets FCC standards for radio frequency interference (RFI) emissions. *Class A certification* applies to mainframes and minicomputers and other computers used in commercial settings; *Class B certification*, which is stricter, applies to personal computers and laptops used in the home and office.

FDDI II

A proposed standard from the American National Standards Institute (ANSI) to enhance the Fiber Distributed Data Interface (FDDI) by providing isochronous transmission for connectionless data circuits and for connection-oriented voice and video circuits.

FDDITalk

Apple Computer's implementation of the FDDI protocol that includes the protocols and drivers for use in an AppleTalk network.

FDDITalk Link Access Protocol (FLAP)

The AppleTalk Data-Link Layer (Layer 2 of the OSI Reference Model) protocol portion of FDDITalk.

Federal Communications Commission (FCC)

A federal agency that develops guidelines for the operation of communications and other electronic equipment. The FCC also allocates bandwidth for FM radio broadcasting and television, long-distance telecommunications, and short-haul transmissions.

Federal Information Exchange (FIX)
A connection between the public Internet and one of the federal government's internetworks.

Federal Networking Council (FNC)
A committee made up of representatives from multiple government agencies that have networks connected to the Internet.

feed
A circuit over which data is sent to a central station or along a network backbone.

feeder cable
A 25-pair cable used to carry voice and data signals.

ferrule
A component that keeps the optical core and cladding of a fiber-optic connection immobile. The ferrule is made of ceramic, plastic or stainless steel, and is glued to the cladding with epoxy.

Fetch
A Macintosh client program used for the File Transfer Protocol (FTP) that features a Graphical User Interface (GUI), drag-and-drop transfers, multiple simultaneous downloads, and compatibility with a variety of system resources, file types, and configurations.

fiber bandwidth
A metric measurement that reflects a fiber-optic cable's capacity to carry data. Fiber bandwidth is expressed in megahertz (MHz) or megabits per second (Mbps) per kilometer.

fiber bundle
A collection of fibers that are routed together in fiber-optic transmissions. The two types of fiber bundles are a *flexible bundle* (which are bundled at either end of a fiber-optic cable, but are free to move between the endpoints) and a *rigid bundle* (which are melted together to form a single rod bent into a specific shape during manufacturing).

Fiber Channel Standard (FCS)
The optical fiber specification in a Fiber Distributed Data Interface (FDDI) network architecture.

Fiber Distributed Data Interface (FDDI)
A high-speed local area network (LAN) standard specified by the American National Standards Institute (ANSI) X3T9.5 committee. FDDI uses fiber-optic cable, which transmits light generated from a laser or Light-Emitting Diode (LED) to realize a data speed of 100 megabits per second (Mbps). An FDDI network uses either multimode or single-mode fiber-optic cable and is built on a dual-ring topology.

Fiber Optic Inter-Repeater Link (FOIRL)
A device used to connect fiber-optic cable to an Attachment Unit Interface (AUI) in an Ethernet installation.

fiber optics
A communications technology that transmits data along a focused beam of light over a glass or plastic fiber. Fiber optics offers an advantage over copper media, in that it allows for greater distances and a higher bandwidth and is immune to electromagnetic interference (EMI).

fiber-optic cable
A transmission medium made of glass or plastic fiber strands, surrounded by a protected jacket. Fiber-optic cable facilitates a high-bandwidth transmission by modulating a focused light source through the fiber.

fiber-optic connector
A connector used to create a physical link between two segments of optical core. Each fiber is held in place by a ferrule and the end of the cut fiber is polished before the connection is made.

Fibre Channel
A fiber-optic channel standard that can also be used for networking. Its three primary uses are clustering, linking processors to storage arrays, and creating a local area network (LAN) backbone. The American National Standards Institute (ANSI) Fibre Channel standard supports several different

grades of fiber-optic cable and uses a 4B/8B signal encoding scheme. Bandwidth can range from 100 megabits per second (Mbps) to 1 gigabit per second (Gbps).

field
The smallest unit of data in a database file or networking packet.

file
A set of records stored on a disk.

File Access Data Unit (FADU)
Part of the Open Systems Interconnection (OSI) File Transfer, Access, and Management (FTAM) service. FADU is a packet that holds information about accessing a directory tree in a particular file system.

File Access Listener (FAL)
A program in Digital Equipment Company's DECnet environment that implements the Data Access Protocol (DAP) and is capable of accepting remote requests for local files issued from any process that can use the DAP.

File Allocation Table (FAT)
An index that includes a list of pointers to show the physical disk areas at which the pieces of a file are located. The FAT groups together files that may be held in multiple, noncontiguous blocks.

file attribute
A particular value associated with a file. The file attribute may indicate what types of actions are allowed to be performed on the file or who may access the file.

file caching
Using system random access memory (RAM) to improve file access time. File caching reserves a portion of RAM to hold frequently accessed files so they do not have to be continually accessed from the physical storage media. Whenever an application requests a file, the operating system first looks in the cache to see whether the file is there. If it is, the file is retrieved from cache instead of from the physical storage device.

file compression

A method used to store more data on the storage medium than would otherwise be possible. This method compresses files that are not used or those used infrequently.

file format

The structure of a file. Different programs and operating systems employ different file formats.

file fragmentation

A process used by the operating system to make use of all available disk space. Files become fragmented when they are stored in several noncontiguous places on a physical disk.

file handle

A number that refers to or identifies a file.

file indexing

The process of indexing File Allocation Table (FAT) entries to access large files faster. File indexing allows an application to go directly to a specific block of a file, instead of scanning through all consecutive blocks.

file locking

A process used to ensure a file is updated correctly before another application or process can access the file. Once a file has been locked, it cannot be accessed by any other connection.

filename

The name used by a file on a disk for reference purposes. Every file in a directory has a unique filename, although files in different directories can use the same name because they are specified along with the directory path.

file node

A 128-byte addressable network entry that includes information about a file. The entry is located in the server's Directory Entry Table (DET) and includes the filename, attributes, file size, creation date and time, and other management data.

file recovery
The process of recovering deleted or damaged files.

file rights
Assigned rights that control a trustee's access to a file and the operations that can be performed on it.

file server
A central computer that runs the network operating system software and stores files that can be accessed by client computers on the same network.

File Server Environment Services
A set of function calls used to let applications set server parameters and view information about the servers. Applications can use these calls to enable or disable transaction tracking, set server time and date, or prohibit or enable users to log in.

File Service Process (FSP)
A file server process that executes file handling requests.

file sharing
A networking feature that enables multiple users to access the same file simultaneously.

file specification (filespec)
A denotation that includes the drive letter, path name, directory name, and filename.

file system
A method used by the network operating system to organize data on the hard disk. The file system gives each file a filename and stores it in a specific location within a file hierarchy for easy access. The file system uses a path or directory structure, which is used to organize files hierarchically.

file transfer

The process of copying a file from one location to another. To transfer a file over the network, the file is divided into packets. Depending on whether the file is being sent between two incompatible operating systems, the file may need to be reformatted or translated upon receipt.

File Transfer Protocol (FTP)

Part of the Transmission Control Protocol/Internet Protocol (TCP/IP) suite of protocols used to transmit information in packets between stations and to prevent errors in the transmission.

File Transfer Service (FTS)

An Application Layer (Layer 7 of the OSI Reference Model) service responsible for handling files and transferring files between locations. File transfer services may include Electronic Data Interchange (EDI), the Message Handling System (MHS), transaction processing, or virtual terminal applications.

File Transfer, Access, and Management (FTAM)

The Open Systems Interconnection (OSI) remote file service protocol used for transferring and accessing files on different types of computers that are also FTAM-compliant.

file-compression program

An application that compresses files so they take up a smaller amount of storage space.

file-conversion program

An application used to convert files from one format into another. A file-conversion program may convert files between the formats of two different applications or between the formats of two different operating systems.

filename extension

The extension that appears after the period in a filename. The extension typically indicates the type of file.

filtering
A task accomplished by a network router. With filtering active, the router discards certain types of packets or packets that originate from, or are destined for, specific locations.

filtering rate
The speed at which packets are checked and discarded by a router.

Finder
An Apple Macintosh application used to start up other programs, to manage documents and applications, and to manipulate files.

Finger
An Internet service used to gather information about a person associated with given user identification information.

firewall
A routing mechanism that prevents certain broadcast messages from passing into a particular network or subnetwork. A firewall is used to prevent outsiders from accessing an intranetwork.

firewire
The Institute of Electronic and Electrical Engineers (IEEE) 1394 standard, originally created by Apple Computer, that offers a high-speed method of connecting peripheral devices to a host computer. It is often used for video equipment.

firmware
Software instructions set permanently into an integrated circuit.

First In, First Out (FIFO)
A processing strategy under which the first element to be added to a queue ("first in") is the first one to be processed ("first out").

first-level file
A file opened at the operating system level with either the open, sopen, or create function.

First-Level Interrupt Handler (FLIH)
A network device that determines which device or channel is the source of an interrupt. After making that determination, the FLIH then invokes a second-level interrupt handler to process the request behind the interrupt.

fix
A piece of add-on code that resolves a bug or defect in a previous release of the software. Fixes are typically incorporated into future releases.

Fixed Priority-Oriented Demand Assignment (FPODA)
A network access protocol that requires stations to reserve slots on the network.

fixed routing
A routing mechanism under which packets are transmitted between source and destination over a fixed, permanent path.

flag
Assigned to a folder or file, a property or value that represents a given condition. A flag consists of a single bit and is usually set to "on" or "off," or "yes" or "no." Flags can be used to filter out packets or to determine access and use rules for a particular file or directory.
Synonym: *attribute*

flag byte
A bit sequence used to mark the start or end of a frame.

flag character
In an X.25 packet-switching network, a character added to the beginning and end of each Link Access Procedure Balanced (LAPB) protocol frame to indicate its boundaries.

flame

Slang for a rude, insulting, and emotionally charged electronic mail (e-mail) message.

flame war

An online discussion that has degenerated into a heated series of personal attacks against the participants.

flamebait

A comment or statement posted to a mailing list, newsgroup, or other online forum intended to elicit highly emotional postings from other participants.

flapping

A problem in routing that occurs when an advertised route between two nodes alternates (or flaps) back and forth between two paths. Flapping usually is caused by a network problem that causes intermittent interface failures.

Flash EPROM

Intel's Erasable Programmable Read-Only Memory (EPROM) technology incorporating a nonvolatile memory storage that can be electrically erased in the circuit and then reprogrammed.

flash memory

A type of nonvolatile random access memory (RAM) that retains its contents after the power for the computer has been shut off. Flash memory can be erased or reprogrammed and is often used to store configuration information.

flash update

An asynchronous routing update sent in response to a change in network topology.

flat name structure

A naming structure that gives each file a unique name. In a flat structure, no logical relationship exists between names; the names are accessible through a table lookup procedure.

flc
A sophisticated version of a fli animation file.

fli
An animation file in Autodesk Animator format that can be viewed on many Web browsers by adding the proper plug-in software. This name is an abbreviation for the slang word for a movie (*flick*).

Floating Point Unit (FPU)
A math coprocessor chip used for floating-point arithmetic.

floating-point coprocessor
A secondary processor that performs floating-point arithmetic faster than the main processor. Some processors integrate the floating point unit directly into the main processor instead of using a separate chip.

flooding
A process used by a link state router to build and maintain a logical map of the entire network by sending a packet with information about its links to all other link state routers on the network. Each link state router then combines its own information with the information gained from other routers.

floppy disk
An inexpensive, polyester-based, low-capacity removable memory disk. Floppy disks are often distinguished as 5 ¼ or 3 ½ disks, which refers to their size (in inches).

flow control
The process used to manage the rate at which data travels between network components. Flow control imposes an optimal transmission rate to minimize network congestion. It is used most often when the transmitting device is significantly faster than the receiving device.

flow-control negotiation
The process of negotiating the window size and maximum packet size of individual calls in each direction.

flux budget
The amount of light that can be lost between adjacent nodes in a Fiber Distributed Data Interface (FDDI) network without causing the transmission to degrade.

focal point
In IBM's Network Management Architecture (NMA), the node (usually a mainframe host) that runs the network management software.

foil shield
A thin aluminum shield that surrounds the dielectric in coaxial cable. The foil shield is surrounded by a braided shield, which is, in turn, surrounded by a plastic or rubber jacket.

folder
An operating system container that holds documents, applications, and other subfolders. A folder is the equivalent of a subdirectory and is used to organize information on the desktop.

followup
A public reply to a Usenet newsgroup posting that includes a link back to the original posting.

font
A set of characters of the same typeface, style, stroke weight, and size. A font should not be confused with a typeface, which refers to the actual design of the characters.

footprint
In satellite communications, the area of Earth covered by a radio signal transmitted from the satellite. In networking, footprint is the amount of random access memory (RAM) that an application uses during execution.

For Your Information (FYI)
A short document containing information about topics of importance to Internet users.

foreground process

A process currently operating and being controlled interactively by the user. A foreground process gets the highest priority from the computer's central processing unit (CPU).

forge

The act of intentionally misrepresenting an electronic mail (e-mail) message so it appears to have come from someone else.

fork

A file component in the Apple Macintosh File System (MFS). The two types of forks are a *data fork* (which holds data) and a *resource fork* (which contains application-specific information).

form (printer)

In NetWare, the name and size of the paper used for a print job.

form (screen)

A specification for the layout of data or menu options on a video screen.

form feed

A print job setting option that requests the printer to add an extra sheet of blank paper at the end of a print job.

format

An operating system process that prepares a data disk for use.

Format Identifier 4 (FID4)

A format used by a transmission header in Systems Network Architecture (SNA) that encapsulates a message between SNA subarea nodes capable of supporting virtual and explicit routes, as well as transmission groups.

formatter

A printer function that converts print data to dot patterns.

forms

World Wide Web (WWW) pages or sections of pages that collect text from a user and send data back to a host or server for processing.

forms-based

World Wide Web (WWW) screens or programs that use forms in a Hypertext Transfer Protocol (HTTP) language to solicit input from a user.

forward channel

A communications path that carries a transmission from a call initiator to a called party.

Forward Error Correction (FEC)

An error-correction mechanism that provides the transmission enough information to enable the recipient to locate and to correct any bit-level errors that occur during transmission.

Forward Explicit Congestion Notification (FECN)

A bit set by a Frame Relay network to indicate congestion is occurring in the packet-forwarding direction.

forward file

A file created to tell an electronic mail (e-mail) program to send any incoming messages to another e-mail address.

forwarding

The process of sending a data packet or message to another destination. Forwarding can take place in a network bridge, router, or gateway. The network device first reads the packet and checks the address and protocol in the packet header, and then forwards it to the destination on the basis of the information it finds.

Fourier transform

A technique that uses a time-series pattern to evaluate the importance of various frequency cycles.

four-wire circuit

A circuit comprised of two pairs of conducting wires and used for telephone communications. One pair is used for transmitting; the other is used for receiving.

fractional T1 (FT1)

A digital communications line derived from a larger 1.544 megabits per second (Mbps) T1 line. A fractional T1 can have a bandwidth of 384, 512, or 768 kilobits per second (Kbps). Up to twenty-four 64Kbps fractional T1 lines can be broken out of a full T1 line.

fragment

A piece of a packet broken down to smaller components for transmission.

fragmentation

The process of breaking a packet into smaller pieces to accommodate the transport requirements of the physical network medium. Fragmentation involves breaking up the data into individual parts, each of which is combined with a header for additional processing.

frame

A packet data format consisting of streams of bits. A frame includes start bits, data bits, an optional parity bit, and stop bits in addition to the payload.

Frame Check Sequence (FCS)

A value used to check for errors in a message transmitted over a network. The FCS calculates a value on the basis of the packet's contents and stores the value within the packet in a separate FCS field. The recipient recalculates the value and compares it against the value contained in the FCS field. If the two numbers match, the transmission is assumed to be error-free.

Frame Control (FC)

A field in a Token Ring data packet that presents a value used to indicate whether the frame is a Media Access Control (MAC) Layer (a sublayer of the Data Link Layer of the OSI Reference Model) management packet or whether it carries logical link control data.

Frame layer

An X.25 layer that transports data over a physical link and corrects link errors.

Synonym: *Link layer*

Frame Reject Response (FRMR)

A frame used to indicate an unacceptable frame has been received.

Frame Relay network

A type of wide area network (WAN) system that uses permanent circuits between end points. Through statistical multiplexing, transmission resources are allocated only when active communications take place over the circuit. Frame Relay implements fast packet switching and offers a high throughput, because Data Link Layer protocols can forego time-consuming error-checking algorithms and leave these to higher protocol layers. Frame Relay includes a cyclical redundancy check (CRC) algorithm to detect corrupted bits, but does not incorporate any mechanisms to correct bad data. Frame Relay is usually used for sending data only and is well-suited to bursty transmissions.

Frame Status (FS)

A field appearing in a Token Ring data packet.

frame switching

The process of transporting High-Level Data Link Control (HDLC) frames over a network.

framing

The process that inserts start and stop bits before and after data has been transmitted. Framing is used in asynchronous communications to delimit data.

Free Buffer Enquiry (FBE)

A field appearing in an Attached Resource Computer Network (ARCnet) frame.

free memory

The portion of computer memory not currently in use. Free memory is what remains after the operating system and device drivers have been loaded.

Free Software Foundation (FSF)
An organization that creates freely available software. The organization is well-known in the UNIX world for its GNU operating environment.

free space attenuation
The amount of signal loss that occurs between sender and recipient in a wireless connection.

freenet
Any of several free online systems. The first one was created at the University of Cleveland, which offers local community information and limited Internet access.

freeware
A software program that (although the author still retains rights or ownership) may be used without payment. Freeware differs from *shareware* (which usually includes a trial period, but requires some sort of payment to the author) and from *public-domain software* (for which the author relinquishes all rights).

frequency
A metric measurement indicating the number of times a cycle repeats within a given time period. Frequency is usually expressed in hertz (Hz).

frequency band
A range of frequencies in which a transmission takes place.

frequency converter
A device used to convert between frequency ranges in a broadband system.

frequency delay
A signaling delay that may occur when signals operating at different frequencies travel at different speeds through a medium. Frequency delay may cause signal distortion, but may be corrected with an equalizer.

Frequency Division Multiple Access (FDMA)
A method of dividing a large bandwidth into multiple channels.

Frequency Division-Multiplexing (FDM)
A type of multiplexing that divides a medium's bandwidth into separate frequency ranges. Each separate frequency is divided by a guard channel, which protects it from interference from the other frequencies.

frequency translator
An analog device used in a broadband cable system. The frequency translator is used to convert one block of frequencies to another.

frequency-agile modem
A type of modem used in broadband systems capable of switching frequencies to allow communications to take place over multiple channels at different times.

Frequently Asked Questions (FAQ)
A collection of commonly asked questions with answers on any given topic, typically found on the Internet.

frogging
The process of inverting signal frequencies in a broadband transmission. Frogging is used to equalize distortion.

front-end application
A network application, typically deployed on a client workstation, which works with a back-end application running on a server.

front-end network
A type of network consisting of specialized, high-performance workstations. A front-end network is usually connected with optical fiber.

Front-End Processor (FEP)
A component in a Systems Network Architecture (SNA) network that controls access to the host computer (usually a mainframe) and is typically

attached to the host by a direct channel. The FEP is used to offload certain tasks from the host.

FTP-by-mail
A process in which a user sends a message to a server to request a file be mailed to the user by way of electronic mail (e-mail). This process is used when only e-mail access to the Internet is available.

full backup
A copy of all files contained in a server. A full backup copies all files, directories, and management information to a separate backup media.

full duplex (FDX)
A process whereby two data streams flow in opposite directions simultaneously. In a full duplex system, the recipient node can send control data back to the sender; the sender continues to transmit data.

full-page display
A monitor capable of displaying a full page of text at one time without requiring the user to scroll up or down.

Fully Qualified Domain Name (FQDN)
The full name for a machine on the Internet. The FQDN includes the machine's name and the domain name.

function keys
Programmable keys on a keyboard that can be assigned to perform specialized tasks.

function management header
An optional field at the beginning of a request unit. The function management header carries logical unit (LU) control information.

Function Management layer

In IBM's Systems Network Architecture (SNA) model, the communications layer that formats presentations and communicates with the Data-Flow Control Layer. End users deal directly with the Function Management Layer.

fusing

A laser printer process that bonds toner to the paper by using a heated fusing roller and a pressure roller to melt the toner and then to press it onto the paper.

F

Fuzzball

An LSI-11 computer system from Digital Equipment Corporation (DEC) that runs Internet Protocol (IP) gateway software, which is used on the National Science Foundation Network (NSFnet) as backbone packet switches.

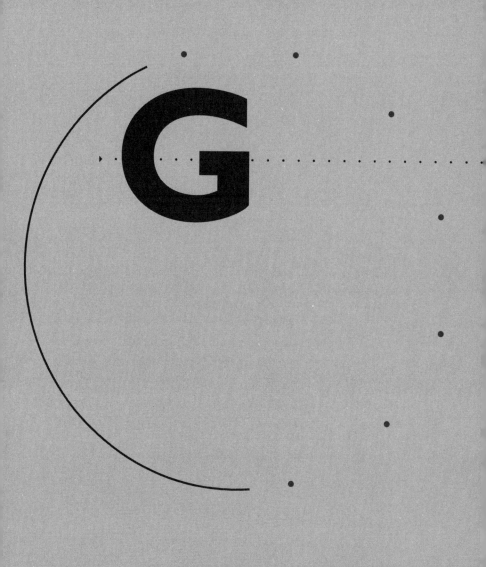

G

Abbreviation for giga, or one billion.

G.703

An electrical and mechanical specification from the Consultative Committee for International Telegraphy and Telephony (CCITT) that defines a connection between a telephone company and Data Terminal Equipment (DTE).

gain

An increase in an electrical signal's voltage as a result of amplification.

garbage collection

Deallocating memory blocks that are no longer in use.

Gatedaemon

A program that routes packets on the Internet and supports several routing protocols.

gateway

A link between two dissimilar networks that maps information between the two networks or subnetworks through a routing table. A gateway is usually a combination of hardware and software, and runs on the following layers of the OSI Reference Model: Application (Layer 7), Presentation (Layer 6), and Session (Layer 5). An *address gateway* connects networks with different directory spaces, a *protocol gateway* connects networks that use different protocols. A third type, the *format gateway*, connects networks that use different representation schemes—for example, American Standard Code for Information Interchange (ASCII) and Extended Binary-Coded Decimal Interchange Code (EBCDIC).

gateway host

In Systems Network Architecture (SNA), a host node that contains a *systems services control point (SSCP)* for a gateway.

gateway NCP

A network-control program (NCP) connecting two or more Systems Network Architecture (SNA) networks. A gateway NCP translates addresses for cross-network data transmissions.

gateway server

A type of server that provides users with network access to resources in remote environments.

Gateway-to-Gateway Protocol (GGP)

A protocol used in MILnet that uses a distributed shortest-path algorithm to specify how core routers exchange reachability and routing information.

gauge

A metric that indicates the diameter of electrical wire. Higher gauge numbers indicate thinner wire.

Gaussian noise

Noise in an electrical signal that results from the vibration of atoms and molecules. Gaussian noise increases with temperature and occurs on all frequencies.

gender changer

A connector used to connect two cables of the same gender (two male connectors or two female connectors).

General Data Stream (GDS)

A format used for mapped data in IBM's Advanced Program-to-Program Communications (APPC) architecture. High-level application data is converted to GDS format before transmission.

General Format Identifier (GFI)

A field in an X.25 packet that indicates the packet's format.

General Help Screen

An online help screen that provides general information about a specific task or function.

general service query

A query that requires a response from every qualified server. The query can specify all servers or servers of a given type. All qualified servers respond to the query with an identification packet.

General-Purpose Interface Bus (GPIB)

A parallel interface often used to connect scientific equipment to computers.

Generic Flow Control (GFC)

A protocol used in Asynchronous Transfer Mode (ATM) networking. GFC ensures all nodes are given access to the transmission medium.

geosynchronous orbit

The orbit of a satellite whose velocity matches the speed of Earth's rotation, causing the satellite's position to remain stationary relative to a specific point on Earth's surface.

gigabit (Gb)

A unit of measurement that usually measures transmission speeds in optical links. A gigabit equals about one billion bits or, more precisely, 2^{10} bits.

gigabyte (GB)

A unit of measurement that measures memory or physical storage. A gigabyte equals about one billion bytes or, more precisely, 2^{30} bytes.

glare

An error condition that occurs in a bidirectional telephone circuit when an incoming and an outgoing call connect because of a crossed connection.

global area network (GAN)

A type of network that spans multiple countries and supports international data formats.

global group
A function of Windows NT Advanced Server that is a group of users who have access to the servers and workstations in their own domain, as well as in other domains.

global kill file
A file that tells a newsreader which articles to skip, applying the same criteria to all newsgroups to which a user subscribes.

global login
A type of login that enables a user to log in to the network itself instead of individual servers. A global login provides access to all network resources.

global name
A name in a network known to all the network's nodes and servers.

global naming service
A network service that provides a way to name the resources attached to a file server. Banyan's StreetTalk service and Novell Directory Services (NDS) use global naming.

global network
An international network that encompasses all offices of a multinational company. Global networks must address unique problems, including working in multiple languages, standards, and currencies.

global tree
A network directory tree using Abstract Syntax Notation One (ASN.1) to represent network-management objects. The tree's main subtrees are administered by the Consultative Committee for International Telegraphy and Telephony (CCITT), International Standards Organization (ISO), and by a joint ISO-CCITT committee.

GNU

A collection of freeware programs from the Free Software Foundation, particularly programs that offer a functional equivalent to the programs and utilities found in UNIX operating systems.

gopher

A distributed Internet service that provides access to hierarchically organized information in a database, catalog, newsgroup, or other system. Gopher servers are accessible through TELNET or through a gopher client. A gopher client can access information on any gopher server through a single menu system.

Gopherspace

A term that encompasses all gopher menus on the Internet.

gov (government)

A suffix attached to the Internet addresses of sites maintained by parts of the government (most likely the federal government) as opposed to a company or educational institution.

Government OSI Profile (GOSIP)

The United States government's representation of the OSI Reference Model. Government contractors usually have to comply with GOSIP, which includes specifications for interoperation among systems and mutual access among users in different government agencies.

grace login

A login that can be performed during the period between notifying a user to change passwords and disabling the user's account if the password has not been changed.

Grade of Service (GoS)

A telephony metric that indicates performance levels, referring to the probability of a delay before a call can be connected.

graded index fiber
A fiber-optic cable that has several layers of cladding, each with a different refractive index. Graded-index fiber provides a cleaner signal than does single-step fiber.

graphical user interface (GUI)
An operating environment that uses graphics to identify its features and controls. GUIs, such as Microsoft Windows, Motif, and Macintosh, present commands and information through a series of icons the user clicks or manipulates. GUI-based applications use a consistent set of menus, dialog boxes, and other graphical components to execute within portions of the screen delineated as windows.

graphical utility
A utility used by network administrators to manage the network through a graphical operating environment, such as Windows or OS/2.

graphics accelerator board
An expansion board with a graphics coprocessor and other video circuitry. To improve system performance, the graphics accelerator board offloads most graphics-processing tasks from the main processor to the graphics coprocessor.

graphics coprocessor
A graphics chip designed to speed the processing of graphics and the display of high-resolution images.

Graphics Interchange Format (GIF)
A graphics format, originally designed for CompuServe Information Services, widely used on the Internet for standalone graphic documents and for graphic elements in Web pages. The GIF (pronounced *jiff*) format specifies a raster view of compressed images.

graphics mode
A video adapter mode that creates screen displays a pixel at a time, instead of a character at a time.

green box
A version of NetWare specific to a locale or created in a foreign language.

Greenwich Mean Time (GMT)
The time at the Greenwich observatory, used as a global standard reference time.
Synonym: *Universal Coordinated Time*

ground
A reference voltage used for other voltages in an electrical system. A ground establishes a common return path for an electrical current. All networks and network segments must be grounded.

ground start
A signaling mechanism used in telecommunications to establish a dial tone and to prevent collisions between incoming and outgoing calls, normally by grounding the circuit in a Private Branch Exchange (PBX).

ground station
Communications equipment that sends and receives signals to and from satellites.
Synonym: *downlink station*

ground wave
A low-frequency radio signal used in wireless communications. The ground wave travels over the surface of the Earth.

group
A set of network users who share applications, have similar needs, and can be managed collectively.

group (telecommunications)
A type of broadband communications channel that consists of twelve 4-kilohertz (KHz) voice channels, for a total of 48KHz. Each channel uses a different carrier frequency. All channels are transmitted simultaneously, using Frequency Division Multiplexing (FDM).

group address
A single address that refers to multiple network devices.
Synonym: *multiple address*

group delay
A communication signal problem caused by nonuniform transmission speeds of a signal's components through a transmission medium.

Group object
A leaf object in the Novell Directory Services (NDS) structure, used to administer network users as a group, rather than as individuals. The Group object lists multiple User objects; an action taken on a Group object applies to every member of the group.

group reply
A response to an electronic mail (e-mail) message sent to the person who sent the original message and to all others who appear on its distribution list.

groupware
A type of software that enables several network users (or small groups of users) to access and manipulate objects concurrently and to work collaboratively on a project. Typically, groupware includes functions for scheduling, messaging, and document management.

GroupWise
Novell's groupware software offering that includes features such as electronic mail (e-mail), directory services, and support for threaded group discussions. Other features include group scheduling, document management, and replication. Users of GroupWise can also manage and track documents; a check-in-and-check-out facility enables several members of the workgroup to access documents from a central repository. An add-on program adds capabilities of workflow management.

guaranteed bandwidth
The capacity of a network to transmit continuously at a given speed. Guaranteed bandwidth is essential for delay-insensitive applications such as voice or video.

guard band
A small band of frequency that separates multiple bands in a broadband transmission. The guard band prevents interference between the multiple communications channels.

guard time
A period of silence that occurs between transmissions in a Time Division Multiplexing (TDM) signaling system. The guard time compensates for signal distortion and helps maintain synchronization.

Guest
A special type of network account that enables unregistered users to access the network. A guest account enjoys only limited access rights.

guided media
Transmission media that constrain or focus the communications signal.

Guidelines for the Definition of Managed Objects (GDMO)
An International Standards Organization (ISO) specification that establishes a type of notation that describes managed objects and the actions taken to manage them.

Gzip
A lossless compression utility for UNIX files, developed by the Free Software Foundation as part of the GNU project. Files that have been compressed with this utility usually have the .GZ suffix.

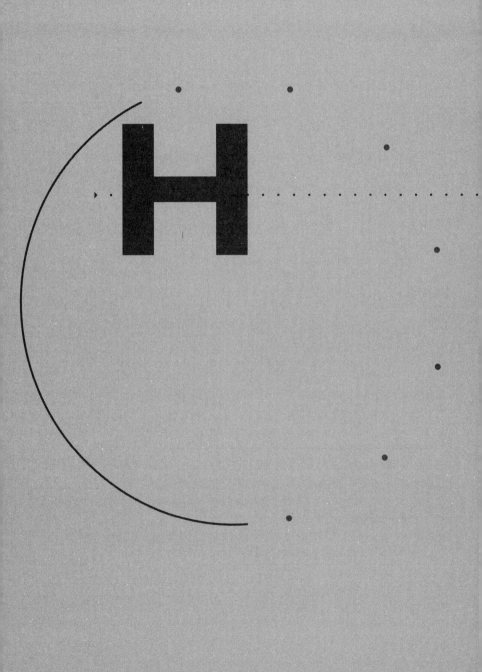

H Channel

A higher-rate Integrated Services Digital Network (ISDN) channel that can be leased as single units, and then subdivided into multiple, lower-bandwidth channels. H channels are appropriate for high-bandwidth transmissions, such as video or graphics.

hacker

Originally, a self-taught computer user who *hacks* through the steps involved in creating a program, running a network, or doing another technology-related task. The term later came to refer to an individual who breaks into other people's computers for the purpose of theft or vandalism.

half bridge

One of a pair of bridges separated by a telecommunications link in a wide area network (WAN). A half bridge is not connected directly to another network but, instead, is connected to another half bridge via telephone or long-distance cable.

half duplex (HDX)

A type of communications in which transmission can go in either direction, but it can only go in one direction at a time. The entire bandwidth is used for the one-way transmission. (By contrast, *full duplex* divides the bandwidth between the two directions.)

half gateway

A device designed to perform half the functions of a full gateway (which is often divided into halves to simplify design and maintenance).

half router

One of a pair of routers separated by a telecommunications link. To nonrouter stations, the pair of routers appears as a single router.

half-open connection

An incomplete connection in which only half of the link is established.

half-session

A component providing data-flow control and transmission control for one session of a network-addressable unit (NAU).

Hamming code

A forward error-correcting technique. Hamming code inserts additional bits at predefined locations in a transmission. The calculated value of these additional bits makes it possible to determine whether an error has occurred during transmission.

hand-held computer

A portable computer, small enough to fit into a hand or pocket. Hand-held computers often have multiple input methods (such as bar-code scanning devices or pen-based mechanisms).

handle

A pointer used to identify a computer resource or feature. The number of handles allowed is limited by the operating system.

hand-off

The transfer of a connection between cells in cellular communications. The hand-off time (which can be from 200 to 1,200 milliseconds) accounts for the short delay sometimes experienced when talking on a cellular telephone.

handset

The part of a telephone that contains the transmitter and receiver, held during use of the telephone.

handshaking

The exchange that takes place between two data communications systems prior to data transmission. The handshaking procedure guarantees the devices on both ends of the connection are synchronized and coordinates each phase of the data-exchange transaction.

hard disk

A magnetic data-storage device. Data can be read from, and written to, a hard disk and the disk can be attached to a stand-alone, local workstation or a networked workstation. The capacity of the hard disk depends on the *cylinders* (concentric storage areas similar to a floppy disk's tracks).

Hard Disk and Channel Reliability

A feature of System Fault Tolerance (SFT) that guarantees the integrity of data through disk-mirroring and disk-duplexing facilities.

hard drive

The storage device that holds the hard disk. The drive rotates the disk at speeds of up to 3,600 revolutions per minute (rpm) and places a read/write head on a thin cushion of air immediately above the disk. The entire unit is sealed to protect it from contaminants.

hard error

A serious error that occurs in a Token Ring network, which could bring down the network.

hard reset

A system reset done mechanically by shutting off the power and turning it back on again or by pressing a reset button.

hard-coded

Software that does not allow future expansion.

hard-disk controller

An expansion board used to control a hard disk drive. A hard-disk controller may manage multiple hard disks, floppy disks, and tape drives within the same system.

hard-disk interface

A way of accessing data stored on a hard disk. Hard-disk interfaces include the ST-506 Interface, Enhanced Small Device Interface (ESDI), Integrated Drive Electronics (IDE), and Small Computer Systems Interface (SCSI).

hard-disk type
A number used to define hard-disk characteristics. The hard-disk type is stored in a computer's Complementary Metal-Oxide Semiconductor (CMOS) random access memory (RAM); it defines the hard disk's number of read/write heads, number of cylinders on the disk, and other information.

hardware
Physical computer devices. Network hardware may include nodes, cabling, and other peripherals, such as printers or storage devices.

Hardware Abstraction Layer (HAL)
A function of Microsoft Windows NT and NT Advanced Server that acts as an interface between the operating system kernel and specific hardware to make NT transportable to other machines.

hardware address
A number assigned to a Network Interface Card (NIC) by a manufacturer or network administrator. The hardware address identifies the local device address to the rest of the network.

hardware interrupt
A request for service, generated by a hardware device.

hard-wired
A system designed in such a way that future expansion has been made impossible.

Harmonica
A cabling device used to convert a 25-pair cable into multiple 2-pair, 3-pair, or 4-pair cables.

Harmonica Block
A wiring block used to connect a limited number of RJ-11 plugs into a single wiring center.

hashing
A way of quickly predicting a file's address by calculating the address in cache memory and on the hard disk. If a workstation must read a file on the server, the server will perform a hash algorithm to predict an address on a hash table.

Hayes-compatible modem
Any modem that recognizes the standard AT command set.

HDLC Distance Host
A means of running the High-Level Data-Link Control (HDLC) protocol over synchronous serial links instead of over special HDLC hardware.

head
In a hard drive, a physical device that reads data from and writes data to the platter. Two heads may exist in the drive, one on each side of the platter. The movement of the head is governed by the disk controller.

head end
The starting point for a broadband transmission to end users. Recipients of the transmission can usually transmit only control and error information back to the head end, but no data can be transmitted.

header
Information at the beginning of a data packet. The header typically includes addressing and control information.

header compression
A set of compression options designed to cut nonessential data from the frame format. Header compression helps to maximize bandwidth on Public Switched Telephone Network (PSTN) connections.

Header Error Control (HEC)
In an Asynchronous Transfer Mode (ATM) cell header, an 8-bit field used to detect errors in the header. The value of the HEC field is calculated using the other 32 bits of the header.

heartbeat
A test function used in Ethernet networks to determine signal quality.

Hello interval
In Open Shortest Path First (OSPF) networks, the number of seconds between transmissions of Hello packets.

Hello packet
In Open Shortest Path First (OSPF) networks, a protocol that establishes and maintains neighbor relationships.

help button
In a graphical user interface (GUI), a feature typically offered on a dialog box to give the user access to context-sensitive, online help about a particular feature.

Help Desk
A central site where queries are answered, sometimes fully or partially automated. A Help Desk is often staffed by support personnel who have the knowledge and resources to answer questions about software or hardware products and to troubleshoot problems. Specialized Help Desk software may offer a prepared body of knowledge or may enable an administrator to put knowledge into the system, so the Help Desk staff can readily locate and disseminate needed information.

help key
A special key used to gain access to online help. The F1 key is usually designated as the help key.

help menu
The part of a graphical utility's menu bar used to access online help.

helper address
An address configured on an interface to which broadcasts received in that interface are sent.

helper application

A program a World Wide Web (WWW) browser calls on to perform a specific task. Most Web browsers now use *plug-in applications* loaded from within the browser.

hermaphroditic

A standard Token Ring connection that has both plug (male) and socket (female) connecting components.

hertz (Hz)

A unit of electrical frequency equal to one cycle per second.

Heterogeneous LAN Management (HLM)

A capability enabling the management of local area networks (LANs) that contain dissimilar devices and run different protocols on different machines.

heterogeneous network

A network using multiple protocols at the Network Layer (Layer 3 of the OSI Reference Model). A heterogeneous network may contain components from different vendors.

hexadecimal

A system of numeric notation used to denote addresses in computer memory. Hexadecimal is a base-16 system in which the numbers 0 through 9 are represented by the numerals themselves, and the base-10 numbers 10 through 15 are represented by letters A through F. A leading *0x* (zero and *x*) or a trailing uppercase *H* indicates a number is hexadecimal. For example, the decimal number 10 would be represented in hexadecimal as either "0xa" or "aH."

HGopher

A Windows client that enables the retrieval and viewing of Gopher files on the Internet. This program enables a user to copy multiple windows into a viewer simultaneously while browsing other windows.

hiccup

An error in transmission that occurs when data has been dropped and must be retransmitted. This is commonly caused by momentary line or port interference, buffer overflow, power loss, or power surge.

Hidden (H) attribute

A DOS or OS/2 attribute that, when switched on, hides files from view in a standard directory listing. This attribute also prevents the specified file from being deleted or copied. In NetWare and IntranetWare, the Hidden (H) attribute may be used on files and directories.

hierarchical addressing

An addressing scheme that partitions a network into sections. One part of each destination address is made up of the section identifier. The destination identifier makes up another part. Hierarchical addressing permits destination identifiers to be reused in different sections.

Hierarchical File System (HFS)

The standard Macintosh file structure used to manage files and directories.

hierarchical name structure

A naming strategy that depends on a hierarchical relationship, as among files or network entities.

hierarchical routing

A type of routing that distinguishes several network levels. The Internet, for example, may contain three routing levels in its hierarchical routing system (backbone, midlevel, and stub).

Hierarchical Storage Management (HSM)

A data-management system that transparently migrates files to progressively less-expensive media, depending on frequency of access. Files accessed most frequently are stored on high-speed media; those accessed less frequently may be stored on tape or optical media. End users need not know the physical location of a file to access it.

hierarchy

A logical structuring of elements in a series of branches emanating downward, starting from a root or top-level node; each successive node can have none, one, or multiple branches leading to subsidiary nodes. Only one path leads from a lower-level node back to the root or top-level node.

high memory

A generic term for memory above conventional memory. High memory can indicate system memory, extended memory, or expanded memory.

High-memory area (HMA)

The first 64K of extended memory between 1,024K and 1,088K. The HMA can be directly addressed by DOS in real mode if a separate device driver is used. HMA provides additional memory addressed directly by DOS and functions in a fashion similar to conventional memory.

High-Performance File System (HPFS)

A file system that supports long filenames and high-level caching mechanisms. HPFS is used by the OS/2 operating system and supports filenames of up to 255 characters. It can accommodate high-capacity hard disks and uses advanced caching methods for faster access.

High-Performance Parallel Interface (HiPPI)

A type of channel connection originally designed to connect supercomputers with mainframes. It has also become useful in high-performance applications such as cinematic special effects and scientific visualization. The connection-oriented mechanism offers transmission rates of up to 1.6 gigabits per second (Gbps). HiPPI can work with several other local area network (LAN) mechanisms to create a high-speed wide area network (WAN).

High Sierra standard

A subset of the International Standards Organization (ISO) 9660 standard often used by CD-ROM manufacturers.

High-Capacity Storage System (HCSS)
A storage system used to extend the NetWare server's storage capacity. HCSS integrates an optical disc library or *jukebox* into the NetWare file system, and transfers files between the server's hard disk (which is faster) and the slower, high-capacity devices contained in the library. The process is completely transparent to the end user, to whom files still appear to be stored on the file server, even if they are stored in the external jukebox. This method migrates data files off the hard disk when data stored on it reaches a specified capacity.

high-end
Any full-featured product, typically the most expensive and feature-rich product in a company's product family.

High-Level Data-Link Control (HDLC)
A bit-oriented, synchronous protocol. HDLC is used in the Data-Link Layer (Layer 2) of the OSI Reference Model. HDLC is similar to Synchronous Data Link Control (SDLC), and is used for high-level, synchronous connections to X.25 packet-based networks. In HDLC, messages are sent in frames of variable sizes.

High-Level Entity Management System (HEMS)
A network-management protocol that was once a prospective standard for the Internet. The Simple Gateway Monitoring Protocol (SGMP) and Common Management Information Services Protocol over TCP/IP (CMOT) were selected instead as Internet standards.

high-level language
A machine-independent programming language that uses English-like syntax. A high-level statement corresponds to multiple assembly-language instructions.

High-Level Language Application Program Interface (HLLAPI)
An application programming interface (API) designed to be used with high-level languages such as C, Pascal, and BASIC. The computer-based API can be

used to establish an interface between a mainframe computer and an application on a personal computer.

high-speed circuit
A telecommunications circuit with a fast transmission rate of 20 kilobits per second (Kbps) or more, a rate faster than what is typically needed for voice communication.

High-Speed Local Area Network (HSLAN)
Any of several high-speed transmission architectures that function at 100 megabits per second (Mbps) or faster. Fast Ethernet, Gigabit Ethernet, Fiber Distributed Data Interface (FDDI), and Asynchronous Transfer Mode (ATM) are all examples of HSLANs.

High-Speed Serial Interface (HSSI)
Serial connections transmitting at more than 20 kilobits per second (Kbps).

high-usage trunk group
A cable group used as the primary path between two switching stations in a telecommunications network.

history list
A list of Uniform Resource Locator (URL) addresses visited during a session on the Internet, with the most recent World Wide Web (WWW) site listed first. Most Web browsers allow entries in the history list to be moved to a *bookmark list*.

history menu
A feature of Novell ElectroText and DynaText that enables users to retrace their steps through a document or documents.

hit
Either a temporary change in the phase or amplitude of a signal that can create distortion and cause errors, or the successful return of an item that meets a specified search criteria.

hogging

A state that occurs when a transmitting node consumes a large percentage of the network's available bandwidth.

hold-down

A state of a route in which the router neither advertises the route nor believes any advertisement about the route for a specified length of time. A hold-down is used to flush out bad information about a route from all routers in the network. When a link to a route fails, the route can be placed in a hold-down mode.

holding time

The amount of time a call is in control of a communications channel.

home directory

A private network directory in a NetWare network. The network supervisor can create a home directory for a user, if the user's login directory maps a drive to the home directory.

home page

The first page (or opening page) of a World Wide Web (WWW) site that typically introduces a visitor to what is available on that site.

home run

A cable running from a wallplate to a distribution frame.

homogeneous network

A network using a single protocol at the Network Layer (Layer 3 of the OSI Reference Model). A homogeneous network runs a single operating system and consists of devices purchased from a single manufacturer.

homologation

The compliance and conformity of a product or a specification to standards established by recognized international organizations, which enables portability of products and services across international boundaries.

hooked vector
An intercepted interrupt vector that points to a replacement interrupt service routine (ISR) instead of the original service routine.

hop
The distance traveled by a packet between routers or other network devices as it travels to its final destination.

hop count
The number of routers or other network devices a data packet must pass through to reach its final destination. One hop equals the transmission of a packet across one router.

horizontal cable
A cable defined by the Electronics Industry Association/Telecommunications Industry Association (EIA/TIA)-568 specification that runs from a wiring closet or distribution frame to a wall outlet in a work area. Horizontal cable is usually installed inside the walls, floors, or ceiling.

host
A network server or central computer to which other nodes, storage devices, or controllers are attached. The host provides services to other computers. In a mainframe environment, a front-end processor or controller may sit between the host and the terminals it controls.

host adapter
A Network Interface Card (NIC) in a host server, used to control a storage device.

Host Adapter Module (HAM)
A driver component used to drive specific host adapter hardware in the NetWare Peripheral Architecture (NPA).

Host Bus Adapter (HBA)
A device that functions as an interface between a host microprocessor and the disk controller. During data storage and retrieval, the HBA is used to

offload tasks from the host microprocessor, thereby improving performance. The HBA, along with its disk subsystems, makes up a *disk channel*. NetWare can accommodate five host adapter channels, with four controllers on each channel and eight drives attached to each controller.

Host Name Database
A database that contains all names, aliases, and network addresses of the computers on the network.

host node
A subarea node that includes a systems services control point (SSCP).

host order
The order in which integers and shorts are stored on a given host processor.

host server
A NetWare or other network server with a host adapter and storage device.

host table
A list that contains Transmission Control Protocol/Internet Protocol (TCP/IP) hosts on a network, along with their network addresses.

host-based network
Any type of network in which control is centralized in a mainframe computer.

Hostname
An Internet term for a machine's name. The hostname is part of the Fully Qualified Domain Name (FQDN).

host-to-host
A layer in the Transmission Control Protocol/Internet Protocol (TCP/IP) suite.

host-to-terminal

A type of connection in which multiple terminals are connected to a single host machine.

Hot Fix feature

A NetWare feature used to protect data in the event of hardware failure. Hot Fix allocates a portion of the hard disk's storage capacity as a redirection area. If the read-after-write verification finds a bad data block on the disk, Hot Fix redirects the data away from the bad block to the redirection area. Hot Fix then marks the block as bad; the server makes no further attempts to store data in the bad block in the future.

hot key

A keystroke or key combination that triggers a particular task.

hot line service

A private, point-to-point telecommunications link. A hot line service does not require dialing.

Hot Potato Algorithm

A network routing algorithm used to route a packet to the output line with the shortest queue.

hot standby

A microwave communications strategy that connects two transmitters and two receivers to an antenna. If one unit malfunctions, the hot standby immediately takes over the duties of the primary unit.

hotlist

A list of World Wide Web (WWW) locations about a particular topic, arranged to enable the user to jump to the Web site (or add to a bookmark list) by clicking an item.

hot-swapping

A Redundant Array of Inexpensive Disks (RAID) technique that deals with the failure of an array by activating a spare drive and rebuilding the data from another drive in the array that has failed.

hub

A network device that modifies transmission signals and enables the network to be expanded. A hub is often located in a wiring closet and is a point of concentration for wiring. An *active hub* amplifies transmission signals; a *passive hub* splits the signals instead. Either type enables workstations to be added to the network, but a passive hub (because it does not amplify) must be connected directly to a station or to an active hub.

hub and spoke

A network topology that connects multiple peripheral components directly to a common central component.

hub card

A multiport card used in a 10BaseT network. A hub card can be used in place of a hub.

Huffman coding

A lossless method of encoding data according to the relative frequency of the data's individual elements. Huffman coding is frequently used for text files and fax transmissions.

Huge Variable-Length Record (HVLR)

A record larger than 64K. Btrieve can perform record operations on portions of a HVLR without having to use the full record.

Hundred Call Seconds (CCS)

A measure of line activity in telephone communications. One CCS is equal to 100 seconds of conversation on a single line. One hour of conversation on a single line equals 36 CCS and 36 CCSs equals one Erlang.

hunt group

A group of telecommunications lines accessed in succession to find the first available line.

hybrid circuit
A telephone wiring circuit in a four-wire cable. The hybrid circuit divides the four-wire cable into 2 two-wire paths.

hybrid mode
In a network using Fiber Distributed Data Interface (FDDI) II network, a mode of operation that enables data and voice to be transmitted over the same network. In hybrid mode, packet-based and circuit-switched services are both available.

Hybrid Multiplexer (HMUX)
In Fiber Distributed Data Interface (FDDI) II networks, a component of the Media-Access Control (MAC) Layer that multiplexes network data from the MAC Layer, as well as time-dependent data, such as voice or video.

hybrid topology
A network based on two or more physical topologies, such as a star-wired ring topology.

hyperlink
A link in a hypertext system used to move to another file or another location within the same file.

hypermedia
A combination of data, text, and other elements in a hypertext system. Hypermedia links together different elements, enabling users to move easily between them. Multiple connections make additional material, resources, and related topics easy to access.

hypertext
A way of retrieving and presenting information on the basis of a dynamic index. Hypertext linkage and retrieval is generally nonlinear and nonsequential, providing a convenient way for users to jump to sections of related text.

Hypertext Markup Language (HTML)

A set of markup codes (or *tags*) inserted in a text file to make the file viewable through a World Wide Web (WWW) browser. The individual tags tell the browser how to display the text. HTML is an official standard; Microsoft, Netscape Communications, and other companies have added proprietary extensions to HTML to enhance its functionality.

Hypertext Transfer Protocol (HTTP)

A collection of rules used for exchanging information on the World Wide Web (WWW), under which any file can contain a hyperlink to another file or another location within the same file.

Hypertext Transfer Protocol Daemon (HTTPD)

A program that exists on a World Wide Web (WWW) server and accommodates client requests for files.

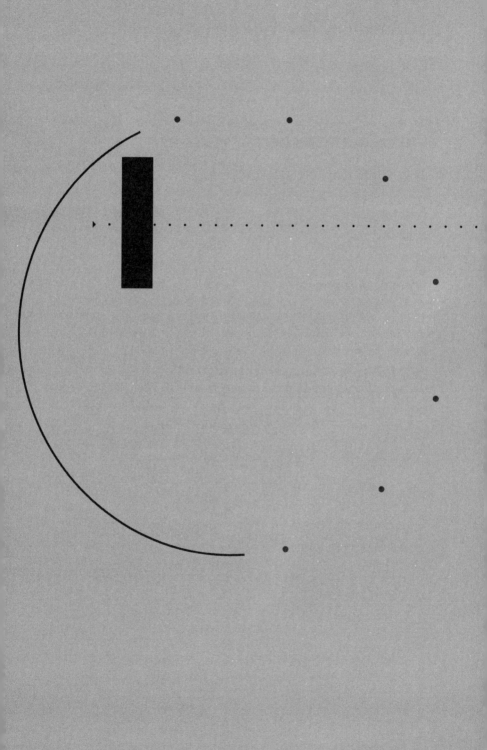

I/O bound
The state that exists when the speed of the input/output (I/O) port limits the speed of a program's execution.

I/O Request Packet (IRP)
A packet used in Windows NT and Windows NT Advanced Server to provide communication between drivers.

IBM cable
The cabling system designed by IBM. Cable types are referred to as Type 1 through Type 9, and are used for Token Ring and general-purpose wiring.

IBM data connector
A type of data connector used in IBM Token Ring networks. An IBM data connector attaches a node to a Multistation Access Unit (MAU), wallplate, or patch panel.

IBM Network Management (IBMNM)
A network management protocol used in an IBM Token Ring network.

ICMP Router Discovery Protocol (IRDP)
A protocol similar to the End System-to-Intermediate System (ES-IS) protocol that enables a host to determine a default gateway by using a router address. The difference between ES-IS and IRDP is the latter uses the Internet Protocol (IP).

icon
A graphical representation of an object, application, or device. A group icon represents several objects, applications, or devices. End users can manipulate the icons—typically by moving a mouse or pointing device—to trigger an action or to access data.

identifier variables

A variable used in a login script. The identifier variable is used to enter in a variable, as opposed to a specific name, in a login script command. As a result, multiple users can use the same script.

idle cell

A cell in an Asynchronous Transfer Mode (ATM) network transmitted to keep network traffic at a specific level.

IEEE 802.x

A family of protocols included in specifications from the Institute of Electrical and Electronic Engineers (IEEE). Table I.1 shows some of the common IEEE 802.x specifications.

T A B L E I . I	*IEEE 802.x Specifications*
SPECIFICATION	**DESCRIPTION**
IEEE 802.1	An access control standard for bridges linking 802.3, 802.4, and 802.5 networks.
IEEE 802.2	The standard specifying the Logical Link Control (LLC) sublayer of the Data-Link Layer (Layer 2 of the OSI Reference Model), for use with 802.3, 802.4, and 802.5 networks.
IEEE 802.3	A standard defining the Medium Access Control (MAC) Layer for a Carrier Sense Multiple Access/Collision Detection (CSMA/CD) bus network, such as Ethernet.
IEEE 802.4	A standard defining the Medium Access Control (MAC) Layer for a token-passing bus network.
IEEE 802.5	A standard defining the Medium Access Control (MAC) Layer for a token-passing ring network model, such as IBM Token Ring.
IEEE 802.6	A standard for metropolitan area networks (MANs) based on fiber-optic rings.

"I'm Alive" Packet

A diagnostic packet sent by a NetWare System Fault Tolerance (SFT) III server. The "I'm Alive" packet is sent over the internetwork connection to enable servers to check each other's status. Every SFT III server sends the packet to other servers over the IPX cable at the rate of 18 times per second.

image file

A file containing a single image sent to a user's computer by a host computer on the World Wide Web (WWW) as part of a Web page.

Immediate Compress (Ic) attribute

A NetWare 4.x directory and file system attribute that causes a file or directory to be compressed as soon as the operating system can do so, without having to wait for a specific event to trigger the compression.

immediate delivery

An electronic mail (e-mail) feature, in which a program sends a message immediately when a user indicates composition is complete.

impairment

The degradation of an electrical signal.

impedance

Resistance to an Alternating Current (AC) in a wire. Impedance is measured in ohms and is a function of signal frequency.

implicit congestion notification

A method of detecting network congestion. Transmission Control Protocol (TCP), for example, uses an implicit congestion notification method to infer when the network is in a congested state.

implicit transaction tracking

A function that works transparently with existing multiuser software, uses record locking, and requires no coding on the part of the developer.

Improved Mobile Telephone Service (IMTS)
A mobile telephony service that enables a mobile telephone user to dial directly to a standard wired telephone.

inband signaling
A transmission containing signal and control information, sent within the regular data channel instead of in a separate frequency.

inbound service advertisement filter
A service information filter used to limit acceptance of service advertisements received by a router.

incremental backup
A data backup methodology that backs up only those files that have been modified or created since the most recent backup.

independent LU
A logical unit (LU) that does not require an active session to another LU within a Systems Network Architecture (SNA) host system.

Independent Telephone Company (ITC)
A local exchange carrier that is not one of the Regional Bell Operating Companies (RBOCs).

index
A key or group of keys used by a database program to sort files.

index balancing
The process of searching for available space in a sibling index page, when one index page becomes full.

index of refraction
A metric indicating the degree to which light travels at a different speed through a particular medium.

Indexed (I) attribute
A NetWare file attribute set when a file exceeds a fixed size and that indicates the file has been indexed for fast access.

inductor
An electrical component used to minimize noise caused by interference. Inductors are typically found in line conditioners or surge protectors.

Industrial, Scientific, and Medical (ISM)
The three ranges of frequency the Federal Communications Commission (FCC) made available for unlicensed spread-spectrum communications. Prior to the FCC's action, which took place in 1985, these frequencies were allocated for industrial, scientific, and medical use.

Industry Standard Architecture (ISA)
An industry standard bus design, commonly used on the IBM PC/XT. The ISA design uses plug-in cards and expansion slots, and can accommodate both 8-bit and 16-bit cards.

Information frame (I frame)
A frame used to transfer packet information and flow-control data.

Information Management Systems (IMS)
IBM's mainframe-based database management and communications software used in Systems Network Architecture (SNA) networks.

Information Systems Network (ISN)
AT&T's high-speed switching network that can accommodate both voice and data, and can be connected to most standard network architectures.

infrared transmission
A type of wireless communications that can be used only in small areas, such as a single office. Light waves below the visual spectrum are used to connect devices in a network, instead of traditional cabling. The devices must have a line-of-sight connection (no obstacles can impede the path between sender and receiver).

Inherited Rights Filter (IRF)

A list of rights that can apply to a NetWare file, directory, or object. The IRF controls the rights a trustee can inherit from parent directories or container objects. In its default state, the IRF allows all rights to be inherited. However, the IRF does not grant rights, but rather only allows or revokes them. The IRF may be ignored if a trustee has an explicit trustee assignment to a given file, directory, or object. The IRF is part of the access control list (ACL); to change an object's IRF, a user must have the Write property right to the ACL property of that object. The IRF is used to prevent rights from automatically moving between objects.

Inherited Rights Mask (IRM)

A NetWare 3.x feature used to filter out specific rights. The IRM is used as a security measure to determine which trustee rights can be carried over into a new subdirectory.

Initial Domain Identifier (IDI)

The portion of a network address, as specified in the OSI Reference Model, that represents the domain.

initialize

The process of preparing a new floppy or hard disk for use. The process erases any previously stored information.

Synonym: *formatting*

inline

A portion of a World Wide Web (WWW) page containing images or sounds that are automatically downloaded as part of the page, rather than shown only when a link to the image or sound is selected.

input

Any type of information that moves into a computer, usually from a keyboard or other input device.

input cursor

A cursor on a NetWare Loadable Module (NLM) screen that indicates the starting column or row position where input is taken. The input cursor and output cursor can be placed in two different locations on the screen, for situations where input is accepted in one field and output is shown in a different field.

input/output (I/O)

The transfer of data between a computer and its attached peripheral devices.

Input/Output Engine (IOEngine)

Part of the NetWare System Fault Tolerance (SFT) III operating system that handles physical processes (such as network input and output), hardware interrupts, and device drivers.

insertion loss

A signal loss, measured in decibels, that occurs at a point of connection.

inside wire

Wiring that runs between workstations and other devices on the customer premises, and the point at which the public wiring starts.

install

To configure hardware or software for use. Software applications usually come with an installation program, which automatically copies all the necessary files into the appropriate directories. The install program may then assist the user in configuring the program to match the target system.

Installable File System (IFS)

A file system that can be dynamically loaded into an existing operating system. An IFS is used to make newer releases of operating systems backward-compatible with older versions.

installation program

An application used to install and configure another application. The installation program may guide the user through a series of configuration options and usually copies all the correct files into the appropriate directories.

Institute of Electrical and Electronic Engineers (IEEE)

A standards organization that establishes networking standards for cabling, electrical topology, physical topology, and access schemes. The IEEE established the 802.5 and 802.3 protocols.

instruction set

A set of machine-language instructions that a processor executes.

Insulation Displacement Contact (IDC)

A cabling contact in which the connector cuts into the cable's insulation to make contact with the wire.

int (international)

A suffix on an Internet address that indicates the address belongs to an international organization.

INT 14H

A personal computer hardware interrupt used to reroute messages from the serial port to the Network Interface Card (NIC). This interrupt is used by some terminal emulation applications.

INT 21H

A DOS interrupt that performs a variety of functions, including getting a segment for use by a control program, reading the computer keyboard, writing to the monitor display, and writing to printer.

integral controller

A controller built into a mainframe computer.

integrated circuit (IC)

A small semiconductor with multiple electrical components.
Synonym: *computer chip*

Integrated Database Application Programming Interface (IDAPI)

A standard for interfaces between front-end and back-end database applications. IDAPI was proposed as an alternative to Microsoft's Open Database Connectivity (ODBC) standard by Borland, IBM, and Novell.

Integrated Digital Access (IDA)

A method of providing access to multiple digital channels.

Integrated Digital Network (IDN)

Any network using digital signaling and digital circuits.

Integrated Drive Electronics (IDE)

An interface standard for hard disk drives that replaces the ST-506 and places controller hardware on the drive for better performance. An IDE bus has a 40-pin connector.

Integrated IS-IS Protocol

A protocol used to establish communications between routers in an autonomous system or routing domain. Integrated IS-IS is a version of the Intermediate System to Intermediate System (IS-IS) protocol that uses a single routing algorithm to support more protocols on the Network Layer (Layer 3 of the OSI Reference Model) than Connectionless Network Protocol (CLNP). The Integrated IS-IS protocol can be used in either a Transmission Control Protocol/Internet Protocol (TCP/IP) or an Open Systems Interconnection (OSI) environment.

Integrated Service Unit (ISU)

A device that combines a channel service unit (CSU) and a data service unit (DSU). The ISU interfaces computers and terminals with Digital Data Service (DDS) lines.

Integrated Services Digital Network (ISDN)

A set of Consultative Committee for International Telegraphy and Telephony (CCITT) standards for digital networking. ISDN involves the digitizing of a telephone network so voice, data, text, graphics, music, video, and other source files can be provided to users from a single terminal over existing telephone wiring. ISDN requires special adapters to translate between analog and digital signals. Transmission rates are based on the amount of multiplexed Bearer channels ("B" channels), which are 64 kilobits per second (Kbps) each. The Basic Rate Interface (BRI) consists of two B channels and a single 16Kbps D channel. The D channel is used to carry signaling information. The Primary Rate Interface (PRI) consists of 23 B channels and one D channel, for a total of 1.536 megabits per second (Mbps).

integrated software
An application program that combines the functionality of different applications (such as a word processor, spreadsheet, and database) into a single offering.

integrated terminal
A terminal that can accommodate multiple transmission streams.

Integrated Voice and Data (IVD)
The integration of voice and data traffic in a single network. Primarily, this consists of the integration of Integrated Services Digital Network (ISDN) and local area network (LAN) architectures, and is overseen by the Institute of Electrical and Electronic Engineers (IEEE) 802.9 working group.

integrity control
A way to guarantee that data is accurate. Methods of integrity control may include concurrency controls and shadow paging.

intellectual property
Any special knowledge or information that can be bought or sold or that can be considered an economic asset to the holder.

intelligent hub
A physical hub device that combines the functions of a hub with processing capabilities.

Intelligent Peripheral Interfaces (IPI)

A hard disk interface that can accommodate a transfer rate of up to 25 megabits per second (Mbps) and offers a high storage capacity.

Intelligent Printer Data Stream (IPDS)

A printing mode in a Systems Network Architecture (SNA) network that provides access to multiple Advanced Function Printing (AFP) features simultaneously.

intelligent terminal

A terminal connected to a mainframe or other central host computer. An intelligent terminal possesses some local computing capabilities and can execute certain tasks independently of the host. However, the intelligent terminal usually lacks local disk storage.

Interactive Voice Response (IVR)

A type of Computer-Telephone Integration (CTI) that enables end users to input information using a touchtone telephone. The IVR system uses a synthesized computer voice to interact with the caller.

Inter-Application Communication (IAC)

A feature of the Macintosh System 7 operating system that permits independent software applications to share information. IAC consists of the Publish-and-Subscribe feature (which enables users to create documents made up of components created by multiple applications) and Apple events (which permits one application to take control over another one).

interconnect company

A company that sells telecommunications equipment for connecting to telephone lines. Equipment sold by the interconnect company must be registered with the telephone company before installation.

Inter-Dialog Gap (IDG)

The minimum gap between dialogs in a LocalTalk network.

Interdomain Policy Routing (IDPR)
An experimental interdomain routing protocol under consideration by the Internet Engineering Task Force (IETF) that encapsulates traffic between autonomous systems (ASs) and routes the traffic according to the policies established by each AS along the path.

Interdomain Routing Protocol (IRP)
An Internet protocol defined by the International Standards Organization (ISO) that routes packets between different domains in an internetwork. Based on the Border Gateway Protocol (BGP), IRP is designed to operate seamlessly with End System to End System (ES-ES) and Intermediate System to Intermediate System (IS-IS) protocols.

Interexchange Carrier (IXC)
A long-distance telephone carrier.

interface
The point at which a physical or logical connection is made between two elements. In hardware, an interface refers to the physical connection between circuits or devices. In software, an interface is a software connection between two applications or two application functions.

Interface Data Unit (IDU)
A data structure specified in the OSI Reference Model. The IDU is a structure passed between layers, when one layer is providing a service to an entity in a higher layer.

interface group
A group of interfaces that permits protocols to request an X.25 virtual circuit (VC) through any interface in the group without having to specify one specific interface.

interface standard
Any standard method of connecting two or more elements with different functions.

interference
An external factor that may adversely influence data being transmitted along a circuit. Interference may come from a variety of sources, including magnetic fields.

Interframe Gap (IFG)
The maximum time period that can exist between consecutive frames or packets.

Interim Local Management Interface (ILMI)
An interface specification from the Asynchronous Transfer Mode (ATM) Forum group that outlines the incorporation of network-management capabilities into the ATM User-to-Network Interface (UNI).

Interior Gateway Protocol (IGP)
A protocol used to exchange routing table information between routers in the Internet. Two IGPs are the Routing Information Protocol (RIP) and the Open Shortest Path First (OSPF).

Interior Gateway Routing Protocol (IGRP)
A protocol used by routers to communicate with each other in an autonomous system having arbitrarily complex topology and consisting of media with diverse bandwidth and delay characteristics. Originally designed by Cisco Systems to work in Internet Protocol (IP) networks, IGRP was later ported to run in the Open System Interconnection (OSI) and Connectionless Network Protocol (CLNP) networks. Because it is a distance vector routing protocol, each router IGRP sends all or a portion of its routing table in a routing update message at regular intervals to each of its neighboring routers. Routers then use this information to calculate distances to all nodes located in the network.

interior router
An AppleTalk network router that routes packets between networks.

InterLATA

A set of telephony services, provided by interexchange carriers, that move between two or more exchanges. Each exchange is known as a Local Access and Transport Area (LATA).

interleave

Transmitting pulses from two or more digital sources in a time-division sequence over a single circuit. When applied to random access memory (RAM), the interleaving process divides dynamic RAM into two separate memory banks, so the processor can read one while the other is being refreshed.

intermediate cross-connect

A cross-connect between wiring closets.

Intermediate Distribution Frame (IDF)

An intermediate wiring location connected to a main distribution frame at one end and to end users on the other end.

intermediate node

A node that can provide intermediate routing services in a Systems Network Architecture (SNA) network.

Intermediate Routing Node (IRN)

A Systems Network Architecture (SNA) subarea node that has the capability of intermediate routing.

Intermediate System (IS)

A network entity specified in the OSI Reference Model that functions as an intermediary between multiple subnetworks.

Intermediate System to Intermediate System (IS-IS)

An Open Systems Interconnection (OSI) link-state routing protocol. IS-IS allows intermediate systems to exchange routing information. The IS-IS protocol floods the network with link-state information to build a complete, consistent picture of the network topology. This protocol uses IS-IS

Hello packets, Link State Packets (LSPs), and Sequence Numbers Packets (SNPs) for data transmission.

internal command
An operating system command that resides in memory. An internal command does not have to be loaded from disk and, therefore, can respond quickly.

internal modem
A modem that plugs into a computer's expansion bus.

internal network
A virtual, logical network made up of the AppleTalk protocol stack and the AppleTalk router.

Internal Organization of the Network Layer (IONL)
A Network-Layer (Layer 3) specification of the OSI Reference Model. IONL divides the Network Layer into three sublayers: Subnetwork Access, Subnetwork-Dependent, and Subnetwork-Independent. The Subnetwork Access sublayer establishes an interface over which data is sent across the subnetwork or network. The Subnetwork-Dependent sublayer assumes a specific subnetwork architecture; the Subnetwork-Independent sublayer provides for internetworking of the layers above itself.

internal PAD
A packet assembler/disassembler (PAD) in a packet-switching network that exists inside a packet-switching node.

internal routing
A routing mechanism used by NetWare to provide access to two or more networks from a single file server. The server has one Network Interface Card (NIC) for each network. This mechanism enables two networks using different protocols to become part of the same internetwork.

International Alphabet 5 (IA5)

A 7-bit code defining the character set used for message transfers in the Consultative Committee for International Telegraphy and Telephony (CCITT) X.400 Message Handling System (MHS). IA5 is similar to American Standard Code for Information Interchange (ASCII), but allows for international characters.

International Consultative Committee for Radiocommunications (CCIR)

A now-defunct agency in the International Telecommunications Union (ITU) that defined radio communications standards. The CCIR was combined with the International Frequency Registration Board (IFRB) to form the International Telecommunications Radiocommunications Standardization Sector (ITU-R).

International Electrotechnical Commission (IEC)

An international standards organization that sets electrical standards.

International Federation for Information Processing (IFIP)

An organization that researches preliminary Open Systems Interconnection (OSI) standardization procedures and is responsible for formalizing the Message Handling System (MHS) specifications found in the X.400 specification.

International Frequency Registration Board (IFRB)

An agency of the International Telecommunications Union (ITU) that allocates frequency bands in the electromagnetic spectrum. This agency was combined with the International Consultative Committee for Radiocommunications (CCIR) to form the International Telecommunications Radiocommunications Standardization Sector (ITU-R).

international numbering plan

A Consultative Committee for International Telegraphy and Telephony (CCITT) telecommunications standard for allocating telephone numbers around the world.

International Reference Version (IRV)
A variation of the IA5 character-encoding mechanism.

International Standardization Organization (ISO)
A Geneva-based organization that develops standards for international data communications, information exchange, and other types of commercial activity. The United States member of ISO is the American National Standards Institute (ANSI). ISO is well-known for the seven-layer Open Systems Interconnection (OSI) model for computer-to-computer communications.

International Standardization Profile (ISP)
A subset of a specification still under review during the formalization process.
Synonym: *functional standard*

International Standards Organization Development Environment (ISODE)
A device used in digital telephone services. The ISODE is made up of the channel service unit (CSU) and the digital service unit (DSU), and is used in place of a modem on a Digital Data Service (DDS) connection.

International Telecommunications Union (ITU)
A United Nations agency that develops international telecommunications standards. The ITU has three subagencies: the Consultative Committee for International Telegraphy and Telephony (CCITT), International Frequency Registration Board (IFRB), and International Consultative Committee for Radiocommunications (CCIR).

internationalization
A process that permits software to be adapted for use with multiple languages.

Internet
The worldwide internetwork formed by the Defense Advanced Research Projects Agency (DARPA) and the Transmission Control Protocol/Internet Protocol (TCP/IP) protocols it uses. Overseeing activities of the Internet are the

Internet Society (ISOC), the Internet Architecture Board (IAB), the Internet Engineering Study Group (IESG), and the Internet Research Study Group (IRSG).

Internet Access Provider (IAP)
A company that provides access to the Internet. The IAP has a point of presence on the Internet and, sometimes, has its own high-speed leased lines.
Synonym: *Internet Service Provider*

Internet address
A 32-bit address assigned to Transmission Control Protocol/Internet Protocol (TCP/IP) Internet hosts that consists of information about the document type and about the protocol used to transport it, the domain name of the machine on which the document is found, and the document's name represented as an absolute path to the file.

Internet Architecture Board (IAB)
The coordinating committee that oversees management of the Internet. IAB consists of two subcommittees: the Internet Engineering Task Force (IETF) and the Internet Research Task Force (IRTF). The IETF recommends standards and protocols for use on the Internet, and the IRTF researches new Internet-related technologies. The Internet Engineering Steering Group (IESG) is the executive committee for the IETF; the Internet Research Steering Group (IRSG) is the executive committee for the IRTF. The former name of this group was the *Internet Architecture Board.*

Internet Assigned Numbers Authority (IANA)
A group, operated by the University of Southern California Information Sciences Institute, responsible for assigning values for networks and attributes, and ensuring every identifier is unique.

Internet Control Message Protocol (ICMP)
Part of the Internet Protocol (IP) used to handle link-level error and control messages. Gateways and hosts use the ICMP to send problem reports concerning datagrams back to the source.

Internet Datagram Packet (IDP)

A protocol for the Network Layer (Layer 3) of the OSI Reference Model. IDP is part of the Xerox Network Systems (XNS) protocol suite that routes data or packets from a variety of transport protocols, such as Routing Information Protocol (RIP), Packet Exchange Protocol (PEP), and Sequenced Packet Protocol (SPP).

Internet Engineering Steering Group (IESG)

The executive committee of the Internet Engineering Task Force (IETF).

Internet Engineering Task Force (IETF)

The Internet Activities Board task force that addresses the short-term engineering concerns of the Internet. The IETF is responsible for the Remote Network Monitoring Management Information Base (RMON MIB), a standard for monitoring network activity.

Internet Header Length (IHL)

A four-bit field in the Internet Protocol (IP) datagram. The value in the IHL specifies the length of the datagram header.

Internet Message Access Protocol (IMAP)

A client/server protocol for receiving electronic mail (e-mail) from a local server. Under IMAP, mail is received and held by an Internet server, and subsequently retrieved, searched, read, or deleted by the client.

Internet message server

Software that provides access to the Internet over network bridges. A dedicated machine is not required to establish this type of connection.

Internet Network Information Center (InterNIC)

A central organization responsible for allocating and maintaining World Wide Web (WWW) domain names. This organization works as a cooperative effort between AT&T, the National Science Foundation (NSF), and Network Solutions, Inc. AT&T supports the Directory and Database Services, which entails overseeing a Directory of Directories, white pages services, and publicly accessible databases. The NSF is responsible for maintaining Net Scout services, which entails the publication of Scout Report and Net-happenings.

Network Solutions sponsors Registration Services, Support Services, and Net Scout Services. The InterNIC Registration Services registers second-level domain names to be used on the Internet. The second-level domain name consists of a unique name (not to exceed 22 characters) followed by a three-letter, top-level domain abbreviation.

internet network library
A library that contains functions used in Transmission Control Protocol/Internet Protocol (TCP/IP) programming.

Internet Network Operations Center (INOC)
A group responsible—in the early days of the Internet—for monitoring and controlling core gateways.

Internet Presence Provider (IPP)
A company or organization that provides access to the Internet. This category of Internet providers includes both Internet Service Providers (ISPs) and internal departments that manage Internet connections for companies, educational organizations, or government agencies.

Internet Protocol (IP)
An industry standard protocol suite. IP permits multivendor nodes in a heterogeneous network to communicate. IP is a Session Layer (Layer 5 of the OSI Reference Model) protocol that defines how packets are organized and handled.

Internet Registry (IR)
A centralized database that holds the network addresses of all autonomous systems on the Internet. The IR is maintained by the Internet Assigned Numbers Authority (IANA).

Internet Relay Chat (IRC)
An Internet service used to hold multiparty conferences.

Internet Research Steering Group (IRSG)
An Internet-related group that oversees the Internet Research Task Force (IRTF).

Internet Research Task Force (IRTF)

An Internet-related group, the function of which is to conduct long-term research.

Internet Router (IR)

A device in an AppleTalk internetwork used to filter and route packets.

Internet Service Provider (ISP)

A commercial organization that provides access to the Internet, sometimes in a package that includes software, consulting, and technical support.

Internet Society

An international organization dedicated to promoting the Internet as a means for communication and collaboration. The Internet Society provides a platform for the discussion of administration issues regarding the Internet.

Internet Standard (IS)

An Internet specification that has been formally evaluated and tested. The specification must first go through the Proposed Standard and Draft Standard stages, where significant testing is implemented, before it becomes an official Internet Standard.

internetwork

Two or more networks connected by routers, bridges, or gateways. All users on an internetwork can use all of the resources of any connected network, so long as the appropriate privileges have been granted. Internetworking may involve connecting two local area networks (LANs), connecting a LAN to a mainframe, or connecting a LAN to a wide area network (WAN).

internetwork link

A connection between two or more networks. The different types of internetwork links include bridges, routers, brouters (bridge/routers), gateways, and switches, which may be used to connect similar or dissimilar networks. Whereas bridges and routers are used to connect identical or similar networks, a gateway can be employed to connect dissimilar networks. A switch, on the other hand, is a type of multiport bridge or gateway used to connect more than two networks.

Internetwork Packet Exchange (IPX)

A Novell communications protocol used to send data packets to a requested internetwork destination. IPX routes outgoing data packets across a network, reads assigned addresses of returning data, and sends it to the proper area within the operating system. IPX is capable of routing data packets through physically different networks and workstations and is a best-effort delivery service.

Internetwork Packet Exchange Open Data Interface (IPXODI)

A module that takes workstation requests the DOS Requester determines are for the network, packages them with addressing information, and transfers them to the link-support layer (LSL). Each packet must have an initialized header, which specifies the target network, origin, and what happens after delivery. IPXODI transmits data packets as datagrams and can, therefore, send them only on a best-effort basis.

Internetworking Unit (IWU)

An intermediate system functioning as an intermediary between two subnetworks.

Interoffice Channel (IOC)

A communications link that exists between two telephone carrier central offices.

interoperability

The ability of multivendor devices in a heterogeneous network to communicate and share data. In an interoperable system, one user does not need to know the particulars of the operating system running on a device from which data is being accessed. Adherence to open standards, as opposed to proprietary protocols, promotes interoperability.

Interpersonal Messaging (IPM)

One of two major components of the X.400 Message Handling System (MHS) that covers ordinary business or personal correspondence. The IPM elements consist of a heading (such as name and address) and a body (the content of the message). IPM messages are sent and received over the

Interpersonal Messaging Service (IPMS). The other major component of MHS is the Message Transfer System (MTS).

Interprocess Communication (IPC)

Methods used to pass information between two programs running on the same computer under a multitasking operating system. IPC may also refer to information being passed between two programs running on a network.

Inter-Repeater Link (IRL)

A cable segment between two repeaters in an Ethernet network. No nodes are attached to the IRL.

interrupt

A halt in a computer process triggered by an external event. The interrupt stops normal processing and can take the form of an internal hardware interrupt, external hardware interrupt, or software interrupt.

Synonym: *trap*

interrupt character

A character, or combination of characters, entered from the keyboard to interrupt processing on the computer.

interrupt controller

An integrated circuit (IC) that processes and prioritizes hardware interrupts.

Interrupt Dispatch Table (IDT)

A table used by the Windows NT and Windows NT Advanced Server operating systems to locate the appropriate routine for handling a given interrupt.

interrupt handler

A software routine executed automatically when an interrupt occurs.

interrupt mode
A printer configuration option that sends a signal through the data port when it is ready to accept another character for transmission to the printer.

Interrupt Request Channel (IRQ)
A signal protocol used by hardware devices. The IRQ allows the hardware device to communicate to the system where attention is required.

Interrupt Request Level (IRQL)
A service of Microsoft Windows NT and Windows NT Advanced Server that reflects a level of priority for interrupt request lines. Interrupts below the specified level are masked; interrupts above the level are handled.

interrupt service routine (ISR)
A routine that processes an interrupt and then returns control to the process that was suspended when the interrupt occurred.

interrupt vector table
A list of addresses for interrupt handlers.

intra-area routing
A term used to describe routing within an area on a DECnet network.

intraexchange carrier
A local telephone company that handles calls within an exchange or intraLATA calls.

intraframe encoding
A compression scheme used in video signal transmission. Intraframe encoding encodes only those parts of the video frame that have changed.

IntraLATA
The telephony circuits within a single Local Access and Transport Area (LATA).

IntranetWare

A software bundle from Novell that includes the NetWare 4.x network operating system, which is designed to create an intranet from an existing network infrastructure. IntranetWare is designed to allow both Internet Protocol (IP) and Internetwork Packet Exchange (IPX) access to intranet resources, such as Web servers, FTP servers, and wide area network (WAN) connections to the Internet. All services of the intranetwork platform are included (such as file, print, directory, messaging, Web publishing, security, connectivity, and management). Like its predecessors, IntranetWare incorporates Novell Directory Services (NDS) for management and security.

intruder

An unauthorized user who has accessed, or is attempting to access, a computer system.

intruder lockout

The act of locking a user account after the NetWare Intruder Limit has been reached or other restrictions have been violated.

Inverse ARP (Address Resolution Protocol)

A protocol that can learn the IP address of a remote node's Data Link Connection Identifier (DLCI).

inverted backbone

A type of network architecture in which the hub and routers sit at the center of the network and network segments are attached to the hub.

Invitation to Transmit (ITT)

A token frame in an Attached Resource Computer Network (ARCnet) network.

Inward Wide Area Telephone Service (INWATS)

An "800" telephone service, where the party being called is billed for the call.

IP address

An Internet Protocol (IP) address is assigned to every system in a TCP/IP network. The IP address is a network-level address and is 4 bytes (32 bits) long. The IP address can be divided into two parts: an IP network address and a local host address. IP addresses are assigned by the Internet Assigned Numbers Authority (IANA) and are hierarchical in nature. The five classes are referred to as Class A through E. Class A is used for large networks, B for medium-sized networks, and C for smaller networks. Class D addresses are reserved for multicast addresses; class E is a reserved class used for experimental purposes.

IP address formats

The 4 bytes (32 bits) in an IP address that identify the type of network connection. The division of the bytes determines the class of the address. IP addresses are often converted from binary format to dotted decimal notation, with each of the 4 bytes converted to the equivalent decimal value from 0 to 255. For example, the address 10001111 01010111 11000111 00100001 converts to the equivalent address of 143.87.199.33. No host address and no network address can consist entirely of bytes with values of 0. The network address of 127 is reserved as a *loopback address* (the message is sent back to the sending process). The final byte in an IP address cannot be 0 or 255.

IP Security Option (IPSO)

A part of the Internet Protocol (IP) that specifies how security levels are defined on a per-interface basis.

IP tunneling

A method used to enable two or more Internetwork Packet Exchange (IPX) networks to exchange IPX packets through an Internet Protocol (IP) internetwork. IP tunneling encapsulates IPX packets in a User Datagram Protocol (UDP) datagram for transmission across the IP internetwork.

IPX address

A network address used in Novell NetWare networks that includes a 4-byte network number, a 6-byte node number, and a 2-byte socket number. The network number is assigned to every segment on the LAN. The node number identifies a specific system and is usually assigned by the manufacturer. The socket number distinguishes processes within one computer.

IPX external network number

A network number used to identify a network cable segment on a NetWare network. The IPX external network is expressed in hexadecimal format, and is between one and eight digits. It is assigned when the Internetwork Packet Exchange (IPX) protocol is bound to a Network Interface Card (NIC) in the server.

IPX internal network number

A network number used to identify a NetWare server. Every server on the network has a unique IPX internal network number. The IPX internal network number is expressed in hexadecimal format and is between one and eight digits.

IPX internetwork address

A 12-byte number used in NetWare networks that is expressed in hexadecimal format and consists of three parts. The first part is 4 bytes and consists of the IPX external network number; the second part is 6 bytes and is a node number; the third part is a 2-byte socket number.

IPX Sockets

A tracked resource that appears as an option in the "Available Options/Resource Utilization" screen of the NetWare 3.12 MONITOR NetWare Loadable Module (NLM). This resource display tracks NLMs that have established a socket connection between two devices, with a different socket handling each type of communication.

isarithmic flow control

A flow-control process that sends permits through a network, the possession of which grants a node the right to transmit information.

IS-IS Interdomain Routing Protocol (IDRP)

An Open Systems Interconnection (OSI) protocol that determines how routers communicate with other routers in different domains.

isochronous

A time-sensitive transmission. Isochronous transmission places a constant time interval between transmissions, regardless of whether they are synchronous or asynchronous. In this manner, asynchronous data can be transmitted over a synchronous link.

Isochronous Media Access Control (IMAC)

A Media-Access Control (MAC) element in the Fiber Distributed Data Interface (FDDI) II architecture. IMAC can accommodate delay-insensitive data, such as voice or video, which is received through a circuit-switched multiplexer.

isoEthernet

The Institute of Electrical and Electronic Engineers (IEEE) 802.9a standard used to transmit delay-insensitive, multimedia traffic over the same wiring used on 10BaseT Ethernet. IsoEthernet uses an encoding scheme common to Fiber Distributed Data Interface (FDDI) to squeeze an extra 6.144 megabits per second (Mbps) of bandwidth out of the 10Mbps 10BaseT connection. This additional bandwidth is used to isolate delay-insensitive traffic from the contention-oriented Ethernet data traffic. IsoEthernet can be deployed using existing cabling and requires a separate isoEthernet hub and isoEthernet network adapter cards.

isolation

A type of power conditioning that protects against noise by using ferroresonant isolation transformers to mitigate voltage irregularities.

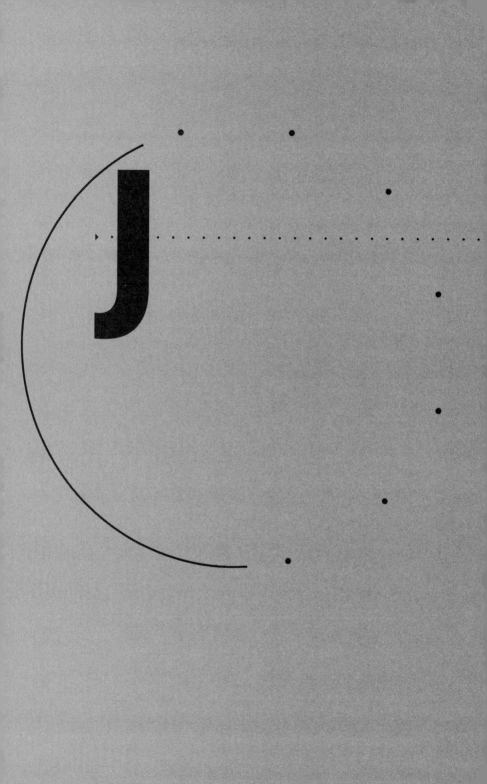

jabber

A meaningless transmission continuously generated by a network device. Jabber is usually the result of a hardware malfunction or user error.

jabber detector

A device that helps to prevent a node from sending continuous and meaningless transmissions in a Carrier Sense Multiple Access/Collision Detection (CSMA/CD) media access network.

jabber packet

An oversized packet (larger than 1,518 bytes) in an Ethernet network that contains a bad CRC (cyclical redundancy check) value. The transmission is meaningless and is usually caused by a hardware malfunction.

jack

A female connector with sockets or slots. A male connector is called a *plug*.

jack in

A term popularized by William Gibson in the novel *Neuromancer* that means to connect to a particular facet of the Internet, to a virtual-reality space, or to an active social information line.

jacket

An outer covering on a cable. The material used to construct this outer covering is a major factor in determining the relative safety of the cable.

jam signal

A signal on an Ethernet network that tells other nodes a packet collision has occurred.

jamming

A radiation in a specific range of frequencies that inhibits or prevents signals in that frequency range from being used. Deliberate jamming is also called *active jamming*; unintentional jamming is also called *passive jamming*.

Japan Standards Association (JSA)

A Japanese equivalent to the American National Standards Institute (ANSI).

Japanese UNIX Network (JUNET)

A Japanese research network used by commercial institutions and organizations.

jargon file

A file containing technical terminology and various idioms inherent to computing.

Java

A programming language released by Sun Microsystems in 1995, used to write general-purpose programs and programs designed to run specifically on the Internet or on intranets. The general-purpose programs (called *Java applications*) can be run standalone. The Internet or intranet programs (called *applets*) must be run from within a Web browser.

Java Development Kit (JDK)

A software development kit (SDK) available from Sun Microsystems that contains development tools to write, test, and debug Java applications and applets.

JavaScript

A Java scripting language from Sun Microsystems and Netscape Communications that facilitates adding interactive features to a Web page.

jitter

A signal variation in timing caused by the constancy of a source clock rate or differences between a source's clock and a receiver's clock. Two types of jitter are *phase jitter* (in which the signal is out of phase) and *amplitude jitter* (in which the amplitude of the signal varies).

Job Control Language (JCL)

A command language providing the required instructions for a specific operating system to run a specific application program.

job server
A server that uses software to manage a network or special-purpose queue of jobs.

Job Transfer and Manipulation (JTM)
A file-transfer service defined in the Application Layer (Layer 7) of the OSI Reference Model and that enables an application to perform data processing on a remote machine.

John Von Neumann Center Network (JVNCnet)
A network in the northeastern United States that provides T1 and slower serial links for midlevel networking services.

Joint Academic Network (JANET)
An X.25 network maintained by academic institutions in Great Britain to provide worldwide electronic mail (e-mail) access through other networks.

Joint Development Agreement (JDA)
A now-defunct agreement between International Business Machines (IBM) and Microsoft Corporation to develop operating system technologies jointly.

Joint Electronic Data Interchange (JEDI)
A task force representing the United Nations in Electronic Data Interchange (EDI) meetings and events.

Joint Photographic Experts Group (JPEG)
An International Standards Organization (ISO)/International Telecommunications Union (ITU) standard that compresses files containing still images. To achieve compression ratio as high as 100:1, JPEG (pronounced *JAY-peg*) first performs a discrete cosine transformation by using frequencies to break down image data. JPEG then quantifies these frequencies to adjust the number of bits used to represent various frequencies (also known as *adjusting the granularity*). JPEG then uses a lossy algorithm (which means the granularity of those frequencies rarely used can be dropped out during the compression) to compress the files.

Joint Technical Committee (JTC)

A committee formed by the International Standards Organization (ISO) and the International Electrotechnical Commission (IEC) to address such issues as the OSI Reference Model.

Jonzy's Universal Gopher Hierarchy Excavation and Display (Jughead)

A program capable of limiting an Internet search to a selection of gopher services by searching only higher-level menus in servers. This search must point to a gopher client on a Jughead server.

journaling

A process that enables fast restarts as needed by logging network system activity.

jukebox

A high-capacity storage device that uses an autochanger to mount and dismount optical disks.

jumbo group

A multichannel telecommunications group that consists of six master groups (collections of a large number of channels). Using 3,600 voice channels, the jumbo group simultaneously transmits over a broadband connection.

jumper

A wire or metal bridge used to close a circuit and establish an electrical connection.

jumper block

A group (also called a *block*) of jumper.

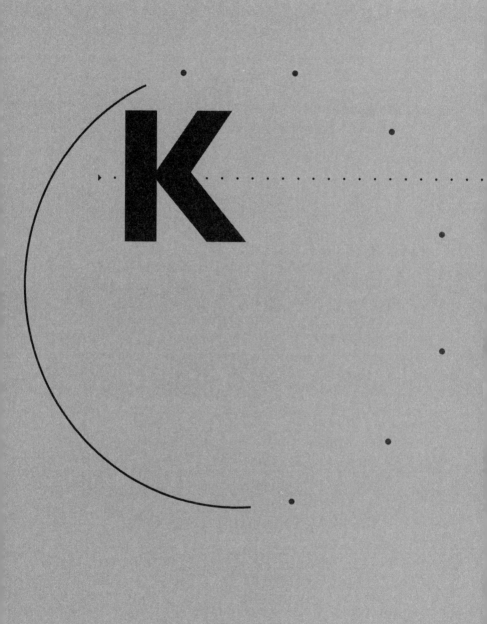

K

An abbreviation for *kilo*, which has a metric equivalent of 1,000. This abbreviation is often combined with other abbreviations in computing, such as *KB* or *Kb*.

k12 newsgroup

A type of newsgroup that discusses topics of interest to elementary through high school students and teachers.

KA9Q

An RFC 1208 specification that implements the Transmission Control Protocol/Internet Protocol (TCP/IP) suite for packet radio systems.

Karn's algorithm

An algorithm improving round-trip time estimations by helping protocols in the OSI Reference Model Transport Layer (Layer 4) distinguish between good and bad round-trip time samples.

keep-alive packet

An Echo Request packet sent to a remote peer, often generating an Echo Response packet being sent back from the remote peer. This is a continuous test at the access interface that is sent at a specified time period.

Kerberos

A network security system that verifies a user is legitimate when logging in to a network and when requesting a service from the network. Using private key encryption methods, Kerberos encrypts transmissions between Kerberos and a user by using special keys called *tickets*. This system was designed at the Massachusetts Institute of Technology (MIT) to provide authentication for users accessing a network from an unattended workstation.

Kermit

A file-transfer protocol commonly used on Bulletin Board Systems (BBSs).

kernel

The core portion of an operating system responsible for managing system resources.

key

A group (or multiple groups) of bytes characterized by physical location in a database record. A key provides the access to a data value and provides a means of sorting database records. In encryption, a key is a conversion algorithm and predefined bit value used to decipher text encrypted in an unreadable form (known as *ciphertext*). The simplest type of encryption uses a single key, and the recipient must know both the encryption algorithm and the key to decrypt the message. *Private-key encryption* uses a private key, which only the sender and recipient know, and a public encryption algorithm. *Public key encryption*, on the other hand, uses two halves of a bit sequence, each one constituting a key: One key is placed in an accessible public-key library; the other key is only known to an individual.

key combination

A combination of keystrokes that provides keyboard access to menu commands. A key combination enables the user to bypass using a mouse to select from menus and may speed user interface with an application program.

K

Key Distribution Center (KDC)

A center responsible for storing, managing, and distributing encryption keys.

Key Management Protocol (KMP)

A protocol used to check security keys in a secure network.

key redefinition

The assignment of different functions to specific keys by an application program.

Key Telephone System (KTS)

An arrangement of multiline telephones that enables users to access a central office or Private Branch Exchange (PBX) by pressing keys. Users can put a caller on hold, call or answer a selected line, talk over an intercom, or transfer calls to another line.

keyboard buffer
Computer system memory used to store the most recently typed keys on a keyboard.
Synonym: *type-ahead buffer*

Keyboard Send and Receive (KSR)
A communication device consisting of a printer and a keyboard. The KSR prints messages as they are received and transmits messages as they are typed at the keyboard.

keyboard template
A plastic overlay fitting over the keys of a keyboard to help a novice user learn the functions of certain keys that are specific to an application program.

keying
The asymmetrical shaping of a component to ensure it is connected properly to another component. A common example of keying is modular telephone jacks.

keystroke information
Information appearing at the bottom of a screen in a DOS menu utility that provides information about the keys available to the user when accessing information on the screen.

keywords
Designated words or terms in a programming language or operating system reserved for particular functions or operations.
Synonym: *reserved words*

kill file
A data file designed to filter out Internet news postings or electronic mail (e-mail) from certain persons or about certain topics.

killer channel
A digital telecommunications channel that overlaps and interferes with other channels because its timing is off.

kilobaud

A unit of measure equaling 1,000 baud.

kilobit (Kbit)

A unit of measure equaling 2^{10} (or 1,024) bits.

kilobits per second (kbit/s)

A unit of measure equaling 2^{10} (or 1,024) bits of data being transferred to and from peripheral devices every second.

kilobyte (KB or K)

A unit of measure equaling 2^{10} (or 1,024) bytes, most commonly used in the context of computer memory or disk storage capacity.

kilobytes per second (kbyte/s, Kbps)

A unit of measure equaling 2^{10} (or 1,024) bytes of data being transferred to and from peripheral devices every second.

Knowbot

A program that tracks down information. This is a combination of the term *knowledge robot*.

Knowbot Information Services (KIS)

An Internet service that queries directory services to retrieve requested information.

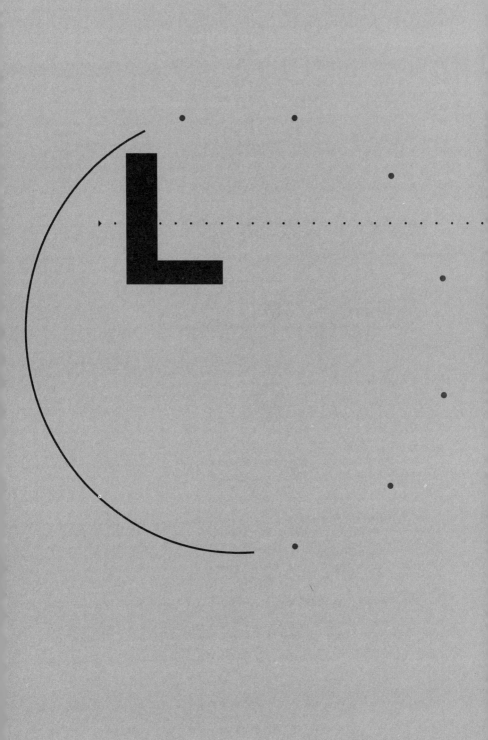

L Multiplex (LMX)
A hierarchy of telecommunications channel groupings representing a group, super group, master group, and jumbo group.

LAN adapter
A circuit board installed on each local area network (LAN) workstation that enables the workstations to communicate with each other and with NetWare servers.

LAN Automation Option (LANAO)
An optional add-on to NetView that simplifies the management of one or more Token Ring networks in the IBM Network Management Architecture (NMA).

LAN Bridge Server (LBS)
A Token Ring network server that tracks and provides access to any bridges connected to the network.

LAN driver
A software component that serves as a link between a server's or a workstation's operating system and the physical parts of a local area network (LAN). Written to the Open Data-Link Interface (ODI) specification, LAN drivers in NetWare 4.x connect directly to the ODI model's Link Support Layer (LSL), which serves as an intermediary between the drivers and communication protocols.

LAN interface board
An interface board installed on each local area network (LAN) workstation that enables the workstations to communicate with each other and with NetWare servers.

LAN inventory package
A software program that automatically creates an inventory of the components and configurations on a local area network (LAN), and then updates the inventory when changes are made to the network.

LAN Manager

A Microsoft server-based network operating system that supports various low-level network architectures (such as ARCnet, Ethernet, and Token Ring). LAN Manager has not been updated since the introduction of Windows NT and Windows NT Advanced Server.

LAN Manager for UNIX (LMU)

A Microsoft server-based network operating system that supports the UNIX operating system.

LAN Network Manager (LNM)

A Systems Application Architecture (SAA) compliant IBM product that manages Token Ring networks by using both the Common Management Information Protocol (CMIP) and the Simple Network Management Protocol (SNMP). While running under OS/2, LNM can act as an entry point for NetView.

LAN Server

IBM's server-based network operating system, based on Microsoft's LAN Manager, which supports servers running in the OS/2 environment.

LAN Traffic Monitor (LTM)

A device that monitors the traffic activity in a local area network (LAN) system.

LAN Workgroup

A server-based connectivity package from Novell that provides NetWare users with transparent access to networked Transmission Control Protocol/Internet Protocol (TCP/IP) resources from their workstations. Features include transparent file sharing, terminal emulation, remote command execution, remote printing, network information utilities, and support for all standard application programming interfaces.

LAN WorkPlace

A desktop connectivity package from Novell that provides concurrent access to Transmission Control Protocol/Internet Protocol (TCP/IP), NetWare, and Internet resources. Features include terminal emulation, graphical file transfer, transparent Network File System (NFS) file sharing, and Netscape Navigator.

LAN/MAN Management Protocol

A local area network (LAN) protocol that provides Common Management Information Service/Common Management Information Protocol (CMIS/CMIP) network management services by implementing them directly into the Logical-Link Control (LLC) sublayer of the Data-Link Layer of the OSI Reference Model. Because it provides Application-Layer (Layer 7) services and bypasses the intervening four layers to use LLC services, LLMP cannot use routers. The original name of this protocol was CMIS/CMIP over LLC (CMOL).

Synonym: *CMOL*

LANalyzer

A software-only network analysis product from Novell that monitors traffic on an Ethernet or Token Ring segment, and then stores information about the segment and each station attached to it. The analysis is often used for planning network growth, monitoring and optimizing network performance, and troubleshooting network problems.

land line

Telephone lines relying on transmissions across wires and cables, as opposed to transmissions via satellite.

language enabling

A process during the internationalization of NetWare that involves isolating message strings (such as error messages and menu items) from the source code and placing them in Language Modules. One of the most valuable uses of language enabling is the capability of retrieving program messages in one of any number of languages at run time.

Language Identification Number (LIN)

A number assigned to non-English versions of NetWare Loadable Modules (NLMs) as a means of identification.

LANstep

A peer-to-peer networking environment from Hayes Microcomputer Products that distributes network services over one or more nondedicated servers. Through a centralized database of available services called LANstep Smart Directory Services, users may access a service by name without having to specify the location of the server providing the services. Although it provides its own operating system, LANstep does allow DOS and Windows applications to execute.

LANtastic

A peer-to-peer operating system from Artisoft that supports networks ranging in size from two nodes to a few hundred nodes. All stations on the network can share files with all other stations or the configuration can be set so one personal computer acts as a dedicated file server. The system runs as a DOS process and uses the DOS file system, but can provide limited multitasking in some configurations.

laptop computer

A battery-operated, portable computer with a flat screen and keyboard that fold together. Some models are equipped with hardware that enables the user to plug the laptop into a desktop computer system.

Large Internet Packet (LIP)

A functionality that increases the size of internetwork packets beyond 576 bytes. Prior to NetWare 4.0, when the workstation initiated a negotiation with the NetWare server and the server detected a router between it and the workstation, the server limited the packet size to 576 bytes. With the introduction of NetWare 4.0 and subsequent versions, LIP enabled the workstation to determine the packet size on the basis of maximum size supported by the router. The larger packet size is supported by Ethernet and Token Ring networks.

Large Internet Packet Exchange (LIPX)

A process that enables larger packet sizes to increase throughput on networks.

Laser Prep file

A file containing a dictionary of PostScript shorthand commands used by the LaserWriter driver on the Macintosh, which downloads the file to initialize the printer before sending a print job. Usually the Macintosh operating system handles this task transparently.

laser transmission

A wireless communications technique in which laser beams of light are transmitted in pulses over a narrow path to a receiver, which translates the pulses into bits. This type of transmission offers high bandwidths and is not subjected to interference or jamming.

Last In, First Out (LIFO)

A programming queuing strategy in which the element added most recently ("last in") is the element removed first ("first out").

last mile

A telephony term used to describe the link between a customer's site and the local telephone company's central office, often the most expensive and least efficient stretch in a telephone company's cabling system.

LASTDRIVE

A DOS command used in the CONFIG.SYS file to specify the maximum number of drives that can be accessed on a computer system, a number often set by networking software.

latency

The amount of time before a requested network or communications channel is available for transmission or the amount of time required for a transmission to reach its destination.

layer

A group of related capabilities or services that build upon each other in an operating, communications, or networking environment. Through a communications process of well-defined interfaces, each layer provides services to the layer above it and uses services of the layers below it. Layers communicate across machines by using a predefined protocol (such as

TCP/IP). However, the communication takes place only at the lowest-level layer on each machine, and then is spread upward to the appropriate layers. Each layer expects to receive certain services from the layer beneath it and provides certain services to the layer above it.

Layer Management Entity (LME)

A mechanism by which the seven layers in the OSI Reference Model can communicate with each other to exchange information and to access management elements at different layers.

Synonym: *hook*

leaf object

A NetWare object that resides at the bottom of the Novell Directory Services (NDS) tree and does not contain any other objects. Certain properties are associated with each type of leaf object and differentiate the various leaf object classes. Table L.1 shows the seven categories of leaf objects supported by IntranetWare and the objects included in those categories.

TABLE L.1	Leaf Objects
LEAF OBJECT CATEGORY	**OBJECTS INCLUDED**
User	User
	User Template
	Group
	Organizational Role
	Profile
Server	NetWare Server
	Volume
	Directory Map
Printer	Printer
	Print Queue
Messaging	Messaging Server
	Message Routing Group
	Distribution List
	External Entity

(continued)

T A B L E L.I	*Leaf Objects (continued)*
LEAF OBJECT CATEGORY	**OBJECTS INCLUDED**
Network Services	Application Auditing File License Service Provider
Informational	AFP Server Computer
Miscellaneous	Alias Unknown Bindery Bindery Queue

leaf site
A computer that receives newsfeeds from Usenet groups on the Internet, but does not pass these feeds on to other computers.

learning router
A router's interface configured to learn its configuration from a configured router on the same network.
Synonym: *non-seed router*

leased line
A communications line leased on a monthly basis from a Public Data Network (PDN) vendor.

Least-Cost Routing (LCR)
A feature of a private branch exchange (PBX) telephone system that selects the most economical path to a destination.

Least Recently Used (LRU)
A file-migration algorithm allowing files that have not been accessed during the longest period of time to be transferred first.

least-significant bit (LSB)

A bit corresponding to the lowest order of two (2^0) in a bit sequence, whose location depends on the context and on the ordering within a word.

legacy wiring

Wiring that has been installed in a business or residence before the installation of a network system.

level 1 routing

An interaction of routers within the same routing area.

level 2 routing

An interaction of routers between established routing areas within an organization that forms a *routing domain* controlled by a single administrative unit.

level 3 routing

An interaction of routers between routing domains controlled by different administrative units.

library NLM applications

A collection of NetWare Loadable Module (NLM) applications that export functions that can be called by other NLM applications.

License Service Provider (LSP) object

In IntranetWare, a leaf object created when a License Service Provider (LSP) is registered with Novell Directory Services (NDS) to represent a server that has loaded the NetWare Licensing Services (NLS) NetWare Loadable Module (NLM). The NLS NLM enables administrators to track and control the use of licensed applications on the network.

lifetime

A representation of the length of time a particular value, feature, or link should be considered valid.

Light-Emitting Diode (LED)

A semiconductor device that converts electrical energy into light. This device is commonly used in calculator displays and as "activity lights" on computers and modems.

light-wave communication

A term describing fiber-optic cables and light generated by Light-Emitting Diodes (LEDs) or lasers.

Lightweight Presentation Protocol (LPP)

A Presentation-Layer (Layer 6 of the OSI Reference Model) protocol for use in the Common Management Information Protocol (CMIP) over TCP/IP (or CMOT) network management scheme. The CMOT scheme was never completed.

Lightweight Protocol

A high-speed internetwork protocol that combines routing and transport services in a more streamlined fashion than traditional Network Layer (Layer 3 of the OSI Reference Model) or Transport Layer (Layer 4) protocols. This protocol uses fixed header and trailer sizes, a more efficient checksum and error-correction method, error checking at endpoints (rather than after each transmission), and connection-oriented transmissions. The overall effect of these features is a faster transmission of data.

Limited-Distance Data Service (LDDS)

A class of telecommunications service that provides digital transmission capabilities over short distances through the use of line drivers instead of modems.

Limited-Distance Modem (LDM)

A short-haul modem designed for high-speed transmissions of more than 1 megabit per second (Mbps) over distances of less than 20 miles.
See also **short-haul modem**

limited resource link

A resource defined by a device operator to remain active only when the resource is being used.

line

A circuit, channel, or link that carries signals for data or voice communications.

line adapter

A communications device designed to convert a digital signal into a form suitable for transmission over a communications channel.

line analyzer

A device used to troubleshoot and monitor load by displaying information about a transmission on a communications channel.

line card

A card that serves as an interface between a communications line and a device.

line circuit

A circuit that determines whether a telephone line is on-hook or off-hook and handles the call origination and termination of the calls.

line conditioner

A device that minimizes voltage-supply fluctuations, detects reversed polarity, detects a missing ground, and detects an overloaded neutral wire.

Synonyms: *voltage regulator, power conditioner, line stabilizer/line conditioner (LS/LC)*

Line Control Register (LCR)

A register in a universal asynchronous receiver/transmitter (UART) that specifies a parity type.

line driver

A communications hardware device that extends the transmission range between computers connected on a leased line. The line driver, which includes a transmitter and a receiver, is used for digital communications. One line driver is required at each end of the communications line.

line group

A term describing multiple telephone lines that can be activated or deactivated as a group.

line hit

A brief burst of interference on an electrical transmission line.

Line Insulation Test (LIT)

A test to check telephone lines automatically for short circuits, grounds, and interference.

line level

The power (measured in decibels) of an electrical signal at a particular point in the transmission path.

line load

A percentage of capacity usage a telephone line gets at a particular time.

line monitor

A telecommunications device that can record and display all transmissions on the line to which it is attached.

Line Printer Daemon (LPD)

A UNIX daemon program that controls printing from a machine or network by knowing to which printer or print queue it is sending a job and by making necessary adjustments.

line-sharing device

A multiplexing device that provides the capability for two or more devices to share the same communications line.

line speed

The transmission speed a telephone line supports at a given Grade Of Service (GOS).

line status
A setting that indicates whether a telephone is on-hook or off-hook.

line-termination equipment
Line cards, modems, multiplexers, hubs, and concentrators that can be used to send telecommunications signals.

line trace
A networking service that logs all activity for later examination and analysis.

Line Turnaround (LTA)
The amount of time in half-duplex communications that it takes to set the line to reverse the transmission direction.

Linear Predictive Coding (LPC)
A voice-encoding algorithm used in narrowband transmissions of secure telephone units (STU-III) that can produce a digitized voice signal at 2,400 bits per second (bps).

line-of-sight communications
A communications process in which a signal from one location is transmitted to another location through the open air without reflection off a satellite or off the Earth.

link
A channel or line (usually a point-to-point line) on a network. In the context of NetWare Link Services Protocol (NLSP), a link is a pointer to Designated Router pseudonode.

Link Access Procedure (LAP)
A bit-oriented, data-link-level protocol from the Consultative Committee for International Telegraphy and Telephony (CCITT), used for communications between devices designated as Data Communications Equipment (DCE) and Data Terminal Equipment (DTE).

Link Access Procedure Balanced (LAPB) Protocol

A bit-oriented, data-link protocol from the Consultative Committee for International Telegraphy and Telephony (CCITT) used to link terminals and computers to packet-switched networks. This protocol is similar to the Synchronous Data-Link Control (SDLC) protocol and is equivalent to the High-Level Data Link Control (HDLC) asynchronous balanced mode.

Link Access Procedure, D Channel (LAPD)

A bit-oriented, data-link protocol from the Consultative Committee for International Telegraphy and Telephony (CCITT) used on the Integrated Services Digital Network (ISDN) D channel.

link connection

Equipment used to provide two-way communication from one link station and to other link stations.

Link Control Protocol (LCP)

Procedures for establishing, configuring, testing, and terminating the operation of data-link connections. LCP also automates the configuration of serial links for bridges and routers over wide area networks (WANs).

link driver

Software that provides an interface between a Network Interface Card (NIC) and the operating system of a computer. The link driver is specific to the type of NIC installed on the computer.

Link Layer

A shortened name sometimes used to refer to the Data-Link Layer (Layer 2) of the OSI Reference Model.

link level

A part of the Consultative Committee for International Telegraphy and Telephony (CCITT) X.25 standard that defines the link protocol. The CCITT recommends the Link Access Procedure (LAP) and Link Access Procedure Balanced (LAPB) protocols.

Link Service Access Point (LSAP)

A Service Access Point (SAP) in the Logical-Link Control (LLC) sublayer of the Data-Link Layer (Layer 2) in the OSI Reference Model.

Link Services Layer (LSL)

A component of the Open Data Link Interface (ODI) model responsible for routing packets between local area network (LAN) boards that use varied multiple-link interface drivers (MLIDs) and protocol stacks.

Link-State Packet (LSP)

In a NetWare Link Services Protocol (NLSP) network, a link-state protocol packet that contains information about all the connections for a router (including information about all neighbors for that packet), broadcast to all other routers in the internetwork.

link-state protocol

A routing protocol under which a router sends information on the state of all its packets to all nodes of the internetwork, thereby reducing routing loops and network traffic. However, this approach does require more memory than the distance vector algorithm.

link-state router

A router that sends a packet containing information about all its links to all link state routers on the network, which use this information to build the network map. The network is said to have "converged" when all link-state routers have the same map of the network.

link-state routing algorithm

An algorithm that builds and maintains a logical map of a network system.

link station

A combination of hardware and software that enables a node to attach to, and provide control for, a link. The two types of link stations are a *primary link station* and a *secondary link station*.

link station address

The sending and receiving addresses for network nodes. Although each sending address must be unique, multiple receiving addresses may be associated with each node.

Link Support Layer (LSL)

An intermediary between drivers for the server or router on a local area network (LAN) and the communications protocols. A component of Novell's Open Data-Link Interface (ODI) specification, the LSL is an intermediate layer between the network interface card's LAN driver and the protocol stacks. The LSL is responsible for directing packets from the LAN driver to the appropriate protocol stack or from any of the available protocol stacks to the LAN driver.

link-level protocol

A set of rules and procedures defining communications methods over a channel, circuit, or link.

Linux

A clone of the UNIX operating system that is a multiuser, multitasking environment designed to work on Intel 386, 486, and Pentium computer systems. Unlike other versions of UNIX, Linux is capable of coexisting with DOS.

liquid crystal display (LCD)

A type of screen display in which electric current is applied to align electrodes surrounding rod-shaped crystals in a special liquid. As current is applied, the orientation of the electrodes changes to produce dark areas on the screen display. This technology is common for portable computers.

list box

A section of a screen display in a graphical utility window that contains a list of items from which to choose.

List object

In IntranetWare, an object that represents an unordered set of object names in the Novell Directory Services (NDS) Directory tree, which enables the user to group other objects logically.

Listen Before Talk (LBT)

A fundamental rule for the Carrier Sense Multiple Access/Collision Detect (CSMA/CD) media-access method. LBT requires that when a node has a packet to send on to the network, it must first listen for a special signal indicating the network is in use. If no such signal is detected, the node can begin transmitting.

Listen While Talk (LWT)

A fundamental rule for the Carrier Sense Multiple Access/Collision Detect (CSMA/CD) media-access method. LWT requires that when a node has a packet to send on to the network, it must first listen for a special signal indicating the network is in use, and it must continue to listen, even while transmitting.

LISTSERV

A group of computer programs that automatically manages mailing lists, distributes messages posted to the list, and adds or deletes members.

little-endian

A term that describes the order in which a word's individual bytes are stored. A little-endian system stores low-order bytes at the lower addresses. Computers with Intel processors (such as the 80286, 80386, and 80486), as well as VAX and PDP-11 computers, use the little-endian system.

load balancing

A scheme that distributes network traffic among parallel paths, providing redundancy while efficiently using available bandwidth.

load sharing

A process in which two or more remote bridges share their traffic load in a parallel configuration, so if one bridge fails, traffic can be routed to the next parallel bridge.

loadable module

A program that is loaded and unloaded from a server or workstation while the operating system is running. Two common types of loadable modules are NetWare Loadable Modules (NLMs) and Virtual Loadable Modules (VLMs).

loading

A process during which NetWare Loadable Modules (NLMs) are linked to the NetWare operating system and system resources are allocated to the NLMs.

loading coil

A device attached to copper cabling that reduces distortion of analog signals. Transmitting digital signals across copper cables is impossible when loading coils are attached.

lobe

A synonym for *node* in the context of Token Ring networks.
Synonym: *node*

Lobe-Attachment Module (LAM)

A Token Ring network box that has multiple interfaces to which as many as 20 lobes (or nodes) can be attached. A LAM is functionally similar to a Multistation Attachment Unit (MAU), although the MAU can have only eight lobes attached. When a LAM is daisy-chained and connected to a Controlled Access Unit (CAU), each CAU can handle as many as 4 LAMs, which yields a potential for 80 lobes.

local

A term used to describe a communications device that can be accessed directly (as opposed to through a communications line), an information-processing operation performed by a computer not installed in a remote location, or a programming variable used in only one part of a program (such as in a subroutine).

Local Access and Transport Area (LATA)

A geographical and administrative area for which a local telephone company is responsible.

local acknowledgment

The process of an intermediate network node terminating a Data-Link Layer (Layer 2 of the OSI Reference Model) session for an end host. Local acknowledgments reduce network overhead.

local area network (LAN)

A system in which personal computers and electronic office equipment are linked together (usually with a wiring-based cabling scheme) within a small area to form a network. Users can then communicate with each other, share resources (such as data storage and printers), and access remote computers or other networks. In a *server-based LAN*, a dedicated server is connected to various workstations, which request services from the server. The network operating system (which determines higher-level protocols and available services) augments the operating system on the workstations, so the server then controls access to some of the network resources. In a *peer-to-peer-based* (or simply *peer-based*) *LAN*, each node in the network can initiate actions, access other nodes, and provide services for other nodes without first acquiring permission from the server. The network operating system often runs under the native operating system of the individual workstations. The *physical topology* of the LAN determines the cabling scheme used to physically connect the nodes of the networks. The *logical topology* of the LAN determines how information is passed from one node to the others on the network.

Local Automatic Message Accounting (LAMA)

An accounting method used by a local telephone company to generate automatic billing for local and toll calls. The method requires the Automatic Number Identification (ANI) capability.

local bridge

A bridge directly interconnecting networks in the same geographical area.

local bus

A 32-bit path directly connecting the central processing unit (CPU) to memory, video, and disk controllers in an IBM (or compatible) personal computer. Local bus architecture allows the transfer of data from the CPU to memory, video, and disk controllers (and vice versa) at the speed of the CPU. This represents an improvement over older bus architectures in which microprocessor speeds outpaced internal bus speeds, slowing the computer and creating a narrow data stream in and out of the CPU. Local-bus architecture is found in Peripheral Component Interconnect (PCI) and Video Electronics Standards Association (VESA) buses.

local carrier

A company that provides local communications connections or long distance connections through an Interexchange Carrier (IXC).
Synonym: *Local Exchange Carrier (LEC)*

Local Channel (LC)

A digital telecommunications link between a customer's site and the central office of the telephone company.

Local Common Gateway Interface (LCGI)

A feature that enables the NetWare Web Server to modify Web pages before sending them to a browser.

local disk

A disk attached to a network workstation rather than to a file server.

local drive

A storage device physically contained in, or attached to, a workstation.
Synonym: *physical drive*

local drive mapping

A path to local media (such as a hard disk drive and floppy disk drives). Some versions of DOS, for example, reserve drives A: through E: for local drive mappings.

Local Exchange Carrier (LEC)

A company that provides local communications connections or long-distance connections through an Interexchange Carrier (IXC).

local group

A Windows NT Advanced Server group that has rights and permissions granted to only the resources of a server in the group's domain.

Local Injection/Detection (LID)

In fiber optics, a device used to align fibers when splicing them together.

local loop

The portion of a communications circuit connecting subscriber equipment to equipment in a local telephone exchange or a local telephone company's central office.

Local Management Interface (LMI)

An interface specification that provides for the exchange of management-related information between a network and a hardware device.

local name

A name known only to a single server or domain in an internetwork or in a network.

Local Network Interconnect (LNI)

A concentrator that supports multiple devices or communications controllers, whether standalone or attached to Ethernet cable.

local printer

A printer attached directly to a port on a network's print server.

local semaphore

An interprocess communication signal between NetWare Loadable Module (NLM) applications running on a single server. Such signals control resources, synchronize thread execution, and queue threads. A local semaphore differs from a *network semaphore*, which applies resources available to servers and workstations on the network.

local transaction program

An application program in a Systems Network Architecture (SNA) network that performs transactions with one or more programs at the logical unit.

Local Area Network Reference Model (LAN/RM)

A description of a local area network (LAN) as defined by 802.*x* specification set of the Institute of Electrical and Electronic Engineers (IEEE).

Local Area Transport (LAT)

A protocol from Digital Equipment Corporation (DEC) that provides for high-speed, asynchronous communication among hosts and terminal servers on an Ethernet network.

Locality (L) object

A NetWare container object that defines geographic locations in the Novell Directory Services (NDS) Directory tree. Because this object is not currently enabled by Novell's NWADMIN or NETADMIN utilities, it is not visible through the current utilities. However, third-party programs are available to define and view this class.

localization

The preparation of hard-copy and online documentation to be used in locations that use non-English languages.

localization toolkit

A package containing the tools third-party vendors need for translating NetWare into non-English versions.

Locally Administered Address (LAA)

A parameter used by a 3174 controller to determine whether a node can access a mainframe computer connected to a Token Ring network.

LocalTalk Link Access Protocol (LLAP)

A link-access protocol found in the AppleTalk suite of protocols and used in LocalTalk networks.

LocalTalk network

A proprietary network architecture from Apple Computer, Inc., consisting of a system of twisted-pair cables, cable extenders, and connectors (DB-9, DIN-8, or DIN-3) that connects computers and network devices to create an AppleTalk network. Using Carrier Sense Multiple Access/Collision Avoidance (CSMA/CA) and the LocalTalk Link Access Protocol (LLAP), up to 255 nodes can be separated by up to 1,000 feet. LocalTalk operates at the Data-Link Layer (Layer 2) and Physical Layer (Layer 1) of the OSI Reference Model.

locked file

A file whose attributes have been set so the file may be opened and read, but not written to, deleted, or changed in any way.

locking

A process to ensure two network users or programs cannot try to access the same data simultaneously. An *advisory lock* issues a warning and can be overridden. A *physical lock* is a control mechanism that cannot be overwritten. With a *file lock*, a file server prevents users from accessing any part of a file, while another user is accessing the same file. With a *record lock*, a file server prevents users from accessing a record in a file, while another user is accessing the same record. With a *logical lock*, logical units (LUs) in a file are inaccessible. With a *physical lock*, sectors or groups of sectors on a hard disk are inaccessible.

log in

The act of entering a username and password to gain access to a network system, such as the Novell Directory Services (NDS) Directory tree or a NetWare server.

Synonym: *log on*

log out

The act of terminating a session on a network system by sending a terminating message or command. The system may respond with informational messages, such as the total resources consumed during the session or the total time between logging in and logging out.

Synonym: *log off*

logical address

A network or node address assigned during installation of a network or addition of a workstation. The installation software assigns a logical address; the hardware manufacturer assigns a hardware address.

logical channel

A mechanism that allows multiple, simultaneous virtual circuits (VCs) across one physical link on a network.

Logical Channel Number (LCN)
A unique number assigned to each virtual circuit (VC) and attached to each packet in a call. The LCN differentiates the packet from other packets generated by users issuing other calls.

logical device name
A name used by the operating system to identify a DOS device.

logical drive
An internal representation used by an operating system to refer to an actual disk device or to a group of directories specified by the DOS SUBST command.

Logical Link Control Type 2 (LLC2)
A protocol and packet format commonly used in Systems Network Architecture (SNA) networks and more widely supported than the Synchronous Data Link Control (SDLC) protocol.

logical memory
Memory that appears contiguous to NetWare 4.x processes, but that may not have contiguous addresses.

logical number
A number assigned by a software installation program to a hardware device. This logical number assignment is made according to such conditions as which other devices are attached to the network and the order in which those devices were attached.

logical partition
A part of a NetWare or IntranetWare physical partition, measured from the beginning of a data area to the end of that same data area.

logical ring
A network that may be cabled physically as a star topology, but is treated logically as a ring topology.

logical topology

A network's logical layout that specifies which path information takes through a network, how the information is transmitted, and how the elements in the network communicate with each other. The two most common types of logical topology are *bus* and *ring*.

logical unit (LU)

A terminal-emulation program or application in a Systems Network Architecture (SNA) network that can communicate with host systems and applications (Type 0, 1, 2, 3, 4, or 7) or with other logical units of the same type (Type 6.0, 6.1, or 6.2).

logical unit Type 6.2

An architectural base for Advanced Program-to-Program Communications (APPC) that supports sessions between two applications in a Distributed Data Processing (DDP) environment.

Logical-Link Control (LLC)

A sublayer in the Local Area Network Reference Model (LAN/RM) that provides an interface and services for the network-layer protocols, and mediates between the higher-level protocols and lower media-access protocols. The LLC resides above the Media Access Control (MAC) sublayer and, when combined, the LLC and MAC sublayers are equivalent to the Data Link Layer (Layer 2) of the OSI Reference Model. The LLC is similar to the Synchronous Data Link Control (SDLC) link-layer protocol.

login

A procedure of entering a username and password to gain access to a network system, such as the Novell Directory Services (NDS) Directory tree or a NetWare server.

login name

A unique name that each user is required to use at login to identify the user.

login restrictions

A set of restrictions on user accounts that control access to the network. In NetWare, login restrictions include a password requirement, account limits, disk space limits, a limited number of connections allowed, and time limits.

login script

A NetWare file containing a list of commands that organize a user's network environment when issued by the user upon logging in to the network. Login scripts can map drives, display messages, set environment variables, and execute programs or menus. *Container login scripts,* which are assigned to Container objects, execute first and set general environments for all users in a container. *Profile login scripts,* assigned to Profile objects, execute after container login scripts and set environments for multiple users. *User login scripts,* assigned to User objects, set environments specific to a single user (such as menu options) and execute after Container and Profile login scripts.

login security

A system that controls initial access to the network and provides continued verification of the identity of the user.

logout

A procedure that terminates access to a network system by breaking the network connection and deleting drives mapped to the network.

Long Fat Network (LFN)

A long-distance network that has bandwidths of several hundred megabits per second, which can cause performance and packet-loss problems with Transmission Control Protocol/Internet Protocol (TCP/IP).

long machine type

A six-letter name that represents a DOS machine brand in NetWare (for example, IBM_PC for an IBM computer). The same long machine type name is used as a subdirectory name when more than one brand of workstation is used (for example, IBM_PC subdirectory for IBM workstations and COMPAQ subdirectory for COMPAQ workstations). If more than one version of DOS is used at various workstations, separate subdirectories must be created for each machine type.

long-haul carrier

A description of the cabling and signaling specifications for a carrier system responsible for long-distance telecommunications signals. Coaxial cabling and analog signaling are characteristics of this carrier; they provide tremendous capacity, but are expensive to use.

long-haul microwave communications

Microwave transmissions over distances of 25 to 30 miles.

long-haul modem

A communications device capable of transmitting information over long distances.

Look-Ahead Queuing

In telephony, an automatic call-distribution feature that involves a secondary queue checking for congestion before traffic is switched to it.

Look-Back Queuing

In telephony, an automatic call-distribution feature that involves a secondary queue checking to see whether congestion on a primary queue has cleared so calls can be returned to the primary queue.

loop

A circuit between a customer's location and a telephone company's central office.

loop timing

In digital communications, a synchronization method that extracts timing information from incoming pulses.

loopback

A diagnostic test that transmits a signal across a medium, while the sending device waits for the return of the signal.

loopback mode

An operating mode that allows testing of a line by sending a signal back to its origin, instead of sending it on to a destination.

loopback plug

A special connector used to perform echo testing.

Loose Source and Record Route (LSRR)

An Internet Protocol (IP) option that enables a datagram's source to specify routing information and to record the datagram route. This option is used as a security measure because it ensures datagrams travel over only those routes that have a level of security commensurate with that of the datagram.

loss

A disappearance of a packet or call during transmission. Loss sometimes occurs during periods of heavy network traffic or because of an addressing error.

loss budget

A combination of all the factors contributing to the loss of a signal between the source and destination.

lossless compression

A data-compression method that rearranges or recodes data in a more compact fashion, in such a way that no data is lost when the file is decompressed.

lossy compression

A data-compression method that discards any data the compression mechanism decides is not needed, which results in the loss of some original data when the file is decompressed.

Lost Calls Cleared (LCC)

A call-handling method in which blocked calls are lost or discarded.

Lost Calls Delayed (LCD)

A call-handling method in which blocked calls are queued for later processing or are delayed.

Lotus-Intel-Microsoft Specifications (LIMS)

A specification that calls for the allocation of expanded memory on special chips, and then maps the expanded memory into 16K pages allocated in the area of system memory between 640K and 1MB. This specification was originally developed by a joint consortium of Lotus, Intel, and Microsoft to work around a restriction on 8086 computers, which could not operate in protected mode because more memory was needed to access addresses above 1MB.

Low-Bit-Rate Voice (LBRV)

A digitized voice signal sent at a transmission speed below a channel capacity of 64,000 bits per second.

low-end

An inexpensive product from the lower end of a company's product list. Such products usually have limited capabilities and features.

Low-Entry Networking (LEN)

A term describing IBM's peer-to-peer configuration for Systems Network Architecture (SNA) networks.

lower memory

The lowest portion of conventional memory, in which the operating system and installable device drivers are commonly loaded.

low-level language

A programming language (such as assembly language) that is close to machine language.

low-level protocol

A protocol at the Physical Layer (Layer 1) or Data Link Layer (Layer 2) of the OSI Reference Model.

low-speed modem
A modem that operates at speeds of 600 bits per second (bps) or less.

LPT
The logical name that DOS assigns to a line printer connected to a personal computer through parallel printer ports.

L-to-T Connector
A telecommunications component used to connect two (analog) frequency division multiplexing (FDM) groups into a single (digital) Time-Division Multiplexing (TDM) group.

lurking
Listening in on a network or internetwork discussion by a user forum, special-interest group, or newsgroup, without participating.

MI3

A telecommunications method used to multiplex 28 T1 channels into 1 T3 channel.

MAC Convergence Function (MCF)

A Distributed-Queue Dual Bus (DQDB) network function that prepares data from a connectionless service.

MacBinary

A Macintosh file-transfer protocol that ensures the proper transmission of Macintosh files over a modem.

Mach

A variation of the UNIX operating system that supports multitasking and multiprocessing. Mach was the first operating system to use a microkernel as an alternative to the traditional operating system kernel.

machine language

A native binary language used internally by a computer. Machine language is the result of high-level programming code being assembled, compiled, or interpreted into a format the computer uses to process instructions.

Macintosh

A personal computer from Apple Computer, Inc., which features a user-friendly graphical user interface (GUI) and uses a proprietary operating system to simulate the user's desktop onscreen display. Because all but the earliest models of the Macintosh have built-in networking capabilities, no Network Interface Card (NIC) or adapters are required.

Synonym: *Mac*

Macintosh client

A Macintosh computer that has been attached to a NetWare for Macintosh network. Using AppleTalk, a Macintosh client can store data on and retrieve data from a NetWare for Macintosh server. A Macintosh client is capable of running executable network files, sharing files with other clients, and monitoring queues.

Macintosh File System (MFS)

A system for storing Macintosh files in a flat structure common on early models of the Macintosh computer. Newer models use a hierarchical file structure, but they can still read disks created with the flat-file structure.

Macintosh files

Macintosh computer files that contain a data fork (information specified by the user) and a resource fork (file information, including Macintosh-specific information, such as the windows and icons used with the file). Macintosh clients on a NetWare or IntranetWare network system access both the data and resource forks of requested Macintosh files because both forks are required for the Macintosh to read the file. Non-Macintosh clients, on the other hand, access only the data fork of a Macintosh file. When Macintosh clients copy Macintosh files from one location to another on a NetWare server (either by using the NCOPY command or by dragging-and-dropping), both the data fork and the resource fork are copied. To store Macintosh files on a NetWare server, the MAC.NAM NetWare Loadable Module (NLM) must be linked with the NetWare operating computer.

Macintosh user

A general term describing a user at a Macintosh workstation.

MacIPX

An implementation of the Internet Packet Exchange (IPX) designed for NetWare for Macintosh networks. Configuration for MacIPX is performed through the MacIPX control panel.

MacNCP

An implementation of the Network Control Protocol (NCP) designed for NetWare for Macintosh networks. Configuration for MacNCP is performed through the MacIPX control panel, which enables a user to specify and verify a user name, a Novell Directory Services (NDS) context, and a preferred Directory tree.

MacNDS

A suite of client software packages for NetWare for Macintosh that includes MacIPX, MacNCP, the NetWare User Authentication Method (UAM), and

NetWare aliases.

macro
A collection of keystroke commands and instructions stored in a file and executed by typing a single command at the command line. A macro automates a complex or repetitive sequence of application commands and is similar to login scripts executed through NetWare.

MacTCP
A Macintosh version of the Transmission Control Protocol/Internet Protocol (TCP/IP) suite used to connect a Macintosh to the Internet and to intranetworks.

mail
In the context of electronic communications, messages sent to one or more recipients by electronic mail (e-mail), voicemail, or videomail. Mail can be read by the recipient at a later time.

mail bridge
A connecting device that filters mail transmissions between networks. Criteria is specified to determine what mail is passed between the networks.

mail delivery system
An electronic mail system that may include a mail server (a program for managing mail delivery), a mail directory (the directory on the network system designated for electronic mail), a mailbox (a user's repository to store messages), and a mail exploder (a program, also known as a *mailbot*, that delivers messages to all recipients on a mailing list).

Mail Exchange record (MX)
A data structure in the Internet Domain Naming System (DNS) that indicates which machines can handle electronic mail for a particular region of the Internet.

mail filter
An electronic mail (e-mail) option that provides for the selection of some

combination of messages to be placed at the beginning of a list, to be forwarded, ignored, and deleted.

mail reflector
An electronic mail (e-mail) feature that sends out messages and documents in response to e-mail requests.
Synonym: *mailbot*

mail server
A program that manages the delivery of electronic mail (e-mail) or other information upon request. A mail server often is considered part of a mail delivery system.

mail stop information
A term describing a facet of addressing in Novell Directory Services (NDS). A mail stop can be recorded for each User object.

Mail Transfer Agent (MTA)
A component of the electronic mail (e-mail) system found in the Transmission Control Protocol/Internet Protocol (TCP/IP) suite. An MTA provides an interface between users (and applications) and the e-mail system, sends and receives messages, and forwards messages between mail servers. Different MTAs communicate with each other using the Simple Mail Transfer Protocol (SMTP). Users interact with MTAs through user agents, which communicate with the MTA using a protocol, such as Post Office Protocol Version 3 (POP3).

mailbomb
Either a large number of files or one very large file sent to an electronic mail (e-mail) address in an effort to crash the recipient's e-mail system.

mailbot
A program that automatically sends out electronic mail (e-mail) messages or automatically replies to e-mail messages. The term is a contraction for *mail robot*.
Synonym: *mail reflector*

mailbox

A repository for the storage of electronic mail (e-mail) messages. A mailbox does not automatically appear as part of an e-mail package, but rather must be configured through a service provider or by the administrator of an interoffice network.

mail-enabled application

An application that includes an electronic mail (e-mail) function and other functions (such as contact-management software, intelligent mail handling, and workflow automation).

mailing list

A type of electronic mail (e-mail) address that remails any incoming mail to a list of recipients, known as *subscribers*. Because mailing lists are topic-specific, subscribers can pick mailing lists of interest.

mailto

A World Wide Web (WWW) page feature that creates a pre-addressed electronic mail (e-mail) form (including a link to the Web page) that visitors may use to return feedback, report errors, or participate in surveys.

Main Distribution Frame (MDF)

A central distribution point (usually a wiring closet) for the wiring of a building. An MDF may be connected directly to a user's workstation or to an intermediate distribution point.

main function

A developer-written function that executes as the initial thread of a NetWare Loadable Module (NLM). Program execution begins with the main function.

main menu

The first menu that appears when running a utility, especially when running a DOS-based utility in NetWare or IntranetWare.

mainframe system

A large-scale, multiuser computer system managing large amounts of data and computing tasks. A mainframe system normally is supplied complete with peripherals and software by companies such as Burroughs, Control Data, IBM, Univac, and others.

Maintenance Operation Protocol (MOP)

A protocol from Digital Equipment Corporation that provides a way to perform primitive maintenance operations on a DECnet network system.

maintenance release

A low-level update to software that includes minor bug fixes or the addition of minor features. A higher-level update that fixes major bugs or introduces major features is called a *major release*. Version numbers on the software indicate the level of the update. For example, software with a release version number of 4.0 indicates a major release; a version number of 4.1 indicates a maintenance release.

major resource

A resource defined by NetWare's Target Service Agent (TSA) and that contains data to be backed up as a group (such as data on a server or volume). A major resource is recognized by the SBACKUP NetWare Loadable Module (NLM).

male connector

A cable connector with pins designed to engage with the sockets on a female connector.

managed object

A network device managed by either network-management software or a protocol suite, such as Simple Network Management Protocol (SNMP).

Management Domain (MD)

An area defined by the X.400 Message Handling System (MHS) from the Consultative Committee for International Telegraphy and Telephony (CCITT) whose message-handling capabilities operate under the control of a single management domain. The two types of MDs are the *Administrative Management Domain (ADMD)* and the *Private Management Domain (PRMD)*.

Management Information Base (MIB)

A database of network-management information and objects used by the Common Management Information Protocol (CMIP) and the Simple Network Management Protocol (SNMP). Each network-management service has its own set of objects for different types of devices or for different network management protocols.

Management Information System (MIS)

A computer-based information system within a company that integrates data from all the departments it serves and provides company management with necessary decision-making data, tracks progress, and solves problems.

management services

Functions for the System Network Architecture (SNA) distributed among network components to manage and control an SNA network.

ManageWise

Novell's network-management software package that includes NetWare and Windows NT server management, desktop management, network analysis, automated network inventory, remote control, software management, and virus prevention. The product is designed to detect and repair such network problems as printing problems, limited access to applications, slow network response time, disk failures, limited storage space on the server, and critical node monitoring. ManageWise also monitors more than 2,000 server conditions, including the network directory, disk drives, volumes, memory, logged-in users, and installed-and-running software.

managing process

Software that initiates network requests for data from managing agents (programs monitoring the activity of workstations) and performs any analysis on the data. The managing process software operates on a dedicated machine known as the *managing station*.

Manchester encoding

A digital scheme used in Ethernet networks to encode data and timing signals in the same transmitted data stream. Manchester encoding uses a mid-bit-time transition for clocking, and a 1 denotes a high level during the first half of the bit time.

manual key

A modified form of the null key used in excluding particular records from a database index. In Btrieve, for example, if every byte of one segment in a manual key contains a null value, then Btrieve excludes the key from the index.

Manufacturing Automation Protocol (MAP)

A specification outlining the automation of tasks in a computer-integrated manufacturing or factory environment. MAP was originally formulated by General Motors to assist in procurement.

Manufacturing Message Service (MMS)

A service, used in automated production lines, enabling a computer application on a control machine to communicate with an application on a slave machine.

map

In the context of NetWare, the assignment of a drive letter or directory path by a DOS or OS/2 client on a NetWare volume. In the context of the Internet, a map is a list of actual addresses used for message delivery in lieu of certain nominal or symbolic addresses. A map also refers to a specific region on a Web page that reports coordinates of any mouse clicks within its border so server programs can respond accordingly.

mapped conversation

A conversation occurring between two transaction programs that are using the Advanced Program-to-Program Communication (APPC) Application Program Interface (API).

mapping
The assignment of a drive letter to a particular logical disk drive.

margin
An allowance for signal loss through attenuation, or simply over time, during a signal transmission.

mark parity
A parity setting in which the parity bit is always set to 1 and as the eighth bit.

markup tag
A formatting or inclusion tag in an editing program that serves as an instruction to a processing or reading program. A markup tag is not visible until the file is passed through an appropriate program. A familiar use of markup tags occurs in the Hypertext Markup Language (HTML) used to create Web pages, where tags represent document layout instructions and links to other places in a file. Markup tags are placed within angle brackets (< >).

masquerade
A threat to network security imposed by either a program that purports to perform a function other than one it is intended to perform or a user pretending to be someone else.

master key password
A security password that controls access to the entire operating system. When a computer system is started, the operating system prompts for the master key password.

master replica
A Novell Directory Services (NDS) Directory replica containing the first instance of partition information, which is used to change the structure of the Directory tree in relation to that partition. Other Directory replica types include read/write replicas, read-only replicas, and subordinate replicas. Although many Directory replicas can exist, only one master replica is allowed; it always is considered the most accurate Directory replica.

mating

The joining of two connectors to complete a circuit or establish a network link. Mating usually occurs between male and female connectors.

maxdata

A term describing the maximum data size for a frame on a network link.

Maximum-Receive Unit (MRU)

An option in the Link Control Protocol (LCP). The MRU enables a sender to inform a peer that the sender can receive larger frames than specified in the default or to request that the peer send smaller frames.

Maximum-Transmission Unit (MTU)

Specified in bytes, the largest packet size that can be sent on a physical network medium. As an example, the MTU for Ethernet is 1,500 bytes.

mean time between failures (MTBF)

A statistically derived average length of time (expressed in thousands or tens of thousands of hours) a computer system or component operates before failing.

mean time to repair (MTTR)

A statistically derived average length of time it takes to repair a failing computer system or component.

media

The plural of medium, a term describing the physical paths over which communications flow (for example, copper wires, coaxial cables, or fiber-optic cables).

Media Access Control (MAC)

One of two sublayers of the Data-Link Layer (Layer 2 of the OSI Reference Model) that controls the use of network hardware and governs access to transmission media. This sublayer is defined in the Institute of Electronic and Electrical Engineers (IEEE) 802.x set of local area network (LAN) standards. The other sublayer in the Data-Link Layer is the Logical Link Control (LLC) sublayer.

media-access method

A strategy on the Data-Link Layer (Layer 2) of the OSI Reference Model that network nodes use to access a network transmission medium. A common media-access method is Carrier Sense Multiple Access/Collision Detection (CSMA/CD).

Media Control Interface (MCI)

An interface used to control multimedia files and devices.

media filter

A device that converts a Token Ring adapter board output signal to work with a specific type of wiring.

media label

A label describing the information contained on electronic media.

media management NLM

A type of NetWare Loadable Module (NLM) that supports NetWare's High-Capacity Storage System (HCSS) by providing access to alternative types of media.

Media Manager (MM)

A NetWare database that tracks all peripheral storage devices and media attached to NetWare servers and enables applications to access or gain information from the devices and media. This database receives input/output requests from applications and converts them to messages compatible with the NetWare Peripheral Architecture (NPA).

media-set ID

Identification information attached to electronic media to help identify their contents. The media-set ID is commonly used for back-up tape cartridges.

medium

Physical components of a network system (usually cables or wires) that carry information from one point to another.

Medium-Attachment Unit (MAU)

A device that detects collisions and injects bits onto the network. The MAU works on the Physical Layer (Layer 1) of the OSI Reference Model and complies with the Institute of Electronic and Electrical Engineers (IEEE) 802.3 standard.

Medium Interface Connector (MIC)

A connector conforming to the Fiber Distributed Data Interface (FDDI) de facto standard.

megabit (Mbit)

A unit of measure equaling 2^{20} (or 1,048,576) binary digits (or bits) often used as an equivalent to 1 million bits.

megabits per second (Mbit/s, Mbps)

A unit of measure equaling 2^{20} (or 1,048,576) bits of data being transferred to and from peripheral devices every second.

megabyte (MB)

A unit of measure equaling 2^{10} (or 1,048,576) bytes most commonly used in the context of computer memory or disk storage capacity. A megabyte equals 1,024 kilobytes.

megahertz (MHz)

A unit of measure equaling one million cycles per second. The speed at which a computer's processor operates (the *clock speed*) is often expressed in megahertz.

memory

A capacity of internal dynamic data storage that can be accessed by a computer's operating system. Read-only memory (ROM) is installed on the computer's motherboard by the manufacturer and contains firmware such as the computer Basic Input/Output System (BIOS). Random access memory (RAM) accepts and holds binary data, including the data being operated on and the program that directs the operations to be performed. RAM stores the information and accesses any part of the information upon request. Table M.1 shows the types of RAM found in DOS.

TABLE M.1	DOS Memory Types
TYPE	**DESCRIPTION**
Conventional Memory (also known as *low DOS memory* or *base memory*)	Located below 640K. Devoted to running programs and applications.
Expanded Memory	Located outside normal address space of DOS. Can be addressed in 16K units (also known as *pages*) in areas known as *page frames*. Designed to store data and numbers. Available for computers that have 8086, 8088, and 80286 microprocessors through memory boards compliant with the expanded memory specification (EMS). Available for computers that have 80386 and 80486 microprocessors through EMS emulators.
Extended Memory	Located above the 1MB address limit of DOS. Used for RAM disks and disk caching routines. Computers that have 80286 microprocessors can address up to 16MB of extended memory. Computers that have 80386 and 80486 microprocessors can address up to 4GB of extended memory. With DOS drivers, extended memory from 1,024K to 1,088K (defined as the high memory area, or HMA) can be addressed. DOS extenders that comply with the extended memory specification (XMS) can address memory above 1,088K.
Upper Memory	Can mean system memory (between 640K and 1,024K), HMA (1,024K to 1,088K), extended memory (above 1,024K), or expanded memory (also above 1,024K).

TYPE	DESCRIPTION
High Memory Area (HMA)	Located in the first 64K of extended memory (1,024K to 1,088K). Can be addressed directly by DOS in real mode by using such device drivers as HIMEM.SYS. Provides additional memory addressed directly by DOS and functions in a fashion similar to conventional memory. Available on computers that have 80286, 80386, and 80486 microprocessors with more than 1,024K of RAM installed.
System Memory (also known as *high DOS memory*, *high memory*, *HMA*, or *upper memory*)	Located between 640K and 1,024K. Not usually addressed by DOS or applications. Can be addressed by computers with 80386 or 80486 microprocessors that use special control programs to make upper memory blocks (UMBs) in system memory.
Upper Memory Block (UMB)	Located between 640K and 1,024K. Directly addressed by DOS and applications. Defined by the XMS specification and created by a driver (such as EMM386.EXE) by converting unused address spaces in system memory to UMBs.

TABLE M. *DOS Memory Types*

memory address
An exact memory location that stores a particular data item or program instruction.

memory allocation
The reservation of specific memory locations in random access memory (RAM) for processes, instructions, and data. During the installation of a computer system, the installer allocates memory for such items as disk caches, RAM disks, extended memory, and expanded memory. Operating systems and applications allocate memory to meet certain requirements, but can use only memory that is actually available. Memory is reallocated between resources to optimize performance.

memory board

An add-on card or board that increases the amount of random access memory (RAM) within a personal computer.

memory buffer

An area of memory that serves as a temporary storage site for data. Buffers often are used to compensate for differences between transmission and processing speeds or to hold data until a peripheral device becomes available.

memory cache

A high-speed memory area on a microprocessor storing commonly used code or data that comes from slower memory. A memory cache eliminates the need to access a computer system's main memory to fetch instructions.

memory chip

A computer chip holding data or program instructions. A random access memory (RAM) chip stores the information temporarily and a read-only memory (ROM) chip stores the information permanently.

memory disk

A designated portion of random access memory (RAM) made to act like a very fast disk drive.

Synonyms: *RAM disk; virtual disk*

memory dump

A printed, displayed, or saved copy of the status of a specific internal memory area in a computer that shows the values of the variables stored in that memory area.

memory management

A process of managing the manner in which a computer handles memory and memory allocation.

memory-management unit (MMU)

The part of a computer microprocessor responsible for managing the mapping of virtual memory addresses to actual physical addresses. The MMU can be a separate chip (as was the case in early Intel or Motorola microprocessors) or part of the central processing unit (CPU) chip.

memory map
The organization and allocation of computer memory. A memory map provides an indication of how much memory is being used by the operating system and underlying application programs.

memory pool
A finite supply of memory (not necessarily contiguous) reserved for specific NetWare function requests and for file caching.

memory protection
A NetWare 4.x process that protects NetWare server memory from corruption by NetWare Loadable Modules (NLMs). This process uses the DOMAIN NLM to create the OS_PROTECTED domain, which provides limited entry points into the default OS domain and, thereby, protects the operating system memory from unauthorized access. The need for DOMAIN.NLM was eliminated in NetWare 4.11.

menu command
A command in a menu source code file indicating the beginning of a menu.

menu utility
A utility enabling NetWare users to access workstation utilities from the DOS or OS/2 operating system.

MERIT
A regional network located in Michigan and affiliated with Advanced Network Services (ANS).

mesh network topology
A physical network topology in which at least two paths lead to and from each network node. This type of topology provides backup connections in the event of connection failures between nodes.

message

A logical grouping of information at the Application Layer (Layer 7) of the OSI Reference Model.

message channel

A form of multitasking, interprocess communication that allows two programs running on the same computer to share information.

Message Digest 5 Algorithm (MD5)

A proposed encryption method for the Simple Network Management Protocol (SNMP) that uses a message, an authentication key, and time information to formulate a checksum value known as a *digest*.

Message Handling System (MHS)

A store-and-forward technology from Novell that handles the sending of electronic mail (e-mail) messages, fax services, calendar and scheduling services, and workflow automation. NetWare Global MHS also offers optional modules for accessing such messaging environments as UNIX, Transmission-Control Protocol/Internet Protocol (TCP/IP), Open Systems Interconnect (OSI), IBM mainframes, Macintosh, and OS/2. MHS has largely been superseded by Novell's GroupWise system.

Message-Oriented Text Interchange System (MOTIS)

A Message-Handling System (MHS) developed by the International Standards Organization (ISO). The basic MOTIS elements are compatible with the Consultative Committee for International Telegraphy and Telephony (CCITT) X.400 MHS specifications.

message packet

A network communications unit of information.

Message Routing Group object

A NetWare and IntranetWare leaf object in Novell Directory Services (NDS) that represents a group of messaging servers that can send and receive messages among themselves.

Message Store (MS)

A component specified in the Consultative Committee for International Telegraphy and Telephony (CCITT) X.400 Message-Handling Service (MHS) in which electronic mail (e-mail) is stored either until it is retrieved by a User Agent (UA) or until an allowable storage time expires.

message-switched network

A network configured so messages from multiple users can travel along the network at the same time. This system stores messages temporarily, and then forwards them through routing (or switching) to a destination. In contrast to *packet-switched networks* (in which individual packets are passed to a destination and reassembled there), a message-switched network collects an entire message before forwarding it to a destination.

Synonym: *store-and-forward network*

message switching

A switching technique that involves sending network messages from node to node, with each message stored at a node until a forwarding path becomes available.

message system

A communications protocol that resides on top of the Internetwork Packet Exchange (IPX) and provides an engine that enables a network node to send messages to other nodes. Access to the message system is provided in a set of Application Program Interfaces (APIs).

Message Tools

A contraction for Message Enabling Tools, a set of programs that manage the enabling and translation of software string resources. These tools extract text strings from such resources as error messages and menu items, displaying them from the source code so they can be translated and reinserted.

Message-Transfer Agent (MTA)

A component specified in the Consultative Committee for International Telegraphy and Telephony (CCITT) X.400 Message Handling Service (MHS) that stores (or forwards) electronic mail (e-mail) messages to a User Agent (UA), another MTA, or to some other authorized recipient.

Message-Transfer Layer (MTL)
A component specified in the Consultative Committee for International Telegraphy and Telephony (CCITT) X.400 Message Handling Service (MHS) that represents one of two sublayers of the Application Layer (Layer 7) in the OSI Reference Model and provides access to transfer services across a network. The other sublayer (which resides above the MTL) is the User Agent Layer (UAL).

Message-Transfer Service (MTS)
A component specified in the Consultative Committee for International Telegraphy and Telephony (CCITT) X.400 Message Handling Service (MHS) that processes requests from Access Units (AUs), Message Stores (MSs), Message-Transfer Agents (MTAs), and User Agents (UAs).

message unit
A unit of data processed by any layer on a network.

Messaging Application Program Interface (MAPI)
A messaging service and mail service interface from Microsoft that provides functions for Microsoft Mail within a Windows application.

Messaging Server object
In NetWare and IntranetWare, a leaf object in Novell Directory Services (NDS) that represents a messaging server that resides on a NetWare server. When NetWare or IntranetWare is first installed, this object is automatically created and placed in the same Directory tree context as the NetWare Server leaf object. Different types of messaging servers provide different types of connectivity or operate in different environments. NetWare 4, for example, includes a NetWare Basic MHS server, which services messages between NetWare 4 network users. A Global MHS server supports communication across asynchronous links with non-MHS environments (such as Simple Mail Transfer Protocol, Systems Network Architecture Distribution Services, and X.400).

Metal-Oxide Varistor (MOV)
A component of an electrical line conditioner or surge protector that intercepts high-voltage spikes from an incoming power supply.

metaverse

A term coined by author Neal Stephenson, which originally meant a virtual electronic reality, but that has grown to mean an abstract universe composed of all ideas, messages, and actions circulating through electronic networks.

metering

A process of tracking software availability and use across a network to ensure software licenses are not being violated or to predict when new copies (or licenses) of a software product must be purchased.

method

A procedure in an object-oriented language that an object executes when it receives a message.

metropolitan area network (MAN)

A network that spans a larger geographical area than a local area network (LAN) but a smaller geographic area than a wide area network (WAN).

MicroChannel Architecture (MCA)

An IBM bus developed for higher models of the PS/2 line of computers that includes 32-bit transfer and software configuration of expansion boards.

microbend

A flaw in fiber-optic cable in which tiny bends have occurred in the fiber, which can affect transmissions.

MicroChannel

A proprietary bus architecture from IBM that allows the use of software to set addresses and interrupts for hardware devices. Expansion boards for MicroChannel Architecture (MCA) are not compatible with machines that have Industry Standard Architecture (ISA) or Extended Industry Standard Architecture (EISA) configurations.

microcode

A set of low-level instructions that specify what a computer microprocessor does when it executes machine-language code.

Microcom Networking Protocol (MNP)

A ten-level set of communications protocols from Microcom used as a standard of data compression, as well as for error detection and correction. The ten levels are as follows:

- ▶ *Levels 1 to 4* define hardware error control.
- ▶ *Level 5* describes a 2:1 data-compression method.
- ▶ *Level 6* describes a communication protocol beginning with V.22 bis modulation and switching to V.29 when possible.
- ▶ *Level 7* describes a 3:1 data-compression method.
- ▶ *Level 8* is undefined.
- ▶ *Level 9* contains a proprietary technique for providing good performance over a variety of types of links.
- ▶ *Level 10* describes an error-control protocol often used on noisy links.

microcomputer

A computer based on a single-chip microprocessor.

microcrack

A flaw in fiber-optic cable in which tiny cracks have developed in the fiber, which can affect transmissions.

microkernel

A streamlined operating system kernel that processes only scheduling, loading, and running of task, while leaving all other operating-system tasks to be run by modules running on top of the microkernel. The microkernel was developed at Carnegie-Mellon University as part of the Mach operating system.

micron

A unit of measure equaling one-millionth of a meter, or 1/25,000 of an inch.

microprocessor

A central processing unit (CPU) that appears on one computer chip.
Synonym: *processor*

Microsoft API (MAPI)

An Application Programming Interface (API) from Microsoft that adds messaging capabilities to any Windows application by handling the details of directory service and message storage and forwarding.

Microsoft Disk Operating System (MS DOS)

A single-user, single-tasking operating system for personal computers that allocates system resources through either a command line or shell interface. Although similar to IBM's PC-DOS, file sizes and names of device drivers do differ between the two systems.

micro-to-mainframe

A connection between a personal computer (or microcomputer) and a mainframe-based network. This connection includes terminal-emulation software that enables the microcomputer to access data and applications on the mainframe system.

microwave network

A wireless network that uses microwave transmissions to transmit signals between nodes on the network.

microwave transmission

A transmission that occurs in a high bandwidth above 1 gigahertz (GHz) in the electromagnetic spectrum and used in a wireless network. A microwave transmission requires a line of sight between the sender and receiver, but can use Earth-based or satellite receivers.

middle-endian

A term that describes the order in which a word's individual bytes are stored. A big-endian system stores high-order bytes at the lower addresses; a little-endian system stores low-order bytes at the lower addresses. Middle-endian systems store somewhere in between.

middleware

Hardware or software that resides between an application program and the computer operating system or the network operating system. Common examples of middleware are a network shell or Common Object Request Broker Architecture (CORBA).

midsplit

A broadband cable system in which the available frequencies are split into two groups, one for transmission and one for reception.

Migrated (M) attribute

An automatically set NetWare status flag indicating a file has migrated.

migration

In the context of the NetWare operating system, the conversion of servers from NetWare 2.x or NetWare 3.x (or from another operating system) to NetWare 4.x. This is not the same as *data migration*, which entails moving files to near-line or offline storage devices. In the context of a NetWare protocol, migration is the conversion of a server, router, or network from the Internetwork Packet Exchange (IPX) protocol to NetWare Link Services Protocol (NLSP), or from TCP/IP to the Open Shortest Path First (OSPF) protocol.

mil (military)

A suffix on an Internet address that indicates the host computer is run under the jurisdiction of the U.S. Department of Defense (DoD).

million instructions per second (MIPS)

A measurement used to gauge the speed of a computer central processing unit (CPU).

millisecond (ms, msec)

A unit of measure equal to one-thousandth of a second.

millivolt (mv)

A unit of measure equal to one-thousandth of a volt.

MILnet

A network appearing on the Internet, originally used for unclassified military information.

minicomputer

A medium-sized computer capable of running multitasking operations and managing more than 100 users simultaneously.

mini-hard disk

A hard disk mounted on a Type III PC Card (also known as a PCMCIA card).

Minimum Spanning Tree (MST)

The shortest set of network or internetwork connections that includes all possible connections, but does not contain any loops.

minor resource

A resource defined by NetWare's Target Service Agent (TSA) that can be located in the Novell Directory Services (NDS) Directory tree below a selected major resource. A major resource is recognized by the SBACKUP NetWare Loadable Module (NLM).

Mirrored Server Engine (MSEngine)

One of two parts of NetWare's System Fault Tolerance III (SFT III) operating system that is responsible for handling such nonphysical processes as the NetWare file system, queue management, and the Directory. The other part of SFT III is the Input/Output Engine (IOEngine). Both the primary server and the secondary server share the same MSEngine. By keeping track of active network processes, the MSEngine provides uninterrupted service if the primary server fails and the secondary server takes over.

Mirrored Server Link (MSL)

A connection in NetWare's System Fault Tolerance III (SFT III) primary and secondary servers that manages server synchronization. The MSL requires a bus extension from the primary Input/Output Engine (IOEngine) to the secondary IOEngine, with a direct connection made through fiber-optic cable.

mirroring

A process of duplicating data from the NetWare partition on one hard disk drive to the NetWare partition on another hard disk drive. This duplication provides fault tolerance for a file system.

misc newsgroup
An Internet newsgroup that discusses topics that do not fit any of the other newsgroup types.

mission-critical application
A computer application vital to the operation of a company.

mnemonic
An easy-to-remember name or abbreviation that represents a long or complex programming instruction.

mobile computing
The establishment of links to a network by remote users.

Mobile-Telephone Switching Office (MTSO)
A central computer that monitors all cellular communication transmissions and adjusts channel assignment to accommodate the fluctuating quality of signals.

Mobitex
A collection of wireless networks maintained by RAM Mobile Data that connects more than 6,000 cities.

modal dispersion
The gradual spreading of a fiber-optic signal with increasing distance.

mode
A set of parameters that defines properties of a network session.

mode name
A name used by a program to request a specific set of network properties the program wants to use for a network session conversation.

modem

A contraction for *modulator/demodulator* that describes a device used to convert digital data into analog (or waveform) signals for transmission along analog signal carriers. The device also converts received analog signals into digital data to be used by a computer. A *digital modem* merely transmits digital signals; it does not translate back and forth between analog and digital formats.

modem eliminator

A device enabling two computers to be linked without the use of modems. In an asynchronous system, a modem eliminator simply may be a null-modem cable connecting the serial ports on two computers. In a synchronous system, a modem eliminator must also provide functions to synchronize communications.

modem server

A synonym for an Asynchronous Communications Server (ACS).

moderated mailing list

A mailing list for which incoming messages have been approved by a designated person.

moderated newsgroup

A newsgroup for which postings have been approved by a designated person.

moderator

A person responsible for reviewing mailing list messages and newsgroup postings and deciding which ones to release to the public.

modifiable

A key attribute that enables a user to modify a key field during an update to a file.

Modified Frequency Modulation (MFM)
An encoding scheme used to record data on 40MB or smaller hard-disk drives.

Modified Modular Jack (MMJ)
A cable developed by Digital Equipment Corporation. The MMJ is a variant of the RJ-xx jacks and is designed for use in premises cabling.

Modify bit
A file attribute set by the operating system when a file is changed, indicating file data has been modified. In NetWare, the Modify bit is called the Archive Needed Attribute and appears as an A whenever file attributes are listed. Modify bits are checked by backup programs to back up only those files for which the Modify bit has been set.

Modify right
In IntranetWare, a file-access and directory-access right that grants the privilege of changing the attributes or name of a file or directory.

Modular Jack (MJ)
A female connector (with sockets or slots) used to connect voice cables to a faceplate. An example of an MJ is a telephone jack.

modularity
Characterized by the quality of being composed of self-supporting pieces that can be used independently of each other.

modulation
The process of converting digital signals to analog signals by modulating a carrier frequency.

Modulation protocol
A protocol that modulates digital signals for transmission over telephone lines and depends on the transmission rates it supports.

module

A self-contained portion of a computer program written, tested, and compiled separately from the main program, which performs a specific operation.

Modulo 8 or 128

A numbering method for packet sequences that controls the numbering of sequential data packets in a window.

More data mark (M-bit)

A bit that is a component of a user packet and, when set, identifies the next packet sent as a logical continuation of the data contained in the current packet.

Most Significant Bit (MSB)

A bit corresponding to the highest power of 2 in a bit sequence. The MSB's location depends on the context and the ordering of bits within a word.

motherboard

The main circuit board in a computer that contains the central processing unit (CPU), a coprocessor (and support chips), device controllers, memory, and expansion slots.

Motif

A graphical user interface (GUI) for UNIX computers.

Motion Pictures Experts Group (MPEG)

An International Standards Organization/International Telecommunications Union (ISO/ITU) standard for compressing video files that requires a fast computer or a plug-in MPEG board for the computer.

mount

The process of inserting a CD-ROM disc into a CD-ROM drive so the Hierarchical File System (HFS) CD-ROM module knows the CD-ROM drive exists.

mouse

A computer input device with one or more buttons, used with programs designed for a graphical user interface (GUI) to move the cursor around the screen display. A mouse can be one of four types: a *bus mouse* (requires a separate expansion board in the computer), a *serial mouse* (plugs into a serial port), a *regular mouse* (plugs into a mouse port), or a *wireless mouse*.

mouse pointer

In programs using a graphical user interface (GUI), a small symbol that appears on the monitor screen, whose movement is controlled by a mouse. The mouse pointer indicates a position on the display screen.

MS Windows client

A NetWare workstation that boots with the DOS operating system and gains access to the network through either the NetWare DOS Requester (in NetWare 4.*x*) or a NetWare shell (in NetWare versions previous to NetWare 4.*x*). While running Windows, the workstation computer (with client software) can perform networking tasks in the Windows environment, including mapping drives, capturing printer ports, sending messages, and changing contexts.

mu-law

A companding standard used in North America for conversion between analog and digital signals in Pulse Code Modulation (PCM) systems.

multicast

A transmission method in which multiple (but not all) nodes on the network receive a copy of a frame or packet.

multicast address

An address referring to multiple network devices.
Synonym: *group address*

Multicast Backbone (MBONE)

A multicast, virtual network that adds live audio and video capabilities to the Internet. An MBONE network is organized as clusters of networks connected by *tunnels* (paths between endpoints that support both multicast transmissions) and multicast Internet Protocol (IP) transmissions.

multi-CPU architecture
A computer architecture in which multiple microprocessors work together on the same task or separately on different tasks.

multidrop connection
A network connection that uses a single line to connect multiple nodes. The Ethernet bus topology uses a multidrop connection.

multidrop line
A line or circuit often found in a Systems Network Architecture (SNA) network that connects several nodes on a single logical link.
Synonym: *multipoint line*

MultiFinder
A multitasking operating system for the Macintosh computer, under which several applications (including background applications) can be open at the same time.

multi-homed host
An Internet connection scheme in which a single machine is connected to multiple data links, possibly over multiple networks.

multihoming
An Intermediate System-to-Intermediate System (IS-IS) addressing scheme that supports the assignment of multiple data links or area addresses.

multilayer
A printed circuit board that has several layers of circuitry laminated together to form a single board.

Multilink Point-to-Point protocol (MP protocol)
An extension of the Point-to-Point Protocol (PPP) used to split a signal, send it along multiple channels, and then reassemble and sequence it at the common destination for the channels.

Multilink Procedures (MLP) protocol

A protocol used in networks that have multiple connections running in parallel. This protocol oversees the use of a point-to-point protocol, such as Link Access Procedure Balanced (LAPB) or High-Level Data-Link Control (HDLC), to help balance the loads on connections.

multimedia

A computer technology that incorporates video, animation, sound, graphics, and text with user interaction.

multimedia extension

Operating system software that extends an application interface to include video, animation, sound, graphics, and text. A multimedia extension also includes commands for synchronization and device control.

Multimedia Multiparty Teleconferencing (MMT)

A process that allows for the transfer of data, voice, and video transmissions in a teleconferencing environment.

Multimode Fiber (MMF)

An optical fiber that supports the propagation of multiple frequencies of light.

multipart

An electronic mail (e-mail) format description indicating the contents of the message represent several different objects.

multipath

A term describing radio communications signals that are reflected back and are out of phase with each other.

multiple access

A term describing simultaneous access to the same file by multiple users on a network. Multiple access usually entails only the reading of files with some sort of locking mechanism employed to prevent users from interfering with each other while trying to modify the file.

multiple-domain network

A Systems Network Architecture (SNA) network that controls multiple system service access points (SSAPs).

Multiple-Link Interface (MLI)

A part of a generic network driver that sits under the Link Support Layer (LSL) in Open Data-link Interface (ODI), which deals with Network Interface Cards (NICs) supporting ODI.

Multiple-Link Interface Driver (MLID)

A device driver that handles the sending and receiving of packets to and from a physical or logical local area network medium. The MLID complies with the Open Data-link Interface (ODI) specification.

Multiple Logical Terminals (MLT)

A feature of the IBM 3174 establishment controller in the Systems Network Architecture (SNA) environment that enables components to support simultaneous multiple network sessions.

multiple name-space support

A method allowing various workstations running different operating systems to create their own familiar naming conventions. Operating systems, such as DOS, Macintosh, OS/2, UNIX, and Windows each have unique naming conventions for files, including name length, allowable characters, case-sensitivity, data and resource forks, length of filename extensions, and so on. This method allows each file stored on a given volume to have a name that any workstation (regardless of the workstation's operating system) can recognize.

Multiple-Protocol Interface (MPI)

The top part of the Link Support Layer (LSL) of the Open Data-Link Interface (ODI) specification that provides support for local area network (LAN) drivers.

multiple protocols

A scenario under which more than one standard is used by a program or operating system for communication between two or more entities on a network.

Multiple Uniform Naming Convention Provider (MUP)

A Windows NT driver that determines which network to access when an application requests permission to open a remote file.

Multiple Virtual Storage (MVS)

An operating system used by IBM computers for large host systems.

multiple-byte character

A character made up of two or more bytes in situations in which a language includes more than the 256 characters that one byte can allow. The American Standard Code for Information Interchange (ASCII) character set includes 256 characters. If a language (such as some Asian languages) includes more than 256 characters, then more than one byte is necessary to accommodate all the characters in that language.

multiplexer

A device that accepts multiple electronic transmission signals and combines them into one high-speed transmission. A *multiplexer*, also known as a *mux*, is often used to allow remote terminals to communicate with front-end processor ports over a single circuit.

Synonym: *mux*

multiplexing

A method allowing a single communications circuit to take the place of several parallel communications circuits.

multiplexor VLM

A Virtual Loadable Module (VLM) that routes calls to a child VLM. The two types of VLMs are *multiplexor VLMs* and *child VLMs*.

multipoint connection

A network connection involving multiple nodes connected by a single line.

multipoint line

A communications line or circuit that interconnects several nodes of a network system.

Synonym: *multidrop line*

multiport repeater

An Ethernet network repeater that connects multiple network nodes in parallel.

multiprocessing

A computer operating system that has the capability to use more than one central processing unit (CPU) in a single computer. The two types of multiprocessing are:

- *Asymmetrical multiprocessing.* The program designer must specify the processor to use when running the program.
- *Symmetrical multiprocessing.* The operating system dynamically assigns tasks to the next available processor.

multiprotocol encapsulation

A method used by protocols on the Network Layer (Layer 3) of the OSI Reference Model, in which a layer adds control information to the protocol data unit (PDU) from the preceding layer. Mutiprotocol encapsulation is also sometimes used to envelop one protocol inside another to facilitate transmission.

Multiprotocol over ATM

An effort of the ATM Forum to standardize protocols to run multiple network layers over Asynchronous Transfer Mode (ATM) networks.

Multipurpose Internet Mail Extensions (MIME)

A specification that enables Internet users to send multipart and multimedia messages. Electronic mail (e-mail) applications that have MIME can send PostScript images, binary files, audio messages, and digital video over the Internet.

multiserver network

A single network with two or more NetWare servers, in which users can access any NetWare server to which they have rights. A multiserver network should not be confused with an *internetwork*, in which two or more networks are linked through a router.

Multistation Access Unit (MAU)
A multiport wiring hub used on Token Ring networks that can connect as many as eight nodes (or lobes) to a ring network. An MAU is also known as a *Controlled Access Unit (CAU)*.

multitasking
The capability of a computer to run more than one application simultaneously and to switch between the applications while they continue to run.

multithreading
A concurrent processing of several threads inside the same program, thus freeing one thread from waiting for another thread to finish processing before it can start.

Multi-User Dimension (MUD)
A multiuser simulation environment in which a user can create things that stay after the user leaves. Other users can interact with these things in the original user's absence, thus building a simulated environment gradually and collectively.

multiuser
A term describing an operating system that supports more than one simultaneous user. Network systems are an example of multiuser environments.

Multiuser Shared Hallucination (MUSH)
An interactive simulation that enables multiple users to add features or objects by using a scripting or programming language.

Multiuser Simulated Environment (MUSE)
A multiuser, computer-moderated, interactive simulation that enables multiple users to add features or objects using a scripting or programming

language. A MUSE usually has more features for users to add with fewer built-in dialogues, implying the interaction is a game.

multivendor network
A network made up of different components manufactured by different vendors.

Musical Instrument Digital Interface (MIDI)
A music file format including strings of messages that can be sent to a sound card, built-in sound system, or external device for translation back into musical notes and rhythms.

MUX Multiplier
A telecommunications device used to funnel multiple signals onto a single channel.

M

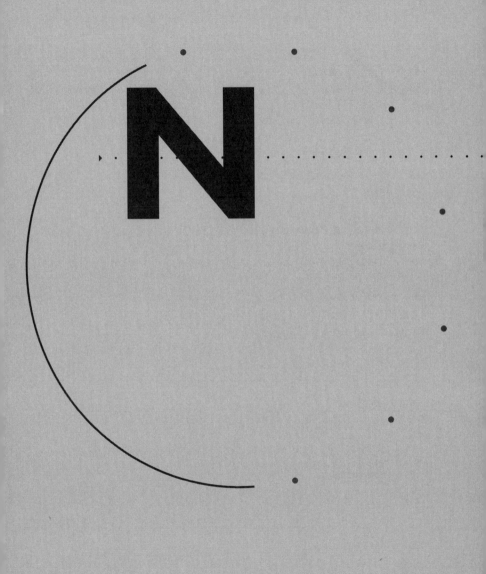

n

An abbreviation for the prefix *nano-* that represents an order of magnitude equivalent to 2^{30}, or about one-billionth.

Nagle's algorithm

A combination of two congestion-control algorithms used in Transmission Control Protocol (TCP) networks. One algorithm reduces a sending window and another limits small datagrams.

name binding

The association of a name for each Network Visible Entity (NVE) with its Internet address.

Name Binding Protocol (NBP)

An AppleTalk protocol that converts entity names into their corresponding Internet addresses. For example, the Macintosh Chooser Desk Accessory and the ATCON NetWare Loadable Module (NLM) use NBP to locate AppleTalk entities.

name caching

A method of using a router to store remotely discovered host names for future use in packet-forwarding decisions.

name context

The position of an object within the Novell Directory Services (NDS) Directory tree.

name resolution

The process of associating a network location with a name assigned by a NetWare network administrator.

name server

A network server that resolves network names into network addresses.

name space NLMs

A set of NetWare Loadable Modules (NLMs) that allow storage of non-DOS files on a NetWare server under a folder name or filename where a user expects to see them, even if the files were created on a platform different from that of the viewing workstation. NetWare uses a different name space for different platforms.

name type

A distinction made between different objects in Novell Directory Services (NDS). For example, the name type of an Organization object is O; an Organizational Unit object is OU.

named pipe

The means by which a client communicates with advanced client-server applications such as Microsoft SQL Server and Microsoft Comm Server software. NetWare Client workstations most frequently communicate with client-server applications by using the Interprocess Communications (IPC) protocol for named pipes.

Named Pipes Extender for DOS

A terminate-and-stay-resident (TSR) program for DOS that extends the capability of DOS in NetWare to include the use of remote named pipes.

Synonyms: *Named Pipes DOS Extender (DOSNP); Named Pipes extender*

name-space format

A filename format unique to a specific operating system. For example, DOS, Macintosh, Network Filing System (NFS), and OS/2 each have different name-space formats.

names directory (ND)

A database that contains the mappings of all Network Visible Entities (NVEs) with their Internet addresses.

names table

A table in each network node that contains the mappings of all Network Visible Entities (NVEs) in that node, complete with their Internet addresses.

naming service

A network service that names resources on the network to access the resources by that name. This enables correspondence between a network entity and a name, rather than the need to remember network addresses. A *local naming service* associates resources to a single server; a *global naming service* associates resources with an entire network or internetwork.

nanosecond (ns)

A unit of measure equal to one-billionth of a second.

Narrowband Analog Mobile Phone Service (NAMPS)

A communications standard from Motorola that combines the Advanced Mobile Home Service (AMPS) cellular standard with digital signaling information.

narrowband

A voice-grade communications transmission channel of 2,400 bits per second (bps) or less.

Narrowband ISDN (NISDN)

A term describing ordinary Integrated Services Digital Network (ISDN) architecture in which narrowband transmissions are used.

National Center for Supercomputer Applications (NCSA)

A University of Illinois at Champaign-Urbana computing center that provides information and resources for the World Wide Web (WWW).

National Computer Security Center (NCSC)

A branch of the United States National Security Agency (NSA) responsible for defining security standards for computer products. The Orange Book produced by the Department of Defense (DoD) lists seven levels of security.

National Information Infrastructure (NII)

A term describing the combination of the Internet and public networks to form a seamless communications Web, including all the necessary protocols, access software, applications software, the information itself, and service providers.

National Institute of Standards and Technology (NIST)

A United States government agency responsible for supporting and cataloging a variety of standards.

Synonym: *National Bureau of Standards (NBS)*

National Research and Education Network (NREN)

A network being developed as a state-of-the-art network for research organizations and educational institutions.

National Science Foundation (NSF)

A United States organization that provides funding for scientific research and controls the National Science Foundation Network (NSFnet) to provide support for educational and scientific research.

National Voluntary Laboratory Accreditation Program (NVLAP)

The United States part of a group of centers that develop automated software to test compliance with X.400 and X.500 standards. Other parts of the group are located in the United Kingdom (the National Computer Center), France (Alcatel), and Germany (Danet GmbH).

NCF file

A NetWare configuration file (NCF) that can be used by the network administrator to automate network server commands. These files are similar to DOS batch files.

NCP Packet Signature

A NetWare security feature that prevents forgery of NetWare Core Protocol (NCP) by requiring the server and the user's workstation to attach a "signature" to each NCP packet, which changes with every packet. If an NCP packet contains an incorrect signature, the packet is discarded without breaking the workstation's connection to the server. This feature protects both servers and workstations from unauthorized access or the attempted use of unauthorized network privileges.

NCP Server object
A Novell Directory Services (NDS) object automatically created for any IntranetWare server being upgraded or installed in IntranetWare that represents any server providing NetWare Core Protocol (NCP) transport and session servers. This object is in a subclass of the Server object.

NE2000
A proprietary Novell Network Interface Card (NIC) used on Ethernet networks.

near-end crosstalk (NEXT)
Interference that occurs close to a connector at either end of a cable. NEXT is usually measured near the source of a test signal.

Nearest Active Upstream Neighbor (NAUN)
A Token Ring node from which another node receives packets and the token. Token Ring nodes receive transmissions only from a NAUN.

NEARnet
A New England-area regional network that connects the National Science Foundation Network (NSFnet), many universities, and several major corporations.

negative acknowledgment (NAK)
A Return signal reporting an error in a message that has been received.

negotiable BIND
A Request/Response Unit (RU) that enables two logical unit-to-logical unit (LU-LU) half sessions to negotiate the parameters of a network session when the LUs are activating a session.

neighbor
Under NetWare Link Services Protocol (NLSP), a router capable of forming an adjacency with another NLSP router. Two NLSP routers are considered neighbors when they can communicate without the aid of an intermediary router.

neighboring router

Two routers in the Open Shortest Path First (OSPF) protocol that share a route to the same network.

net (network)

A suffix on an Internet address that indicates the address belongs to a network provider or a consortium of research laboratories. Internet Service Providers (ISPs) often have names with the .net suffix.

NET.CFG

NetWare's workstation boot file containing configuration values that adjust the operating parameters of the NetWare DOS Requester, Internet Packet Exchange (IPX), and other workstation software. Created with an American Standard Code for Information Interchange (ASCII) text editor, NET.CFG must be included on the workstation's boot disk with other boot files. NET.CFG (which is similar to the CONFIG.SYS file in DOS) replaces the SHELL.CFG file used in earlier versions of NetWare.

NETBIOS.EXE

A NetBIOS driver in the NetWare Client for DOS and MS Windows program. NETBIOS.EXE is an emulator that enables NetWare Internetwork Packet Exchange (IPX) to interface with two NetBIOS interrupts. This driver is an emulator because it does not transmit NetBIOS packets, but rather the packets are encapsulated as IPX packets, which are themselves transmitted.

NETINFO.CFG

In NetWare, an executable batch file that resides on the server and stores LOAD and BIND commands associated with protocol configuration when the INETCFG NetWare Loadable Module (NLM) is used to configure the protocols. If INETCFG is not used, the LOAD and BIND commands are placed in the AUTOEXEC.NCF file. The NETINFO.CFG file is located on the NetWare partition of the server's hard disk.

netiquette

A set of unwritten rules that govern the use of electronic mail (e-mail) and other network services. The term is a contraction of "network etiquette."

netizen
A term that describes a citizen of the Internet, or someone who uses network resources.

Netnews
A term used to describe Usenet newsgroups.

NetPartner
An AT&T network-management system that monitors voice and data links for wide area networks (WANs).

Netscape Navigator
A World Wide Web (WWW) browser from Netscape Communications that features a variety of plug-ins for increased functionality, as well as multiplatform support. The plug-ins provide three-dimensional, multimedia, and collaboration tools, as well as providing the capability to listen to Audio Interchange File Format (AIFF), Musical Instrument Digital Interface (MIDI), waveform audio, and multimedia audio files. The Navigator Mail and News software provides extended support for Hypertext Markup Language (HTML) files.

NetSync cluster
A group that includes one NetWare 4.x server running the NETSYNC4 NetWare Loadable Module (NLM) and up to 12 NetWare 3.x servers attached to it.

NetView
An IBM software product that monitors Systems Network Architecture (SNA) networks. NetView includes access services, a performance monitor, a session monitor, a hardware monitor, a status monitor, a distribution manager, a host command facility, a Help Desk facility, and customization facilities. This product runs as a Virtual Telecommunications Access Method (VTAM) application on the mainframe computer serving as the network manager.

NetWare
A local area network (LAN)/wide area network (WAN) operating system from Novell that uses the NetWare Core Protocol (NCP), Internetwork Packet

Exchange (IPX), and Sequenced Packet Exchange (SPX) protocols to share services transparently across dissimilar platforms. NetWare servers can support DOS, Windows, UNIX, and OS/2 clients, or Macintosh workstations. The Novell Directory Services (NDS) feature provides a scheme for arranging the entire network into a unified structure, as well as organizing network resources for easy access and centralized administration of the network.

Since its introduction in the early 1980s, NetWare has been released in a number of versions, including the following:

▶ *NetWare 86.* The first shipped version of NetWare designed for Intel 8086 processors used a modified implementation of the Xerox networking software called the Internetwork Packet Exchange (IPX).

▶ *NetWare 2.* This release included a modification to the Xerox networking software called Sequence Packet Exchange (SPX) and provided support for the Macintosh.

▶ *NetWare 3.* This release is a client-server implementation written to support the Intel 80386 processor. NetWare 3 is a 32-bit implementation of NetWare and includes support for additional Network Interface Cards (NICs), encapsulation of IPX/SPX packets within a Transmission Control Protocol/Internet Protocol (TCP/IP) network, and a number of bug fixes. NetWare 3.12 is the latest release of this version.

▶ *NetWare 4.* This release features an Enterprise LAN/WAN support, a global naming scheme (NDS), improved remote access capabilities, enhanced security features, and central network administration. NetWare 4.11 is the latest release of this version.

▶ *IntranetWare.* This latest release features the NetWare 4.11 operating systems, along with added Internet capabilities, including a Web server, NetBasic tool, Netscape Navigator Web browser, and Novell Java platform. In addition, the NetWare Distributed Printing Services (NDPS) has been introduced.

NetWare Access Server
Novell's application-server software that network managers use to provide users on remote networks and local area networks (LANs) with access to all NetWare LAN resources, including Systems Network Architecture (SNA) and Transmission Control Protocol/Internet Protocol (TCP/IP) applications.

NetWare Administrator (NWADMIN) utility

In NetWare 4.*x* and IntranetWare, a Windows and OS/2 workstation utility that performs supervisory tasks available in the FILER, NETADMIN, PARTMGR, and PCONSOLE utilities. The NetWare Administrator utility enables a network supervisor to create users and groups; to create, delete, move, and rename Novell Directory Services (NDS) objects; to assign rights in the Directory tree and in the file system; to set up print services; and to set up and manage NDS partitions and replicas. This utility uses a Graphical User Interface (GUI) and runs as a multiple-document interface (MDI) application. By using a menu bar and a browser, supervisors can view the file system of a server in the current Directory tree, open a container object and view the objects within it, view an object dialog (which provides object details) of a container object, and view an object dialog of a leaf object.

NetWare Asynchronous Services Interface (NASI)

Specifications for accessing NetWare communications servers. The NASI Software Developer's Kit (SDK) can be used to build applications running on this interface.

NetWare C Interface for NLM applications

A core set of NetWare Loadable Module (NLM) Application Programming Interfaces (APIs) for NetWare Loadable Modules (NLMs). These APIs provide a direct programming link to the operating system services for NetWare 3.*x* and NetWare 4.*x*.

NetWare Client for DOS and MS Windows

Software connecting DOS and Windows workstations with the NetWare network to enable users at those workstations to use network resources. The four terminate-and-stay-resident (TSR) programs that are the core components of the DOS and Windows environment include the Link Support Layer (LSL), the NetWare DOS Requester, the ODI LAN driver, and the transport protocol.

NetWare Client for OS/2

Software that connects OS/2 workstations with the NetWare network to enable users at those workstations to use network resources. NetWare Client for OS/2 directs network requests from the workstations to the network and enables applications servers to communicate with their workstations without using a NetWare server.

NetWare Connect

A NetWare add-on product that enables remote users of Windows, DOS, and Macintosh computers to dial in and access all resources available on a NetWare network, which also enables network users to dial out to connect to remote computers, bulletin boards, X.25 and Integrated Services Digital Network (ISDN) services, and other asynchronous hosts.

NetWare Connection

A monthly user publication produced by NetWare Users International (NUI) that provides a forum for the exchange of information among CNEs and other users of NetWare and related products.

NetWare Core Protocol (NCP)

Procedures followed by a server's NetWare operating system to accept and respond to workstation requests. NCPs exist for every service a station might request from a server. Requests are formed using the exact guidelines of a specific service protocol and the server handles the request according to the protocol rules. Requests commonly serviced include creating or destroying a service connection, manipulating directories and files, opening semaphores, altering the Novell Directory Services (NDS) Directory tree, and printing.

N

NetWare desk accessory

A Macintosh desk accessory that enables a NetWare for Macintosh user to send messages to other users, as well as to view or administer print jobs from a Macintosh workstation.

NetWare Directory

A NetWare system database that includes information about all the objects in Novell Directory Services. The information appears in a hierarchically organized tree structure.

Synonyms: *NetWare Directory Database; Directory; Directory tree*

NetWare Directory Database (NDD)

A NetWare system database that includes information about all the objects in Novell Directory Services. The information appears in a hierarchically organized tree structure.

Synonyms: *NetWare Directory; Directory; Directory tree*

NetWare Directory partition

A logical division of the NetWare Directory database that forms a unit of data in the Directory tree. This unit is then used to store and replicate Directory information. Each partition contains a container object, all objects contained therein, and data about those objects (such as properties and rights). The Directory partition neither contains any information about the file system nor about the directories contained in the file system. To optimize the capability (through distributed operations) of accessing different areas of the Directory, each Directory partition can be replicated and stored at many locations.

NetWare Directory replica

A copy of a NetWare Directory partition that provides a means for storing the NetWare Directory Database (NDD) on several servers across the network without having to duplicate the entire database for each server. An unlimited number of replicas can be created for each Directory partition and can be stored on any server. Directory replicas eliminate a single point of failure on the network and provide faster access to information across a wide area network (WAN) link. The four types of Directory replicas are the master replica, read/write replicas, read-only replicas, and subordinate replicas.

NetWare DOS Requester

A group of Virtual Loadable Module (VLM) files and a single executable file (VLM.EXE) that together provide NetWare support for DOS and Windows client workstations. The VLM files are grouped into the DOS Redirection Layer, the Service Protocol Layer, and the Transport Protocol Layer. The VLM Manager (VLM.EXE) controls communication and memory issues between the individual layers; it is also responsible for loading the required VLMs and for disbursing requests to individual modules.

Synonym: *Virtual Loadable Module (VLM) client*

NetWare for Macintosh

A collection of NetWare Loadable Modules (NLMs) that provide file handling, printing, network administration, and AppleTalk routing for Macintosh clients on a NetWare network. These NLMs enable Macintosh users to access such network resources as Novell Directory Services (NDS), applications, and network printers to use NetWare features while working in the Macintosh environment.

NetWare for SAA

A group of NetWare Loadable Modules (NLMs) making up a gateway package that provides connectivity to Systems Network Architecture (SNA) networks. With proper access privileges, users can gain access to applications and data on mainframe or midrange computers while working under the DOS, Windows, OS/2, or UNIX operating systems, or while working on a Macintosh computer. NetWare for SAA supports up to several hundred sessions for each gateway.

NetWare for UNIX

A software program that enables users working under the UNIX operating system to use the features of a NetWare network (such as file handling, printing, and backup services). Formerly known as Portable NetWare, NetWare for UNIX is sold by third-party vendors.

NetWare Hub Services

A software package from Novell that manages any hub card that complies with the NetWare Hub Management Interface (HMI) standard.

NetWare Internet Access Server (NIAS)

An enhanced version of the NetWare Multiprotocol Router that offers a single wide area network (WAN) connection and Internetwork Packet Exchange/Internet Protocol (IPX/IP) gateway functions.

NetWare/IP

A group of NetWare Loadable Modules (NLMs) providing Internet Protocol (IP) support for NetWare 3.x and NetWare 4.x servers. NetWare/IP enables a NetWare server to function as a gateway between NetWare and Transmission Control Protocol/Internet Protocol (TCP/IP) networks.

NetWare Licensing Services (NLS)

A distributed, enterprise network service enabling NetWare administrators to monitor and control the use of licensed applications on a NetWare network. The enterprise service architecture of this service consists of client components that support different platforms and system components that reside on network servers. NLS also includes a license metering tool and libraries that export licensing service functionality to developers of other licensing services.

NetWare Link Services Protocol (NLSP)
Novell's derivation of the Intermediate System-to-Intermediate System (IS-IS) link-state routing protocol that transfers information between routers and makes routing decisions on the basis of that information. NLSP routers exchange link information (such as network connectivity, path costs, Internetwork Packet Exchange network numbers, and media types) with peer routers to build and maintain a logical map of the network. NLSP multicasts routing information only when a route is changed or service on the network is changed. NLSP routers use the Routing Information Protocol (RIP).

NetWare Link/X.25
Novell's implementation of X.25 for the NetWare Multiprotocol Router.

NetWare Lite
A DOS-based, peer-to-peer version of the NetWare network operating system that makes drives, files, and printers available to all DOS and Windows users in the network. Although it supports up to 255 nodes on the network, NetWare Lite is limited to a maximum of 25 simultaneous users. NetWare Lite has been replaced by the Personal NetWare product.

NetWare Loadable Module (NLM)
One of a set of NetWare programs that is loaded (some automatically) and unloaded from server memory while the server is running. When an NLM is loaded, the program is dynamically linked to the operating system and the NetWare server allocates a portion of memory to it. The amount of memory allocated depends on the task the NLM is designed to perform. Control of the memory and all other allocated resources are returned to the operating system when the NLM is unloaded. While some NLMs (such as utilities) can be loaded, used, and then unloaded, others (such as local area network drivers and disk driver NLMs) must be loaded each time the server is started. Commands to load the latter NLMs are stored in the STARTUP.NCF and AUTOEXEC.NCF files.

NetWare managed node
A NetWare 4.x server that has the NetWare Management software enabled, thus making more information available to management-console software than is available with Internetwork Packet Exchange/Sequenced Packet Exchange (IPX/SPX) function calls.

NetWare Management Agent (NMA)

A group of NetWare Loadable Module (NLM) programs that provides information about the configuration of a server (including the NLM programs installed, printers, print queues, hard disks, disk controllers, and drivers), statistics on server traffic, statistics on server memory, and specifications on alarm settings for server errors and events. By loading the NetWare Management Agent, network administrators can monitor, manage, and maintain all network servers from a single console.

NetWare Management System (NMS)

A system that manages a NetWare network by using a network-management protocol and building a map of network resources. NMS has been replaced by the ManageWise product.

NetWare MHS Services

Services that enable users to exchange electronic mail, share calendars, schedule events, and so on, electronically across a NetWare network. To provide these services, NetWare uses a messaging server, a Distribution List object, a Message Routing Group object, an External Entity object, and a Postmaster.

NetWare Mobile

An integrated client environment for mobile computing and remote access that provides access to available services on a NetWare network. NetWare Mobile includes an enhanced dialer (to simplify NetWare network connections), a Mobile File assistant (to help manage files), location profiling, and graphical administration tools.

NetWare Monitor

In NetWare for OS/2, a graphical utility that runs under OS/2 Presentation Manager and monitors resources on a NetWare for OS/2 server.
Synonym: *PMMON*

NetWare Multiprotocol Router

A software-based bridge and router combination (brouter) that can concurrently route Internetwork Packet Exchange (IPX), Transmission Control Protocol/Internet Protocol (TCP/IP), and AppleTalk across both local area networks (LANs) and wide area networks (WANs). The NetWare Multiprotocol Router operates on personal computers with 80386, 80486, or Pentium microprocessors, and supports Ethernet, Token Ring, Fiber Distributed Data Interface (FDDI), fast Ethernet, and ARCnet network topologies.

NetWare Multiprotocol Router Plus

Software that provides wide area network (WAN) connectivity for dispersed heterogeneous networks over T1, fractional T1, X.25, and low-speed synchronous leased lines. This product replaces NetWare Link/64, NetWare Link/T1, and NetWare Link/X.25.

NetWare Name Service (NNS)

A predecessor to Novell Directory Services (NDS) that consisted of a set of specialized utilities designed to work with NetWare 2 and NetWare 3 networks to provide a more transparent access to resources in NetWare installations. NNS is no longer available or supported.

NetWare NFS

A collection of NetWare Loadable Modules (NLMs) that transparently integrates UNIX systems with NetWare 4.x file systems and resources. NetWare NFS provides UNIX users with access to the NetWare environment from their native UNIX operating system. NetWare NFS uses the Network File System (NFS) Application-layer protocol from Sun Microsystems.

NetWare NFS Gateway

Software installed on a NetWare server that enables NetWare clients to access files on a Network File System (NFS) server and makes the files appear as though they are on the NetWare server.

NetWare operating system

Novell's network operating system that runs on the server and provides to the NetWare network file and record locking, security, print spooling, and interprocess communications, while determining performance, multivendor support, and reliability of the network.

NetWare partition (disk)

A partition created on each NetWare network hard disk, from which NetWare volumes are created. A NetWare disk partition is a subdivision of a hard disk and should not be confused with a NetWare Directory partition.

NetWare Peripheral Architecture (NPA)

An extension of the Media Manager (MM) that provides broader and more flexible driver support for host adapters and storage devices. NPA distinguishes between two types of driver support: Host Adapter Module (HAM) and Custom Device Module (CDM). The HAM drives the host adapter hardware and provides functionality to route requests to the bus where a specified device is attached. The Host Adapter Interface (HAI) provides an interface for HAMs to communicate with the MM. The CDM drives storage devices or autochanges attached to a host adapter bus. The Custom Device Interface (CDI) provides an interface for CDMs to communicate with the MM.

NetWare protocols and transports

Components of NetWare software that enable client workstations and servers to communicate and be understood on the network. A protocol manages data and a transport manages application messages. Protocols provided with NetWare Client software include Address Resolution Protocol (ARP), Bootstrap Protocol (BOOTP), Internet Control Message Protocol (ICMP), Internetwork Packet Exchange (IPX), Management Information Base (MIB), Network Basic Input/Output System (NetBIOS), Remote Program Load (RPL), Reverse Address Resolution Protocol (RARP), Sequenced Packet Exchange (SPX), System Network Architecture (SNA), Transmission Control Protocol (TCP), User Datagram Protocol (UDP), and Xerox Network System (XNS).

NetWare Requester for OS/2

Software running on an OS/2 workstation that enables the workstation to connect to a NetWare network and application servers to communicate with the workstations without involving NetWare.

NetWare rights package

A feature of the Rights utility that provides a particular set of NetWare rights. Among the available rights packages are User, Owner, Private, Drop, View Only, and Custom.

NetWare Runtime

A single-user version of the NetWare 4.x operating system that can be used as a dedicated applications server with NetWare Loadable Modules (NLMs) installed on it, thus freeing the remaining NetWare servers for other network tasks. Network clients attach to an NLM running on top of NetWare Runtime. That NLM provides to the client required services through Application Program Interfaces (APIs).

NetWare server

A computer that runs the NetWare operating system software, regulates communications among personal computers attached to it, and manages such shared network resources as printers and volumes.

NetWare Server for OS/2

Device drivers allowing the NetWare 4.x operating system to operate as a nondedicated server on a computer running under the OS/2 operating system. NetWare Server for OS/2 runs as an independent operating system on an OS/2 computer. Although it is not a process controlled by OS/2, it does share the hard disk, memory, and CD-ROM drive with OS/2. NetWare Server for OS/2 works with NetWare Client for OS/2.

NetWare Server object

A leaf object in Novell Directory Services (NDS) that represents a server running NetWare on the network and can be referenced by other objects (such as a Volume object) to help identify their locations.

NetWare Server TSA

A Target Service Agent (TSA) that passes requests for data generated within SBACKUP to the NetWare server where the data resides, and then returns to SBACKUP the requested data through the Storage-Management Data Requester (SMDR).

NetWare shell

A NetWare program, loaded into the memory of each workstation, which builds itself around DOS to intercept the workstation's network requests, and then reroute them to a NetWare server. The NetWare shell works only on versions prior to NetWare 4.0.

NetWare SQL

An access system for relational databases, based on Structured Query Language (SQL), and residing at the NetWare server as a NetWare Loadable Module (NLM). This NLM enables users to run applications that are designed to manage shared data files.

NetWare STREAMs

A set of NetWare services that enables user processes to create STREAM messages, to send the messages to neighboring kernel modules and drivers, and to receive the contents of such messages from kernel modules and drivers.

NetWare TCP/IP

A group of NetWare Loadable Modules (NLMs) that implement the Transmission Control Protocol/Internet Protocol (TCP/IP) suite to provide routing services for workstations by using the TCP/IP format.

NetWare Telephony Services

A software/hardware package designed to integrate a NetWare network with a telephone private branch exchange (PBX).

NetWare Tools (OS/2) utility

In IntranetWare, an OS/2 workstation utility that provides access to network resources. This utility enables users to map drives, manage printer connections, manage the Directory tree, manage server connections, display network users, and send messages.

NetWare TSA (OS/2)

In IntranetWare, an OS/2 workstation module that allows the hard drive on the workstation to be accessed by the SBACKUP utility or another backup program for backup to the network. This utility enables users to specify which users can access a particular workstation hard drive, the password for access to the hard drive, and which partitions on the hard drive are available for backup.

NetWare UAM

A User-Authentication Method (UAM) that provides password encryption, allows Novell Directory Services (NDS) authentication, and enables NetWare users to enter passwords longer than six characters while working on a Macintosh workstation.

NetWare UNIX Client (NUC)

Software that enables the NetWare operating system to provide services to UnixWare users and applications and allows UnixWare users to access remote directories, files, and printers on NetWare servers, as if they were in the UNIX environment.

NetWare utilities

In NetWare, the server console, workstation, or file-management programs used to perform specific tasks on the network. Server console utilities execute on the server console, workstation utilities execute on the workstation (although they are installed on the server), and file-management utilities execute programs to manipulate files. NetWare utilities are often NetWare Loadable Modules (NLMs) or Virtual Loadable Modules (VLMs).

NetWare volume

A physical amount of NetWare server hard disk storage space that has a fixed size. A NetWare volume sits at the same level as a DOS root directory, the highest level of the NetWare directory structure.

NetWare Web Server

A component of IntranetWare integrated with Novell Directory Services (NDS) to provide the capability of building a World Wide Web (WWW) site on a corporate intranetwork and the Internet. Through NDS authentication and multiple-access control, the NetWare Web Server provides security to prevent unauthorized break-ins from inside or outside an organization. A Secure Sockets Layer (SSL) uses public key/private key encryption to encode the entire dialogue between the Web browser and the NetWare server. The NetWare Web Server also includes Internet Protocol (IP) address, username, host name, directory, document, NDS user, and NDS group filters.

NetWare-encrypted password

A password encoded by the NetWare User Authentication Method (UAM) software on a Macintosh workstation before it can be sent to the NetWare server.

NetWire

An electronic information service from Novell that provides access to product information, services information, and time-sensitive technical information for NetWare users. NetWire began as Novell's forum on CompuServe and has since been integrated with the Novell Support Connection in the World Wide Web (WWW).

network

A group of computers communicating with each other, sharing peripherals, and accessing remote hosts or other networks. For example, a NetWare network (consisting of workstations, peripherals, and one or more NetWare servers) provides users with the capability to send messages between workstations, share files, and protect files through a security system. Workstations are often called *nodes* (or *lobes*) and connect to one or more *servers*. The physical layout of a network is called a *topology*, the means of connection is often by *cables*, and the means of communication between nodes is often through *protocols*. Different types of network classifications include campus area networks (CANs), global area networks (GANs), local area networks (LANs), metropolitan area networks (MANs), and wide area networks (WANs).

Network Access Controller (NAC)

A device that provides access to a network either for another network or for remote callers.

network adapter

Hardware installed in workstation and server computers that enables them to communicate on a network.
Synonym: *Network Interface Card (NIC)*

network address

An eight-digit, hexadecimal number that uniquely identifies a network cable segment or a unique number that represents a network device.

network addressable unit (NAU)

A logical unit (LU), physical unit (PU), or system services control point (SSCP) that is the origin or the destination of information transmitted through the path control network in a Systems Network Architecture (SNA) network.

network administration

Management tasks (including assigning addresses to devices, maintaining network data files across a network, and setting up of internetwork routing) related to the software and hardware connecting a network. Network administration can also include system tasks related to server management (including starting up and shutting down the network system, adding or removing user accounts, and backing up and restoring network server data).

network analyzer

A software product, or a combination of software and hardware, that monitors the activity of a network and the workstations attached to the network and provides summaries or long-term trends of network activity and performance. The software-hardware combination may include a Network Interface Card (NIC) used to test the network directly.

Network Application Support (NAS)

Specifications from Digital Equipment Corporation designed to use international standards to support a uniform environment for software running on different platforms. The NAS specifications contrast with IBM's Systems Application Architecture (SAA) in that SAA provides proprietary protocols to support multiple platforms.

network architecture

A framework of principles that facilitates the operation, maintenance, and growth of a communications network by isolating user programs and applications from network details. Network architecture includes protocols and software that help to organize functions, data formats, and procedures for a network system. Common network architectures include Attached Resource Computer Network (ARCnet), Asynchronous Transfer Mode (ATM), Ethernet, Fiber Distributed Data Interface (FDDI), and Token Ring.

network backbone
A central cabling system that attaches servers and routers on a network and handles all network traffic. Because of its configuration (all servers connected to a central cable), the network backbone often decreases the time needed for transmission of packets and the amount of traffic on a network.

Network Basic Input/Output System (NetBIOS)
Generically, the standard protocol used as an interface for applications developed to run peer-to-peer communications on an IBM personal computer network and a Token Ring network. The NetWare Client for DOS and MS Windows program includes a NetBIOS driver that is an emulator allowing NetWare Internetwork Packet Exchange (IPX) to interface with two NetBIOS interrupts. This driver is an emulator because it does not transmit NetBIOS packets; rather, the packets are encapsulated as IPX packets, which are themselves transmitted.

Network Basic Input/Output System Extended User Interface (NetBEUI)
An implementation of IBM's Network Basic Input/Output System (NetBIOS) transport protocol that communicates with a network through Microsoft's Network Driver Interface Specification (NDIS) for the Network Interface Card (NIC). Microsoft's LAN Server and LAN Manager use NetBEUI.

network board
A circuit board installed in a NetWare network workstation computer to allow it to communicate with other workstations and with a NetWare server.
Synonym: *Network Interface Card (NIC); network adapter*

network communication
The process of workstations on a network requesting data and services from another workstation through a communications medium such as a cable.

Network Communications Control Facility (NCCF)
A component of IBM's NetView network-management software that monitors and controls the operation of a network.

network computing
A multivendor networking environment incorporating local area network (LAN) and wide area network (WAN) technologies to provide enterprise network connectivity.

network connection software
Software files that must be loaded on network workstation computer for the workstation to be connected to the network.

Network Control Block (NCB)
A packet structure used in the NetBIOS transport protocol.

Network Control Center (NCC)
A designated network workstation in charge of network management, which receives reports from agent processes running on workstations.

network control program (NCP)
A program that provides routing, error control, testing, and addressing of Systems Network Architecture (SNA) devices.

Network Control Protocol (NCP)
A program, such as NetWare Core Protocol (NCP), that manages basic networking functions for a network.

Network Control System (NCS)
A software tool that monitors and modifies network activity. NCS software is generally found on older network systems that incorporate a low-speed, secondary data channel created with Time-Division Multiplexing (TDM).

network device driver
Software that controls the coordination between the physical functions of a Network Interface Card (NIC) and other workstation hardware or software on a network.

network direct printer
A printer or print queue server from a third-party vendor that connects directly to a network, such as NetWare. Installation utilities, usually supplied by the vendor, configure the device to recognize network print components and communicate with the network.

network directory
A directory located not on the computer being used, but rather on another computer in a network.
Synonym: *shared folder*

network drive
An internal representation used by an operating system to refer to an actual disk device or to a group of directories specified by the DOS SUBST command.
Synonym: *logical drive*

Network Driver Interface Specification (NDIS)
A specification developed jointly by 3Com and Microsoft to standardize the interface used between a Network Interface Cards (NIC) and the underlying operating system, as well as to provide protocol multiplexing so multiple protocol stacks may be used at one time.

Network Entity Title (NET)
Network addresses defined in the OSI Reference Model and used in Connectionless Mode Network Service (CLNS) networks.

Network File System (NFS)
An optional NetWare product that is a distributed file system protocol used to access NetWare file systems and NetWare print queues on UNIX systems.

network hardware

Hardware used to create a network that includes computers (for both workstations and servers) and related equipment (including circuit boards, keyboards, and monitors), connection equipment (including cables, wiring centers, connectors, repeaters, transceivers, bridges, routers, and gateways), and auxiliary components (including peripheral devices, safety devices, and tools).

Network Information Center (NIC)

A central authority responsible for assigning all Internet addresses.
Synonym: *Internet Network Information Center (InterNIC)*

Network Information Services (NIS)

A UNIX security and file-access database usually found in the UNIX host files /etc/hosts, /etc/passwd, and /etc/group.
Synonym: *Yellow Pages*

network interface

A boundary that exists between a network carrier and a local installation.

Network Interface Card (NIC)

A hardware interface between a device (such as a printer or computer) and the network transmission media that communicates through drivers with network node software (such as a network shell or operating system) on one end and with network cabling to separate nodes on the other end. Chips on the board provide support for different varieties of network architectures (such as Ethernet or Token Ring), which, in turn, determine features and restrictions for the NIC. On the outgoing end of the connection, a NIC (in a workstation) translates user requests into a form suitable for transmission across the network. On the incoming end of the connection, the NIC monitors the network and checks to see whether the packet's destination address matches the NIC node address, if the packet's destination address indicates it is being broadcast to all nodes on the network, or if the packet's destination address indicates it is being multicast to a group of nodes on the network.
Synonyms: *LAN adapter; LAN card; network board; network interface board; Network Interface Module (NIM); Network Interface Unit (NIU); network adapter*

Network layer (OSI model)

The third layer (Layer 3) in the OSI Reference Model. The Network layer ensures information arrives at its intended destination and smooths out differences between network media so higher layers in the model (the Transport, Session, Presentation, and Application Layers) do not need to account for the distinctions.

network management

A process that ensures consistent reliability and availability of a network and the timely transmission of data across a network. Network management can be assigned to dedicated devices or to general-purpose devices.

Network Management Architecture (NMA)

In IBM's NetView package, a centralized, mainframe-oriented model for network management. NMA provides configuration management, problem management, performance and accounting management, and change management.

Network Management Entity (NME)

Software or hardware in the Open Systems Interconnect (OSI) network-management model that provides a network node with the capability to collect, store, and report data about the node's activity.

Network-Management NLM

A NetWare Loadable Module (NLM) that tracks information about network equipment, warns of impending problems, and enables remote management of the network.

Network Management Protocol (NMP)

A protocol from AT&T that controls certain network devices (such as modems or T1 multiplexers).

network-management services function

A set of programs in a Systems Network Architecture (SNA) network that receive network-management data, alert information, and problem determination statistics from Network-Management Vector Transport (NMVT) Request/Response Units (RUs).

Network-Management Vector Transport (NMVT)

A protocol in Systems Network Architecture (SNA) networks used to exchange network management data.

network modem

A modem equipped with a Network Interface Card (NIC) that is directly connected to a network as a node. Remote callers access the network through this node.

network monitoring

A network-management function that constantly checks the network and reports any problems.

network name

A symbolic identifier the network uses to identify a Network-Addressable Unit (NAU), a link station, or both.

Network News Transfer Protocol (NNTP)

A protocol used by news servers, interactive enough to enable the servers to select which newsgroups and articles they want. This protocol saves on network traffic and on file deletions.

network node (NN)

A personal computer (either a server or workstation), router, printer, or fax machine connected to a network by a Network Interface Card (NIC) and a local area network (LAN) driver.

network number

A number that uniquely identifies a network cable segment. In an AppleTalk network, the network number is a decimal integer between 1 and 65,279. In a NetWare network, the network number is a hexadecimal number that starts with the character pair 0x or 0X and is specified with or without trailing zeros. In a Transmission Control Protocol/Internet Protocol (TCP/IP) network, this is simply the number of the network.

Synonym: *IPX external network number*

network numbering

A system of numbers that identifies servers, Network Interface Cards (NICs), and cable segments on a network. In NetWare, this system includes an IPX external number (which identifies a network cable segment), an IPX internal network number (which identifies an individual NetWare 4.x server), and a node number (which identifies an NIC).

Network Operating Center (NOC)

An organization or a site responsible for the maintenance of a network.

network operating system (NOS)

Software installed on a network server that coordinates network activities, regulates who can access which files on the network, who can make changes to data, and who can use network resources (such as a shared printer).

Network Packet Switch Interface (NPSI)

An interface used in Systems Network Architecture (SNA) networks.

network printer

A printer shared by workstations (or nodes) across a network.

Network Printing Alliance Protocol (NPAP)

A proposed bidirectional protocol standard that enables the exchange of configuration information and other data independent of the Printer-Control Language (PCL) or the Page-Description Language (PDL) in use on the network.

network queue

A group of network jobs waiting to be processed. *Jobs* contain data only interpreted by the job creator or the job server.

network range

A continuous range of decimal integers between 1 and 65,279 (such as 1–10) assigned to each extended network supporting AppleTalk.

network search drive mapping
A pointer to a directory that contains applications, operating system files, and so forth, which enable execution of a program even if it is not physically located in that directory. The mapping enables the operating system to locate the file.

network server
A dedicated computer on a local area network (LAN) that provides access to (and storage for) files and data, while also managing shared resources for the network.

Network Services Access Point (NSAP)
The location in the OSI Reference Model through which a Transport Layer (Layer 4) entity can get access to Network Layer (Layer 3) services. Each NSAP is assigned a unique network address.

Network Services objects
A group of Novell Directory Services (NDS) leaf objects that enable a network administrator to manage a network. This group includes the User Template object (which is used to create User objects), the Application object (which enables the management of applications as objects), the Auditing File object (which enables the management of an auditing log file as an object), and the License Service Provider object (which represents a network server with the NetWare Licensing Services NetWare Loadable Module loaded).

Network Services Protocol (NSP)
A proprietary protocol from Digital Equipment Corporation (used in DECnet networks) that works on the Transport Layer (Layer 4) of the OSI Reference Model.

network station
A machine linked to a network that may be either a workstation or a server. **Synonym:** *node*

network supervisor
A generic term describing the person responsible for configuring the NetWare server, workstations, user access, printing, and so forth.

network topology

The physical arrangement of nodes on a network, including such topologies as bus topology, cascaded bridge, distributed star, hybrid, logical, mesh, physical, ring, star, star-wired ring, and tree.

network traffic

A transmission data load carried by network connections or channels.

Network Visible Entity (NVE)

An AppleTalk network resource or process accessible through the Datagram Delivery Protocol (DDP).

network-aware application

An application created on a network that can access such network services as printing.

network-byte order

A byte order commonly used in AppleTalk networks, which specifies integers must be stored most significant byte first.

Network-Network Interface (NNI)

The interconnection used in a frame relay network that enables users who are subscribing to different frame relay providers to communicate with one another.

NETx.COM

A network shell program for versions prior to NetWare 4.x, used to establish a connection with the operating system running on the NetWare server. Earlier versions of the program were named NET3.COM, NET4.COM, and NET5.COM, which correspond to the major versions of DOS 3, DOS 4, and DOS 5. NETx.COM was replaced in later versions of NetWare with the NetWare DOS Requester.

newbie

A term used to describe a person who is new to the Internet or to a particular area of the Internet, particularly someone who is new to a Usenet newsgroup.

News

An Internet information-sharing service that enables users to exchange messages about topics of mutual interest and to view messages posted by other users.

Synonyms: *Netnews; Network News; Usenet News*

news newsgroup

An Internet newsgroup that discusses topics about Internet newsgroups.

news server

An Internet computer that accesses Usenet newsgroups and enables the user to read the information contained in the newsgroup.

Newsadmin (news administrator)

A person responsible for managing system Usenet newsgroups (including deciding which newsgroups to carry, how long to keep bulletins, and the exchange of newsfeeds with other systems) for an Internet Service Provider (ISP) or for an internal intranetwork site.

newsgroup

A distributed bulletin board system (BBS) on the Internet that provides discussion groups and information about particular topics.

newsgroup kill file

A file telling a newsreader which articles a user wants to read and which to discard.

newsreader

A program that retrieves, organizes, and displays messages or articles from newsgroups. A newsreader can select newsgroups, select newsgroup articles, provide viewing of newsgroup articles, and post articles (or responses to an article). Types of newsreaders include character-based, windowed, threaded (which arrange articles so the evolution of original article and responses can be viewed), and online (which provides viewing while connected to the Internet).

Next Station Addressing (NSA)

In a Fiber Distributed Data Interface (FDDI) network, an addressing mode by which a workstation can send a packet to the next workstation in the ring without having to know that workstation's network address.

NeXTSTEP

An object-oriented variant of the UNIX operating system in which only a microkernel operating system stays loaded, while other services are provided in modules that can be loaded as needed. NeXTSTEP supports Transmission Control Protocol/Internet Protocol (TCP/IP) networks and includes software that enables a NeXTSTEP machine to access file and print services on a NetWare or AppleTalk network.

nitwork

A term describing the collection of details that must be considered to keep a network functioning properly.

NLM global data items

NetWare Loadable Module (NLM) data items for which only one value has been assigned, which are global to all the thread groups and threads of the NLM. If a change is made to the values of NLM global data items, all thread groups and threads in the NLM are affected.

NLM screens

Regular or popup screens that appear during the execution of a NetWare Loadable Module (NLM) and contain instructional or error information about the NLM or about the function the NLM is performing.

nn

A UNIX newsreader that features a fast summary presentation of pending articles and is popular at some academic sites with direct UNIX connections.

node

Any addressable entity on a network (including any device assigned a network address and capable of sending and receiving information) or an endpoint of a link or junction common to two or more links on a network. The term sometimes refers to an actual device such as a server, router, workstation, or network printer. Nodes can also be host processors, communications controllers, or terminals. If a node is not a computer, it must have a Network Interface Card (NIC) preinstalled.

node address
A combination of a node number with the network number to form a unique node address.

node number
A unique 8-bit node number acquired dynamically by a node when it connects to the network (which the node tries to use when it reconnects to the network). A node number is assigned to a Network Interface Card (NIC). Each node must have at least one NIC, by which the node is connected to the network. Depending on the type of NIC, node numbers are assigned in different ways. For example, node numbers for Ethernet and Token Ring NICs are preset by the manufacturer. Node numbers for ARCnet NICs are set with jumpers and switches.

node schematic
A graphical representation of a node (or NetWare server) that displays network boards, server disks, volumes, queues, users, NetWare Loadable Modules (NLMs), and event and alert messages. This representation is the main graphical display in the NetWare Management System (NMS) software.

Node-to-Node Routing
A method that routes a packet from its source node to its destination, instead of touting a packet to the router nearest to the destination node.

noise
An unwanted low-voltage, low-current, high-frequency signal that occurs between two points in a transmission circuit.

Noise-Equivalent Power (NEP)
Amount of optical power needed by a fiber-optic receiver to produce an electric current as strong as the receiver's base noise level.

Nominal Velocity of Propagation (NVP)
A speed expressed as a percentage or fraction of the speed of light in a vacuum, used to measure signal movement through a cable.

nonblocking functions
Functions that do not cause a caller to relinquish control.

nonblocking mode
A mode of execution that allows a function to return immediately if a specific event is not pending or has not occurred.

Synonym: *asynchronous execution*

nondedicated router
An external router that can function simultaneously as a router and as a workstation.

nondedicated server
A network server that runs the network functions and performs as a workstation.

nondisruptive test
A network-management diagnostic or performance test that can be run in the background and has little or no effect on normal network activity.

nonextended AppleTalk network
An AppleTalk network not supporting Phase 2 extensions (such as zone lists and network ranges).

non-Macintosh client
A NetWare term describing a DOS, Windows, or OS/2 client communicating with the network through an Internetwork Packet Exchange (IPX) connection.

non-Macintosh user
A NetWare term describing a user working at a DOS, Windows, OS/2, or UNIX workstation.

nonpreemptive environment

A fast, real-time, multitasking network environment in which threads are scheduled according to priority levels and are executed on a run-to-completion basis.

nonrepudiation

A network-security measure in which a sender cannot deny having sent a message and a recipient cannot deny having received the message.

Non-Return to Zero (NRZ)

A binary encoding scheme that represents ones and zeros as opposite and alternating high and low voltages, with no return to reference (or zero) voltage between encoded bits.

Non-Return to Zero Inverted (NRZI)

A binary encoding scheme that inverts a signal on a one and leaves the signal unchanged for a zero. A change in voltage indicates a one bit and the absence of a change in voltage indicates a zero bit.

non-seed router

A router's interface configured to learn its configuration from a configured router on the same network.

Synonym: *learning router*

nonshareable

A term describing a file, device, or process available to only one user at a time.

nonswitched line

A connection between systems or devices that can be made without dialing.

nonvolatile memory

A type of computer memory that retains its contents when a computer is shut down. For example, read-only memory (ROM), erasable programmable read-only memory (EPROM), and electrically erasable programmable read-only memory (EEPROM) are all nonvolatile memory types.

Nonvolatile RAM (NVRAM)
Random access memory (RAM) that retains its contents when a computer is shut down, sometimes used to store configuration information.

Normal (N) attribute
A file attribute set by the NetWare operating system to indicate no other NetWare attributes have been set.

Normal Response Mode (NRM)
A High-Level Data Link Control (HDLC) mode used on links with one primary station and one or more secondary stations, which allows secondary stations to transmit only if they first receive poll information from the primary station.

normal termination
A termination resulting in the successful execution of a program.

Northwest Net
A regional network in the Northwest United States, Alaska, Montana, and North Dakota that connects all major universities in the region, as well as such major corporations as Boeing International and Sequent Computer.

notarization
The use of a notary (a trusted third party) to verify a communication between two entities is legitimate.

notebook computer
A portable computer with a flat-screen display and keyboard that fold together for easier transportation. Notebook computers can run from battery power or can be plugged in to an alternating current (AC) power source. Notebook computers often use Personal Computer Memory Card International Association (PCMIA) expansion connections for additional peripheral devices such as modems, fax modems, and network connections.

notwork

A term describing a network that is not functioning properly or not functioning at all.

Novell Alliance Program

A partnership formed between Novell and professional service companies that provides customers with comprehensive network design and support services.

Novell *AppNotes*

Novell's monthly technical journal that includes information about designing, implementing, and managing NetWare-based computer systems.

Synonym: *NetWare Application Notes*

Novell AppWare

A software layer developed by Novell that makes network services more easily available to all developers, regardless of the operating system or user interface for which the developers are writing. AppWare is no longer sold by Novell.

Novell Authorized Education Centers (NAEC)

An independent training organization that meets Novell education standards and is authorized to teach Novell-developed courses with Certified Novell Instructors (CNIs).

Novell College Credit Program (NCCP)

A program in which Novell issues an official transcript upon completion of NetWare certification courses reviewed by the American Council on Education (ACE), which may result in college course credit being awarded for taking the courses and passing the certification examinations.

Novell Consulting Services (NCS)

A department at Novell providing custom software development, network auditing, network systems design, and distributed application-design services.

Novell Directory Services (NDS)

In NetWare and IntranetWare, a relational database distributed across the entire network that provides global access to all network resources, regardless of their locations. NDS uses a distributed database (called the *NetWare Directory database* or simply the *Directory*) to store all network resources as objects. Users log in to a multiserver network and view the entire network as a single information system, which improves user productivity and diminishes administrative costs.

NDS organizes users, groups, printers, servers, volumes, and other physical network devices into a hierarchical tree structure. The NDS tree (also known as the *Directory tree*) is what enables resources to be managed and displayed in a single view. Figure N.3 shows an example of an NDS Directory tree. The Directory tree is managed through objects and their associated properties.

NDS replaces the bindery found in NetWare 3.*x* networks. NDS is distributed and can be replicated on multiple servers, whereas the bindery in NetWare 3.*x* is a flat structure in which resources belong to a single server.

Novell Distributed Print Services (NDPS)

An IntranetWare distributed service designed for complex print-management and production requirements, which consists of client, server, and connectivity components seamlessly linking and sharing network printers with applications. With NDPS, the NetWare Administrator provides management and control of printers, eliminating the need to create and configure Print Queue, Printer, and Print Server leaf objects.

Novell DOS 7

A version of DOS developed by Digital Research (at the time, a subsidiary of Novell) that provides improvements in the memory-management, multitasking, and networking capabilities of other versions of DOS and includes utilities to improve system performance through disk compression.

Novell Educational Academic Partner (NEAP)

A college or university that provides Novell-authorized courses in a semester- or quarter-length curriculum and is authorized to teach Novell-developed courses with Certified Novell Instructors (CNIs).

Novell ElectroText

Online NetWare documentation that provides access to documents from a NetWare workstation. This documentation includes all manuals in the NetWare 4.*x* documentation set (except the *Quick Access Guide*).

Novell OEM Partners

Original Equipment Manufacturers (OEMs) in partnerships with Novell that provide sales and support services for NetWare networks.

Novell Support Connection

A CD-ROM that contains Novell technical information documents, Novell Labs hardware and software test bulletins, online product manuals, Novell *Application Notes*, the Novell Buyer's Guide, Novell corporate information, and patches, fixes, and drivers for NetWare.

Synonyms: *Novell Support Encyclopedia (NSE); Novell Support Encyclopedia, Professional Edition (NSEPro)*

Novell Technical Support (NTS)

A Novell department consisting of customer support representatives and support engineers that provides service to end users and to independent service providers.

Novell Virtual Terminals (NVT)

A two-part application program enabling DOS clients to access applications running on a NetWare Application server. One part of the program is for the DOS system and the other is for the UnixWare Application server.

NS header

A part of the network services (NS) Request/Response Unit (RU) that identifies the type of RU.

N-Series connector

A connector similar to a threaded-nut connector (TNC) but with a fatter barrel and a thinner plug, used to connect thick coaxial cables in a thick Ethernet network.

NT Application object

A Novell Directory Services (NDS) leaf object used to represent any object using Windows NT as the workstation operating system.

NT File System (NTFS)

The native file system for the Windows NT operating system featuring up to 256 characters for filenames, a system of permissions for file sharing, a transaction log, the OS/2 file allocation table (FAT), and the OS/2 High-Performance File System (HPFS).

NuBus

A bus specification providing expansion capabilities for a Macintosh computer that supports 32-bit data and address transfer. Slots on the Macintosh for NuBus are used to provide video capabilities, extra memory, and networking capabilities.

null key

A key field in Btrieve that can be a user-defined character. Btrieve distinguishes between any-segment null keys (called a *manual key*) and all-segment null keys (simply called *null keys* in earlier versions of Btrieve). The *any-segment null key* does not include a particular record in the index if the value of any key segment of that record matches a null value. The *all-segment null key* excludes a particular record from the index only if the value of all key segments of that record matches a null value.

null modem

A serial cable and connector with a modified RS-232 configuration that enables two computers to communicate directly without a modem as an intermediary device. The pin configuration of the connecting cable is crossed over so the wires used for sending by one computer are used for receiving data by the other computer.

Numerical Aperture (NA)

A range of angles over which a fiber-optic core can receive incoming light.

NUT

An interface for NetWare Loadable Modules (NLMs) in NetWare 3.x that must be loaded on NetWare 3.x servers for some NLMs to operate.

NWSNUT

An interface for NetWare Loadable Modules (NLMs) in NetWare 4.x that must be loaded on NetWare 4.x servers for some NLMs to operate.

Nyquist Sampling Theorem

A theorem that postulates it is possible to reconstruct analog signals from samples if enough samples are taken.

NYSERNet

A New York state network using a T1 backbone to connect the National Science Foundation Network (NSFnet), many universities, and several major corporations.

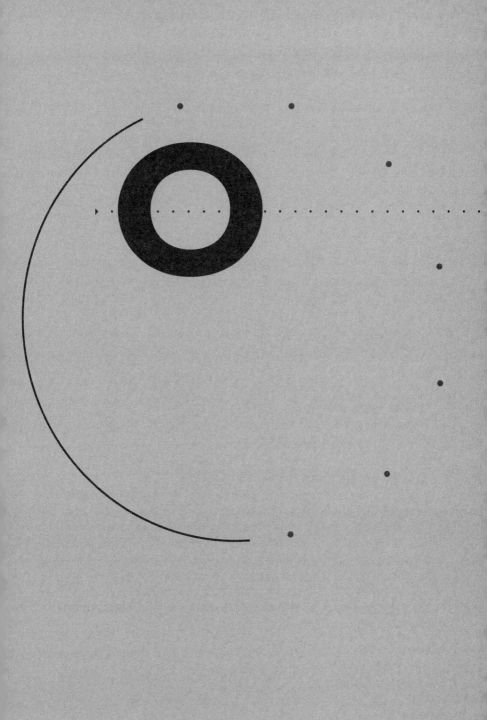

object

A structure in Novell Directory Services (NDS) that stores information about a network resource. An object consists of categories of information (or *properties*), as well as the data in those properties. Objects can represent *physical entities* (such as a user or a printer) or *logical entities* (such as groups or print queues). The object stores information about the entity, but it is not the actual entity itself. The two types of objects are *container objects* (which hold other objects) and *leaf objects* (located at the ends of branches and do not contain other objects). Leaf objects have a common name, but container objects are referred to by their Organizational Unit name, Organization name, or Country name. The *complete name* of an object consists of its common name (if it has one), followed by a period, followed by the name of the container object, followed by a period, and so on, up through all container objects to the [Root] object of the Directory tree. The *context* of an object is the position of the object within its container object. Moving objects from one container to another is called *changing contexts*.

object class

A defined list of objects (such as servers, users, and print queues) found in Novell Directory Services (NDS).

object instance

An instance of an object type bound to a value. This term is used in the context of network management.

Object Linking and Embedding (OLE)

A specification defining how Microsoft Windows applications can link (to a document file) a reference to an actual object or embed an object (into a document file) by making a copy of the object at the desired location. This specification requires OLE support to be written into the Windows applications; the lowest version of OLE used by any of the applications determines the capabilities of the application interface. The OLE specification enables objects from different programs to be linked and embedded in a separate application; it also enables the user to edit the object using the application that created the object.

Object Request Broker (ORB) .

A service developed by the Object Management Group (OMG) as part of the Common Object Request Broker Architecture (CORBA) specification that enables existing applications to communicate with object-oriented applications. An ORB enables applications to request network services without first knowing the directory structure of the environment from which the service is being requested.

object rights

An object's assigned qualities that define what control the object has over directories, files, or other Novell Directory Services (NDS) objects.

object-oriented

Any computer system, operating system, programming language, application, or Graphical User Interface (GUI) that supports the use of objects.

object-oriented graphics

Images constructed from individual components (such as lines, arcs, circles, and squares) that are defined mathematically rather than as a set of dots. Users may manipulate a part of the image without redrawing and may resize or rotate the image without any distortion.

Synonyms: *vector graphics; structured graphics*

object-oriented program (OOP)

A programming model in which the program is viewed as a set of self-contained objects (objects containing both data and code) interacting with other objects by passing messages from one to another. This model also enables the programmer to create procedures that work with objects whose exact type may not be known until the program is run. Objects are incorporated in the program by making them part of a layered hierarchy.

octet

A group of eight binary digits that are operated on as a unit. This term generally is used when describing frame or packet formats.

Synonyms: *byte; character*

odd parity

A communications error-checking method in which the sum of all the 1 bits in the byte plus the parity bit must be odd. When the total is already odd, the parity bit is set to 0. When the total is even, the parity bit is set to 1.

ODI/NDIS Support (ODINSUP)

An interface that enables the Open Data-Link Interface (ODI) to coexist with network driver-interfaces that comply with the Network Driver-Interface Specification (NDIS). ODINSUP permits the connection of a workstation to dissimilar networks; the networks can appear as one. NDIS protocol stacks can communicate through the ODI Link-Support Layer (LSL) and Multiple-Link Interface Driver (MLID), which permits both NDIS and ODI protocol stacks to coexist on the same system and to use a single MLID. ODINSUP enables a user to use a wider variety of programs without being concerned with compatibility and without having to reconfigure or reboot a workstation to switch from one network to another.

Off Hook (OH)

An indication that a telephone line is in use.

offline

The condition of a computer system or peripheral device that is unavailable for use.

offline mail reader

A program that enables a user to read and reply to electronic mail (e-mail) messages from a local copy of the message in the user's mailbox by retrieving messages from the mailbox on the host machine and storing the message on a local disk or in memory until the user is ready to read it.

offline newsreader

A newsreader that can download files from a newsgroup and can enable a user to review the postings at a later time. This results in lower connect charges, but it may result in usage of a significant amount of system storage space.

offline UPS
A backup uninterruptible power supply (UPS) unit not configured to activate automatically should a power outage occur.

offspring count
The number of subdirectories and files located in a directory.

ohm
An electrical unit of resistance that is the counterpart to friction, represented by the uppercase Greek letter omega (Ω). For example, a resistance of 1 ohm passes 1 ampere of current when 1 volt is applied.

on-demand call
A call activated by the presence of data traffic directed to, or through, a remote peer system.

on-demand connection
A type of connection that uses static routing information to advertise the presence of an exterior network and provides occasional access to a remote system (as opposed to permanent access). This type of connection minimizes a connection expense and maximizes network resources.

on-demand SVC
A virtual circuit, shut down after data has been transmitted over a Switched Virtual Circuit (SVC), which remains down until more data is queued up for sending (at which time a connection is re-established).

on-the-fly switching
A switching process performed on the spur of the moment, while the switch is busy or continuously active.

ones density
A measurement that compares the number of ones in a transmission with the total number of digital time slots transmitted. Certain specifications restrict the number of consecutive zeros that may appear in a transmission.

one-time login

A configuration of the network operating system that enables a user to enter a username and password when the computer starts up; that entry enables login to the network.

online

A term describing the capability to perform operations on a computer, the availability of a peripheral device to be used, or a communications computer connected to a remote computer over a network or modem link.

online help

The availability of information about network functions and concepts from any workstation on the network.

online UPS

A backup uninterruptible power supply (UPS) unit configured to activate automatically should a power outage occur.

open

A networking environment in which the specifications for elements or interfaces have been made publicly available for third-party vendors to create compatible or competing products. This term may also describe a gap or separation in the conductive material of a cable.

Open Application Interface (OAI)

A telephonic interface that can be programmed and changed to affect the operation of a private branch exchange (PBX).

open architecture

An architectural design that makes network hardware and software compatible with components from a variety of vendors.

open circuit

A medium's transmission path that has been broken, which usually prevents network communication.

Open Database Connectivity (ODBC)
A Microsoft Applications-Program Interface (API) defining how databases are accessed in the Windows environment.

Open Data-Link Interface (ODI)
A driver specification developed by Novell to enable a single workstation to communicate transparently with several different protocol stacks, while using a single local area network (LAN) board and a single LAN driver. ODI enables a workstation to access several protocol-specific applications and services at the same time and also enables communication between devices with different frame formats. The ODI architecture consists of three major components: Multiple-Link Interface Driver (MLID), Link-Support Layer (LSL), and communication protocol stacks.

Open Document Architecture (ODA)
An Open Systems Interconnection (OSI) specification (ISO 8613) from the International Standards Organization (ISO) defining how documents (especially documents containing fonts, graphics, and text) are electronically transmitted. This specification outlines three levels of document representation: Level 1 (for text-only data), Level 2 (for text and graphics generated in a word processing program), and Level 3 (for text and graphics generated in a desktop publishing program). The specification primarily addresses the logical representation of the document.

Open Network Computing (ONC)
A distributed computing model that uses the Network File System (NFS) of Sun Microsystems for handling files distributed over remote locations by using Remote Procedure Calls (RPCs). This model is supported in most UNIX environments, including Novell's UnixWare.

Open Network Node (ONN)
A part of the Advanced Peer-to-Peer Internetworking (APPI) standard that provides directory and routing services for Advanced Peer-to-Peer (APPN) end nodes and low-entry nodes.

open pipe

A path between a sender and a receiver in a circuit-switched and leased-line communications network that indicates data can flow directly between two locations, rather than being broken into packets and routed by various paths.

Open Shortest Path First (OSPF)

A link-state internal gateway protocol that is part of the Transmission Control Protocol/Internet Protocol (TCP/IP) suite. Using link-state advertisements, OSPF routers exchange information (such as information about the attached interfaces, metrics used, and other variables) about the state of their network connections and links. Using this information to construct the topology of the internetwork, the OSPF routers can then determine routing information for delivery of packets. All this information is stored in a link-state database, which the router examines for each destination to select the shortest path to serve as the route to that destination.

open system

A networking system in which the specifications for elements or interfaces have been made publicly available for third-party vendors to create compatible or competing products.

Open System Testing Consortium (OSTC)

A European organization responsible for developing a test suite for testing conformance to the International Telecommunications Union (ITU) X.400 Message-Handling System (MHS) recommendations.

Open Systems Interconnection (OSI)

An international program created by the International Standards Organization (ISO) and the Consultative Committee for International Telegraphy and Telephony (CCITT) to standardize data networking and to facilitate the interoperability of multivendor equipment. Under this standardization, an *open system* is one that supports the OSI Reference Model for connecting systems on a network and for transmitting information on these systems.

Open Systems Message Exchange (OSME)

An IBM application that provides the capability to exchange messages complying to the International Telecommunications Union (ITU) Message Handling System (MHS) X.400 specification.

operating system (OS)
Software that manages a computer system by such tasks as controlling data storage, controlling input and output to and from the keyboard (or other peripheral devices), and controlling the execution of compatible applications.

operating system protected (OSP) domain
A reserved portion of system memory used to run untested third-party NetWare Loadable Modules (NLMs) on NetWare 4.1 servers.

Operation, Administration and Management (OAM) package
A menu-based interface in UnixWare used to access a suite of system administration and maintenance utilities. These utilities can monitor network performance, detect network defects, protect the network operating system, report on network failures, and localize network faults.

operator hold
A hold placed by a print queue operator on a print job.

optical character recognition (OCR)
A capability provided by a standard optical scanner and special software that enables a computer to recognize printed or typed characters.

optical disc
A type of removable media that can be one- or two-sided, read-only or read-write, and is used as the media type for the High-Capacity Storage System (HCSS).

optical-disc library
A high-capacity storage device that uses an autochanger mechanism to mount and dismount optical discs.
Synonym: *jukebox*

optical drive

A device that provides mass storage through optical or magneto-optical encoding of data. Common types of optical drives include Compact Disc Read-Only Memory (CD-ROM), Write Once, Read Many (WORM), Erasable Optical (EO), Optical Read-Only Memory (OROM), and Magneto Optical (MO).

Optical Fiber, Nonconductive Plenum (OFNP)

A specification from the Underwriters Laboratory (UL) that defines certain safety criteria for optical fiber.

Optical Fiber, Nonconductive Riser (OFNR)

A specification from the Underwriters Laboratory (UL) that defines certain safety criteria for optical fiber.

optical switch

A high-speed communications switch that uses light to carry out a switching function.

Optical Time Domain Reflectometer (OTDR)

A fiber-optic communications tool that tests a light signal and analyzes the cable carrying it by sending out a light signal and checking the amount and type of light that reflects back.

Orange Book

A document originally entitled "The Department of Defense Trusted Computer System Evaluation Criteria" (TCSEC) and designed to provide network-security guidelines for developers and administrators. By listing basic requirements for very low and very high levels of security, the Orange Book provides evaluation criteria for different divisions of security. Criteria are hierarchically divided into Divisions D, C, B, and A. Division A represents the division representing systems with the most comprehensive security. Divisions C and B also have subdivisions known as *classes*, hierarchically arranged within divisions.

order of magnitude

A change in the numerical value of a number, reflected as a multiple of a reference value. The two most common reference values are expressed as decimal (base 10) or binary (base 2) values. Prefixes indicating orders of magnitude are often combined with computer measurements (for example, a *kilobyte* represents 1,000 bytes) as a means of expressing a large number of the unit of measurement. Table O.1 lists some common orders of magnitude used in computing environments.

TABLE O.1 *Orders of Magnitude*

MEASUREMENT	ABBREVIATION	BINARY	DECIMAL	EXAMPLE
exa-	E	2^{60}	10^{18}	1,000,000,000,000,000,000
peta-	P	2^{50}	10^{15}	1,000,000,000,000,000
tera-	T	2^{40}	10^{12}	1,000,000,000,000
giga-	G	2^{30}	10^{9}	1,000,000,000
mega-	M	2^{20}	10^{6}	1,000,000
kilo-	K	2^{10}	10^{3}	1,000
milli-	m	2^{-10}	10^{-3}	0.001
micro	μ	2^{-20}	10^{-6}	0.000001
nano-	n	2^{-30}	10^{-9}	0.000000001
pico-	p	2^{-40}	10^{-12}	0.000000000001
femto-	f	2^{-50}	10^{-15}	0.000000000000001
atta-	a	2^{-60}	10^{-18}	0.000000000000000001

org (organization)

A suffix on an Internet address, indicating the address belongs to a noncommercial organization. The collection of all addresses of this type is sometimes called an *org domain* or an *org hierarchy*.

Organization (O) object

In Novell Directory Services (NDS), a container object required in every Directory tree. An Organization object designates a company, a division of a company, a university or college with several departments, and so on. An Organization object must be placed directly below the [Root] object in the NDS hierarchy, unless a Country or Locality object is used.

Organizational Person object

A Novell Directory Services (NDS) leaf object that is one of two subclasses defined in the X.500 standard (the other is the Residential Person object). The Organizational Person object defines anyone who either represents, or is in some way associated with, a particular organization.

Organizational Role object

A Novell Directory Services (NDS) leaf object that defines a position or role with an organization object or a container object. Object or file rights are granted to the role itself and not to the occupants who may belong to the role.

Organizational Unit (OU) object

A Novell Directory Services (NDS) container object that allows the organization of leaf objects and represents a division, a business unit, or a project team. Organizational Unit objects contain other Organizational Unit (OU) objects, leaf objects, or any NDS object type except the [Root], Country, or Organization objects.

Origin server

A World Wide Web (WWW) server on which a particular resource resides or can be created.

original equipment manufacturer (OEM)

The original manufacturer of hardware subsystems or hardware components. The OEM often contracts to supply subsystems or components to a value-added reseller (VAR).

originate mode

A mode on a device initiating a call and waiting for a remote device to respond.

OS kernel

The core of an operating system that provides the most essential and basic system services (such as memory management).

OS/2

A 32-bit operating system from IBM that uses a graphical user interface (GUI), supports true preemptive multitasking, multiple threads, and nonsegmented memory addressing. OS/2 provides support for the DOS File Allocation Table (FAT) and its own High-Performance File System (HPFS), as well as such add-on file systems as the CD-ROM File System (CDFS). Two useful features of OS/2 are long filename support and extended attribute support.

OS/2 client

A computer that runs on the OS/2 operating system platform and connects to the network by using the NetWare Client for OS/2 software. This computer has the capability to store and retrieve data from the network, as well as to run executable network files.

OS/2 Requester

Part of the software that connects a computer running the OS/2 operating system to a NetWare network. The OS/2 Requester enables OS/2 users to share network resources.

OSI Government Systems Interconnection Protocol (OSI GOSIP)

A specification based on the OSI Reference Model that must be followed for purchases made for government installations, particularly purchases that involve networking products or services.

OSI Implementers Workshop (OIW)

A regional workshop representing North America for implementers of the OSI Reference Model. Other workshops include the European Workshop for Open Systems (EWOS), which represents Europe, and the Oceania Workshop (AOW), which represents the Asiatic region.

OSI Internet Management (OIM)

An organization responsible for specifying ways in which the protocols of the OSI Network-Management Model can be used to manage Transmission Control Protocol/Internet Protocol (TCP/IP) networks.

OSI network address

A network address in the OSI Reference Model associated with an entity in the Transport Layer (Layer 4). The address, which may be up to 20 bytes long, contains a standardized initial domain part and a domain-specific part (which falls under the control of the network administrator).

OSI Network-Management Model

Concepts and guidelines developed by the International Standards Organization (ISO) to be used as a basis for various aspects of network management. The basic configuration outlines a manager system communicating with a managed system to manage a resource contained in, or controlled by, the managed system. The three real-world building blocks for this model include a manager, agent, and managed object. This model defines how the Common Management Information Protocol (CMIP) can be used effectively to manage all kinds of resources. The four major components of the OSI Network-Management Model are as follows:

- *Systems Management Application Process (SMAP)* carries out the network management functions on a single machine.

- *Systems Management Application Entity (SMAE)* communicates with other network nodes (including the network manager) through Common Management Information Protocol (CMIP) packets.

- *Layer Management Entity (LME)* provides network management functions.

- *Management Information Base (MIB)* contains the network management information received from each node.

A task passes from SMAP through the Systems Management Interface (SMI) to the SMAE. Within the SMAE, the Systems Management Application Service Element (SMASE) contains the System Management Function Areas (SMFAs) and the Systems Management Functions (SMFs). The SMFAs include Accounting Management, Configuration Management, Fault Management, Performance Management, and Security Management. The SMFs include Access Control, Account Metering, Alarm Reporting, Event Reporting, Log Control, Object Management, Relationship Management, Security Alarm Reporting, Security Audit Trail, State Management, Summarization, Test Management, and Workload Monitoring. The SMASE functions rely on the Common Management Information Service Element (CMISE) to perform certain services, including Action, Cancel Get, Create, Delete, Event Report, Get, and Set. The CMISE relies on the Association Control Service Element (ACSE) and the Remote Operations Service Element (ROSE) to accomplish some of its tasks. SMASE can also bypass CMISE completely and use the Application Service Element (ASE) to perform services.

Synonym: *ISO Network Management Model*

OSI presentation address

A network address in the OSI Reference Model associated with an entity in the Application Layer (Layer 7). The OSI presentation address consists of an OSI network address and of selectors identifying Service Access Points (SAPs) for the Presentation Layer (Layer 6), Session Layer (Layer 5), and Transport Layer (Layer 4) of the OSI Reference Model.

OSI Reference Model

A computer network system model developed by the International Standards Organization (ISO) to standardize the interconnection of open computer systems (computer systems open for communication with other systems). The model defines seven specific layers, specifies how each layer can be addressed, and outlines the specific services and protocols each layer can use. Each layer of the model uses certain protocols and certain exchange units. The seven layers of the OSI Reference Model are shown in Table O.2.

TABLE O.2	*OSI Reference Model*
LAYER	**DESCRIPTION**
Application (Layer 7)	Provides services to application processes outside the scope of the OSI Reference Model (such as word processing programs or spreadsheet programs). This layer identifies and establishes the availability of communications partners, synchronizes the applications, establishes agreement on procedures for error control and data integrity, and determines the existence of sufficient resources for the intended communication.
Presentation (Layer 6)	Used to negotiate and establish the encoding of values for transferring structured data types (an operation called *transfer syntax*). This layer is responsible for communicating with the Session Layer and for managing the transfer syntax.
Session (Layer 5)	Establishes a network connection between users by managing ordinary data transport and providing enhanced services to certain applications. Some of the services provided are dialogue control (which means managing whose turn it is to communicate across the network), token management (which means managing the exchange of tokens to determine which side can perform critical operations), and synchronization (which means inserting checkpoints into the data stream to monitor the transmission of data).
Transport (Layer 4)	Accepts data from the Session Layer, splits it into smaller units (if necessary), and ensures accurate arrival at the destination. Through this layer, a source computer communicates with a destination computer, using message headers and control messages. This layer provides connection management services (which allow a Transport Layer user to create and maintain a data path to a correspondent Transport Layer user) and data transfer services (which provide a way to exchange data between a pair of Transport Layer users).

TABLE O.2	*OSI Reference Model (continued)*
LAYER	**DESCRIPTION**
Network (Layer 3)	Routes information from one networked computer to another. These computers may be located on the same network or on different networks. Of primary concern is how packets are routed from source to destination; this layer ensures congestion does not occur on the network and heterogeneous networks can communicate with each other.
Data-Link (Layer 2)	Provides a reliable means of data transmission across the Physical Layer by breaking the data into frames, transmitting the frames sequentially, and processing the acknowledged frames sent back by the receiver. This layer provides error control by creating and recognizing frame boundaries and errors associated with this information. Special bit patterns are attached to the beginning and ending of the frames and are constantly checked for accuracy.
Physical (Layer 1)	Provides a physical connection (as well as a means to activate and deactivate the connection) for the transmission of data among network entities. Design issues considered here are mechanical, electrical, and procedural interfaces, as well as the physical transmission medium. The services provided include the establishment of a connection and the transmission of bits over a physical medium to the Data-Link Layer.

In addition to the seven major layers, the OSI Reference Model also includes sublayers within the Data-Link Layer (Layer 2) and Network Layer (Layer 3). The sublayers within the Data-Link Layer are as follows:

▶ *Media Access Control (MAC),* the lower sublayer, controls media-access issues such as whether to use token passing and contention.

▶ *Logical Link Control (LLC),* the higher sublayer, controls issues such as error control, flow control, and framing.

OSINET

An association responsible for the international promotion of Open Systems Interconnection (OSI) in vendor architectures.

outbound service-advertisement filter
A filter that limits the service advertisements propagated by the router to a selected set of services at a selected set of networks.

outframe
The maximum number of outstanding frames allowed in a Systems Network Architecture (SNA) server at any time.

out-of-band communication
A diagnostic or management process that uses frequencies outside the range being used for data or message communications.

output
Data sent by a computer to a peripheral device (such as a console, hard disk, or printer).

output cursor
A cursor indicating the starting row and column position on the computer display screen where the output goes when a function that writes to the display screen is called.

Output Feedback (OFB)
A Data-Encryption Standard (DES) operating mode.

outsourcing
A policy of subcontracting a company's data processing operations to outside vendors, rather than maintaining internal departments to perform the operations.

owner name
An assigned password that protects data files from unauthorized access by Btrieve applications. The owner name can be set through the Btrieve Maintenance utility.

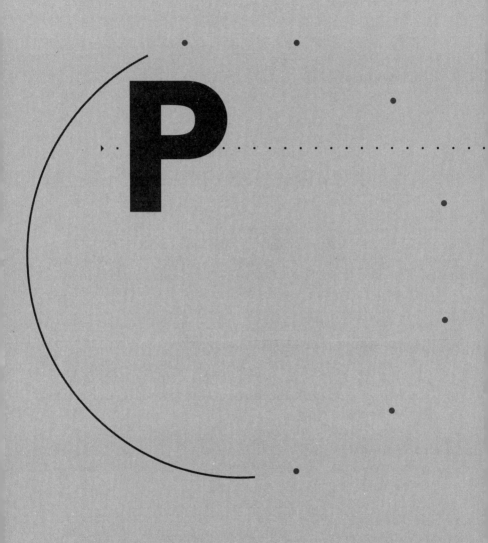

pacing

In a Systems Network Architecture (SNA) network, a method of controlling network traffic by limiting the amount of data a program can send or receive at one time to prevent overrunning of logical unit (LU) buffers.

pacing window size

In a Systems Network Architecture (SNA) network, the number of Request/Response Units (RUs) a program is allowed to send before permission is required to send more.

packet

A unit of information used in network communication. Messages sent between network devices are formed into a header and data portion that together make up a packet. Headers are appended to the data portion as the packet travels through the communication layers. The packet might contain a request for service, information on how to handle the request, and the data to be serviced. If a message exceeds a maximum packet size, it is partitioned and carried as several packets. When the packets arrive at the prescribed destination, the packets are reassembled into a complete message, the headers are stripped off in reverse order, and the request is serviced.

packet assembler/disassembler (PAD)

A device or program that creates packets of data for transmission and removes data from received packets. The PAD is most common in Consultative Committee for International Telegraphy and Telephony (CCITT) X.25 packet data networks.

packet buffer

An area where incoming packets are held until a receiving device can process the data.

packet burst

A method of transmitting data across a NetWare network in which data is collected and sent as a unit in a single high-speed transmission.

Synonym: *burst mode*

Packet Burst Protocol (PBP)

A protocol (which is built on top of the Internetwork Packet Exchange) that speeds the transfer of multiple-packet NetWare Core Protocol (NCP) file reads and writes between a workstation and a NetWare server by eliminating the need to sequence and acknowledge each packet. Because it enables a server or workstation to send a whole set (or burst) of packets before it requires acknowledgment, PBP is more efficient than the one request-one response protocol used in early versions of NetWare and it reduces network traffic. Dropped packets are monitored by PBP; retransmissions are only performed for missing packets.

packet driver

A program for computers operating in the DOS and Windows environments that connects network software to Network Interface Cards (NICs).

Packet Exchange Protocol (PEP)

A Xerox Network Systems (XNS) protocol used at the Transport Level (Level 4 of the OSI Reference Model).

packet filter

A process in which bridges perform such traffic-control functions as limiting protocol-specific traffic to one segment of the network and isolating electronic mail (e-mail) domains. After a network administrator sets packet-filter specifications for each bridge, the bridge can either accept or reject any packet matching the specifications.

packet forwarding

The copying of a packet from one interface to another through the use of an intermediate system.

packet frame

Information added to a packet to ensure the packet is properly and accurately transmitted across a network. The format of the information contained in the packet frame depends on the physical medium on which the data travels.

Packet InterNet Groper (PING)

A program that tests the accessibility of destinations by sending the destinations an Internet Control Message Protocol (ICMP) echo request and waiting for a reply.

Packet Layer

Under the X.25 specification of Consultative Committee for International Telegraphy and Telephony (CCITT), the layer of a packet-switched network that controls call setup and clearing, packet transfer, and network facility selection.

Packet-Level Procedure (PAP)

A full-duplex protocol for the transfer of packets between a computer and a modem on an X.25 network.

Packet Level Protocol (PLP)

A full-duplex protocol specifying the details of data transfer between a sender and receiver on an X.25 network that supports error detection and correction, packet sequencing, and transfer-rate adjustment.

packet-receive buffer

A special area set aside in the NetWare server's memory that temporarily holds data packets arriving from various workstations until the server is ready to process and send them to their destinations. Although the default range of packet-receive buffers (set during server installation) should be satisfactory, the following parameters may be set during installation to increase the range: Maximum packet buffers, Minimum packet receive buffers, and New packet receive buffer time.

packet-switched network

A configuration of independent, interconnected computers that use packets to transmit information to each other.

Packet Switch Node (PSN)

A dedicated machine that accepts and routes packets in a packet-switching network.

packet switching
The division of data communications messages into finite-sized packets, which are forwarded over different circuit paths and reassembled into the message before the message is passed on to the receiving terminal or device.

page
A collection of information (such as text, graphics, and sounds) organized for presentation on the World Wide Web (WWW). Also, a contiguous chunk of memory of a predefined size that may be allocated on an as-needed basis, usually in some area of random access memory (RAM).

Page-Description Language (PDL)
Commands that control the reproduction of text and graphic images on a printed page. Adobe PostScript is an example of a PDL.

paged memory-management unit (PMMU)
A specialized microprocessor chip that manages virtual memory.

page-mode RAM
A system in which specialized Dynamic Random Access Memory (DRAM) microprocessor chips divide memory, so consecutive accesses to memory addresses in the same chunk of memory, result in a page-mode cycle that takes about half the processing time of a regular DRAM cycle.

P

pager
A feature that breaks up information solicited from the World Wide Web (WWW) into chunks that can be viewed one screen at a time. Also, a contiguous chunk of memory of a predefined size that may be allocated on an as-needed basis, usually in some area of random access memory (RAM).

paging
A NetWare feature that allows memory to be assigned noncontiguously (rather than in large blocks of contiguously addressed pages) by using memory segmentation. *Page tables* map physical addresses to logical memory; each table entry corresponds to a *memory page* (equivalent to 4K of random access memory). A group of page tables is known as a *domain*. Paging in NetWare is used for memory protection.

palmtop computer

A "miniature," battery-operated, portable computer that can be held in the palm of one hand, which usually experiences less power duration from their batteries and does not include floppy disk drives or hard disk drives.

parallel channel

A channel with a channel-to-control unit input/output (I/O) interface, using bus-and-tag cables as a transmission medium.

parallel port

A printer interface that transmits data in parallel, 7 or 8 bits at a time. The parallel port is often used to connect a parallel printer to a computer workstation.

parallel printer

A printer that accepts data routed on a bus in parallel format (7 or 8 bits at a time), rather than in serial format (1 bit at a time).

parallel printer interface

An interface that accepts data routed on a bus in parallel format, 7 or 8 bits at a time. The parallel printer interface is faster and easier to configure than a serial printer interface. If the printer cable extends beyond ten feet, however, the data transfer can be unreliable.

parallel processing

A computing method in which two or more microprocessors operate simultaneously while working on different aspects of the same program and sharing the computational load for high-speed processing.

parallel sessions

Two or more concurrently active network sessions between the same two logical units (LUs) in a Systems Network Architecture (SNA) network, with each session capable of having a different set of session parameters.

parallel transmission

A simultaneous transmission of all bits that make up a character or byte.

parameter
A critical item of information required by a program, utility, or Application Programming Interface (API) to perform a prescribed operation.

Parameter RAM (PRAM)
An area of random access memory (RAM) in an AppleTalk network that stores configuration information (such as a node network address).

parent
A data set that can have subordinate data sets.

parent container
In NetWare or IntranetWare, a high-level container object holding other objects in the Novell Directory Services (NDS) Directory tree. The three types of parent containers are Country, Organization, and Organizational Unit.

parent directory
A directory structure in a hierarchical directory system that appears immediately above a subdirectory or current directory. The double period (..) symbol is shorthand for the name of the parent directory.

parity
A method that uses an extra or redundant bit, inserted after the data bits but before the stop bit (or bits), to check for errors in transmitted data. Parity settings on both communicating computers must match. Types of parity include Even, Mark, None, Odd, and Space.

P

parity bit
An extra (or redundant) bit in a byte (8 bits) used for error checking in data transmission.

parity checking
A checking method applied to a character or a series of characters that adds a parity bit to check for data-transmission errors.

Partial Sequence Number PDU (PSNP)

A Protocol Data Unit (PDU) that requests Link-State Packets (LSPs) from one Intermediate System (IS) to another.

partition

Either a logical division of the NetWare Directory database (NDD) or a logical unit into which the hard disk on a personal computer or a NetWare server can be divided. In NetWare, a partition forms a distinct unit of data in the Directory tree used to store and replicate Directory information. Although each NetWare Directory partition consists of a container object, all objects contained in it, and information about those objects, these partitions do not contain any information about the file system or about the directories and files contained there. With partition management, a user can create, merge, and move Directory partitions; display partitions and partition details; add, delete, synchronize, and display Directory replicas.

passive concurrency

A type of concurrency control in which a task does not perform any type of explicit locking.

passive coupler

In fiber-optic communications, an optical signal redirector that splits a signal as requested and passes the weakened signal on to all fibers, which results in signal loss.

passive hub

A device that splits a transmission signal and allows more workstations to be added to a network topology.

passive star coupler

An optical-signal redirector in fiber-optic communications, created by fusing multiple optical fibers together at their meeting point, which is used as the center of a passive-star network topology.

passive star topology

A network configuration in which multiple nodes are connected to a central hub that passes signals on, but does not process the signal in any way. This is the opposite of an *active star topology*, which processes signals before passing them on.

password

Characters typed in by a user when logging in to a network. NetWare enables the network supervisor to specify whether passwords are required, to assign passwords to users, to specify whether passwords must be unique, and to specify whether passwords must be changed periodically.

Password Authentication Protocol (PAP)

A method of validating a network node's inbound call by comparing an exchange of peer ID/password pairs against a list of authorized pairs.

password file

A file containing all the passwords used to log in to a network. This file is usually encoded to restrict access to sensitive network data.

password protection

A protection scheme that guards network access by requiring one or more passwords before a user is allowed to log in.

patch

An additional segment of programming code that improves how a product works for a specific situation and that may or may not be included in a future release of the product.

patch cable

A cable used in Token Ring networks that connects Multistation Access Units (MAUs) to each other.

patch panel

A wiring center that provides for the interconnection of twisted-pair or coaxial cables without connecting the cable to a punch-down block.

path

The complete location (including drive, directory, and subdirectory) of a file or directory in a file system.

Path-Control Layer (SNA model)

The third layer (Layer 3) in the Systems Network Architecture (SNA) communications model. The Path-Control Layer creates a logical channel between two network nodes.

path-control network

The routing portion of a Systems Network Architecture (SNA) network.

path cost

An arbitrary value used by a routing algorithm to determine the best path to a destination.

Path Information Unit (PIU)

A packet created in a Systems Network Architecture (SNA) network when the Path-Control Layer (Layer 3) adds a transmission header to a basic information unit (BIU) from the Transmission-Control Layer (Layer 4).

pathname

Identification of a file that includes the server name, volume, directory path, and filename.

payload

The data portion of an Asynchronous Transfer Mode (ATM) packet (or cell).

PC Card

A card conforming the Personal Computer Memory Card International Association (PCMCIA) standard that uses a 68-pin connector with longer power and ground pins (which always engage before the signal pins).

PCMCIA modem

A modem that works on a PC Card.

PDU Lifetime

A value indicating the number of routers a protocol data unit (PDU) can use before it reaches its destination. If the PDU exceeds this value, it is discarded. PDU Lifetime is invoked to keep PDUs from continuously traveling around a network without ever reaching a destination.

Peak Load

A value expressed in one of several performance measures (such as number of packets or bits per second) that defines a maximum amount of traffic a network can handle.

peer

A device that has equal communications capabilities with another device.

peer hub

A hub installed on a Network Interface Card (NIC) that plugs into an expansion slot on a computer.

peer layers

In a layered network architecture, corresponding layers on two connected nodes that communicate with each other at a particular layer, using a protocol supported by that layer.

peer-to-peer

A type of direct communication between two devices on the same communications level of a network without intervention by any intermediary devices (such as a host or server).

peer-to-peer network

A network in which each node can initiate actions, access other nodes, and provide services for other nodes without first acquiring permission from the server. The network operating system often runs under the native operating system of the individual workstations.

pen computer

A computer that accepts handwriting as input, incorporating pattern-recognition software that translates marks made on the computer screen with a special pen-like stylus. The stylus can also be used to make menu selections.

Pentium

Intel's 64-bit microprocessor chip, the next-generation follow-up to the 80486 microprocessor chip. Features include an 8K instruction code, data caches, a built-in floating-point coprocessor, a memory-management unit (MMU), and dual pipelining (which allows the processing of more than one instruction per clock cycle).

performance management

As defined by the International Standards Organization (ISO) and the Consultative Committee for International Telegraphy and Telephony (CCITT), a part of the OSI Network Management Model that performs the following functions: monitors daily activity on the network; gathers and logs data on the basis of daily activity of the network; stores the performance data in a database to be used for network optimization and expansion; analyzes the performance data to identify bottlenecks; and changes configuration settings of the network to optimize performance.

performance tuning

The capability to monitor and analyze the performance of a computer system and to adjust the configuration of the system to obtain optimum performance.

peripheral

A CD-ROM drive, fax machine, hard-disk drive, modem, optical drive, printer, tape drive, or other device that can be attached to a file server, workstation, standalone server, or the network itself to provide additional services to network users.

Peripheral Component Interconnect (PCI)

An Intel specification defining a local bus that allows as many as ten PCI-compliant expansion cards to be plugged into the motherboard of a computer. One of the expansion cards must be a PCI controller card, which exchanges information with the computer's processor and enables certain intelligent PCI adapters to perform tasks concurrently with the main processor by using bus mastering techniques.

peripheral node
In a Systems Network Architecture (SNA) network, a node that depends upon an intermediate or host node to provide network services for its dependent logical units (LUs), but that has no intermediate routing function assigned to it.

peripheral router
A router that connects a network to a larger internetwork.

PERL
A script programming language designed to process system-oriented tasks in the UNIX environment. This language is widely used to create Common Gateway Interface (CGI) programs that can be ported between the NetWare Web Server and UNIX servers.

permanent SVC
A switched virtual circuit (SVC) that remains in a connected state until a user or application disconnects it.

permanent swap file
A file used to store parts of running programs that have been swapped out of memory to make room for other running programs. Once created, a permanent swap file can be used repeatedly in virtual-memory operations that use hard-disk space in place of random access memory (RAM).

permanent virtual circuit (PVC)
A communications path between two fixed end points continuously available and similar to a leased line.

permission
A privilege to access certain system resources, granted to a user on the basis of rights given to the user's account by the network administrator.

Person object

A Novell Directory Services (NDS) leaf object that contains the more common attributes of the Organizational Person and Residential Person objects.

Personal Communications Services (PCS)

A class of applications that includes wireless communications for users of portable computers.

Personal Computer Memory Card International Association (PCMCIA)

A nonprofit organization formed in 1989 that developed a standard for credit card-sized, plug-in adapters designed for use in portable computers. In addition to hardware standards, the organization also established Socket Services software to provide a standard interface to the hardware, as well as Card Services software to coordinate access to PC Cards.

personal digital assistant (PDA)

A battery-operated palmtop computer (which means it fits in the palm of one hand) that features a pen-based interface for personal organization software with fax and electronic-mail (e-mail) facilities.

Personal Identification Number (PIN)

A unique number or code assigned to identify individuals as they perform network transactions (such as banking from an automated teller machine).

Personal Information Manager (PIM)

A software package that integrates word processing, database, and other modules to enable users to store notes, memos, names and addresses, appointments, to-do lists, and other organizational activities.

Personal NetWare

Peer-to-peer network software released by Novell in 1994 that provides DOS and Windows users with the capability to share printers, files, and other resources, and to run standard applications. Personal NetWare replaced NetWare Lite.

pervasive computing
The concept that computers will be readily available in most environments, all computers will have the capability to interconnect with other computers, and users will have access to other users and information from anywhere at any time. The basis for this interconnection will be networking and internetworking, and the tools necessary for this interconnection will be easy to use.

peta
An order of magnitude that represents 10^{15} in the base-10 system or 2^{50} in the base-2 system.

phase
A reference (expressed in degrees or radians) to a portion of an entire signal period used to offset the start of a signal.

phase jitter
A distortion of signal phase caused by random fluctuations in signal frequency, which makes it difficult to synchronize the signal.

Phase Lock Loop (PLL)
In a Token Ring network, a function that automatically ensures accurate signal timing.

PhoneNet
A telephone wire version of AppleTalk whose adapters and wiring are less expensive than those found in LocalTalk.

photodetector
A fiber-optic communications component that registers incoming light; its sensitivity has an influence on the transmission properties of a connection.

photodiode
In fiber-optic communications, the receiver component that converts light signals into electrical signals.

physical address
The address of a network device as defined in the Data-Link Layer (Layer 2) of the OSI Reference Model.

physical connection
A hardware connection between two computer devices.

Physical Contact (PC)
A term describing a condition where cable and fiber elements in optical fiber are actually touching and making a connection.

Physical Control Layer (SNA model)
The first layer (Layer 1) in the Systems Network Architecture (SNA) communications model. The Physical Control Layer provides a serial or parallel interface to the network.

Physical Delivery Access Unit (PDAU)
In an X.400 Message Handling System (MHS) specified by the Consultative Committee for International Telegraphy and Telephony (CCITT), an application process that enables a Message-Transfer System (MTS) to deliver an image of a letter to any location accessible through the MHS.

physical drive
A physical (as opposed to conceptual or logical) device in a computer that performs actual magnetic or optical operations on the storage medium. The physical drive may be divided into several *logical drives* (logical processes that function as though they were separate disk drives).

Physical Layer (OSI model)
The first layer (Layer 1) in the OSI Reference Model. The Physical Layer details the protocols that govern transmission media and signals.

Physical-Layer Convergence Procedure (PLCP)
In the Distributed-Queue Dual-Bus (DQDB) network architecture, a function that maps high-level packets into a uniform format for transmission through a particular configuration.

Physical Layer Signaling (PLS)

The highest component of the Physical Layer (Layer 1) in the OSI Reference Model that provides an interface between the Physical Layer and the Media-Access Control (MAC) sublayer of the Data-Link Layer (Layer 2).

physical-media dependent (PMD)

A physical layer in most networking architectures responsible for the actual connection between two locations.

physical medium

In the OSI Reference Model, a medium that provides a physical means of transmitting data. An interface for the physical medium is supplied at the bottom of the Physical Layer (Layer 1) of the OSI Reference Model; the model itself does not provide specifications for physical media.

physical memory

Random access memory (RAM) chips installed in a computer system. NetWare addresses physical memory in 4K blocks called *pages*.

physical network management (PNM)

The maintenance and management of the physical components of a network, such as computers, cabling, connectors, power supply, telephones, fax machines, and other devices.

P

physical node address

The address of a file server's Network Interface Card (NIC) on a local area network (LAN).

physical partition

A hard-disk partition that has been created for the use of the operating system. The hard disk can contain several physical partitions for numerous operating systems.

physical topology

A wiring layout for a network that specifies how network elements are electrically interconnected and what happens when a network node fails. The three main types of physical topology are a *logical bus topology* (including bus, star, and tree topologies), a *logical ring topology* (including Token Ring), and a *hybrid topology* (a combination of different topologies). Physical topologies are also classified by the manner in which nodes are connected to each other, including a *point-to-point connection* (in which two nodes are directly linked together) and a *multipoint connection* (in which multiple nodes are connected to a single node).

physical unit (PU)
In Systems Network Architecture (SNA), a node that supports one or more logical units (LUs).

piggybacking
A transmission that includes acknowledgment packets within ordinary data packets.

pin
In some types of cable connectors, the male lead (usually one of many leads running through the cable).

Pine
A mail program used on an electronic mail (e-mail) reader called *elm* for systems operating in the UNIX environment.

ping packet
A packet containing an Echo message or Echo Reply message sent by using the Internet Control Message Protocol (ICMP) to monitor the performance of network nodes.

pinout
The function associated with a specific pin; each pin in a multipin connector has a pinout.

pipe
A section of computer memory used by one command to pass processing information to a second command.

pipelining
The fetching and encoding of instructions to ensure a processor need not wait to carry out the instructions; as soon as one instruction is executed, another instruction is ready.

piping
A process in which the output of one program becomes the input for another program.

pkgadd
A UnixWare command to simplify the process of installing third-party software and extensions for the operating system.

PKZIP
A shareware file-compression program for computers that run in the DOS environment. PKZIP enables users to compress several files into one ZIP file. Files are decompressed by using the PKUNZIP shareware program. (A Windows version of this program is called *WinZip*.)

Plain Old Telephone Service (POTS)
A standard analog telephone service provided by many telephone companies.

Plastic-Clad Silica (PCS)
Optical fiber that features a glass core and plastic cladding.

platform
A generic reference to all possible choices for some specific part of a computing environment (such as the NetWare network operating-system platform or the DOS operating-system platform).

platform-specific routers
Routers used on a specific type of network architecture, usually proprietary.

platter

A round metal surface on a hard disk. Multiple platters may be stacked on a hard disk with a read/write head for each side of the platter with the group of read/write heads moving in unison to the same track number on each platter side.

plenum

A type of air shaft or duct used for ventilation in a building.

plenum cable

A cable that runs through a plenum. Subjected to stringent standards, plenum cable must have a jacket made of fire-resistant material that does not exude toxic chemicals when exposed to heat.

plesiochronous

Corresponding events in digital signaling that happen at the same *rate* in two timing-synchronization systems, but not necessarily at the same *time*. Although the clocks on the two systems run at the same speed, they are not synchronized to the same time reference.

plotter

A graphics-rendering device used to draw charts, diagrams, and so on.

plug

A male connector with pins that fit into the sockets of a female connector.

Plug and Play

A standard defining automatic technique that simplifies the process of configuring a personal computer, often found in Industry Standard Architecture (ISA) expansion boards. The standard was developed jointly by Compaq Computer Corporation, Microsoft, Intel, and Phoenix Technologies.

plug-in

A software program installed with, or inside of, another program, designed to add optional functionality.

point of presence (POP)
A connection serviced by a local or long-distance telephone company.

point-to-point connection
A direct connection between two network nodes without any intervening nodes or switches, or a direct connection between two networks.

point-to-point line
A switched or nonswitched communication line or circuit that connects a single node in a remote network with another node.

Point-to-Point Protocol (PPP)
An industry-standard protocol enabling point-to-point transmissions of routed data from router to router, or from host to network, on local area networks (LANs) by using a synchronous or asynchronous serial interface. PPP is a successor to Serial-Line Interface Protocol (SLIP).

Point-to-Point Protocol Remote-Node Services (PPPRNS)
A protocol that supports Point-to-Point Protocol (PPP) connections to remote network nodes.

poison-reverse updates
Routing loops sent to defeat large routing loops and to indicate specifically that a network or subnetwork is unreachable, rather than implying a network is unreachable by excluding it in routing updates.

polarity
A designation indicating a logical unit (LU) is the *contention winner* or *loser* in a network that complies with Systems Network Architecture (SNA). When a requesting LU indicates it should be the loser in the event of a contention, the responding LU will automatically accept the status of contention winner.

poll interval
A time interval (expressed in seconds) between the nonbroadcast, multiaccess network transmission of a Hello packet to a network neighbor that has become inactive.

polled mode

A printer configuration option that allows a port driver to check (or poll) the data port periodically to determine whether the data port is ready to accept data for transmission to a printer. Status of the port is indicated with a flag and queries are made at each timer tick (18 times per second) on the central processing unit (CPU). Although it may significantly slow other tasks at a workstation, polled mode does eliminate any possibility of interrupt conflicts among different network hardware configurations by enabling users to set up a printer without having to determine to which interrupt the port is set or even if the port supports interrupts.

polling

Contacting the nodes on a network, periodically and sequentially, by sending an inquiry to ask whether a given node wants to transmit; if it does, the node returns an acknowledgment to enable the transmission to start. The three common types of polling are *roll-call polling* (a master station locates the next node to call by consulting a polling list), *hub polling* (one node in *poll mode* polls the next node in a sequence), and *token-passing polling* (a sequenced node receives a token and can transmit or pass the token to the next device in the sequence).

POP server

A program that uses the Post Office Protocol (POP) to transfer electronic mail to and from an e-mail client program on a network. The address of the POP server is often required when securing and configuring an Internet account with an Internet Service Provider (ISP).

popup screen

A menu or other graphical display laid over the screen currently displayed on a computer monitor.

port

In hardware, a connecting component allowing a microprocessor to communicate with a compatible peripheral. In software, a memory address identifying a physical circuit used to transfer information between a microprocessor and a peripheral.

port driver

A software driver responsible for routing jobs from the print queue and through the proper port to a printer. NetWare 4.*x* and IntranetWare use the NPRINTER NetWare Loadable Module (NLM) as a port driver.

port multiplier

A concentrator that connects multiple devices to a network.

port number

The number assigned to network computers to identify them while they communicate on the Internet.

port selector

A hardware device (or software) responsible for selecting—either randomly or according to predefined criteria—a particular port for use in a communications session.

port switching

Transparently switching from one port to another in response to port malfunction or overload.

portable

The capability to move a program easily from one computing environment to another with minimal changes.

P

portable computer

A battery-powered computer designed to be carried easily from location to location. Types of portable computers include *laptop computers* (which have an extended battery life), *notebook computers* (smaller than a laptop and can fit into a briefcase), and *palmtop computers* (often specifically designed for a particular function, but small enough to fit in the palm of a hand).

portable modem

An external modem with a compact design that enables easy transportation and can be plugged into any computer.

Portable Operating System Interface (POSIX)

A standard originally developed by the Institute of Electrical and Electronics Engineers (IEEE) to provide a common interface to UNIX systems. POSIX now encompasses the interface between applications and operating systems in a variety of environments.

post office

An intermediate storage location for messages in a Message-Handling System (MHS) where messages are held until they are retrieved by a user or sent to a designated destination.

Post Office Protocol (POP)

Conventions and rules according to which electronic-mail (e-mail) programs running on a computer workstation (called an *e-mail client*) communicate with e-mail server programs on the network (called a *mailbox*). Messages sent to the client are stored in the mailbox for later retrieval by the client.

Post, Telephone, and Telegraph (PTT)

A government agency found in many European countries that provides postal, telephonic, telegraphic, and other communications services.

postamble

A sequence of bits or fields—which may include an error-checking field, specific flags, or a predefined bit sequence—to indicate the end of a message or packet.

Synonym: *trailer*

posting

In the context of NetWare, a method in which an Advanced Program-to-Program Communications (APPC) process enables a transaction program to check whether a specific amount of data is available in the receive buffer of a logical unit (LU). In the context of Internet communications, a posting is an article in a newsgroup.

Postmaster

A NetWare user who has the Supervisor access right to the NetWare Message-Handling Service (MHS) Messaging Server object, the Read access right to the Message Routing Group in which the NetWare MHS Messaging Server object is located. In Novell Directory Services (NDS), the Postmaster also has the Supervisor access right to the Mailbox Location, Mailbox ID, and E-Mail Address properties for users of the NetWare MHS Messaging Server object. When certain types of errors occur, Basic NetWare MHS sends a message to the Postmaster's electronic-mail (e-mail) box.

Postmaster General

A NetWare user who has the Supervisor access right to the NetWare Message Routing Group in which the user resides and who can add a messaging server to, or remove it from, the Message Routing Group. More than one Postmaster General can be assigned to a Message Routing Group.

PostScript

A Page-Description Language (PDL) from Adobe Systems that uses text coding to control fonts, text formatting, graphic images, page layout, and other aspects of printed images. PostScript is implemented on several different types of printers and applications.

PostScript Printer-Definition file (PPD)

A file that contains model information about a PostScript printer, which a print spooler can use to answer PostScript queries from a network.

power budget

A measurable difference between the power of a transmitter and the sensitivity of a receiver. Power budget determines the amount of signal loss that can be allowed in a transmission and the maximum distance a signal can reliably travel.

power conditioning

Methods used to protect sensitive network hardware components from the ill effects of a disruption in electrical power supply (known as a *power disturbance*).

power supply

A computer component that converts the electrical power supplied at a wall outlet into a lower voltage for use by the computer.

power surge

A sudden increase in line voltage usually caused by a nearby electrical appliance or by the restoration of power after an outage.

power-on self test (POST)

Computer diagnostic programs designed to ensure that major system components are present and operating correctly. These programs are stored in read-only memory (ROM) and loaded before the operating system when the computer is started up. When the POST detects a problem, system startup is halted and a message is displayed on the screen.

PowerPC

A microprocessor chip with Reduced Instruction Set Computing (RISC) architecture, jointly developed by Apple Computer, IBM, and Motorola. The PowerPC features 32-bit processing, which enables it to handle more than one set of instructions at a time.

preamble

A sequence of bits or fields in a message or packet, containing source and destination addresses, information about packet type or size, special signals, or a predefined bit sequence to indicate the start of the message or packet.

Synonym: *header*

preemptive multitasking

A method whereby an operating system executes a task for a specific period of time (determined by a preset priority), preempts the task, and provides another task with access to the central processing unit (CPU) for a prescribed amount of time. In this type of processing, no task is allowed to exceed its allotted time interval.

pre-imaging

Storing the image of a file page before updating a record on the page.

Premises Distribution System (PDS)
Either a cabling system encompassing an entire building or the name of AT&T's premises wiring system.

premises network
A network confined to a single building, but that encompasses the entire building.

Presentation Layer (OSI model)
The sixth layer (Layer 6) in the OSI Reference Model. The Presentation Layer is responsible for communicating with the Session Layer (Layer 7) and for managing the negotiation and establishment of the encoded values for the transfer of structured data types.

Presentation Services Layer (SNA model)
The sixth layer (Layer 6) in the Systems Network Architecture (SNA) communications model. The Presentation Services Layer provides data information and formatting services to the network.

primary half-session
The half session on the network node that sends a session activation request.

Primary Interexchange Carrier (PIC)
A long-distance telephone service carrier to which a user may subscribe.

primary link station (PLS)
In a network that complies with the Synchronous Data-Link Control (SDLC) protocol, the link station that controls the link. The PLS initiates communications with another PLS or with a secondary link station (SLS). Each link has only one PLS.

primary logical unit (PLU)
A logical unit (LU) containing the primary half-session for a particular LU-to-LU session.

Primary-Rate ISDN (PRI)

One of two service categories provided by an Integrated-Services Digital Network (ISDN) that provides bearer channels (also known as B channels) and data channels (also known as D channels), both of which are capable of speeds of 64 kilobits per second (Kbps). When combined, the 1.544 megabits-per-second (Mbps) speed is equivalent to that of a T1 channel. The other service category provided by ISDN is known as *Bit Rate Interface* (BRI).

primary server

A NetWare System Fault Tolerance III (SFT III) server that network stations see, and the one to which they send requests for network services. (Routers send packets to the primary server because it is the only server they see.) The .IOEngine in the primary server determines the order and type of events sent to the MSEngine. Only the primary server can send reply packets to network workstations. By contrast, the SFT III secondary server is the server activated after the primary server. Either server may function as a primary server; system failure determines the role of each. When the primary server fails, the secondary server becomes the new primary server. When the failed server is restored, it becomes the secondary server.

primary station

In such protocols as High-Level Data-Link Control (HDLC) and Synchronous Data-Link Control (SDLC), a station that performs management functions, controls the transmission activity of secondary stations, and receives responses from secondary stations.

Synonym: *primary link station*

Primary time server

A server responsible for synchronizing the time with at least one other Primary time server (or Reference time server) and for providing the time to Secondary time servers and workstations.

print-device definition

A function or mode, defined in a Printer-Definition File (PDF), which corresponds to a printer, plotter, or other peripheral. A print-device definition supplies the necessary control sequences for setting or resetting the printer and for controlling such features as boldface, emphasis, italics, print size, font selection, and colors. It enables the user to specify modes for use in print-job configurations, which prepare the printer for a print job, combine functions, reset the printer to default settings, and so forth. Print definitions are required for proper performance by a printer and must be imported into NetWare print services by using the NetWare Administrator or PRINTDEF utilities.

print driver

A software driver that converts print jobs into a format recognizable by the type of printer being used.

print header

Transport-control codes that precede data to a print queue and match the modes defined by the NetWare PRINTDEF utility. The default size for a print header is 64 bytes.

print job

A file sent by Novell Directory Services (NDS)—or through bindery services—and stored in a print-queue directory to await printing. Each print job is assigned a unique filename: a variation of the first four characters of the print-queue directory identification, four more numerals, and a .Q filename extension. Print jobs are handled on a first-in, first-out (FIFO) basis by the print queue.

print-job configuration

A set of options used to determine how a job is printed. These options can include the printer to be used, the print queue to be used, the number of copies to print, and whether to use a banner page, specific printer form, and print-device mode. In NetWare, print-job configurations can be created through the NetWare Administrator and PRINTCON utilities.

print-job list

A list accessible from NetWare's PCONSOLE, NETUSER, or NetWare Administrator utilities that shows all print jobs currently in the print queue.

Print Manager

A print-job-management utility in Windows 3.x that queues any documents to be printed on a network printer. This utility enables users to change the order of the print queue or to remove print jobs from the queue. Print Manager only works with Windows applications.

print queue

A network directory that stores print jobs and has a printer, which receives the print jobs from the print server assigned to it. When the printer is ready, the print server removes the print job from the directory (print queue) and sends it to the printer. The only limitation on the number of print jobs a print queue can hold is disk space. In NetWare, all print queues are assigned names; each is a random number (representing the print-queue identification seen through the NetWare Administrator utility) followed by the .QDR extension. All print-queue directories in NetWare contain files (with .SYS and .SRV filename extensions) that are flagged as system files and hidden files.

print-queue operator

A user (usually designated by the NetWare network administrator) who can edit other users' print jobs, delete print jobs from the print queue, modify the print-queue status, and change the order in which print jobs are serviced.

print-queue polling time

A time interval a print server waits between checking the print queue for jobs that are ready for printing.

print-queue sampling interval

In NetWare, a time period specified in the PCONSOLE utility as the amount of time a print server waits between checking the print queues for print jobs ready to be printed. The default is 15 seconds.

print server

A program that takes print jobs from a print queue and sends them to a network printer. In NetWare 4.x and IntranetWare, print servers run through the PSERVER NetWare Loadable Module (NLM) on a NetWare server; they can service up to 255 printers that have any number of print queues assigned. In NetWare 3.x, print servers are loaded through either PSERVER (on a file server) or PSERVER.EXE (on a dedicated workstation).

Print Server object

In Novell Directory Services (NDS), a leaf object representing a network print server. This object should be placed in the same container as printers and print queues with which it is associated.

Print Server operator
A user (or member of a group) delegated rights by the NetWare network administrator to manage the print server by controlling notify lists, printers, and print-queue assignments.

print spooler
Operating system software that coordinates the print jobs sent to a shared printer when the printer is busy.

print tail
Transport-control codes that follow a print header to a print queue and match modes defined by the NetWare PRINTDEF utility. The default size for a print tail is 16 bytes.

printer
A peripheral or piece of hardware used to produce printed material. A printer may be attached directly to the network, to the printer port of a NetWare server, or to the printer port of a computer workstation. A network printer-port driver is required to pass a print job from the network to the printer; the type of driver depends on the method of attachment to the network. Printers attached directly to the network store their own printer-port drivers.

P

Printer-Access Protocol (PAP)
A part of the AppleTalk protocol suite that enables Macintosh clients and NetWare for Macintosh servers to communicate with printers on an AppleTalk network.

Printer-Control Language (PCL)
A Page-Description Language (PDL) used by the Hewlett-Packard Laserjet and other compatible printers.

printer definition
A set of printer control characters specific to a particular brand or model of printer and used to format printer output to bold, italics, and centered text.

printer emulation

A printer characteristic that enables the printer to behave like a printer from another manufacturer by changing modes.

printer form

An option in NetWare print services that allows the designation of a form to indicate the type of paper on which a job is to be printed. If the paper loaded in the printer does not match the printer-form designation, the job is not printed.

printer mode

A sequence of print functions that defines the style, size, boldness, and orientation of typefaces used in a printed file.

Synonyms: *printer command; control sequence; escape sequence*

Printer object

In Novell Directory Services (NDS), a leaf object representing a physical printing device on the network. Every printer should have a corresponding NDS object, which should be placed in the same container as those of the users who print to it.

printer server

An AppleTalk Print Services (ATPS) entity that services a single print queue and sends jobs to a single printer on an AppleTalk network.

printing

The process of transferring data from computer files (in the form of print jobs) to a print queue, through a print server, and, finally, to a printer for output on paper. Several printers can be shared across a network to facilitate printing from all nodes.

Priority Access Control Enabled (PACE)

A proprietary variant of the Ethernet architecture designed to set priorities for the transmission of time-sensitive materials; the highest priority is granted to data that must be sent at a constant rate to be readable. PACE was developed by 3COM and other collaborators.

priority queuing
The setting of priorities for frames in an output queue on the basis of various routing features, such as packet size and interface type.

Privacy-Enhanced Mail (PEM)
One of two enhancements to Internet mail message formatting introduced in RFC 822 that provides mechanisms for encrypting, signing, and authenticating messages to ensure electronic mail is reasonably secure from intruders. The other enhancement was Multipurpose Internet Mail Extensions (MIME).

Private Automatic Branch Exchange (PABX)
A telephone system offering automatic switching and other communications capabilities. Because almost all telephone systems are now automatic, this term is often replaced with a synonym, Private Branch Exchange (PBX).

Private Branch Exchange (PBX)
A telephone system that provides interoffice connections from one extension to another, as well as connections to an external telephone network. PBX switching can be automatic or manual (done by an operator).

private-key encryption system
An encryption method that uses a conversion algorithm and predefined bit value (called a *key*), known only to the sender and the receiver.
Synonyms: *one-key encryption; single key encryption*

private leased circuit
A leased communications circuit that is always available and connects a company communications network with a remote site.

Private Management Domain (PRMD)
An electronic-mail system or a Message-Handling System (MHS), operated by a private organization, which complies with the X.400 communications model.

Private Network-to-Network Interface (PNNI)

A routing information protocol that enables multivendor Asynchronous Transfer Mode (ATM) switches to be integrated in the same network.

Privilege Attribute Certificate (PAC)

A certificate that specifies the privileges granted to a user and is checked to determine whether the user should be granted access to a requested service (or to the network).

privilege level (microprocessor)

A scheme for protecting Intel microprocessors that assigns addresses to specific tasks and, from within the tasks, protects the operating system (and special processor registers) from access by applications. Four privilege levels are defined within a task. Ring 0, the innermost ring, is assigned as the most trusted level. Ring 3, the outermost ring, is least trusted and is available to applications. Rings 1 and 2 are reserved for the operating system and its extensions. Privilege levels are maintained by circuitry found in the memory management unit (MMU).

Synonym: *protection ring*

privilege level (network)

Rights granted to a user by the network administrator so the user can execute various functions on the network.

privileged mode

A mode of the operating system that enables certain device drivers and the operating system to manipulate parts of the system (such as memory or input/output ports).

PRN

A logical device name assigned to a printer in the DOS and OS/2 environments. This assignment usually is made to the parallel port, known on most systems as LPT1.

probe

An AppleTalk network packet sent to the remote end of the network to request an acknowledgment from the end node. This packet is used to determine the end of the network and to verify the node is functioning properly.

problem-determination statistics (PD Stats)
Under Systems Network Architecture (SNA), statistics used by the network-management function to determine and diagnose problems associated with the communication links used for network sessions.

process
A program (or portion of a program) that executes on a host computer in a multitasking network environment.

Processor-Direct Slots (PDS)
A general-purpose expansion slot in Macintosh computers that is connected directly to the microprocessor instead of indirectly by a bus (such as with a NuBus system).

Professional Developers Program (PDP)
A joint program between Novell and independent developers of computer applications to provide direct access to various NetWare services and centralized network resources. PDP has been replaced by the Developer Net program.

P

Profile login script
A script that sets the NetWare environment for a group of users who have identical login script needs. If Profile login script is used (it is optional), it executes after a Container login script and before a User login script.

Profile object
In Novell Directory Services (NDS), a leaf object containing a login script that can be used by users who must share common login-script commands, but are not located in a portion of the Directory tree. The Profile login script executes after the Container login script and before the User login script.

program
Specially coded instructions that perform a specific task when carried out by a computer.

program link

An icon or symbol that appears on a monitor screen and, when double-clicked, runs preset executable files. Program links often are used to display graphics or to download files.

Program Manager

A Windows 3.*x* shell that enables a user to organize programs and applications, to create groups, and to serve as the basis for running the Windows 3.*x* program.

programming language

A language used specifically to create a program of instructions a computer can execute to perform a prescribed task.

promiscuous mode

An operatiing mode on a Network Interface Card (NIC) that allows any packet to be passed to a higher layer, regardless of whether the packet has been addressed to a node.

prompt

A character or message appearing on the computer monitor display screen that requires a response from the user. Examples of prompts include the DOS prompt (displays the current drive letter followed by the ">" symbol), the OS/2 prompt (displays the current drive mapping in brackets), and the NetWare server console prompt (displays a colon). The DOS and OS/2 prompts can be customized; the NetWare prompt cannot be changed.

propagation delay

A value indicating the amount of time required for a signal to pass through a component (or from one component to another).

property

Characteristics of objects in Novell Directory Services (NDS) that hold information about the object. NDS requires only those properties entered when a new object is created (such as properties that name the object or properties required to create the object). A property can contain multiple values (such as the Telephone Number property, which contains numerous telephone numbers).

property groups
A group of Novell Directory Services (NDS) properties organized by function.

property rights
Rights that apply to an object property in Novell Directory Services (NDS).

proprietary server
A server used with hardware and software from a particular vendor; a proprietary server runs a proprietary operating system.

proprietary software
Software designed specifically to run on a particular computer system and not readily available to the public.

protected mode
A mode that provides multitasking capabilities by allocating memory to various processes that run concurrently; memory used by one process is not allowed to overlap memory used by another process. Computers equipped with Intel's 80286, 80386, 80486, and Pentium microprocessors run in protected mode by default. However, computers equipped with these microprocessors can also be set to run in *real mode*, which means they are subjected to the same memory constraints of an 8086 machine (only 1MB of memory and only one process or application running at one time).

protocol
Conventions or rules that determine how a program or operating system communicates between two endpoints. A protocol defines the procedures to follow as data is being transmitted or received across a network, including the format, timing, sequence, and error checking used on the network.

protocol address
An address in the Network Layer (Layer 3) of the OSI Reference Model. The protocol address refers to a logical (rather than physical) network device.

protocol analyzer
A hardware-software combination (or simply software) used to capture and examine network traffic.

protocol client
An application or a protocol that solicits and receives the services of another protocol.

Protocol-Control Information (PCI)
Protocol-dependent information added to a data packet in the OSI Reference Model before the packet can be passed to a lower level for processing.

protocol converter
A hardware-software combination used to connect two dissimilar networks by converting from one protocol to another.

Protocol Data Unit (PDU)
A packet exchanged between devices within a specified layer of the OSI Reference Model. A PDU communicates with the same layer of the OSI Reference Model on another machine.

protocol-dependent
A process or component based on a software address or available in the Network Layer (Layer 3) of the OSI Reference Model, which is specific to the protocol used in the Network Layer.

Protocol element
A command for performing File Transfer Protocol (FTP) operations at the protocol level.

protocol field compression
A process that reduces Protocol ID field from the 2-byte framing standard set by the High-Level Data-Link Control (HDLC) Protocol to a single byte.

Protocol field compression is one way to reduce unnecessary overhead when using low-bandwidth links.

Protocol ID (PID)
A field in a Subnetwork Attachment Point (SNAP) header that helps to identify a distinct routed or bridged protocol.

Protocol-Independent Routing (PIR)
The routing of packets without regard to packet format or the protocol being used.

protocol stack
A suite of protocols that includes all layers required to perform transmission and receipt of data packets.

protocol suite
A collection of networking protocols providing all communications and services required to enable computers to exchange messages and other information. A protocol suite usually accomplishes this by managing physical connections, communications services, and application support.

protocol translator
A means—whether software or a network device—of converting one protocol into another similar protocol.

P

provider options
Options made available through a particular transport provider (such as Datagram Delivery Protocol or AppleTalk Data Stream Protocol), accessible only through the Transport Layer Interface (TLI).

proxy
An element responding on behalf of another element and requesting the use of a particular protocol.
Synonym: *proxy agent*

proxy ARP

The process of a router replying to an Address-Resolution Protocol (ARP) request from a host on behalf of the ARP target host. This process was effective in subnetted Internet Protocol (IP) networks with hosts that did not recognize the subnetting; knowledge of subnets was limited to subnet routers, and the hosts could see only the IP network. When the subnet routers reply to ARP requests from hosts on behalf of other hosts (on other subnets reachable through the router), the hosts that originate the requests need not know about the subnets attached to the network. This use of proxy ARP is called *ARP subnet routers*. Because most IP hosts now understand subnetting, the use of ARP subnet routers has been minimized. The most common use of proxy ARP today is in *stub networks*.

proxy protocol

A protocol used on the World Wide Web (WWW) whenever a proxy server initiates communication with another proxy server through a firewall.

proxy server

A server that acts on behalf of another server.

pseudo hop count

Under NetWare System Fault Tolerance III (SFT III), the number of hops a primary server adds to the true hop count when advertising the route to the Mirrored Server Engine (MSEngine). A pseudo hop count becomes necessary when the SFT III servers reside on different network segments and the hop count for one server is higher than for another server. The primary server advertises an artificially high hop count (the true hop count plus a pseudo hop count) to ensure packets are rerouted properly if one server fails. If the primary server does fail, the surviving server advertises the true hop count, which is immediately recognized by routers as the best route to the MSEngine. The *total hop count* (true hop count plus pseudo hop count) cannot exceed 16.

pseudo preemption count

A NetWare system parameter determining the number of times threads are allowed to make file read or write system calls before a relinquish is forced.

pseudo preemption time

A NetWare system parameter indicating the amount of time (in 0.84-microsecond increments) a NetWare Loadable Module (NLM) process may run before it is forced to relinquish control.

pseudo volume

In NetWare for Macintosh, the process of a CD-ROM copying files from a compact disc to the server's hard disk, and then creating a partition (the pseudo volume). Although the pseudo volume looks like a separate volume on the Macintosh desktop, it now contains the CD-ROM files and directory structure.

pseudonode

Under NetWare Link-Services Protocol (NLSP), a fictitious router that represents an entire local area network (LAN) in the link-state database.

pseudo-switched link

In a Public Switched Telephone Network (PSTN), a dial-up communications link established by using a pair of synchronous modems.

pseudoterminal

A computer terminal that does not really exist. Some programs, such as Telnet, may use a pseudoterminal to log in a user and run commands.

PU 2.1

In a peer-oriented network, a type of physical unit (PU) that connects Systems Network Architecture (SNA) nodes.

public data network (PDN)

A data network available for use by the general public.

PUBLIC directory

A directory created on the SYS: volume during NetWare installation that enables general access to the network, as well as containing NetWare utilities and programs for network users. The location of this directory for DOS users is SYS:PUBLIC; for OS/2 users, the location is SYS:PUBLIC/OS2.

public files

NetWare utilities, help files, some message and data files, and any other files that must be accessed by all NetWare users. The files usually are located in the SYS:PUBLIC directory for DOS users and the SYS:PUBLIC/OS2 directory for OS/2 users.

public key encryption system

An encryption method that uses a conversion algorithm, a predefined bit value (called a *key*) known only to a single user, and a key known by the public.

Synonym: *double-key encryption*

public service provider

An Internet service provider (ISP) offering connection time that can be paid for by the hour or by the month.

Public Switched Telephone Network (PSTN)

A telephone communications service provider with switched-circuit lines that offers unrestricted access; an attribute that emphasizes the importance of inbound authentication for a network.

[Public] trustee

A special trustee in NetWare that can be added to any Novell Directory Services (NDS) object, directory, or file, and which, by default, includes the Read right and the File Scan right. When [Public] becomes a trustee of an object, directory, or file, all NDS objects effectively are granted rights to that object, directory, or file. [Public] must always be entered enclosed in brackets; its use is restricted to trustee assignments. Like any other trustee, [Public] may be added or deleted, and an Inherited-Rights Filter (IRF) blocks inherited rights for [Public].

pulse

A brief variation in voltage or current level, characterized by the amplitude of change and the duration of the change. A pulse *rise time* is measured as the amount of time needed to change the level from 10 percent to 90 percent of maximum; a *fall time* is measured as the amount of time needed to change the level from 90 percent back down to 10 percent.

Pulse Amplitude Modulation (PAM)
A digital-to-analog conversion scheme in which a modulating wave modulates the amplitude of a pulse stream.

pulse carrier
A signal used as the basis for pulse modulation; it consists of a series of rapid, constant pulses.

Pulse Code Modulation (PCM)
The transmission of analog information that has been sampled into digital form and encoded with a fixed number of bits.

pulse density
A measurement that compares the number of ones in a transmission with the total number of digital time slots transmitted. Certain specifications restrict the number of consecutive zeros that may appear in a transmission.

Pulse Time Modulation (PTM)
Encoding an analog signal for conversion to digital format by varying a time-dependent feature of a pulse.

punch-down block
A device with metal tabs used to puncture the casing on twisted-pair cable and to make electrical contact for wires on the cable, thereby establishing a *cross-connection* between the block and other blocks or connections with specific devices.

purge
The removal of previously deleted files from a disk or directory.

Purge (P) attribute
A NetWare file system attribute that causes NetWare to purge a directory or file when it is deleted.

Q.920/Q.921
Specifications for Integrated Services Digital Networks (ISDNs) that define the User to Network Interface (UNI) in the Data Link Layer (Layer 2) of the OSI Reference Model.

Q.931
A recommended standard from the Consultative Committee for International Telegraphy and Telephony (CCITT) that defines signaling to set up an Integrated Services Digital Network (ISDN) connection.

Q.93B
A recommended standard from the Consultative Committee for International Telegraphy and Telephony (CCITT) that defines signaling to set up an Asynchronous Transfer Mode (ATM) connection.

quad
A cable that has two twisted pairs of wires (four in all) with each wire being separately insulated.

quad-shield cable
Coaxial cable that has four layers of shielding (alternating layers of foil and braid shields) used in industrial settings where heavy electrical interference can occur.

quadbit
A group of 4 bits that are transmitted, processed, and interpreted as a single bit.

quadrature amplitude modulation
A data-encoding technique for modems operating at 2,400 bits per second (bps) that uses a combination of phase and amplitude change to encode multiple bits on a single carrier signal.

quadrax cable
A hybrid of triaxial and twinaxial cable that has both extra wire with dielectric and extra shielding.

Qualified Link Level Control (QLLC) protocol

A protocol enabling Systems Network Architecture (SNA) packets to be transmitted over X.25 links.

Qualifier bit (Q-bit)

A component of a user packet that determines whether the user data field contains data for the user or high-level control information.

Quality of Service (QoS)

A set of parameters in Asynchronous Transfer Mode (ATM) networks describing a transmission with such values as allowable delay variation in cell transmission and allowable cell loss versus total cells transmitted.

quantizing

The digital signal process of converting a Pulse Amplitude Modulation (PAM) signal to a Pulse Code Modulation (PCM) signal.

quarter-inch cartridge (QIC)

Standards developed by the Quarter-Inch Cartridge Drive Standards trade association that specify tapes commonly used in backup operations. Two of the most common are a QIC 40 (a tape that writes 10,000 bits per inch on 20 tracks) or QIC 80 (a tape that writes 14,700 bits per inch on 28 tracks) to back up as much as 250MB of compressed information from a small-to-medium hard disk system. The QIC 1350 tape format can back up as much as 1.35GB of compressed information and the QIC 2100 tapes can back up as much as 2.1GB of compressed information.

quartet signaling

A 100BaseVG Ethernet strategy developed by Hewlett-Packard and AT&T, which simultaneously uses four wire pairs and relies on the fact that the pairs need not be used for sending and receiving at the same time. Demand priority in the 100BaseVG implementation enables hubs to handle the network access for network nodes, so wire availability is guaranteed.

query

A message that inquires about the value of some variable or set of variables.

query language

A programming language found in database management systems (DBMSs) that enables a user to extract and display specific information from the database. The Structured Query Language is an international query language.

queue

An area of the network operating system that contains a list or line formed by items waiting for service (such as tasks waiting to be performed, stations waiting for connections, messages waiting for transmission, or jobs waiting to be printed).

Queue Management Services (QMS)

A built-in component of the NetWare operating system that provides developers with a set of Application Program Interface (API) calls to handle queue operations from any type of application. QMS is commonly used for print servers, batch job servers, archive servers, file copying servers, and compiling servers.

Queue object

A NetWare leaf object representing a print queue on the network or, more specifically, the directories where print jobs are sent to be serviced by a printer.

queue operator

A NetWare user who has rights to manage all jobs in a queue. The queue operator can view information about the queue and jobs in the queue, place a print job on hold, release the print job from a hold, determine the date and time a job prints, and delete a print job.

queue sampling interval

A time period the print server waits between checking the print queues for jobs that are ready and waiting to be printed.
Synonym: *queue polling time*

queue server mode

An operating mode found on network-direct printers and hardware queue servers that allows the device to access the print queue directly.

queue services
Services that allow applications to create and manipulate queues for controlling jobs and services on the network.

queue user
A NetWare user who can place his or her own print jobs on hold, release the print jobs from a hold, determine the date and time jobs are to be printed, and delete print jobs.

queuing delay
A time period that data must wait before transmission onto a statistically multiplexed physical circuit.

queuing theory
Scientific principles applied to the formation or lack of formation of network congestion or congestion at an interface.

QuickTime
An architecture developed by Apple Computer that works with time-based data types (such as sound and video) to synchronize multiple tracks of sound and pictures. QuickTime is a common data format that can be created on one type of computer and played back on another. Versions are available for both Macintosh and Windows.

Q

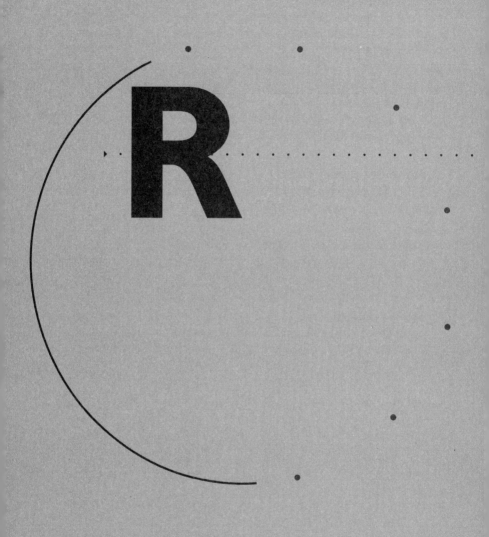

rack-mount server

A motherboard installed into a large rack to provide power to several computers and that supports symmetric multprocessing. A rack mount server is often used in large network installations where many servers would clutter limited space.

radio button

A round button in a graphical utility that represents a selection option and, when selected, appears on the monitor display screen as a darkened circle.

Radio Frequency (RF)

A generic reference to frequencies that respond to radio transmissions (such as Cable Television and broadband networks).

radio frequency interference (RFI)

A noise source often caused by cordless telephones, intercoms, or electrical motors.

radio network

A wireless network in which communications are accomplished with single-frequency or spread-spectrum radio wave transmissions broadcast in all directions.

RAM chip

A semiconductor storage medium that can be either dynamic RAM (whose capacitors must have their electrical charge refreshed every millisecond) or static RAM (whose capacitors retain their charge as long as power is applied).

RAM disk

An area of computer memory managed by a special device driver and used as a simulated disk with a higher operating speed than a regular hard disk. Because random access memory (RAM) is volatile, a RAM disk loses all its contents when power is turned off for the computer.

random access

A process in which a storage device can go directly to a required memory address without having to read from the beginning each time data is requested. A random access device reads information directly by accessing the appropriate memory address.

random access memory (RAM)

An internal dynamic storage area of a computer's memory that can be addressed by the operating system. This area of memory is used by programs and drivers to execute instructions and to hold data temporarily. The three common types of RAM are Dynamic RAM (DRAM), which must be periodically refreshed; Static RAM (SRAM), which retains contents as long as power is supplied; and Video RAM (VRAM), which provides memory for graphics processing or temporary image storage.

RC5 encryption algorithm

A secret-key encryption algorithm using a variable-length key and relying heavily on data-dependent rotations of bit values for its encoding method. This algorithm uses separate algorithms for expanding the secret key, performing encryption, and performing decryption.

rcp

A command (Remote Copy) used on UNIX systems to copy files from one computer to another.

Read Only (Ro) attribute

A NetWare file attribute indicating the file can be read and written to, if other rights assignments allow it.

R

Read Only replica

A NetWare Directory replica used to view, but not to modify, information about the Directory.

Read right

A NetWare directory, file, and property right that grants a user the right to open and read directories and files, as well as the right to read the values of a property.

Read Write (Rw) attribute

A NetWare file attribute that produces a status flag indicating a file cannot be compressed because of insignificant space savings.

Read/Write replica

A NetWare Directory replica used to read or update information about the Directory (such as adding or deleting objects).

read-after-write verification

A method used to ensure that data written to the hard disk matches the original data still residing in computer memory. If a match is made, the data is released from computer memory. If a match is not made, the hard disk block location is recognized as bad. In NetWare, Hot Fix then redirects the data to a good block location within the Hot Fix Redirection Area.

read-only

A file mode that enables viewing the contents of the file, but does not enable a user to insert, update, or delete any information.

read-only memory (ROM)

Computer memory chips whose contents can be executed and read, but cannot be changed. The four types of ROM are Electronically, Erasable, Programmable ROM (EEPROM), in which old data is erased by writing over it; Erasable Programmable ROM (EPROM), in which old data is erased by shining ultraviolet light on the chip; Programmable ROM (PROM), which can be programmed once, but cannot be changed after programming; and Mask ROM (MROM), which is programmed during manufacturing and cannot be changed.

real mode

A mode on computers with an Intel 80286, 80386, or 80486 microprocessor that allows the computer to emulate a computer with an 8086 microprocessor.

real time

A computer system that generates output almost simultaneously with corresponding inputs.

reassembly
The putting back together of a datagram message at the destination after it has been fragmented either at the source or at an intermediate node.

reboot
The process of restarting a computer and reloading the operating system.

rec (recreation)
A suffix on an Internet address that indicates the address belongs to a subject group including mainstream sports, culture, and entertainment. However, this Internet hierarchy can contain more exotic topic areas that may be unsuitable for younger users.

Receive Data (RXD)
As defined by the RS-232-C standard, a hardware signal that carries data from one device to another.

Receive Only (RO)
A setting that indicates a device can receive transmission data, but cannot transmit any data.

receiver
The one of three major communications system components designed to capture or store transmission data, and then convert it to visual or acoustic form. The other two major components in a communications system are a transmitter and a communications channel.

Receiver Ready packet
A control packet sent to Data Terminal Equipment (DTE) that indicates a receiving DTE is ready for a call.

reconfiguration burst
A special bit pattern transmitted repeatedly over an Attached Resource Computer Network (ARCnet) whenever a node wants to force the creation of a new token or when a new node is added to the network.

record

A set of logically associated data items in a database, usually the unit transferred between an application and a database management system (DBMS). A record is often a collection of database fields.

record locking

A NetWare operating system feature that prevents different users from gaining simultaneous access to the same record in a shared file. This feature prevents overlapping disk writes in a multiuser environment.

rectifier

A device designed to convert alternating current (AC) into direct current (DC).

recursion

The capability of a programming language subroutine to call itself.

recursive

A term used to describe commands or routines that call themselves.

recursive copying

A process that copies a specified source directory to a destination directory in a manner that keeps all directories and files exactly as they were on the source logical drive.

Red Book

A term used to describe the telecommunications standards published by the Consultative Committee for International Telegraphy and Telephony (CCITT) in 1985. Also, a term used to describe the National Security Agency's "Trusted Network Interpretation" companion to the Orange Book.

red box

A package containing the standard U.S. format English version of Novell products.

redirect

A process in the Internet Control-Message Protocol (ICMP) or the End System-to-Intermediate System (ES-IS) protocol that enables a router to tell a host to use another router for better effectiveness.

redirection

A diversion of data or other signals from a default or intended destination to a new destination.

redirection area

A space on a hard disk set aside for the Hot Fix feature to send data redirected from faulty disk blocks.

Synonym: *Hot Fix Redirection Area*

redirection reference

A mapping of a logical device name (such as LPT1) to a network printer that makes it possible for an application that is not network-aware to send print jobs to a network printer.

redirector

A networking program that intercepts requests from another program or from a user and directs them to the appropriate environment.

redistribution

The process of allowing routing information from one routing protocol to be distributed in update messages from another routing protocol.

Reduced Instruction Set Computing (RISC)

A microprocessor chip that recognizes usually fewer than 128 assembly language instructions. RISC is commonly used in workstations because it can be designed to run faster than a Complex-Instruction-Set Computing (CISC) chip.

redundancy

A duplicate capacity used when a failure occurs; also, having more than one path to a signal point.

Redundant Array of Inexpensive Drives (RAID)

A disk subsystem architecture combining two or more standard physical drives into a single logical drive to achieve data redundancy. This architecture is used to provide fault tolerance if one or more drives fail. Table R.1 shows the different levels of RAID architecture.

TABLE R.1	RAID Architecture Levels
LEVEL	DESCRIPTION
RAID 0	This level (which incorporates data striping, disk spanning, or bit interleaving) includes data written block by block across each drive or data blocks written to the next available disk.
RAID 1	This level (which incorporates disk mirroring or disk duplexing) includes two hard disks of equal capacity that duplicate the contents of one another.
RAID 2	This level (which data striping or bit interleaving) includes bits written to different drives with checksum information written to special checksum drives.
RAID 3	This level (which incorporates data striping, bit interleaving, and parity checking) includes bits written to different drives and a single parity bit written to a parity drive.
RAID 4	This level (at which data striping, bit interleaving, and parity checking take place) includes data written to different drives, a single parity bit written to a parity drive, and an entire block (sector) of data written to each hard disk each time.
RAID 5	This level (which incorporates data striping, bit interleaving, and distributed parity) includes data written to different drives, an entire block (or sector) of data written to each hard disk each time, and parity data added to another sector.

reentrant

A program technique allowing one copy of a program to be loaded into memory and shared with another program. Reentrant code is often used in operating system service routines (so only one copy of the code is needed) and in multithreaded applications (where different events take place concurrently in the computer).

Reference time server

A NetWare server responsible for providing a time to which all other time servers and workstations synchronize.

referential integrity (RI)

An assurance that when a Structured Query Language (SQL) field in one table references a field in another table, changes to these fields will be synchronized.

refractive index

A measurement indicating the degree to which light will travel at a different speed in a given medium.

Synonym: *index of refraction*

register insertion

A media-access method in which a node that wants to transmit inserts a register (or a buffer) containing a packet into the data stream of a ring at an appropriate point in the stream. This method is used in older ring topologies, but has been replaced in newer ring networks with token passing.

registered resources

Network resources that can be monitored and managed by a management software program designed to work with NetWare Management Agent. The registration process involves key software, hardware, and data components identifying themselves to the NetWare Management Agent.

regulation

A power-conditioning process (such as that used by an Uninterruptible Power Supply) that protects against blackouts and brownouts.

relational database

A database model with data organized as a set of two-dimensional tables represented by rows (which represent records, or collections of information about a specific topic) and columns (which represent fields, or items that make up a record). Data in a relational database always appears from the point of view of the user.

Relative Distinguished Name (RDN)
In NetWare or IntranetWare, a context from an object to another object in the Novell Directory Services (NDS) Directory tree.

relay
An electrical switch designed to allow a small current to control a larger current.

relay point
A point in a packet-switching network at which packets or messages are switched to other circuits or channels.

relaying
One of two major functions of the Network Layer (Layer 3) of the OSI Reference Model that moves data between a source and destination along a path determined by a routing process. The other major function of the Network Layer is routing.

release timer
A device used by an exactly once transaction under AppleTalk Transaction Protocol (ATP) to determine when to eliminate entries from its transactions list.

reliability
A ratio of expected keep-alive packets to received keep-alive packets used as a routing metric. A high ratio indicates a reliable line.

Reliable Transfer
A transfer mode in the OSI Reference Model that guarantees either a message will be transmitted without error or a user will be notified if the message could not be transferred without error.

Reliable Transfer Service Element (RTSE)
An Application Service Element (ASE) in the Application Layer (Layer 7) of the OSI Reference Model that ensures Protocol Data Units (PDUs) are transferred reliably between applications.

remote access

Access to network resources that are not physically located on the same site network topology.

Remote Access Services (RAS)

A Windows NT service that provides limited wide area networking (WAN) capabilities, such as remote access and packet routing. Types of WAN connections supported by RAS include Integrated Services Digital Networks (ISDNs), modems, and X.25 links.

remote boot

A method in which NetWare uses a remote image file to boot a diskless workstation (a client workstation that does not need a floppy or hard drive to function on the network). The diskless workstation relies on a Programmable Read-Only Memory (PROM) chip installed in its Network Interface Card (NIC) to communicate with the boot server.

remote bridge

A bridge connecting physically disparate network nodes on a wide area network (WAN).

Remote Common-Gateway Interface (RCGI)

A feature that allows the NetWare Web Server to modify Web pages before sending them to a browser.

remote computing

Computing performed from a remote location by way of either a remote node (where a user dials in through an access server and becomes another node on the network) or remote control (where a user dials in from a remote location to access his or her own computer).

remote console management

The ability of a NetWare network supervisor to manage servers from a workstation by using console commands as if the supervisor were at the server console: scanning directories and editing text files in both NetWare and nonNetWare partitions on a server, transferring files to (but not from) a server, shutting down a server, or installing or upgrading NetWare on a remote server. Remote console management is accomplished by using the RCONSOLE utility.

remote-control program
A program that provides an interface between two computers so when they are linked together (by way of a serial cable, modem-to-modem communication link, or network connection), one computer can control the operation of the other computer. Each computer runs a copy of the remote control program.

Remote Database Access (RDA)
An Open Systems Interconnection (OSI) specification outlining remote access to databases located across a network.

remote dialback
A security feature available on networks that have dial-in access.

remote digital-loopback test
A modem capability that allows an entire circuit to be tested.

Remote File Service (RFS)
A Distributed File System (DFS) network protocol allowing computer programs to use network resources as though they were local services.

Remote Job Entry (RJE)
The transmission of data and commands from a remote location to a centralized host computer to facilitate processing.

Remote Network Monitoring (RMON)
A proposed standard for the use of remote monitors designed to supplement network management information obtained and used in the Simple Network-Management Protocol (SNMP), particularly by providing functions for getting information about operation and performance of entire networks (or subnetworks) on an internetwork.

remote node
A form of remote access on Internet Protocol (IP) and Internet Protocol Exchange (IPX) networks in which a device dials in to the network and acts like a peer on the target network.

Remote Operations Service Element (ROSE)
An Application Service Element (ASE) in the Application Layer (Layer 7) of the OSI Reference Model that supports interactive cooperation between two applications. An application that requests the association is known as an *initiator* (or an *invoker*); responding to the request is known as the *responder* (or *performer*). Once an association is established, the applications must agree on one of five operation classes. Although ROSE provides a mechanism to enable applications to cooperate, it does not provide a means for carrying out the actual operations.

Remote Password Generator (RPG)
A device that generates a unique password each time a user logs in to a network by using a special number created by the network and the user's Personal Identification Number (PIN).

remote printer
A NetWare network printer not directly attached to a network server, but attached instead to a workstation or directly to the network.

remote-printer mode
An operating mode for network-direct printers or hardware queue servers connected to a printer, and then to the network (or installed in a port at the printer) to function in a manner similar to a workstation running the NetWare 4.*x* NPRINTER or NetWare 3.*x* RPRINTER utilities. Devices configured for remote printer mode are then controlled by a NetWare print server.

R

Remote Procedure Call (RPC)
A mechanism allowing a procedure on one computer to be used in a transparent manner by a program running on another computer.

Remote Program Load (RPL)
A process in which an image of a bootable floppy disk is stored on a NetWare volume so remote boot workstations can use the image to start up at the system prompt. A Programmable Read-Only Memory (PROM) chip in the Network Interface Card (NIC) of the workstation allows the workstation to communicate with the boot server. When the workstation is started, it uses the boot image to load the DOS system and the NetWare Client files required to connect to the network.

Remote Reset
A Novell software program that enables a user to boot a DOS workstation from a remote boot image file on a NetWare server.

remote resource
Any device available through the network, even though it is not attached to a local node.

Remote Source-Route Bridging (RSRB)
A process of sending a packet over a wide area network (WAN) route that has been predetermined entirely in real time prior to the sending of the packet.

remote terminal
A terminal geographically located away from a network, usually connected to the network by way of a modem and telephone line.

remote user
A user, geographically located away from a network, who accesses the network by way of a modem and telephone line.

remote workstation
A stand-alone computer or a workstation that connects to a local area network (LAN) by a router or through a remote asynchronous connection.

Rename Inhibit (Ri) attribute
A NetWare directory and file attribute producing a status flag that prevents any user from renaming the directory or the file.

Rename right
A NetWare object right granting a user the right to change the name of an object, which, in effect, changes the naming of the property.

repeater
A device functioning at the Physical Layer (Layer 1) of the OSI Reference Model that indiscriminately passes all signals from one network segment to another and reconditions the signal to extend the distance between two hosts.

replacement variable
Variables entered in batch files that are replaced by defined parameter values entered in the command line when the batch file is executed.

replica
A copy of a NetWare Directory partition that provides a means for storing the NetWare Directory Database (NDD) on several servers across the network without having to duplicate the entire database for each server. An unlimited number of replicas can be created for each Directory partition and can be stored on any server. Directory replicas eliminate a single point of failure on the network and provide faster access to information across a wide area network (WAN) link.

replica synchronization
A process that ensures replicas of the NetWare Directory partition contain the same information as other replicas of that partition.

R

repudiation
A denial by either a sending node that a network transmission message was sent or by a receiving node that a network transmission message was received.

Request for Comments (RFC)
A procedure in the Internet community that involves the submission of a series of documents containing protocol descriptions, model descriptions, and experimental results for review by experts.

Request To Send (RTS)

A hardware signal sent from a potential transmission sender to a destination, which indicates the transmitter is ready to send a transmission. The receiver sends a Clear To Send (CTS) signal when it is ready to receive the transmission.

Request/Response Header (RH)

Control information preceding a Request/Response Unit (RU), which specifies the type of RU and contains control information associated with that RU.

Request/Response Unit (RU)

A message unit containing such control information as a request code, function management headers, end-user data, or a combination of these types of information.

requester

A workstation program that passes requests from an application to a server-based application.

reservation protocol

A communications protocol that enables a network node to assume exclusive control of a channel for a limited period of time.

reserved memory

The area of DOS memory between 640K and 1MB used to store system and video information.

Synonym: *upper memory*

reserved word

A designated word or term in a programming language or operating system reserved for particular functions or operations.

Synonym: *keyword*

Reset request packet

A control packet sent to Data-Terminal Equipment (DTE) to request the resetting of a virtual call.

residual error

A communication error that occurs or survives despite the presence of a system error-correction mechanism.

resistance

The opposition to the flow of electricity in a circuit.

resource

Any of a variety of manageable components of a network.

resource fork

Part of a Macintosh file that contains file resources, including Macintosh-specific information (such as the windows and icons used with the file). The resource fork is one of two parts of a Macintosh file; the other part is the data fork.

Resource object

An object class in Novell Directory Services (NDS) that identifies the logical resources available on the network.

resource tag

Operating system tags used to ensure allocated NetWare server resources (such as screens and allocated memory) are properly returned to the operating system upon termination of a NetWare Loadable Module (NLM). The NLM requests a resource from the NetWare server for each kind of resource it uses and then assigns it a resource tag name.

R

responder

A socket client in AppleTalk Transaction Protocol (ATP) that performs a service for a requester and sends a TResp packet as notification the service was performed.

response mode

A communications mode in which a device receives a call and must respond to the call.

response time

The amount of time elapsing between sending a network transmission request and actually receiving the data.

response unit

A response by a logical unit (LU) to one or more request units that indicates the successful receipt of data or indicates an error condition.

responsible LU

A logical unit (LU) that deactivates a session when it is no longer being used by two LUs for a conversation.

Restart Request packet

A control packet sent to Data-Terminal Equipment (DTE) to request the restarting of a virtual call.

restore

To retrieve data previously copied or backed up to a storage medium.

resynchronization

A NetWare process in which servers that comply with System Fault Tolerance III (SFT III) are returned to a mirrored (identical) state. *Mirroring* is the process of duplicating data from the NetWare partition on one hard disk drive (a primary server) to the NetWare partition on another hard disk drive (a secondary server). When a primary server fails, the secondary server takes over. When both servers are restored to operation, they resynchronize memory images and mirror disks automatically. Both servers are continually polling each other so each server is aware of the state of the other server. If a server runs in an unmirrored state, it searches for a partner. When it detects a partner on the other end of a mirrored server link, it automatically attempts to synchronize with the other server and return to a mirrored state.

retry count

A number representing how many requests the Network Basic Input/Output System (NetBIOS) transmits for connections or how many failed communications it retransmits.

return (reflection) loss
A value expressed as a ratio in decibels (dB) that indicates the amount of a signal lost because it is reflected back toward the sender.

return band
A one-directional, Frequency-Division Multiplexing (FDM) channel over which a remote device responds to a central controller.

Return to Zero (RZ)
A self-clocking, signal-encoding method that involves voltage returning to a neutral (or zero) state halfway through each bit interval.

Return to Zero Inverted (RZI)
An inverted version of Return to Zero (RZ) in which 1 and 0 are exchanged in the signal descriptions.

Reverse Address-Resolution Protocol (RARP)
A process that determines an Internet address from a Data-Link address in a Transmission-Control Protocol/Internet Protocol (TCP/IP) network. This process provides the reverse functionality of an Ethernet function in which a router determines an 8-bit Media Access Control (MAC) or local Data-Link Layer (Layer 2 of the OSI Reference Model) address for a device with which it is attempting to communicate. The process of determining the local Data-Link address from an Internet address is known as *address resolution*.

reverse charging
A facility specified in a Call Request packet by the calling Data-Terminal Equipment (DTE). Reverse charging is the equivalent of a collect telephone call.

ribbon cable
A type of cable—typically used for connecting internal disks or tape drives—that has wires placed side-by-side in the insulation material, rather than being twisted together inside a circular insulation.

rights

Qualities that determine what a Novell Directory Services (NDS) object can do with directories, files, other objects, or properties of objects. An object can only perform operations if it has the rights to perform those operations; these rights are granted to a specific directory, file, or object by *trustee assignments*. Each object has a list of who has rights to the object and what rights the object has to other objects. *Directory rights* apply to the NetWare file system directory (as well as subdirectories within the directory) and are considered part of the file system. *File rights* only apply to the file to which they are assigned. A trustee must have the Access Control right to a directory or file to grant directory or file rights to other objects. *Object rights* apply to NDS objects, but do not affect the properties of an object. *Property rights* apply to the properties of an NDS object. A trustee must have the Write, Add Self, Delete Self, or Supervisor right to the Access Control List property of the object to grant object or property rights to other objects.

ring

The attachment of network nodes in a closed loop with data being transmitted from node to node around the loop, always in the same direction.

ring group

A collection of Token Ring interfaces on one or more routers in a bridged Token Ring network.

Ring In/Ring Out (RI/RO)

A port through which a Token Ring Multistation Access Unit (MAU) can be connected (Ring In) and a port through which the MAU can be connected to another MAU (Ring Out).

Ring Indicator (RI)

A signal that indicates an incoming call.

ring latency

In a Token Ring or Institute of Electronic and Electrical Engineers (IEEE) 802.5 network, the amount of time required for a signal to propagate once around a ring.

ring monitor

A centralized management tool used on Token Ring or Institute of Electronic and Electrical Engineers (IEEE) 802.5 networks.

ring topology

A network topology that has the characteristics of a logical topology (packets are transmitted sequentially from node to node in a predefined order) and a physical topology (each node is connected to two other nodes). In a ring topology, nodes are positioned in a closed loop. Information is transmitted on a one-way path around the loop so a node receives packets from exactly one other node, a node transmits packets to exactly one other node, and the initiating node is the last to receive a packet. Each node in the ring can act as a repeater, thus capable of boosting a transmission signal before passing it along. Cable requirements are minimal for a ring topology. If one node fails, however, the entire ring fails and, because communication is one way, diagnosing or troubleshooting problems becomes difficult.

RIP (IPX)

NetWare's implementation of the Router Information Protocol (RIP) with Internet Packet Exchange (IPX) protocol.

RIP (TCP/IP)

A distance vector gateway protocol for Transmission Control Protocol/Internet Protocol (TCP/IP) networks in which routers determine and use the most efficient routes to nodes on the network. The TCP/IP Routing Information Protocol (RIP) router periodically broadcasts messages that contain routing update information about each network it can reach and the cost (or the number of hop counts) to reach that network. The routing update information is kept in the routing table, with the router that sent the routing update message remembered as the next router (or hop) on the route to the network. A router determines the destination route on the basis of the fewest hop counts needed to reach the destination. TCP/IP allows a maximum of 15 hop counts to reach a destination.

RIP II (TCP/IP)

A Routing Information Protocol (RIP) enhancement that includes the subnetwork mask in its routing information. RIP is unable to advertise information about subnetworks, so routers are limited to advertising-only networking (and not subnetworking) routes. RIP II can support subnets and can be used in those network topologies requiring variable-length subnet masks.

rise time

A time increment an electrical signal takes to go from 10 percent of its level to 90 percent, which is used when setting the upper limit on the maximum transmission speed supported by the signal.

riser cable

Cable strung vertically, such as in an elevator shaft of a building. Because such areas can be a source of electrical interference, optical fiber is usually the cable of choice for riser cables.

Rivesi, Shamir, Adleman (RSA) Algorithm

A patented public-key encryption algorithm bearing the name of its inventors.

RJ-xx

A modular connection mechanism that allows for up to eight wires dedicated to carry different signals. The three most common types of RJ-xx mechanisms are *RJ-11*, a four-wire (two-pair) connection with the two central wires being tip (green wire) and ring (red wire) lines; *RJ-12*, a six-wire (three-pair) connection that uses the same-sized plug (male component) and jack (female component); and *RJ-45*, an eight-wire (four-pair) connection commonly used for data transmission over unshielded twisted-pair (UTP) cable and leased-line telephone connections.

rlogin

A remote login service found on Berkeley Software Distribution (BSD) UNIX operating systems comparable to the Internet's Telnet service.

roamer

A cellular telephone user who uses services in multiple calling areas during the course of one call.

robot

A program that automatically performs a task ordinarily performed by a person. A *mailbot* is an example of a type of robot.

roll-back

The database process of aborting a transaction and undoing all changes made to a file during the transaction. Roll-back restores a file to the state it was in prior to the transaction.

roll-forward

The database process of re-creating data in the database by rerunning all the transactions listed in a transaction log.

roll-in

The process of transferring data from an auxiliary memory to the computer's central memory.

ROM BIOS

Software that provides routines to perform basic input/output (I/O) operations on an IBM or IBM-compatible computer.

root bridge

A device appointed by a spanning tree to determine which managed bridges to block in the spanning tree topology.

R

root directory

In a hierarchical directory structure, the highest directory level. In NetWare, the root directory is the volume.

Root Mean Square (RMS)

A value associated with Alternating Current (AC) voltage as it is actually measured. This value can be calculated by multiplying the peak voltage in the circuit by 0.070707.

[Root] object

A Novell Directory Services (NDS) container object that provides the highest point of access to different Country and Organization objects and allows trustee assignments granting rights to the entire NetWare Directory tree. The Country, Organization, and Alias objects can be created at the [Root] object. The [Root] object is merely a placeholder that contains no information.

Round Trip Time (RTT)

The total amount of time a network communication travels from the source to the destination and back, including the amount of time required to process the message at the destination and to generate a reply. Routing algorithms sometimes use RTT in calculating the most efficient route.

route

A path through an internetwork determining which computers are accessible from other computers across the network.

route discovery

A process that determines possible routes on a source-routing network from the source to a destination node.

route extension

A Systems Network Architecture (SNA) path from the destination subarea node through peripheral equipment to a network addressable unit (NAU).

routed protocol

A protocol for which a router understands the logical internetwork as perceived by the protocol so the router can then route that protocol.

router

A workstation or NetWare server that runs software to manage the exchange of information between network cabling systems. A NetWare router, which runs on a NetWare server, connects separate network cabling topologies or separate networks by way of the server's NetWare operating system. By default, NetWare automatically routes Internet Packet Exchange/Sequenced Packet Exchange (IPX/SPX) packets, although it can be enabled for nonrouting Transmission Control Protocol/Internet Protocol (TCP/IP) and AppleTalk protocols. The two types of routers are a *local router*, used within the cable limitations of a local area network (LAN) driver, and a *remote router*, connected beyond its driver limitations or through a modem.

Router Discovery Protocol

A feature of the Transmission Control Protocol/Internet Protocol (TCP/IP) suite that enables hosts to find routers on locally attached networks and alleviates the need to configure hosts with a routing table or a default router.

routing

The process of moving information (in the form of data packets) across an internetwork from source to destination. This process occurs at the Network Layer (Layer 3) of the OSI Reference Model and can be contrasted to *bridging*, which occurs at the Data Link Layer (Layer 2). Routing involves the determination of the most efficient routing path and the transport of packet information through the network. Routing algorithms use *metrics* (such as hop counts or path lengths) to determine the optimal path to a destination and to store routing information in *routing tables*. These tables help to determine the optimal path to a destination. Transportation of the packet is accomplished by determining the address of the destination and sending the packet to that destination address.

routing area

An administrative domain of Internetwork Packet Exchange (IPX) networks that all have the same area address. The routing area provides users with access to services in the Network Layer (Layer 3) of the OSI Reference Model.

routing bridge

A bridge used on the Media Access Control (MAC) sublayer of the Data Link Layer (Layer 2) of the OSI Reference Model, which uses methods from the Network Layer (Layer 3) to determine the topology of a network.

routing buffer

A portion of NetWare file server random access memory (RAM) used as a temporary storage area of packets until they can be processed by the server or sent on to the network.

Synonym: *communication buffer*

routing domain

A collection of routing areas connected by level 2 routers. Routers within the same domain communicate by way of a common intradomain routing protocol known as an *Interior Gateway Protocol* (IGP), such as Intermediate System-to-Intermediate System (IS-IS) protocol. Routers in different domains communicate by way of a common interdomain routing protocol known as an *Exterior Gateway Protocol* (EGP), such as the IS-IS Interdomain Routing Protocol (IDRP).

Routing Information Field (RIF)

A field that appears in an Institute of Electronic and Electrical Engineers (IEEE) 802.5 packet header and is used by a source-route bridge to determine through which Token Ring network segments a packet must transmit.

routing information filter

A filter designed to restrict the exchange of routing information between routers to provide more network security and to reduce network bandwidth consumed by the periodic exchange of routing information between routers.

Routing Information Protocol (RIP)

A routing protocol in which routers use routing tables to determine the most cost-efficient route (the route involving the fewest hops) to a destination. RIP routers periodically broadcast messages that contain routing update information about each network it can reach and the cost (or the number of hop counts) to reach that network. The routing update information is kept in the routing table that includes the ultimate destination, the next hop on the way to that destination, and a metric (indicating the distance in the number of hops to the destination). The router that sent the routing update message is considered the next router (or hop) on the route to the network. A router determines the destination route on the basis of the fewest hop counts needed to reach the destination. As changes occur to the network (such as topology changes), a new route to a destination may prove to be more cost-efficient. Thus, the routing tables are constantly updated and routers always choose the most efficient route to a destination. TCP/IP allows a maximum of 15 hop counts to reach a destination.

Routing Information Table

A table containing information (such as network numbers, routes to a particular destination, and metrics associated with those routes) a router uses to determine the best possible route to use to forward packets to destinations.

routing metric

A measurement that determines the preference between two routes generated by the same protocol to the same destination. Metric information includes reliability, delay, bandwidth, load, Maximum Transmission Units (MTUs), communications costs, and hop count.

Routing-Table Maintenance Protocol (RTMP)

An AppleTalk routing protocol in the Transport Layer (Layer 4) of the OSI Reference Model that provides for the moving of packets between networks, RTMP was derived from the Routing Information Protocol (RIP).

routing update

A message sent by a router at prescribed intervals of time to indicate network reachability and associated cost information.

RS/6000

A set of 32-bit chips used in IBM Reduced Instruction Set Computing (RISC) workstations that features a superscalar design with four separate 16K data-cache units and an 8K instruction cache. Together with Apple and Motorola, IBM developed a single-chip version of the RS/6000 called the PowerPC.

R

RS-232-C

A recommended standard interface from the Electronic Industries Association (EIA) that defines electrical, functional and mechanical characteristics of asynchronous transmissions between Data-Terminal Equipment (DTE) and a peripheral device. The RS-232-C is a 25-pin or 9-pin DB connector.

RS-422

A recommended standard interface from the Electronic Industries Association (EIA) that defines electrical and functional characteristics of balanced serial interface, but does not specify a connector. The RS-422 is used on the serial port of a Macintosh computer.

RS-423

A recommended standard interface from the Electronic Industries Association (EIA) that defines electrical and functional characteristics of unbalanced serial interface, but does not specify a connector.

RS-449

A recommended standard interface from the Electronic Industries Association (EIA) that defines electrical, functional, and mechanical characteristics of synchronous transmissions in a serial binary data interchange. The RS-449 is a 37-pin or 9-pin DB connector.

RS-485

A recommended standard interface from the Electronic Industries Association (EIA) that defines electrical and functional characteristics of balanced serial interface, but does not specify a connector. The RS-485 uses tri-state drivers, rather than the dual-state drivers found in the RS-422, and is used in multipoint applications.

RS-530

A recommended standard interface from the Electronic Industries Association (EIA) that defines electrical and functional characteristics of serial binary data transmission, either synchronously or asynchronously. The RS-530 uses a 25-pin DB connector.

run length limited (RLL)

An encoding scheme used to store information on a hard disk that effectively doubles the hard disk's storage capacity in contrast with older schemes such as Modified Frequency Modulation (MFM).

runt packet

A packet that has too few bits.

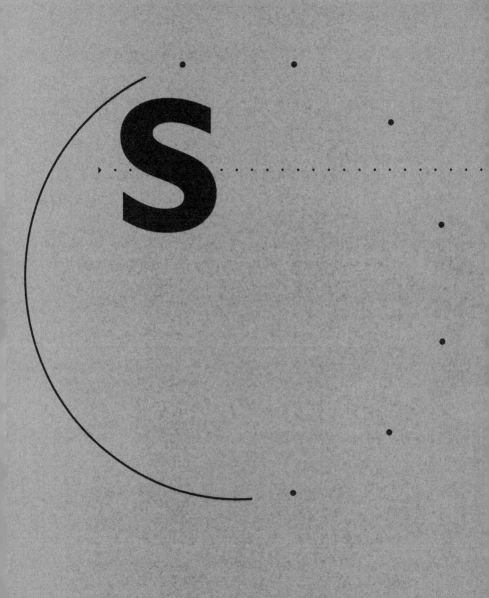

safety device
A device designed to protect network system hardware from drastic deviations or fluctuations in the electrical power supply.

sag
A drop in line voltage between 70 percent and 90 percent of the nominal voltage over a short period of time.

salvageable files
NetWare files deleted by users that are recoverable.

same-server migration
A method of using a single network server to upgrade a network to NetWare 4.x; a workstation hard disk temporarily holds bindery information.

Sampled Servo (SS)
A recording technique for compact discs in which the contents are stored on a single, spiral track.

SAP filtering
A Service Advertising Protocol (SAP) scheme in which a user can filter multiple Novell Directory Service (NDS) objects by first finding a server and opening its bindery to reveal the names of more objects.

Scalar Processor Architecture (SPARC)
A 32-bit Reduced Instruction Set Computing (RISC) processor from Sun Microsystems used in SPARCstation workstations.

scaling
The process of adding more nodes to expand a network.

scattering
A method of communication or of gathering information in which an intelligent fixed disk device controller issues multiple simultaneous requests to different drives connected to the same controller.

schema

The rules defining how the Novell Directory Services (NDS) Directory tree is created and how information is stored in the Directory database. The schema defines attribute information, inheritance, naming, and subordination. *Attribute information* concerns the different types of information that can be associated with an object. *Inheritance* specifies which objects can inherit the properties and rights of other objects. *Naming* determines the structure of the directory tree. *Subordination* determines the location of objects in the directory tree.

sci newsgroup

An Internet newsgroup that discusses scientific topics.

screen attributes

A set of attributes that determine the behavior of a screen.

screen-handling services

Services that make it possible to manage special features of the logical screen of a server, including the ability to create new screens with a variety of different attributes and the ability to manipulate the screen.

script

A small program invoked at a particular time, such as a login script or a macro program that contains commonly used or frequently used commands.

scroll

To move text up and down on a screen display while reading it.

scroll bar

A bar in a graphical utility beside a list box that enables the user to move up and down the list.

SCSI bus

A Small Computer System Interface (SCSI) with a 50-pin connector (as opposed to an Integrated Drive Electronics, or IDE, 40-pin connector) that connects Host Bus Adapters (HBAs) to controllers and hard disks. An SCSI bus requires both the use of proper termination equipment and proper addresses for all connected peripheral devices.

SCSI terminator

A device used in Small Computer System Interface (SCSI) connections that prevents signals from echoing on the SCSI bus.

search

A query of information on a network or in a database.

search criteria

Values specified when making a search query that tell the network system or database to match the requested values.

search drive

A drive supported only from DOS workstations that the NetWare operating system searches when a requested file is not found in the current directory. This feature enables a user to access an application file or data located in a directory other than the current directory.

search engine

A World Wide Web (WWW) location that uses search criteria specified by a user to compile a list of Web sites that mention words or phrases specified in the search criteria. Some search engines use Web robots to search through and index hypertext documents available on the WWW; others simply gather information available from indexes.

search mode

A mode specifying how a program uses search drives when looking for a data file.

search path

A list indicating to the operating system which directories to search if a requested program is not found in the current directory.

seat

Configuration of a telephone line, port, and telephone on a computer system.

secondary half-session

A half-session on a node that receives the session-activation request.

secondary link station (SLS)

A link station (other than the primary link station) that can exchange data with a primary link station, but not with other secondary link stations.

secondary logical unit (SLU)

A logical unit (LU) containing the secondary half-session for a particular logical-unit-to-logical-unit (LU-LU) session.

secondary server

A NetWare System Fault Tolerance (SFT) III server, which receives a mirrored copy of the memory and disk from the primary server (the first server activated on the system), is activated after the primary server, and splits multiple-read requests with the primary server. Unless it is on the same network segment as the primary server, the secondary server acts as a router for the local network segments to which it is directly attached. If it is on the same network segment as the primary server, the secondary server does not perform any routing. The designation of primary server versus secondary server is handled by the system. When the primary server fails, the secondary server becomes the new primary server. When the failed server is restored, it becomes the new secondary server.

Secondary time server

A NetWare server that provides the time to workstations after it has received the time from a Single Reference, Primary, or Reference time server.

secret key encryption

A data-encryption scheme used to encrypt and decrypt messages in which a single key is known only to the sender or receiver.

sector
A subdivision of a track on a hard disk drive.

Secure Electronic Transactions (SET) protocol
A protocol developed by VISA and MasterCard that allows credit card transactions to be conducted across the Internet.

Secure Sockets Layer (SSL) protocol
A protocol designed by Netscape Communications that provides for encrypted authenticated communications across the Internet between World Wide Web (WWW) browsers and servers. A Uniform Resource Locator (URL) beginning with "http" indicates an SSL connection is used. With an SSL connection, each side is required to have a Security Certificate, the information from which is used to encrypt a message. This ensures the following: Only the intended recipient can decode the message; the message has not been tampered with; and the message did, indeed, originate from the source from which it claims to have come.

secure transmission
An exchange of messages with the assurance that the message was sent by the person or system from which it claims to be sent and only the intended recipient can read the message. A secure transmission mode is common on many Web browsers.

security
Elements in NetWare and IntranetWare that control access to the network or to specific information on the network.

Security Certificate
Information used by the Secure Sockets Layer (SSL) protocol to establish a secure connection. To create a valid SSL, both sides must have a valid Security Certificate. The information contained in a Security Certificate includes to whom the certificate belongs, who issued the certificate, some sort of unique identification (such as a serial number), dates the certificate is valid, and an encrypted "fingerprint" that can be used to verify the contents of the certificate.

security equivalence
A Novell Directory Services (NDS) property of every User object that lists other objects. A user is granted all rights any object in that list is granted, including object rights, file rights, and directory rights.

Security Management
One of five network management domains described in the OSI Network Management Model that controls access to network resources according to local guidelines to protect against intruders. To accomplish this control, all access points to the network are defined and efforts are made to ensure these points cannot be breached or compromised. Access points include the network nodes, cables, air waves, and programs. An authentication process (not specified in the OSI Network Management Model) restricts access by unauthorized users and alarm signals are used to alert of any breach or compromise to network security.

seed router
An AppleTalk router that defines the range of network numbers for all routers in a network segment. Each AppleTalk network segment is required to have at least one seed router.
Synonym: *configured router*

seek time
The amount of time that elapses while a hard disk drive's read/write head searches for a given track.

segment
A discrete portion of a network or a local area network (LAN) that has no routers or bridges.

segmentation
Setting a maximum limit for the amount of memory to be used by a process. Segmentation assigns memory from a large block of physically contiguous memory.

Segmentation and Reassembly (SAR)
A process involving data frames being segmented into Asynchronous Transfer Mode (ATM) cells at the transmitter and reassembled into the original format at the receiver.

Selected Property rights
An option allowing the assignment of property rights to individual Novell Directory Services (NDS) objects in a NetWare Directory tree.

selector
A value used at a specific layer of the OSI Reference Model to distinguish each of the Service Access Points (SAPs) through which an entity at that level provides services to the layer above it.

semaphore
In multiprocessor environments, an integer value used to prevent data corruption by coordinating the activities of programs and processes. Semaphores help to synchronize interprocess communications by ensuring certain event sequences do or do not occur. Semaphores can also be used to restrict the number of users who have access to a resource by setting an upper limit. When the upper limit is reached, the semaphore denies access by additional users. An *event semaphore* allows a thread to tell other threads an event has occurred and it is safe for the threads to resume execution. A *mutual exclusion semaphore* protects system resources from simultaneous access by several processes. A *multiple wait semaphore* allows threads to wait for multiple events to take place or for multiple resources to become free.

sense code
Code indicating what type of error has occurred in the running of a program, which is sent to a partner node in function management headers or negative responses.

sequence number
A number appearing in the bitmap/sequence header of an AppleTalk Transaction Protocol (ATP) header of a Transaction Response (TResp) packet that indicates the position of the TResp packet in a TResp message.

Sequenced Packet Exchange (SPX)

A NetWare protocol that enhances the Novell Internetwork Packet Exchange (IPX) protocol. To ensure successful packet delivery, SPX requests verification from a destination that data has been received, compares a verification value to a value calculated before transmission, and, by matching those two numbers, acknowledges the packet arrived and that it arrived intact. SPX also has the capability of tracking data transmissions consisting of more than one packet (a transmission that has been split into several packets). If no acknowledgment is received within a specified amount of time, SPX retransmits the packets. If retransmissions fail to produce an acknowledgment, SPX notifies the operator the connection has failed. SPX is derived from the Xerox Packet Protocol.

Sequenced Packet Protocol (SPP)

In the Xerox Network System (XNS), a protocol for the Transport Layer (Layer 4) of the OSI Reference Model.

sequential access

An access method used by some storage devices in which the device starts at the beginning of the medium to find a specific storage location.

serial

Performing tasks one after the other.

serial communication

Transmission of data from one device to another, one bit at a time, over a single line.

Serial Line Internet Protocol (SLIP)

An Internet protocol designed to run Internet Protocol (IP) over serial lines that connect two network systems. SLIP is being replaced by Point-to-Point Protocol (PPP).

serial port

A port (typically COM1 or COM2 on IBM-compatible systems) that allows the asynchronous transmission of data, one bit at a time.

serial printer
A printer that uses a serial interface to a network. Because a serial printer accepts data transferred a bit at a time and assembled into bytes using handshaking techniques, it may perform slower than a parallel printer.

serialization
A process of assigning serial numbers to software to prevent unlawful duplication of the product.

server
A network computer used by multiple users to share access to files, printing, communications, and other services. In a large network, a server may run the network operating system (such as a *NetWare server* running the NetWare operating system). In smaller networks, the server may run a personal computer operating system in tandem with peer-to-peer networking software.

server console
A monitor-keyboard combination that enables a user to view network traffic, send messages, set configuration parameters, shut down a network server, and (in the case of NetWare) load and unload NetWare Loadable Module (NLM) programs.

Server Message Block (SMB)
Microsoft's distributed file system network protocol that allows a computer to use the files and resources of another computer as if the two computers were locally connected.

server mirroring
A NetWare System Fault Tolerance (SFT) III configuration in which a secondary (identical) server immediately takes over network operations when a primary server fails. The two servers must be connected by a mirrored server link and, as long as this link is in place, can reside on different network segments.

Server object
A Novell Directory Services (NDS) leaf object that represents a server.

server protocol

Procedures and processes a network server follows to accept and respond to service requests from workstations.

Server Session Socket (SSS)

In AppleTalk networks, a protocol in the Session Layer (Layer 5) of the OSI Reference Model used that contains the number of the socket to which the Session Layer packets are sent.

Server Side Includes (SSI)

Commands that enable authors of World Wide Web (WWW) pages to insert variables in the Web pages (such as text from another file or the current date and time).

server-based network

The use of one or more network nodes as dedicated servers through which other nodes must go to access resources on other workstations.

service

A task or operation made available through an application or systems program that includes network services (or those including file services to control file access and storage), print services, communications services, fax services, archive services, and backup services.

Service Access Point (SAP)

An interface between layers in the OSI Reference Model through which an entity at a particular layer can provide services to the processes at the layer above. SAPs, which are assigned by the Institute for Electrical and Electronic Engineers (IEEE), each have their own unique address that can also be used as the access point to the service's user (that is, the entity at the next highest level). SAPs are often labeled according to the layer being discussed (for example, PSAP for the Presentation Layer, SSAP for the Session Layer, TSAP for the Transport Layer, NSAP for the Network Layer, DSAP for the Data Link Layer, and PhSAP for the Physical Layer).

S

Service Advertising Protocol (SAP)
A Novell protocol used by servers to advertise their services to the network, which allows routers to create and maintain a database of current internetwork server information. Routers broadcast SAP updates to all other routers on the network to keep all routers synchronized. Workstations broadcast SAP request packets to query the network to find a server.

service bureau
A company that provides support services (such as data processing or software development) as an outside vendor to its customers, thus providing a means for companies to avoid high equipment and personnel costs associated with running similar in-house services.

Service Data Unit (SDU)
A packet passed as a service request parameter from one layer in the OSI Reference Model to a layer below it.

Service Hypertext Transfer Protocol (SHTTP)
A secure version of the Hypertext Transfer Protocol (HTTP) that provides encryption services, a digital signature, and authentication. SHTTP provides end-to-end secure communications.

service information filter
A filter that restricts service access by filtering out any packets that advertise the services. A service information filter keeps applications from discovering the locations of services, but does not restrict access to the services if the application already knows their locations.

service point
Software through which a non-IBM device or a network can communicate with a network manager in IBM's Network Management Architecture (NMA) model.

service provider
A company or individual who provides access to a network or to another service. Service providers are distinguished by the modem speeds they can handle, whether the access telephone number is local or long-distance, the

types of access protocols they support, and, in the case of an Internet Service Provider (ISP), the range of Internet usage capabilities they support.

servlet
A small, specialized server program, particularly a program acting as a component or helper application for larger software applications.

session
Either a connection between two network addressable units (NAUs) or the time between turning on a computer and turning it off.

session activation
The exchange of an activation request and a positive response between network addressable units (NAUs).

session deactivation
The exchange of a deactivation request and a response between network addressable units (NAUs).

session file
A file that contains the names and locations of NetWare for Macintosh entities most frequently used and the utility used to work with each one.

Session Layer (OSI model)
The fifth layer (Layer 5) in the seven-layer OSI Reference Model. The Session Layer allows dialog control between end systems and handles problems that are not communication issues.

session parameters
Parameters specifying or constraining protocols between two network addressable units (NAUs).

session partner
Either of two network addressable units (NAUs) participating in a network session.

settle time

The time it takes to stabilize the head on a hard disk drive above the track.

shadow RAM

Random access memory (RAM) located in upper memory that can be used as a place into which data and code can be copied from the computer system's read-only memory (ROM).

shareable

A term used to describe a file, device, or process available to multiple users that they can use simultaneously, if necessary.

Shareable (Sh) attribute

A file attribute set by the NetWare operating system that allows a file to be accessed by more than one user at a time.

shared memory

Memory involved in an interprocess communication accessed by more than one program running in a multitasking operating system. Memory management units, such as semaphores, are responsible for ensuring applications do not collide or try to update from the same information at the same time.

shared process

A process that can be serviced by a single server for multiple stations, all of which can communicate with the server.

shared services

Computer functions and resources used by multiple clients simultaneously from anywhere on the network.

shared media network

A network configuration in which all nodes share the same line, thus making only one transmission possible at one time. Adding nodes to a shared-media network increases network traffic, but does not increase capacity.

shareware
Computer programs made available to users for a trial period before the user is expected to pay a set amount to the shareware provider.

shell
Software that serves as the interface between the user and the operating system. The DOS operating system has a DOS command interpreter and the DOSSHELL program; Windows uses the Program Manager as a shell. The Macintosh environment uses the Finder; the UNIX environment uses the C shell and the Bourne shell. In Novell environments, the NetWare shell is an early version of the DOS client software.

shell account
An Internet account that allows a local computer to act as a terminal on a multiuser UNIX network connected to the Internet, which allows the use of all UNIX commands and the ability to store and process information on the host computer. The downside to a shell account is the inability to use a point-and-click interface or to view graphics, and that files are downloaded to the hard disk of the UNIX host machine (which means files must be downloaded from the host machine to the local computer).

shield
A sheath wrapped around a conductor wire and insulator in coaxial and twisted-pair cabling that helps to prevent external signals and noise from interfering with the signal transmission through the cable.

Shielded Distributed Data Interface (SDDI)
A network configuration that uses shielded twisted-pair (STP) cabling for the Fiber Distributed Data Interface (FDDI) architecture and protocols.

shielded twisted-pair (STP) cable
A cable with a foil shield and copper braid surrounding pairs of wires that have a minimum number of twists per foot of cable length. Although it is considered bulky, STP is used for high-speed transmissions over long distances and is often associated with Token Ring networks.

short

A cabling condition in which excess current flows between two wires because of an abnormally low resistance between the two wires.

short circuit

The accidental completion of a circuit at a point too close to its origin to allow normal or complete operation.

short machine type

A four-letter (or shorter) name that represents a DOS machine brand in NetWare (for example, IBM for an IBM computer). The same short machine type name is used with overlay files (for example, with IBM$RUN.OVL and CMPQ$RUN.OVL). The default short machine type, which is set in the NET.CFG file with the SHORT MACHINE TYPE parameter, is IBM.

shortcut

A keystroke (or keystroke combination) that is the equivalent of selecting a menu item or a small Windows 95 file that acts as a pointer in to a program, data file, or location on a network.

Shortest Path First (SPF)

A routing strategy in which packets are passed between routers according to the distance to the destination.

shortest-path routing

A routing algorithm that calculates paths to all network destinations wherein the shortest path is determined by the cost assigned to each link.

short-haul modem

A modem used to transmit information only over short distances (such as from one side of a building to another).

sideband

A modem frequency band either just above or just below the frequency used by the carrier signal in the modulation process that converts data along analog signals.

sign-trailing separate (STS)
A numeric data type in the COBOL programming language, represented as an American Standard Code for Information Interchange (ASCII) string. STS is right-justified and padded with leading zeros; it has the sign byte at the end.

signal
A change in voltage or current over time described by the levels the current reaches and by the pattern with which the level changes over time. A *peak* is the highest level reached by a signal. A *signal pattern* is described as a waveform representing the level over time, with a *sine waveform* representing a clean signal and a *square waveform* representing an encoded digital bit. A signal can be either an *electrical signal* (one emanating from a power source) or a *digital signal* (one representing a data transmission).

Signal Quality Error (SQE)
A signal sent from the transceiver to the attached machine in an Ethernet 2.0 or 802.3 network to indicate the transceiver's collision-detection circuitry is working properly.
Synonym: *heartbeat*

Signal-to-Crosstalk Ratio (SCR)
A ratio value representing the decibel level of a signal to the noise in a twisted-pair cable. The SCR is calculated specifically as the ratio between near end crosstalk (NEXT) and the attenuation on a cable.

signal-to-noise ratio (SNR)
A measure of signal quality that uses a ratio between the desired signal and the unwanted signal (or noise) at a specific point in a cable.

Simple Gateway Monitoring Protocol (SGMP)
A network management protocol that was the precursor to the Simple Network Monitoring Protocol (SNMP).

Simple Mail Transfer Protocol (SMTP)
A standard electronic mail (e-mail) protocol that provides specifications for mail system interaction and control message formats.

Simple Network Management Protocol (SNMP)

An Application-Layer (Layer 7 of the OSI Reference Model) protocol that specifies a format for collecting network management data and the exchange of that data between devices. Using Desktop SNMP services, a NetWare workstation can send status information to an SNMP management program running on an Internetwork Packet Exchange (IPX) or Transmission Control Protocol/Internet Protocol (TCP/IP) network. The two types of devices that make up the SNMP architecture are SNMP *agents* (background processes that monitor operation of the device and communicate with the outside world) and SNMP *managers* (network management stations that collect messages from SNMP agents, generate reports, and handle data). The five operations on which SNMP functions are based as follows: *GetRequest*, used by an SNMP manager to poll an agent for information; *GetNextRequest*, used by an SNMP manager to request the next item in a table or array; *SetRequest*, used by an SNMP manager to change a value within an agent's Management Information Base (MIB); *GetResponse*, used by an SNMP agent to satisfy a request from a manager; and *Trap*, used by an SNMP agent to notify a manager of an event.

Simple Network Time Protocol (SNTP)

A variant of the Network Time Protocol (NTP) in which the correct time is obtained from an official source and disseminated to servers across the network. The major appeal of this protocol is simplicity, as it is not regarded as highly accurate (only to within several hundred milliseconds).

simplex

A communications mode that allows information to be transmitted in only one direction. Although the receiver may be able to send control and error signals, it cannot send data to the sender.

Simplified Access Control (SAC)

Access-control guidelines presented in the Consultative Committee for International Telegraphy and Telephony (CCITT) X.500 Directory Services model.

single large expensive disk (SLED)

A storage method that uses only a single, high-capacity disk as a storage location.

Single Reference time server

The sole source of time on the NetWare network that provides time to Secondary time servers and to workstations.

single session

The only session connecting two logical units (LUs) in a Systems Network Architecture (SNA) network.

Single Sign-On (SSO)

A network login strategy in which a user needs only a single-user ID and password to access any machine, application, or service on a network, provided the user has proper access and usage privileges.

Single-Attachment Concentrator (SAC)

A Fiber Distributed Data Interface (FDDI) network concentrator serving as a termination point for a Single-Attachment Station (SAS) and attaching to the FDDI network through a Dual-Attachment Concentrator (DAC).

Single-Attachment Station (SAS)

A Fiber Distributed Data Interface (FDDI) network node that lacks the physical ports necessary to attach directly to both the primary and secondary rings on the network, which, instead, attaches to a concentrator.

single-frequency transmission

A transmission method using radio waves in which the signal is encoded within a narrow frequency range and in which all energy is concentrated at a particular frequency range. Single-frequency transmissions are susceptible to jamming and eavesdropping.

S

single-mode fiber

A fiber with a narrow diameter, through which lasers are used to transmit signals. Only one route is used for the light wave to pass through the cable, making single-mode fiber popular in networks that transmit over long distances (such as telephone networks).

single-step multimode fiber

An optical fiber that has only a single layer of cladding and a core wide enough to allow multiple light paths through at one time.

single-user system

A computer system designed to be used by only one user at a time. A single-user system is often a personal computer running DOS, System 7, OS/2, Windows 3.x, Windows 95, or Windows NT.

site

A group of computers (or even a single computer) that hosts a particular data collection, a set of World Wide Web (WWW) pages sharing a common entry-point address, or another network resource.

site license

A software-licensing agreement that applies to all installed copies of a software package at a specific location, rather than individual licenses for each copy of the software program. A site license may allow unlimited copies for internal use or may limit the number of copies covered by the license agreement.

skin effect

A term used to describe the condition in the transmission of data at a fast rate over twisted-pair cable in which current flows most on the outside surface of the wire, thereby increasing resistance. Skin effect often results in a loss of signal.

sliding-window flow control

A flow-control method in which a receiver grants permission to a transmitter to transmit data until a window is full, at which time the transmitter must stop the transmission until the receiver advertises a larger window. This type of flow control is common in transport protocols.

slot time

The maximum amount of elapsed time between the receipt of a packet by the first node on an Ethernet network and the receipt of a packet by the last node.

slots

A media-access method found in older ring topologies in which a ring is divided into fixed-sized slots that travel around the ring.

slotted ring

A ring topology using slots as the media-access method. This topology was popular in the 1970s, but has been replaced by the Token Ring topology.

SMA connector

A fiber-optic connector using a threaded-coupling mechanism to make the connection that can be used with either multimode or single-mode fiber. SMA connectors have been designed to meet military specifications.

Small Computer Systems Interface (SCSI)

An industry standard outlining the interconnection of peripheral devices (such as hard disk drives and tape backup systems) and their controllers to a microprocessor. The standard defines both hardware and software specifications for communication between a host computer and a peripheral device. A large degree of compatibility between SCSI (pronounced *scuzzy*) devices is common.

smart hub

An Ethernet or ARCnet network concentrator that has certain network management facilities built into the firmware to allow a network administrator to control and plan network configurations.

Synonym: *intelligent hub*

smart terminal

A terminal connected to a larger computer, having limited (or no) local disk-storage capacity and limited capability to perform operations independently of the larger computer.

SMS Data-Service Unit (SDSU)

A data service unit that provides access to Switched Multimegabit Data Service (SMDS) through a High Speed Serial Interface (HSSI) or through some other serial interface.

SMS Storage Device Interface (SMSDI)

A set of NetWare routines that allows the SBACKUP NetWare Loadable Module (NLM) to access various storage devices and media. When more than one storage device is connected to the host, SMSDI provides SBACKUP with a list of available and unavailable storage devices and media, which SBACKUP then displays so the user can select an available backup device.

SNA Character Stream (SCS)

A printing mode in the Systems Network Architecture (SNA) model that provides various printing and formatting capabilities.

SNA Distribution Services (SNADS)

A Systems Network Architecture (SNA) store-and-forward file and document handling service that uses Advanced Program-to-Program Communication (APPC) protocols to transport data.

SNA gateway

A hardware or software device connecting a Systems Network Architecture (SNA) mainframe host to a local area network (LAN).

SNA Network Interconnection (SNI)

An IBM gateway that connects multiple Systems Network Architecture (SNA) networks.

SNMP trap handler

A trap handler used in the Simple Network Management Protocol (SNMP).

soc newsgroup

An Internet newsgroup that discusses social topics.

socket

The portion of an internetwork address within a network node that represents the destination of an Internetwork Packet Exchange (IPX) packet. Novell reserves socket number 451h for NetWare Core Protocol (NCP), 452h for Service Advertising Protocol (SAP), 453h for Routing Information Protocol (RIP), 455h for Network Basic Input/Output System (NetBIOS), 456h for diagnostics, and 8063h for Novell Virtual Terminal (NVT).

socket client
A process or function that can make use of a socket to request and receive information and network services.

socket number
A unique value assigned to a socket, the maximum size of which depends on the number of bits allocated for the number.

soft error
An error in a Token Ring network that is not considered serious or a threat to the performance or continued operation of the network.

software
Application programs that enable computers to perform functions and tasks.

software handshaking
A process in which control codes (XON and XOFF) in data are used to control the flow of data through the cable.

software interrupt
A signal to the computer processor generated by an instruction in a software program that tells the processor to suspend and save its current activity, and then to branch to an interrupt service routine (ISR).

software license
An agreement to abide by certain prescribed conditions (such as defined rights of the user and limited liability of the software publisher) in the use of a software program.

software piracy
Illegally copying and distributing copyrighted software products.

Solaris

An operating system from SunSoft designed for UNIX environments, which supports a graphical user interface (GUI), electronic mail (e-mail), Network File System (NFS), and Network Information Services (NIS).

Source Address (SA)

A packet header field whose value represents the address of the node sending the packet.

Source Route Bridging (SRB)

An algorithm providing a means to bridge local area networks (LANs) that assumes the complete source-to-destination route is placed in all frames being sent across the network and that the frames can be stored and forwarded as indicated by the appropriate frame field. This type of bridging is often found in Token Ring networks.

Source Route Translational Bridging (SR/TLB)

A bridging method in which source and route nodes can communicate with a transparent bridge station with help provided by an intermediate bridge that translates between the two bridge protocols.

source route transparent bridging

A proposed IBM bridging scheme that merges the transparent and Source-Route Bridging (SRB) strategies into one device to satisfy the needs of all nodes on the network. No translation would be performed between the bridging protocols.

source routing

IBM's method of routing frames through a network composed of multiple local area networks (LANs) by specifying in each frame the route it is to follow. End stations determine the route through a discovery process supported by source route bridges. NetWare source routing programs allow bridges on IBM Token Ring networks to forward NetWare packets.

source server

A server from which data and bindery files, as well as other information, can be migrated to a NetWare 4 destination server during an upgrade.

spanning

A technique involving the placement of frequently used segments of a file system or database on separate disks to improve input/output.

spanning tree

Either a network segment that has no logical loops or a network structure that has a root node and one path connecting all other nodes on the network. Used in bridged networks, this tree structure allows bridges to make routing decisions on the basis of the routing distance a path must span.

spanning tree algorithm

On a multilooped, bridged network, a technique used to find the most desirable path between network segments. When multiple paths exist, this algorithm determines the most efficient path and limits the link between two networks to this single active path. If the path fails, the algorithm reconfigures the network to activate another path.

SPARCstation

A group of UNIX workstations from Sun Microsystems that range from small desktop systems to tower servers in multiprocessor configurations. The SPARCstation is based on the Scalar Processor Architecture (SPARC) processor.

sparse file

A file with at least one empty block, often created by a database program. Some operating systems save the entire file (including empty blocks) to disk. NetWare, however, conserves disk space by providing the capability to save only the portions of sparse files that contain data, rather than entire files with empty blocks.

special-interest group (SIG)

A group, often part of a user group or other organization, that shares information about a specific topic.

spectral width

A range of light frequencies emitted by laser.
Synonym: *laser line width*

speed matching

The capability of a destination device to use a buffer that allows a high-speed source to transmit data at its maximum rate, even if the destination device is a lower-speed device.

spider

A program that attempts to visit every World Wide Web (WWW) site or other network node to collect the information necessary to create an index or map.

Synonyms: *crawler; robot*

spike

The occurrence of more than twice the nominal peak voltage in a line, usually caused by lightning and lasting a short while.

Synonym: *impulse*

splice

A transient signal, usually of high amplitude, that lasts a short period of time.

split cable system

A broadband wiring scheme that incorporates a single cable bandwidth being divided between transmission and receiving capabilities. Common splits include a subsplit, midsplit, and highsplit.

split-horizon routing

A routing technique in which routers do not advertise routes discovered through an interface out through the same interface, because neighboring routers using that same interface already know the information. Because split horizon routing reduces routing traffic on the network, it is commonly used by distance vector routing protocols.

split pair

The sending of a signal over wires from two different pairs in twisted-pair cabling, instead of over wires in the same pair.

splitter
An analog device that breaks a signal into multiple derived signals.

spooler
A device or software program that provides a queuing system for files waiting to be printed, so files can be printed while the computer performs other tasks.

spread-spectrum transmission
The distribution of a radio transmission signal over a broad frequency range; the distribution pattern is based on either frequency hopping or on direct sequence coding.

SS7
A standard from the Consultative Committee for International Telegraphy and Telephony (CCITT) that is applied to out-of-band signals. SS7 offers fast call setup and sophisticated information and transaction capabilities.

SSCP-LU session
A session between a system services control point (SSCP) and a logical unit (LU), in which the session enables the LU to request the SSCP to help initiate a logical-unit-to-logical-unit (LU-LU) session.

SSCP-PU session
A session between a system services control point (SSCP) and a physical unit (PU) in which the session enables SSCPs to send requests to, and receive messages from, individual nodes to control the network configuration.

ST (Straight Tip) connector
A fiber-optic cable developed by AT&T, used in premises wiring and in networks.

ST-506
An interface drive type from Seagate Technologies, which may be used in personal computer systems with less than 40MB disk capacity and features a relatively slow data-transfer rate of 5 megabits per second (Mbps).

S

stack manager
A software process that mediates between a driver for a Network Interface Card (NIC) and drivers for higher-speed protocols. Although typically loaded at the file server, this process may also be loaded at a gateway or workstation.

standalone
A computer or peripheral not connected to a network.

standalone hub
An external hub with its own power supply that usually is a box with connectors for the attachment of nodes and possibly includes special connectors for linking to other hubs.

standard
Rules or procedures agreed upon by industry participants.

Standard Message Format (SMF)
A standard set of rules defining both the format of messages and how third-party application and gateway programs can interface with Message Handling Service (MHS) messaging products in NetWare.

Standby Monitor (SM)
A network node, usually found in Token Ring networks, which serves as a backup to the Active Monitor (AM) and is ready to take over in a timely and correct manner if the AM fails.

standby power supply (SPS)
An emergency power source (usually including a battery charger, battery, and inverter) designed to deliver a limited amount of power to a file server or other device in the event of a total loss of power. The SPS monitors power coming in from power lines (the primary source) and, as long as that power is sufficient, bypasses the battery. When the primary source fails, the SPS switches to battery power (the secondary source) in a time period short enough usually to avoid data loss.

star coupler

A coupler used to split a signal into more than two derived signals.

star topology

A network topology in the shape of a star that has a wiring hub (or concentrator) in the center of the configuration and the network nodes arranged around the hub, representing the points of the star. Each node in the network requires its own cable. The star topology does not adhere to any of the Institute of Electrical and Electronic Engineers (IEEE) standards for network configuration.

StarGroup

A network operating system from AT&T that usually runs on UNIX systems and provides support for common protocol suites, Systems Network Architecture (SNA) and asynchronous gateways, X.25 network routers, and other capabilities. StarGroup is based on the Microsoft LAN Manager.

StarLAN

An AT&T network operating system that implements Carrier Sense Multiple Access/Collision Detection (CSMA/CD) protocols on twisted-pair cabling, which transmits at one megabit per second (Mbps). StarLAN 10 is a 10Mbps Ethernet version that uses twisted-pair or fiber-optic cabling.

start bit

A bit used to start asynchronous communications timing that is not required in synchronous communications.

Start Delimiter (SD)

A field that appears in a Token Ring data or token packet.

start-stop transmission

A method of transmission that synchronizes each character individually. No fixed interval exists between transmitted characters; start bits and stop bits coordinate the data flow.

startup disk

A disk containing all the necessary startup files to enable the computer to begin operation.

Synonym: *boot disk*

star-wired ring topology

A hybrid physical topology that combines the features of a star topology with those of a ring topology, connecting individual nodes to a central hub as an internal ring within the hub. The hub constitutes the ring, which must remain intact for the network to function. Advantages to a star-wired ring topology are that disconnecting a faulty node from the internal ring is relatively easy, fault isolation is relatively easy, the network layout is flexible and relatively easy to expand, individual hubs can be connected to form larger rings, and wiring to the hub is flexible.

state

A mode in Advanced Program-to-Program Communication (APPC) that determines which verbs a program is allowed to issue.

Stateless Protocol

A protocol in which individual transactions may be repeated without affecting prior or future transactions, because each transaction is independent of its predecessor and its successor.

Static Random Access Memory (SRAM)

A type of random access memory (RAM) that can store only about one-fourth as much information as dynamic RAM (DRAM), but features access times of 15 to 30 nanoseconds, which is much faster than DRAM. Both DRAM and Static RAM (or SRAM) retain their contents as long as power is applied and they do not need constant refreshment.

static routing

A method in which a Routing Information Table is manually updated, rather than being updated automatically by the network system.

statically assigned socket
A socket with a number in the range of 1 through 127, reserved for use by clients such as the lower-level AppleTalk protocols.

station
A server, router, printer, fax machine, or any computer device connected to a network by a Network Interface Card (NIC) and a communications medium.

station address
A number that uniquely identifies a Network Interface Card (NIC).
Synonym: *node number*

Station Management (SMT)
In a Fiber Distributed Data Interface (FDDI) network, a component made up of services that ensure the correct operation of various network elements. SMT includes frame services, connection management, and ring management.

station restrictions
Account login restrictions imposed on a user that specify to which workstation(s) a user can log in.

statistical multiplexing
A method in which line time is dynamically allocated to each of the various attached terminals, according to whether the terminal is active or inactive at a particular moment. A statistical multiplexer is capable of analyzing traffic density and dynamically switching to a different channel pattern to speed up the transmission.
Synonym: *stat mux*

Statistical Time-Division Multiplexing (STDM)
A data-transmission method allowing the X.25 interface to maximize the use of bandwidth by dynamically allocating on demand portions of the available bandwidth to active devices. The X.25 interface provides a better throughput than Time-Division Multiplexing (TDM).

S

stop bit

A signal indicating the end of a character or, in the context of a serial data transfer, the distinction where one character starts and another stops.

storage device

A device (such as an external tape backup unit) used to back up data from a server or a workstation.

storage-device driver

Software designed to control the operation of a storage device attached to a compatible host adapter.

storage-device interface (SDI or SMSDI)

A set of routines that enables the NetWare SBACKUP utility to access various storage devices and media. If more than one storage device is attached to the host, the SDI provides SBACKUP with a list of storage devices and media.

storage-device support driver

Software used with a Device-Independent Backup Interface (DIBI) and a storage-device driver.

Storage Management Data Requester (SMDR)

A NetWare feature that passes commands between the SBACKUP utility and Target Service Agents (TSAs).

Storage Management Services (SMS)

Services that allow data to be backed up and restored independently of the hardware and file systems normally used for backup and storage. Table S.1 shows SMS-compliant NetWare Loadable Module (NLM) programs and other software that run on NetWare servers.

T A B L E S . I	SMS Programs for NetWare
PROGRAM	**DESCRIPTION**
SBACKUP utility	Provides backup and restore capabilities.
Storage-Management Data Requester (SMDR)	Passes commands between the SBACKUP utility and Target Service Agents (TSAs).
SMS Device Interface (SMSDI)	Passes commands between the SBACKUP utility and the storage devices and media.
Device drivers	Act on commands passed from the SBACKUP utility through the SMSDI to control the mechanical operation of storage devices and media.
Target Service Agents (TSAs)	Take data requests generated by the SBACKUP utility and pass them to the NetWare server (where data resides) and then return requested data back through SMDR to the SBACKUP utility.
Database TSAs	Take data and command requests from the host server (where SBACKUP resides) and the database (where the data resides) and then return requested data back through SMDR to the SBACKUP utility.
Workstation TSAs	Take data and command requests from the host server (where SBACKUP resides) and the workstation (where the data resides) and then return requested data back through SMDR to the SBACKUP utility.
Workstation Manager	Receives "I am here" messages from workstations available to be backed up and maintains an internal list of the names of these workstations.

S

---

store-and-forward

A technique used in message switching that entails messages being stored temporarily at intermediate points across the network before being transmitted to the next destination. This method is commonly used on networks that are unavailable at all times and enables users to take advantage of off-peak rates when traffic and costs might be lower.

store-and-forward switch

A switch designed to first check a packet's integrity by confirming the Media Access Control (MAC) address in an internal address table before sending it on to its destination port.

straight-tip connector

A connector for fiber-optic cable that maintains the alignment of the ends of connected fibers and facilitates an efficient transmission of light signals.

stream

A full-duplex connection between a task and a device that can include an encapsulated processing module or a second-level file opened for data transmissions.

stream I/O services

Services for standard read and write file operations in which data can be transmitted as characters, strings, blocks of memory, or under format control.

streaming

A transmission mode that allows a receiving system to begin processing or displaying the content of a file before an entire file has been received. When used with Internet files, this mode enables the user to hear, see, or interact with time-based multimedia files that have long playing times without waiting for similarly long download times.

StreetTalk

A distributed global naming and directory service on the Banyan Systems Virtual Network System (VINES) operating system.

StreetTalk Directory Assistance (STDA)

A popup window in StreetTalk that displays the name of every node or device attached to the network, as well as other information about the node or device.

string

A series of alphabetical characters or a category of data types used to store strings.

string manipulation functions

Functions designed to manipulate strings of characters.

striping

Interleaving file systems or databases across multiple disks on a network in an effort to improve input/output performance.

Structure-Management Information (SMI)

A component in the Internet Protocol (IP) network-management model that specifies how information about managed objects is to be represented.

Structured Query Language (SQL)

A query language developed by IBM for the management of relational databases. Adopted by Oracle Corporation, SQL contains about 60 commands used to create, modify, query, and access data organized in tables. Used as either an interactive interface or as embedded commands in an application, SQL is an American National Standards Institute (ANSI) and International Standards Organization (ISO) standard.

structured wiring

A planned cabling system for enterprise networks, expected to include provisions for both voice and data communications.

STS bit

A bit set in the AppleTalk Transaction Protocol (ATP) header of a Transaction Response (TResp) packet to force the requester to retransmit a Transaction Request (TReq) packet immediately.

stub network

An Internet Protocol (IP) network serviced by a proxy server, using a subset of an existing IP network address.

suballocation

A process of storing data in small blocks to save disk space.

subarea

The portion of a Systems Network Architecture (SNA) consisting of a subarea node and any peripheral nodes or other links attached to it.

subarea node

A communication controller or host on a Systems Network Architecture (SNA) network that handles complete network addresses.

subchannel

A subdivision of a communication channel based on broadband frequency and creating a separate channel.

subdirectory

A directory appearing below another directory in a file system hierarchy. (The *root directory* is commonly the highest directory in a file hierarchy and is the directory from which all other directories must branch.)

Sub-Distribution Frame (SDF)

An intermediate wiring center connected by backbone cable to a Main Distribution Frame (MDF).

subnet layers

Network layers used by devices that relay transmissions between other devices. In the OSI Reference Model, subnet layers are the Physical Layer (Layer 1), Data-Link Layer (Layer 2), and the Network Layer (Layer 3).

subnet mask

In the Internet Protocol (IP) addressing scheme, a group of selected bits that identifies a subnetwork. All members of the subnetwork share the same mask value.

Synonym: *subnetwork address mask*

Sub-Network Access Protocol (SNAP)

In the OSI Reference Model, a protocol used on the middle three sublayers of the Physical Layer (Layer 1), the Data Link Layer (Layer 2), and the Network Layer (Layer 3). The SNAP provides access to (and transfers data to) the *subnetwork*.

subnetwork

A portion of a backbone network partitioned by repeaters, bridges, or routers. Nodes on a subnetwork use a single protocol to communicate with each other. The subnetwork, which may include both nodes and routers, is connected to a larger network through an intermediate system that may use a routing protocol to communicate with nodes outside the subnetwork.

subnetwork address mask

An indication of how an Internet Protocol (IP) address is divided into subnetwork addresses and local host addresses. The network mask contains a 32-bit number with all ones for network and subnetwork portions of the complete IP address and all zeros for the host address portions.

Subnetwork Point of Attachment (SNPA)

A data-link address used to configure a Connectionless Mode Network Service (CLNS) route for an interface.

Subnetwork-Dependent Convergence Protocol (SNDCP)

In the OSI Reference Model, a protocol used on the middle three sublayers of the Physical Layer (Layer 1), the Data-Link Layer (Layer 2), and the Network Layer (Layer 3) to handle details or problems relating to the subnetwork to which the data is being transferred.

Subnetwork-Independent Convergence Protocol (SNICP)

In the OSI Reference Model, a protocol used on the middle three sublayers of the Physical Layer (Layer 1), the Data-Link Layer (Layer 2), and the Network Layer (Layer 3) to provide the routing and relaying capabilities needed to get data to its destination.

Subnetwork Protocol (SP)

A subnetwork-layer protocol that provides the transfer of data through the local subnet. Some systems may require an adapter module to be inserted between the Internet Protocol (IP) and the SP to reconcile dissimilar interfaces.

subnetwork, Level x

A network level created by dividing an oversized internetwork into a number of smaller networks to help routers keep track of routing information. For example, a *level 1 subnetwork* is managed by a *level 1 router*. All networks in this division are treated as part of the same network. Transmissions to a machine on one of the networks would be sent to the address of the level 1 router, rather than to the address of an individual network.

subordinate object

A Novell Directory Services (NDS) object located within another object.

subordinate replica

A NetWare Directory replica automatically placed on a NetWare server when a parent Directory partition has a master, read/write, or read-only replica, and the child Directory partition does not.

subscribe

To sign up as a customer of an Internet Service Provider (ISP), add a name to a mailing list, or add a newsgroup to the list of pending articles a newsreader program presents to a user.

subscriber connector (SC)

A device that connects two components by plugging one connector into the other and establishes a connection that must be broken (for example, by pressing a button or releasing a hatch). An SC works with either single-mode or multimode fiber.

substring

A subdivision of a string.

subvector

In Systems Network Architecture (SNA), a data segment that is part of a message vector, consisting of a length field, a key describing the vector type, and other subvector-specific data.

superpipelining

A preprocessing method in which two or more execution stages are divided into two or more pipelined stages to improve microprocessor performance.

superscalar

A type of architecture for microprocessors, containing more than one execution unit and allowing the microprocessor to execute more than one instruction per clock cycle. The microprocessor determines whether an instruction can be executed in parallel with the next instruction in line; if it detects no dependencies, it executes the two instructions.

superserver

A high-performance computer specifically designed to be used as a network server and characterized by scalable input/output (I/O) channels, complex multiprocessing features, several central processing units (CPUs), large amounts of error-correction memory, cache memory, fault-tolerant features, and a large hard disk storage capacity.

superuser

A special UNIX privilege level for system managers that provides unlimited access to all files, directories, and commands.

supervisor

A person who is responsible for the administration and maintenance of a network, database, or both. Normally a supervisor has access rights to all volumes, directories, and files.

Supervisor right

A NetWare directory, file, object, and property right that grants a user all rights to directories, files, objects, and properties.

See also **access rights.**

Supported Gateway

A protocol supported by the Messaging Server object in Novell Directory Services (NDS).

suppression

A power-conditioning technique that protects hardware against transients. The most common suppression devices are surge protectors that include circuitry to prevent excess voltage.

surface test

In NetWare, a test run by the INSTALL program to search a hard disk's NetWare partition for bad blocks. A *destructive test* destroys data as it makes several passes over the disk surface while reading and writing test patterns. A *nondestructive test* pre-reads and saves existing data, reads and writes test patterns, and then writes data back to the hard disk. Volumes on the hard disk must be dismounted before the surface test can be run.

surge

A sudden increase in line voltage that usually lasts a short period of time and may be destructive.

surge (packet-switched network)

A temporary increase in required bandwidth, measured in relation to a guaranteed bandwidth called the Committed Information Rate (CIR).

surge suppressor

A power-conditioning device placed between a computer and the Alternating Current (AC) line connection to protect the computer from power surges.

swap file

A file on a hard disk used to store parts of running programs temporarily that have been swapped out of memory to make room for other running programs.

See also **swapping.**

swapping

A process that involves exchanging one item for another item, which may occur with memory, processes, data disk space, and so on.

switch

An option that modifies the way a computer carries out a command.

switch (data)

A device that reroutes data to its destination, commonly found in switching networks where data is grouped and routed on the basis of predetermined criteria.

switch block

A set of switches mounted to form a single hardware component that can be used to control system configuration data or to set system addresses.

switch (Ethernet)

A device designed to direct traffic among several Ethernet networks. Normally this device has multiple ports with which to connect subnetworks and multiple processors to handle traffic through the switch.

switched 56

A circuit-switched telecommunications service operating at 56 kilobits per second (Kbps) that can be leased from long-distance service providers.

switched digital access

A method in which a local telecommunications carrier mediates a connection to a long-distance line, connecting the user directly to the local carrier and, from there, connecting to a long-distance carrier.

switched line

A network node connection established by dialing in to the network.

Switched Multimegabit Data Services (SMDS)

A packet-switched service that offers high-speed data throughputs for metropolitan area networks (MANs). Described in a series of specifications produced by Bell Communications Research (Bellcore), this service uses the SMDS Interface Protocol (SIP) between a user device and SMDS network equipment. SMDS is being adopted by both long-distance carriers and providers of telecommunications equipment.

switched network

A network in which temporary connections are established between two nodes when necessary. The routing of transmissions through these temporary connections is known as *switching* and is used for networks on which many nodes may be accessing the network simultaneously. The three most common types are circuit-switched networks, message-switched networks, and packet-switched networks.

Switched T1

A circuit-switched telecommunications service over a T1 line with a bandwidth of 1.544 megabits per second. The transmission may go through a multiplexer that breaks it down and transmits it across several slower channels.

switched virtual circuit (SVC)

A circuit established dynamically using call setup and call clearing procedures, which remains in a connected state until a user or application shuts it down.

switching element

A device that controls the mapping, scheduling, and forwarding of data during the transmission of a packet into a node and along the appropriate path to the packet's destination. The switching element consists of an *input controller* that synchronizes each input with an internal clock, an *output controller* that queues and buffers inputs, and an *interconnection network* that provides a means of getting from an input channel to an output channel.

switching hierarchy

A hierarchy of five switch levels (or exchanges) that establish connections for long-distance telephone calls. The five levels are regional centers (or regional points), sectional centers (or sectional points), primary centers (or primary points), toll centers (or toll points), and end offices.

synchronization

The process of ensuring that replicas of a NetWare Directory partition contain the same information as other replicas of that partition (*replica synchronization*) or all servers in a Directory tree report the same time (*time synchronization*).

synchronization level

A specification that indicates whether corresponding transaction programs exchange confirmation requests and replies.

synchronization services

Services that provide applications with the capability to coordinate access to network files and other network resources.

synchronous

A data-transfer mode in which information is transmitted in blocks (or frames) of bits separated by equal time intervals. Both sending and receiving computers must precisely control the timing. This requires that special characters be embedded in the data stream to begin synchronization and to maintain synchronization during the transmission.

Synchronous Data Link Control (SDLC)

A protocol developed by IBM in the mid-1970s that supports a variety of link types and topologies. SDLC can be used with point-to-point and multipoint links, bounded and unbounded media, half-duplex and full-duplex transmissions, and circuit-switched and packet-switched networks. SDLC identifies *primary* network nodes as those controlling the operation of other stations and *secondary* network nodes as those being controlled by a primary network node. These nodes can be placed in a *point-to-point configuration* (which involves only a primary and secondary node), a *multipoint configuration* (which involves one primary and multiple secondary nodes), a *loop configuration* (which involves a primary node connected to the first and last secondary nodes in a loop topology), and a *hub go-ahead configuration* (which involves the primary node using an outbound channel and the secondary nodes using an inbound channel).

Synchronous Optical Network (SONET)

A high-speed, fiber-optic network that provides an interface and mechanism for optical transmission of data. SONET features transmission rates from 51.84 megabits per second (Mbps) to 2.488 gigabits per second, an 810-byte packet frame, the capability of transmitting 80,000 frames per second, a four-layer (Photonic, Section, Line, and Path) hierarchy for implementation and management of frame transmissions, adjustable timing and framing during transmission, and support for drop-and-insert capabilities.

Synchronous Transfer Mode (STM)

A transport method used in broadband Integrated Services Digital Networks (ISDNs) that uses Time Division Multiplexing (TDM) and switching methods with up to 50 megabits per second (Mbps) of bandwidth for synchronous transmissions.

Synchronous Transfer Mode-x (STM-x)

Any of several channel capacities (denoted by x) that are defined by the Synchronous Digital Hierarchy from the Consultative Committee for International Telegraphy and Telephony (CCITT).

syntax
Rules of spelling and grammar applied to a programming language or to an operating system, including the exact sequence of command elements required for the command to be interpreted correctly.

syntax error
An error that occurs in a programming language or operating system syntax of commands (for example, a misspelling).

SYS volume
The first volume created during NetWare server installation, it contains the SYSTEM, PUBLIC, LOGIN, MAIL, DELETED.SAV, QUEUES, NLS, and ETC directories.

System 7
A major revision to the operating system for the Macintosh computer, released in May 1991 featuring 32-bit addressing, aliases, and an Apple menu that could contain applications, the Applications menu, Balloon Help, colorized three-dimensional windows, faster printer drivers, built-in file sharing, and QuickTime.

system administrator
A person responsible for the daily operation and maintenance of the network system, including planning future expansions, installing new hardware and software, adding and removing users, backing up the system, assigning and changing passwords, monitoring system performance, and training users.

System (Sy) attribute
A directory and file attribute with which the NetWare operating system marks directories or files for its own exclusive use.

system connect
The act of physically connecting to a host computer or to a network.

system console screen

A monitor display screen from which NetWare server console commands can be entered at the command line.

system crash

The point at which a network system becomes inoperable or no longer functions properly.

SYSTEM directory

A directory (SYS:SYSTEM) created during the installation of NetWare that contains operating system files, NetWare Loadable Module (NLM) files, and utilities for managing the network. The ADMIN user or a user with ADMIN equivalent rights has rights to the SYS:SYSTEM directory.

System Fault Tolerance (SFT)

A data-protection scheme in NetWare that provides procedures enabling a user to recover from hardware failures automatically. Table S.2 shows the three levels of SFT protection. Note, each level of protection includes the previous levels (for example, SFT III includes SFT I and SFT II).

TABLE S.2 *SFT Levels*

LEVEL	NAME	DESCRIPTION
SFT I	Hot Fix	Provides protection against data being saved to faulty blocks on the server's hard disk.
SFT II	Disk Mirroring or Duplexing	Provides protection against hard disk failures by pairing two hard disks on the same channel (disk mirroring) or on different channels (disk duplexing).
SFT III	Server Mirroring	Provides protection from server failure through the use of a secondary (identical) server that immediately assumes control of network operations when the primary server fails.

System ID

A six-byte hexadecimal number used to identify a NetWare Link Services Protocol (NLSP) router.

System-Independent Data Format (SIDF)

A format used by the SBACKUP utility in NetWare that allows all data backed up with SBACKUP to be read by other backup applications with the capability of reading and writing in SIDF.

System login script

A type of login script that sets general environments for all users in NetWare 2.x and NetWare 3.x. The Container login script replaces the System login script in NetWare 4.x.

system memory

System random access memory (RAM) located between 640K and 1,024K not usually addressed by DOS or applications. System memory can be addressed by computers with 80386 or 80486 microprocessors that use special control programs to make upper memory blocks (UMBs) in system memory.

system prompt

A monitor screen display that indicates the operating system is ready to receive a command.

system redundancy

Duplication of key system components to protect against failure. System redundancy in NetWare is provided in System Fault Tolerance (SFT) III through mirrored network servers. Redundant cabling, power supplies, disk storage, gateways, routers, Network Interface Cards (NICs), mirrored server links, and printers provide protection against other failures.

system slide

Cabling that runs from a computer or network to a distribution frame.

Systems Application Architecture (SAA)

A set of IBM standards introduced in 1987 that defines a set of interfaces (and protocols) for future IBM software. The three main components of SAA are *Common User Access* (CUA), which provides a Graphical User Interface (GUI) definition for products designed for object-oriented environments; *Common Programming Interface* (CPI), which includes a set of application programming interfaces (APIs) and Structured Query Language (SQL); and *Common Communications Support* (CCS), which provides a common set of communications protocols.

Systems-Management Application Entity (SMAE)

A component of the OSI Network Management Model that implements the network management services and activities at the Application Layer (Layer7) in the network node.

Systems Management Application Process (SMAP)

Software in the OSI Network Management Model that implements the network-management capabilities in a single node.

Systems-Management Application Service Element (SMASE)

A component that performs the work for a System Management Application Entity (SMAE) in the OSI Network Management Model.

Systems-Management Function (SMF)

Services provided to manage particular network domains in the OSI Network Management Model. SMFs include Object Management, State Management, Relationship Management, Alarm Reporting, Event Report Management, Log Control, Security Alarm Reporting, Security Audit Trail, Access Control, Accounting Metering, Workload Monitoring, Summarization, and Test Management.

Systems-Management Function Area (SMFA)

One of five domains defined in the OSI Network Management Model, including Accounting Management, Configuration Management, Fault Management, Performance Management, and Security Management.

Systems Network Architecture (SNA)

A hierarchical, single-host network structure introduced by IBM in 1974 that includes descriptions of the logical structure, formats, protocols, and operational sequences for data transmission through, and configuration of, wide area networks (WANs). The SNA model divides a hierarchical structure into seven layers, with each layer performing a specific function. Table S.3 shows the seven layers and provides a brief description of each.

TABLE S.3 *SNA Model*

LAYER	DESCRIPTION
Transaction Service (Layer 7)	Provides network management services, such as distributed database access and document interchange.
Presentation Service (Layer 6)	Formats and transforms data for compatibility between different presentation media and coordinates the sharing of network resources.
Data Flow Control (Layer 5)	Synchronizes data flow, coordinates the exchange of data, and groups data into units.
Transmission Control (Layer 4)	Performs error-control functions, coordinates the pace of data exchanges to match processing capacities, and encodes data for security.
Path Control (Layer 3)	Creates a logical channel between two nodes and controls data traffic on the network. Nodes perform routing and congesting control.
Data-Link Control (Layer 2)	Controls the transmission of data between adjacent network nodes over a single line. Nodes activate and deactivate links on command from their control points, as well as managing link-level data flow.
Physical Control (Layer 1)	Provides adjacent network nodes with either a parallel or serial interface. Includes both data communications equipment within nodes and the physical links (connections) between them.

S

The three lower levels of the model (Physical Control, Data-Link Control, and Path Control) are collectively referred to as the *transport network*. The distributed components of these three layers are responsible for transporting data through the network on behalf of network addressable units (NAUs), which are components that can establish temporary, logical connections with each other.

Systems Network Architecture Management Services (SNA/MS)

A network management strategy based on the Systems Network Architecture (SNA) model to help plan, organize, and control an SNA network. This model includes the five categories of Problem Management, Performance and Accounting Management, Configuration Management, Change Management, and Operations Management.

Systems Network Architecture/Synchronous Data Link Control (SNA/SDLC)

A communications protocol in the Systems Network Architecture (SNA) model that transfers data between a host and a controller.

Systems Operator (Sysop)

A person responsible for the physical operation of a computer system or a network resource who decides backup procedures and when maintenance should be performed on the system.

systems services control point (SSCP)

A control point in a host node that provides network services for dependent nodes.

SystemView

A comprehensive network management package introduced by IBM in 1990, designed to replace NetView. SystemView supports more networking models than does NetView.

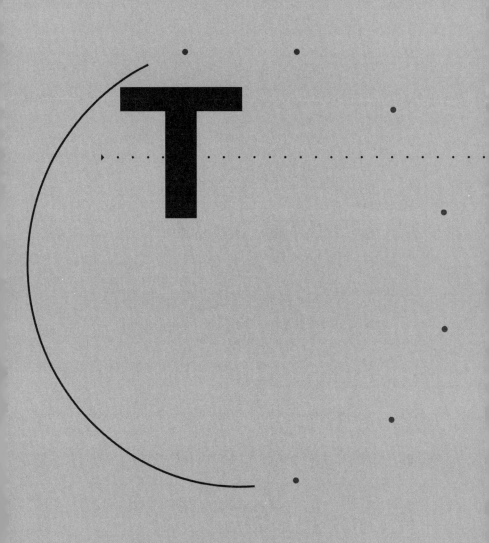

T

An abbreviation for tera-, which has a value of 2^{40} or 10^{12}, equivalent to about 1 trillion in the United States measuring system.

T1

A high-speed leased line developed by Bell that is capable of transmitting telephone signals at up to 1.544 megabits per second (Mbps) in the United States. Theoretically, a T1 line should be able to transmit a megabyte of information in less than ten seconds. Although not fast enough to transmit full screen, full-motion video (which requires 10Mbps), T1 is the fastest speed commonly used to connect networks to the Internet.

T1 Carrier

A digital communications carrier used in North America, Australia, and Japan. Originally developed by AT&T to transmit voice conversations, it has been expanded to include data and image transmissions.

T1 multiplexer

A statistical multiplexer designed to split the 1.544-megabit-per-second (Mbps) T1 bandwidth into 24 separate 64 kilobit-per-second (Kbps) channels of digitized voice or data communications.

T2

A communications service that provides the equivalent of 4 T1 channels, or 96 channels transmitting at 64 kilobits per second (Kbps) for a total bandwidth of 6.3 megabits per second (Mbps). Although not available commercially, this point-to-point service is used within telephone company networks.

T3

A communications service that provides the equivalent of 28 T1 channels, or 672 channels transmitting at 64 kilobits per second (Kbps), for a total bandwidth of 44.736 megabits per second (Mbps). T3 is sometimes used to connect major nodes on the Internet and to form high-traffic internal networks.

T4

A communications service that provides the equivalent of 168 T1 channels, or 4,032 channels transmitting at 64 kilobits per second (Kbps), for a total bandwidth of 274.176 megabits per second (Mbps). This point-to-point service is used for both voice and data transmissions.

talk

An Internet newsgroup that conducts endless arguments about a wide range of topics.

tank circuit

A Token Ring network circuit that ensures accurate signal tracking and prevents the degradation of the signal.

tap

A connector used to attach cable without blocking the passage of information along that cable.

tape backup unit

An internal or external tape drive used to back up data from hard disks.

tape cartridge

A self-contained storage module for magnetic tape, which is frequently used as a backup storage medium.

tape drive

A peripheral device that reads from—and reads to—magnetic tape, often used as a backup medium for computer network systems. Because many backup software programs read the tape sequentially (always starting from the beginning of the tape to search for data), the tape drive is considered a slow backup device.

tape server

The combination of a tape drive and software that can back up files to—and restore files from—the tape drive. A tape server may include *archiving* capabilities to identify files that have not been accessed for a predetermined amount of time and may back up such files, as well. No dedicated machine is required for a tape server.

target

A server, workstation, or service on the NetWare network that has a Target Service Agent (TSA) loaded, which allows the target to have all its data backed up or restored.

target coding

Coding used by an application receiving a transmission on a network. Such an application must be running on a network node capable of using all seven layers of the OSI Reference Model.

target device

Devices aimed at performing specific functions. As an example, servers or workstations can contain files targeted for backup.

target server

A network server from which data is backed up or to which data is stored. Typically, the data is received from another network device.

Target Service Agent (TSA)

A program designed to process data that moves between a specific target and a backup engine that complies with NetWare's Storage-Management Services (SMS). When using the SBACKUP utility, the host server sends requests to the TSA. Next, the TSA receives and processes the commands from SBACKUP. Then the target operating system can handle the request for data, pass the data request to the target, receive the requested data from the target, and return it to SBACKUP in standard SMS format.

Target Service Agent resources

Categories of data created by each NetWare Target Service Agent (TSA) and classified as either *major resources* or *minor resources*. These resources vary with each TSA, so the SBACKUP utility processes these resources in different ways.

Target Token-Rotation Time (TTRT)

A parameter value in a Fiber Distributed Data Interface (FDDI) network that specifies how much time passes before every node on the network gets access to the token.

task

Collectively, an independent program and the network resources it uses (such as an operating-system process or part of an application).

Task Manager

A Novell DOS program designed to manage multitasking and task switching operations.

task number

A unique number assigned to an individual program on a multitasking workstation.

task switching

A process that switches between applications, suspending one application in the background while running another.

T-connector

A T-shaped coaxial cable connector that connects two thin Ethernet cables and also provides a third connector for the Network Interface Card (NIC).

TCP/IP Transport Software

NetWare operating-system software that includes a set of drivers having an interface with the Multiple-Link Interface Driver/Open Data-Link Interface (MLID/ODI) drivers at the bottom layer and an interface with the Berkeley-socket Application Programming Interface (API) at the top layer.

T

Technical Advisory Group (TAG)

A committee of the Institute of Electrical and Electronic Engineers (IEEE), responsible for providing general recommendations and technical guidance to other IEEE committees.

Technical and Office Protocol (TOP)

A version of Ethernet developed by Boeing Corporation and used in an engineering environment. TOP provides standardized protocols and services for use in real-world situations that may involve the exchange of formatted data or access to such data from remote locations. To accommodate a variety of file types, TOP provides Application Programming Interfaces (APIs) that are built upon the OSI Reference Model, including Product-Definition Interchange Format (PDIF), Office Document Architecture (ODA), Office Document Interchange Format (ODIF), Computer-Graphics Metafile Interchange Format (CGMIF), Graphics Kernel System (GKS), and File Transfer, Access, and Management (FTAM) files.

Technical Service Alliance (TSA)

A collaborative effort between Novell and numerous companies to solve technical problems for customers they share.

tee coupler

A coupler with three ports, used to split an incoming signal into two outgoing signals. A tee coupler is commonly used in bus topologies.

telecommunications

The electronic transmission of all types of information from one location to another over a communications link.

Telecommunications Industries Association (TIA)

An organization responsible for establishing cable standards for networking.

teleconferencing

Linking audio, video, or computer systems by a communications channel to enable individuals who are geographically separated to participate in a discussion or meeting from a remote location.

telephony

A generic term used to describe the general field of voice telecommunications.

Telephony API (TAPI)
An Application Programming Interface (API) that enables Windows applications to set up and control telephone calls. Developed jointly by Intel and Microsoft, TAPI functions independently of the telephone network and does not define a data-transmission method when a call is in progress.

teleservices
Services that are defined for communications between two Integrated Services Digital Network (ISDN) endpoints. Common teleservices include telefax, telephony, teletext, telex, and videotex.

Telnet
In the Transmission Control Protocol/Internet Protocol (TCP/IP) suite, a protocol that governs character-oriented terminal traffic in the Application Level (Level 7) of the OSI Reference Model.

temperature sensor
A sensor located inside a computer that, when the temperature reaches a certain level, automatically turns on the computer's fan.

temporary swap file
A swap file created on a temporary basis that uses several noncontinuous pieces of hard-disk space. A temporary swap file does not occupy hard-disk space if the application that created it is not running.

terabyte (TB)
A unit of measure equaling 2^{40} (or approximately 1 trillion) bytes, most commonly used in the context of computer memory or disk-storage capacity.

termid
In Systems Network Architecture (SNA), an identification for a cluster controller on a switched line.

terminal
A combination of a keyboard and display monitor capable of sending and receiving data over a communications link.

Terminal-Access Controller (TAC)
An Internet host computer designed to accept terminal connections from a dial-up line.

Terminal-Access Controller Access System (TACACS)
A system designed by experts from the Defense Data Network (DDN) to restrict access to Terminal-Access Controllers (TACs) on the DDN.

Terminal Adapter (TA)
A device designed to mediate between an Integrated Services Digital Network (ISDN) and devices that are not ISDN-compatible.

terminal-cluster controller
A device designed to connect one or more personal computers to a Front End Processor (FEP) for a mainframe computer.

terminal emulation
A software program or method of operation that enables a microcomputer to function as a dumb terminal attached to a mainframe computer, usually to facilitate telecommunications.

terminal server
Software that provides a transparent connection between a terminal and one or more host computers. This server may provide multiple terminals with access to a host or it may provide terminals with the capability of switching between sessions on different host machines.

terminate-and-stay resident (TSR)
A DOS program that remains in memory even when it is not actively running; a TSR can run while other applications are displayed on the monitor screen. Macintosh versions of TSRs are known as *Inits*.

termination
The placement of a terminating resistor at the end of a line, bus, chain, or cable to prevent signals from being reflected or echoed. If a signal echoes back along a line, bus, chain, or cable, it may become corrupted. In NetWare, the

use of a Small Computer Systems Interface (SCSI) to connect a server's Host Bus Adapter (HBA) to a disk subsystem requires the termination of the bus, as do the hard disks connected to the respective controllers. Newer SCSI devices have automatic termination.

text file
A file composed of text characters from the American Standard Code for Information Interchange (ASCII) character set and encoded in a format recognizable by most computers.

text mode
A video adapter mode used in personal computers. A personal computer in text mode displays characters on the screen from the built-in character set, but does show graphics or a mouse pointer.
Synonym: *character mode*

text utility
In NetWare 4.*x* software, one of two main types of utility (the other is *graphical*). Text utilities include *Command-Line Utilities (CLUs)* and *menu utilities*.

ThickNet
Coaxial cable with a diameter of 1 centimeter (0.4 inch), used to connect Ethernet network nodes at distances up to about 1,000 meters (about 3,300 feet).

thickwire
Coaxial cable that measures about half an inch in diameter.

ThinNet
Coaxial cable with a diameter of 5 millimeters (0.2 inch) that is used to connect Ethernet network nodes at distances up to about 300 meters (about 1,000 feet).

thinwire
A thin coaxial cable similar to cable used for television and video connections.

Thomas-Conrad Network System (TCNS)

An implementation of the Attached-Resource Computer Network (ARCnet) architecture developed by Thomas-Conrad that transmits at 100 megabits per second (Mbps). TCNS includes both ARCnet drivers and drivers for other operating environments; it requires the use of special Network Interface Cards (NICs). Although TCNS does use shielded twisted-pair (STP) or fiber-optic cables, it does not support unshielded twisted-pair cables (UTP).

thrashing

Disk activity so excessive that the system spends all its time swapping pages in and out of memory and spends no time executing an application. This may be caused by a poor system configuration that creates an undersized swap file or by insufficient installed memory in the computer.

thread

A concurrent process that is actually part of a larger process or program. Multitasking operating systems allow single programs to contain several threads that all run at the same time.

thread global data items

A set of data items that have separate values for each thread. Data items for one thread cannot be referenced by another thread.

thread group

A group of one or more threads as defined by a program designer.

thread of execution

A separate execution within a program that either performs a request or polls for the occurrence of some event. Although polling threads are always running, they relinquish control after going through one polling loop.

threaded newsreader

A newsreader that enables the user to read groups of related articles (known as *threads*). This enables a user to choose to read or not to read a thread at a time, rather than one article at a time.

threaded nut connector (TNC)
A connector that is threaded and screws into a jack to create a tight connection.

three-way handshake
A synchronization process for activities occurring when two protocols establish a connection. The three steps involved are the caller sending a packet requesting a connection, the called node returning a connect confirmation packet, and the caller sending an acknowledgment packet.

threshold
An attribute used in network management to indicate a cutoff point between significant (or critical) events and nonsignificant events.

throughput
A measurement of the total amount of useful information processed or communicated during a specific time period. Normally this measurement is made according to the total number of bits transmitted in a second, including all bits transmitted or retransmitted.

throughput class
A class negotiation that specifies, on a per-call basis, the throughput of data that can be transferred on a virtual circuit (VC) at speeds of 75 bits per second (bps) to 64 kilobits per second (Kbps).

throughput negotiation
A facility specifying whether to allow negotiation (on a per-call basis) of throughput for data that can be transferred on a virtual circuit (VC).

tick
A time delay measuring about 1/18 of a second (or precisely 18.21 ticks per second). In NetWare, ticks are used to indicate how long it takes to reach the network. The number of ticks appears as part of each network entry in a Router Information Protocol (RIP) packet.

tight buffer

A layer stretched tightly over fiber-optic cable cladding to keep the fiber from moving around.

Time-Division Multiple Access (TDMA)

A method of communications in which a channel is made available to multiple parties simultaneously. Each party is allocated a time slot; its duration depends on two factors: (1) the number of parties who want to transmit and (2) the priority assigned the party to whom the time slot is allocated. Transmission packets must be reassembled at the receiving end.

Time-Division Multiplexing (TDM)

Data transmission that dedicates a fixed bandwidth of the network medium to connected devices, regardless of whether the devices are active.

time-domain reflectometery (TDR)

A technique used to diagnose cabling faults, calculating the length of the cable by measuring the time a reflected pulse takes to return to the TDR and multiplying that measurement by the Nominal Velocity of Propagation (NVP).

time functions

Functions providing the capability to obtain and manipulate times and dates across the network.

time server

A designated NetWare server that performs a particular time synchronization function. The four types of time servers are as follows:

- *Single Reference time server* determines the time for the entire network and provides time to Secondary time servers and to workstations. This time server is the only source of time on the network.

- *Primary time server* synchronizes time with at least one other Primary or Reference time server and provides time to Secondary time servers and to workstations, as well as voting with other Primary or Reference time servers to determine a common network time. At least one other Primary or Reference time server that the Primary time server can contact is required.

- *Reference time server* provides the time to which all other time servers and workstations synchronize, a time that may be synchronized with an external time source. Reference time servers vote with other Primary or Reference time servers to determine a common network time. A Reference time server, however, does not adjust its internal clock. Instead, the internal clock of the Primary server is adjusted to be synchronized with that of the Reference time server. Only one Reference time server is usually installed on a network.

- *Secondary time server* obtains the time from a Single Reference, Primary, or Reference time server, adjusting its internal clock to synchronize with network time. Secondary time servers also provide time to workstations.

time-slice multitasking

A multitasking process in which the operating system assigns the same small time period to each process in turn.

time stamp

A unique code that includes the time and identifies an event that occurs in the NetWare Directory, such as when a password is changed or a Novell Directory Services (NDS) object is renamed. The NDS event must have a time stamp so Directory replicas can be updated correctly. NDS uses time stamps to establish the order of events, record "real world" time values, and set expiration dates.

time synchronization

A method that corrects inherent deviation of the time kept by clocks in all servers of a NetWare Directory tree, so all servers report the same time and provide a time stamp to order Novell Directory Service (NDS) events.

timeout condition

An error condition that occurs after a specified amount of time has elapsed without an expected event taking place. The error condition prevents the procedure from hanging up the computer system.

tip

One of the two wires in a twisted-pair wire; the other wire is called a *ring*.

TN3270

Terminal-emulation software that allows a terminal to appear to the system as if it were an IBM 3270 model 2 terminal.

token

A special packet used in some media-access methods that is passed from node to node along a network according to a predefined sequence. The node possessing the token gets access to the network.

token bus topology

A network architecture that uses token passing in a physical-bus configuration that connects its nodes in a logical ring, The token bus architecture supports both coaxial and fiber-optic cable in carrier-band or broadband networks. Transmission speeds in this type of network can reach 20 megabits per second (Mbps).

Token-Holding Time (THT)

A parameter value used in Fiber Distributed Data Interface (FDDI) networks to adjust access to the network by specifying how long a node can hold the network token before it must be passed along to the next node in the sequence.

token passing

The circulation of an electronic token throughout a network to prevent multiple nodes from simultaneously transmitting on the network. A node must be in possession of the token before it can transmit across the network. Token passing is commonly used in Fiber Distributed Data Interface (FDDI), Token Ring, and Token Bus networks to avoid packet collisions.

Token Ring

The IBM version of a local area network (LAN); its ring structure uses a token-passing protocol of 4 to 16 megabits per second (Mbps) to regulate network traffic and to avoid packet collisions. A Token Ring network with telephone wiring can support up to 72 devices; the same topology with shielded twisted-pair (STP) cabling can support up to 256 nodes, in star-shaped clusters of up to 8 nodes. Each cluster is attached to the same Multistation Access Unit (MAU). All MAUs are connected to the main ring circuit. One particular node on the ring—the *Active Monitor* (*AM*)—generates the token that starts the network communication process. Other nodes serve as *Standby Monitors* (*SMs*) that track the activity of the AM and determine among themselves which is to replace the AM in case of failure. A Token Ring network also performs such special activities as beaconing, neighbor notification, ring insertion, ring purging, and token claiming.

Token-Ring Interface Coupler (TIC)

A device designed to provide direct connections between a Token Ring network and various types of mainframe equipment, including Front-End Processors (FEPs), AS/400s, and 3174 terminal cluster controllers.

token ring topology

A local area network (LAN) with a ring structure that uses a token passing to regulate network traffic and to avoid packet collisions. A controlling computer institutes token passing, which controls a node's right to transmit across the network. A node captures a token, sets its status to *busy*, and adds a message with a destination address. Every other node reads the token to determine whether it is the intended recipient; the actual recipient node collects the token, extracts the message, and returns the token to the sender. The sender then removes the message and resets the token to a *free* status, which indicates the token can be used by the next node in the sequence.

TokenTalk

An implementation of the AppleTalk protocol over Token Ring networks. TokenTalk is defined at the Physical Layer (Layer 1) and Data-Link Layer (Layer 2) of the OSI Reference Model and uses the TokenTalk Link-Access Protocol (TLAP) to access the network. TokenTalk supports both 4 megabits per second (Mbps) and 16Mbps networks.

TokenTalk Link-Access Protocol (TLAP)

The protocol that enables TokenTalk to access a network.

top-level domain

A level of the Internet Domain-Naming System (DNS) that appears as a child of the root domain (the highest level in the DNS). The Internet DNS uses domain syntax to help translate *hostnames* (which include the top-level domain as the rightmost component of the address) into *host addresses*. Top-level domains include generic worldwide domains, generic United States domains, and country domains. ISO-3166 defines two-letter and three-letter top-level domains from around the world. Table T.1 shows the generic domains.

T A B L E   T . I   *Generic Top-Level Domains*

DOMAIN	DESCRIPTION
COM	Generic worldwide domain used for commercial organizations.
NET	Generic worldwide domain used for network service providers and Internet administration authorities.
EDU	Generic worldwide domain used for educational institutions, particularly four-year colleges and universities.
INT	Generic worldwide domain for organizations established through international treaties.
ORG	Generic worldwide domain for organizations not fitting into other generic worldwide domain categories.
GOV	Generic United States domain for agencies of the federal government.
MIL	Generic United States domain for the U.S. Department of Defense.

The U.S. top-level domain is divided into several subdomains, which are shown in Table T.2.

T A B L E   T . 2   *U.S. Top-Level Domain Subdomains*

SUBDOMAIN	DESCRIPTION
FED	Agencies of the federal government.
DNI	Organizations with a presence in multiple states or regions.
CC	Community colleges with a statewide presence.
CI	City government agencies.

TABLE T.2	U.S. Top-Level Domain Subdomains (continued)
SUBDOMAIN	**DESCRIPTION**
CO	County government agencies.
GEN	Organizations that do not fit into any other category.
K12	Public school districts.
LIB	Libraries.
STATE	State government offices.
TEC	Vocational and technical schools.

topology

The physical layout of a network, including the cabling, workstation configuration, gateways, and hubs. The three basic types of topology are the *star topology* (workstations connected to a server but not to each other), *ring topology* (the server and workstations are cabled together in a ring), and *bus topology* (all workstations and the server are connected to a central cable). Each of these basic types has variations; some may be combined to create *hybrid topologies.*

TP0

Under Opens Systems Interconnection (OSI), a connectionless Transport Protocol (TP) in class 0 used for reliable transport over subnetworks.

TP4

Under Opens Systems Interconnection (OSI), a connectionless Transport Protocol (TP) in class 4 used for reliable transport over subnetworks.

Traceroute

A program that provides a map of the path a packet travels during transmission from source node to destination node.

track

A physical division of the platter on a hard disk that appears as a concentric circle where data can be stored.

traffic

A flow of messages and data usually measured in bits transferred over a given time period by a communications channel or link.

traffic descriptor

In Asynchronous Transfer Mode (ATM), an element specifying the parameter values for Virtual Channel Connection (VCC) and Virtual Path Connection (VPC) that can be negotiated by entities involved in the connection.

Synonym: *user-network contract*

trailer

A part of a packet that includes the error-detection fields that follow the data contained in the packet. The header is the part of the packet that precedes the data contained in the packet.

transaction

A set of related operations constituting a logical unit of work. An application performing the transaction must specify whether all or none of these operations be performed.

transaction backout

The backing out of a transaction because of a system failure resulting from hardware problems and power outages, problems with applications running on a workstation, or user intervention at a workstation.

Transaction Bitmap

Under AppleTalk Transaction Protocol (ATP), a field that appears in a Transaction Request (TReq) packet to indicate how many buffers the requester has reserved for the packets that constitute the Transaction Response (TResp) message.

transaction identifier (TI)

Under AppleTalk Transaction Protocol (ATP), a 2-byte integer that appears in the header of a Transaction Request (TReq) packet in a transaction. The transaction identifier uniquely identifies a request.

Transaction Release packet (TRel)

Under AppleTalk Transaction Protocol (ATP), a packet sent in response to a Transaction Response (TResp) packet to indicate the requester received the entire response message.

Transaction Request packet (TReq)

Under AppleTalk Transaction Protocol (ATP), a packet sent by a socket to request a responding packet perform an action and return a response.

Transaction Response message

Under AppleTalk Transaction Protocol (ATP), a message consisting of up to eight Transaction Response (TResp) packets.

Transaction Response packet (TResp)

Under AppleTalk Transaction Protocol (ATP), a packet sent in response to a Transaction Request (TReq) packet to specify the results of the requested operation.

Transaction Services Layer (SNA model)

The seventh layer (Layer 7) of the Systems Network Architecture (SNA) model. The Transaction Services Layer provides distributed network-management services such as database access and document interchange.

Transaction-Tracking System (TTS)

A NetWare system designed to protect data from corruption by backing out incomplete transactions that result from the failure of a network component. A transaction may be saved improperly due to a power interruption, failure of server or workstation hardware, software, or a transmission component (such as a hub, repeater, or cable). TTS makes a copy of the original data before it is overwritten by new data; when a transaction is backed out, data returns to the state it was in before the transaction began. TTS can protect against data corruption in any type of application that issues record-locking calls and stores information in records (including traditional databases, some electronic-mail applications, and some appointment schedulers in workgroup applications).

Transactional (T) attribute

A file attribute set by the NetWare operating system that indicates the file is protected by the Transactional-Tracking System (TTS).

transactions list

A list that contains all recently received transactions, used to implement *exactly-once transactions* and maintained by responders that comply with AppleTalk Transaction Protocol (ATP).

transceiver

A device that can transmit data, receive data, and convert from an Attachment-Unit Interface (AUI) Ethernet connection to another type of cabling. This term is a contraction of *transmitter/receiver*.

transceiver cable

A cable, found primarily in Ethernet systems, that connects a Network Interface Card (NIC) to a transceiver.

transfer mode

A mode in which telecommunications data is transferred or switched (or both) in a network.

transfer time

The amount of time it takes a backup power supply to switch to auxiliary power in a power outage affecting a network node.

transit bridging

A bridging technique that encapsulates a frame being sent between two similar networks via a dissimilar network.

translation bridging

Bridging that resolves differences in header formats and protocol specifications. Translation bridging is required on networks with dissimilar protocols for the Media Access Control (MAC) sublayer of the OSI Reference Model.

transmission code

A set of rules that govern how data is represented during a transmission. Examples include Extended Binary-Coded Decimal-Interchange Code (EBCDI), which represents data as 8-bit code, and American Standard Code for Information Interchange (ASCII), which represents data as 7-bit code.

Transmission-Control Layer (SNA model)

The fourth layer (Layer 4) in the Systems Network Architecture (SNA) model. The Transmission-Control Layer performs error-control functions, coordinates the pace of data exchanges to match processing capacities, and encodes data for security. This layer establishes, maintains, and terminates SNA sessions, sequences all data messages, and handles flow control for the session.

Transmission Control Protocol (TCP)

In the Internet Protocol (IP) suite, a transport protocol that provides connection-oriented, full-duplex streams of data and uses the IP for delivery.

Transmission Control Protocol/Internet Protocol (TCP/IP)

A suite of networking protocols that enables dissimilar nodes in a heterogeneous environment to communicate with one another. TCP/IP protocols handle media access, packet transport, session communications, file transfer, electronic mail, and terminal emulation. This suite and related applications were developed for the Department of Defense (DoD) during the 1970s and 1980s specifically to enable different types of computers to exchange information with each other. TCP/IP is currently mandated as the official DoD protocol and is widely used on UNIX platforms.

T

transmission group

In Systems Network Architecture (SNA), one or more parallel communications links treated as one communication facility for routing purposes.

Transmission Header (TH)

In the Systems Network Architecture (SNA) model, an element added to the basic information unit (BIU) at the Path-Control Layer (Layer 3).

transmission medium

The physical path (cabling, wires, microwaves, satellite transmissions) over which a transmission is carried.

transmission mode

One of four modes in which communication between a sender and a receiver can take place. The four modes are as follows:

▶ *Simplex.* One-way communication in which the sender can use the entire communication channel.

▶ *Half duplex.* One-direction communication—but going both ways—in which a sender can use the entire communication channel. To change directions, a special signal is issued and acknowledged.

▶ *Full duplex.* Two-way communication that goes both ways simultaneously. The sender and receiver each only get half the communication channel.

▶ *Echoplex.* Error-checking mode in which characters typed for transmission are returned to the sender's screen from the receiver for direct comparison with what was typed.

Transmit Data (TXD)

A hardware signal carrying information from one device to another, defined by the RS-232-C standard.

transparent

Capable of operating without being evident to the user.

transparent bridging

A scheme in which bridges pass frames one hop at a time, basing their hops on tables that associate end nodes with bridge ports. The presence of the bridges is transparent to the network's end nodes.

transparent LAN

A networking service in which two local area networks (LANs) can communicate over telecommunications links without having to handle the long-distance connection explicitly.

transport client
An application or protocol that accesses Transport-Layer Interface (TLI) services.

transport endpoint
A channel that provides an endpoint for communication between a transport user and a transport provider.

Transport Layer (OSI model)
The fourth layer (Layer 4) in the OSI Reference Model. The Transport Layer provides reliable, end-to-end delivery of data and detects errors in the sequence of transmission.

Transport-Layer Interface (TLI)
An Interprocess Communication (IC) mechanism providing protocol-independent support for server applications. In NetWare, the TLI is an Application Programming Interface (API) that resides between the STREAMS utility and user applications.

transport provider
A protocol, such as Datagram-Delivery Protocol (DDP) or AppleTalk Data-Stream Protocol (ADSP), that provides the services of the Transport-Layer Interface (TLI).

Transport Service Data Unit (TSDU)
A user data unit transmitted between two clients of a transport connection.

transport user
An application or protocol that accesses Transport-Layer Interface (TLI) services.

traps
Under Simple Network Management Protocol (SNMP), operations used by an SNMP agent to notify an SNMP manager that major events have occurred.

tree structure

A flexible data structure representing the hierarchical organization of information. A tree consists of a *root* element with one or more elements branching out directly below it. Often the root is an abstract entity that has a purpose, but no real content. The elements below the root (also known as a *parent directory*) are called *children*; a child can, in turn, have children of its own beneath it. Various types of network directories are often represented in the tree structure.

tree topology

A hybrid physical topology combining features of star and bus topologies. The starting end of the tree is the *head end* or *root end*. When several buses are daisy-chained together, branches are possible at the connections.

Synonyms: *distributed bus topology*; *branching tree topology*

trellis-coded modulation (TCM)

A quadrature amplitude-modulation technique that encodes data as a set of bits associated with both phase and amplitude changes. TCM is typically used in modems that operate at speeds of 9,600 bits per second (bps) or higher.

triaxial cable

Coaxial cable consisting of an inner braid surrounded by an inner jacket, surrounded, in turn, by an outer copper braid, which is surrounded by an outer jacket. The extra shielding in triaxial cable provides grounding and improved protection.

Trivial File Transfer Protocol (TFTP)

A version of the Transmission Control Protocol/Internet Protocol (TCP/IP), but without password protection or user-directory capabilities.

trunk

A transmission channel used to connect two switching devices.

Trunk-Coupling Unit (TCU)

A physical device enabling a Token Ring network station to connect to a trunk cable.

trustee

In NetWare or IntranetWare, a user or group granted the rights needed to work with a directory, file, or object.

trustee assignment

Rights granted to NetWare or IntranetWare objects that are part of the directory, file, or object to which they grant access. In Novell Directory Services (NDS), a trustee assignment is stored in a *trustee list*, which, in turn, is stored in the object's Access-Control List property. The [Public] trustee assignment is special: Anyone who tries to access a file, directory, or object without any other rights is allowed only the rights granted to the [Public] trustee. Rights for files and directories are granted in the same manner, but rights to objects are different and have no effect on directories and files. Conversely, trustee assignments for files and directories have no effect on rights granted for objects. A trustee assignment for a file or directory enables a user to see the path to the root directory of the volume. A trustee assignment for an object does not automatically show the user the Directory tree to the root. Through *inheritance*, a trustee assignment to a directory, file, or object can provide access to the directory, its files, its subdirectories, or to the subordinate objects.

trustee node

An addressable, 128-byte entry found in NetWare's Directory Entry Table (DET), containing information about a trustee. A trustee node is maintained by the server.

trustee rights

Privileges granted to a user or group for a specific volume, folder, or file in NetWare. Trustee rights determine the kinds of tasks the trustee can carry out.

tunneling

Encapsulating and de-encapsulating one protocol in another. Specific definitions vary. In AppleTalk, tunneling is the process by which a router that supports the AppleTalk Update-Routing Protocol (AURP) encapsulates AppleTalk packets in Internet Protocol (IP) packets. The router then sends the resulting packets across the network under Transmission Control Protocol/Internet Protocol (TCP/IP) to a router that supports AURP. In NetWare's Internetwork Packet Exchange (IPX) protocol, tunneling is the process by which a router running the IPTUNNEL or IPRELAY driver encapsulates IPX packets in User-Datagram Protocol/Internet Protocol (UDP/IP) packets, sending the resulting packets across the TCP/IP network to another router that runs IPTUNNEL or IPRELAY. The receiving router then removes the IP and AURP or UDP headers of the packets and forwards them to their destinations.

Turbo File-Allocation Table (Turbo FAT)
A special File Allocation Table (FAT) index used when a file exceeds 64 blocks and must be quickly accessed.

TUXEDO
A Novell software program, originally developed by UNIX Systems Laboratory, which provides a high-level interface for transaction-management services in client-server systems. TUXEDO provides the capability of transferring data among platforms that differ in the way they represent data, while also monitoring and managing those transactions. Development and support for TUXEDO has been transferred to BEA Systems, Inc.

twinaxial cable
A coaxial cable that has two cables inside a single insulating shield, commonly used with IBM AS/400 minicomputers.

twisted-pair cable (TP)
Cable with two or more pairs of insulated wires twisted together at a rate of six twists per inch; one wire carries the signal and the other is grounded. The two types of TP are shielded twisted-pair (STP) and unshielded twisted-pair (UTP).

Twisted-Pair Distributed Data Interface (TPDDI)
A network architecture that implements the capabilities of Fiber Distributed Data Interface (FDDI) capabilities on twisted-pair cabling.

twisted-pair wiring
In balanced circuits, two wires spun around each other (usually loosely) to help alleviate any induced noise.

Twisted-Pair, Physical-Media Dependent (TP-PMD)

An implementation of the Fiber Distributed Data Interface (FDDI) standard that can attain 100 megabits per second (Mbps) standard on unshielded twisted-pair (UTP) cabling.

Type 1 operation

A connectionless operation as defined by the Logical-Link Control (LLC) standard set by the Institute of Electronic and Electrical Engineers (IEEE).

Type 2 operation

A connection-oriented operation as defined by the Logical-Link Control (LLC) standard set by the Institute of Electronic and Electrical Engineers (IEEE).

Type code

A four-character code that identifies the nature of a Macintosh file. Every Macintosh file has a Type code and a Creator code.

Type of Service (ToS)

A byte in the header of an Internet Protocol (IP) packet that specifies the kind of transmission being requested, including the delay, throughput, and reliability of the desired transmission.

type-ahead buffer

Computer system memory used to store the most recently typed keys on a keyboard.
Synonym: *keyboard buffer*

T

unbalanced configuration

A configuration in the High-Speed Data-Link Control (HDLC) protocol that includes one primary station and multiple secondary stations.

unbinding

A NetWare process that removes a communication protocol from Network Interface Cards (NICs) and from local area network (LAN) drivers.

unbundled software

An application or feature of an application sold separately from a computer system (in the case of an application) or from an application (in the case of a feature of an application).

undervoltage

An electrical condition in which a voltage supply falls below its nominal value.

unicast address

An address that specifies a single network device.

Unicode

A 16-bit character representation defined by the Unicode Consortium that allows characters for multiple languages to be represented and supports up to 65,536 characters. NetWare stores all objects and their attributes in the Directory database in Unicode representation. DOS and OS/2 clients, however, use 256-character code pages, and not every character used on a given code page represents correctly on a workstation using a different code page. If a user changes code pages, a different set of Unicode translation tables are required to run NetWare utilities and to manage the Directory database. Therefore, when managing objects created in different code pages, object names and properties must be limited to characters common to all applicable code pages.

unified messaging

A telephony service local area networks (LANs) in which messages or information are accessed in a transparent manner (the messages or information can be displayed regardless of the format).

Synonym: *integrated messaging*

Unified Network Management Architecture (UNMA)

A network management architecture developed by AT&T that relies on distributed processing. Based on Open Systems Interconnection (OSI) protocols, UNMA serves as an operating environment for the AT&T Accumaster Integrator network-management package. It provides a framework for dealing with nine management functions, including accounting management, configuration management, fault management, performance management, and security management, which correspond to the OSI Network Management Model. The other management functions are integrated control, operations support, planning capability, and programmability.

Uniform Resource Locator (URL)

An Internet address that consists of information about the document type and the protocol used to transport it, the domain name of the machine on which the document is found, and the document's name represented as an absolute path to the file.

Uniform Service Ordering Code (USOC)

A commonly used sequence for wiring pairs.

uninterruptible power supply (UPS)

A backup unit that provides uninterrupted power in the event of a power outage. An *online UPS* actively modifies power as it moves through the unit so, if a power outage occurs, the unit is already active and continues to provide power. An *offline UPS* monitors the power line and, when power drops, the UPS is activated. If a UPS is attached to a server, the server can properly close files and rewrite the system directory to disk.

unipolar

An electrical characteristic of internal signals in digital communications equipment that literally means one polarity.

unique password

A password unlike any other password used to log in to the NetWare network. If the network is configured to accept only unique passwords, it rejects any new password identical to one of the last eight passwords (or any password used for at least one day).

unity gain
The use of amplifiers to balance signal loss with signal gain in broadband networks.

universal asynchronous receiver/transmitter (UART)
An electronic module designed to combine the circuitry for transmitting and receiving. A UART is required for asynchronous communication over a serial line.

universal in-box
A central delivery point for electronic mail (e-mail), faxes, and other types of electronic communication.

Universal Naming Convention (UNC)
A syntax used to specify a path to network resources that includes the server and volume name.

universal synchronous receiver/transmitter (USRT)
An electronic module combining the circuitry for transmitting and receiving. A USRT is required for synchronous communication over a serial line.

UNIX
An operating system originally developed by Dennis Ritchie and Ken Thompson at AT&T Bell Laboratories that allows a computer to handle multiple users and programs simultaneously. Since its development in the early 1970s, UNIX has been enhanced by many individuals and companies, particularly by computer scientists at the University of California, Berkeley (known as Berkeley Software Distribution UNIX, or BSD UNIX). This operating system is available on a wide variety of computer systems, ranging from personal computers to mainframes, and is available in other related forms. AIX is an implementation that runs on IBM workstations, A/UX is a graphical version that runs on Macintosh computers; Solaris runs on Intel microprocessors. UnixWare is the Novell implementation of UNIX. NetWare for UNIX is an Original Equipment Manufacturer (OEM) version of NetWare that can run on a UNIX host.

UNIX client

A UNIX computer connected to a NetWare network that stores and retrieves data from the server and runs executable network files. A UNIX client provides multitasking capabilities for multiple clients on a single station. To enable other NetWare clients to access UNIX applications, the UNIX client includes Internetwork Packet Exchange/Sequenced Packet Exchange (IPX/SPX) and NetWare Core Protocol/Internetwork Packet Exchange (NCP/IPX) protocols.

UNIX-to-UNIX Copy Program (UUCP)

An Application Layer (Layer 7 of the OSI Reference Model) protocol used by consenting UNIX systems to communicate with each other. This dial-up, store-and-forward protocol formed the basis for mail and news exchange during the early days of internetworking.

UnixWare

Novell's implementation of the UNIX operating system. A Personal Edition of UnixWare is a single-user system for applications and an Application Server version is a multiuser, server system. UnixWare has been transferred to the Santa Cruz Operation (SCO) for future development and support.

Unknown object

A leaf object representing a Novell Directory Services (NDS) object that has been corrupted and cannot be identified as belonging to any other object class.

unloading

A NetWare process that unlinks NetWare Loadable Modules (NLMs) from the operating system.

unnumbered frame

A frame used for system administration (such as link startup and shutdown, as well as mode specifications) in the High-Level Data-Link Control (HDLC) protocol.

unreliable

A term often used to indicate packet delivery on a network has not been verified.

U

Unsequenced Acknowledgment (UA)

A packet acknowledging the receipt of a Set Mode command in NetWare networks.

unshielded cable

Cable that has no outer foil shield to protect against electromagnetic interference (EMI) or radio-frequency interference (RFI).

unshielded twisted-pair cable (UTP)

Cable containing two or more pairs of twisted copper wires; the greater number of twists, the lower the crosstalk. UTP is available in both voice-grade and data-grade versions. Ease of installation and low material cost make this cable appealing, but drawbacks include limited signaling speed and shorter maximum cable-segment length.

Unspecified Bit Rate (UBR)

An Asynchronous Transfer Mode (ATM) service category that does not include the notion of a per-connection negotiated bandwidth. UBR does not make any traffic-related service guarantees.

up time

The time during which a computer or other device is functioning, but not necessarily available for use.

upgradable computer

A computer system designed to be upgraded when newer technology becomes available. Systems may differ in the degree that circuitry must be changed and how the upgrade is accomplished.

upgrade

A process involving the installation of a newer and more powerful version of hardware or software on a computer system.

upload

A communications process involving the sending of files from one computer to another computer over a network or modem.

Upper Layer Protocol (ULP)

A protocol in the OSI Reference Model that is higher than the current reference point, often the next-highest protocol in a particular protocol stack.

upper memory

DOS memory located above 640K and below 1024K, addressable by 16-bit microprocessors, keeping parts reserved for DOS and Basic Input/Output System (BIOS) functions.

Synonym: *reserved memory*

upper memory block (UMB)

A block of DOS memory between 640K and 1024K addressed by DOS and applications and defined by the Extended Memory Specification (XMS). The unused portion of this memory area is known as the UMBs and is used to store terminate-and-stay-resident (TSR) programs and to load device drivers.

UPS monitoring

A NetWare process in which a server ensures that an uninterruptible power supply (UPS) unit is attached and functioning properly. In a power failure, NetWare notifies users and, after a timeout period specified in the SERVER.CFG file, the server logs out remaining users, closes open files, and shuts itself down.

Upstream Neighbor's Address (UNA)

The address of a Token Ring network node from which a given node receives frames. Given the ring structure of the network, this address is unique at any given time in the operation of the network.

upward compatibility

The capability of software to function with other, more powerful products likely to become available in the future. Upward compatibility is made possible by adherence to design standards.

US Classification Levels

A set of classification levels established by the federal government for messages and information transmitted across the Internet, which includes Top

Secret, Secret, Confidential, and Unclassified. The classification level is specified in 8-bit values assigned to each level.

Usenet

A cooperative network initiated in 1979 that includes more than 10,000 hosts and a quarter million users and provides a distributed conferencing service for users. The thousands of distributed bulletin boards on this network display messages according to hierarchical categories known as *newsgroups* and are accessed by users with *newsreader* programs. Individual Internet Service Providers (ISPs) determine which newsgroups to offer and with which systems to exchange messages. Newsreader programs use the Network News Transfer Protocol (NNTP) to translate messages.

user

Someone who is authorized to log on to a network or database (or both) when security is installed and who has access rights to files and directories.

User Access Line (UAL)

A line in an X.25 network that provides a connection between Data Terminal Equipment (DTE) and a network. The user's data communications equipment (DCE), which may be a modem or multiplexer, provides the necessary interface to the network.

user account

A NetWare security feature that determines under what name the user logs in to the network, the groups to which the user belongs, and the trustee assignments made to the user. This account is maintained by the network supervisor for every user on the network.

User Agent (UA)

An application process in the Consultative Committee for International Telegraphy and Telephony (CCITT) X.400 Message Handling System (MHS) that provides user access to a Message Transfer Service (MTS).

User Agent Layer (UAL)

An upper sublayer of the Application Layer (Layer 7) of the OSI Reference Model that provides an interface between user interaction and the Message

Transfer Layer (MTL) of the Consultative Committee for International Telegraphy and Telephony (CCITT) X.400 Message Handling System (MHS).

User-Authentication Method (UAM)

A NetWare feature that compares the user name and password entered by a user at login with information stored in the NetWare Directory database, and then grants or denies the connection according to whether the comparison matches. NetWare supports an Apple Standard UAM and a NetWare UAM.

User Datagram Protocol (UDP)

A Transport Layer (Layer 4 of the OSI Reference Model) protocol in the Transmission Control Protocol/Internet Protocol (TCP/IP) suite. UDP is not connection-oriented and does not acknowledge data receipt. This protocol is less reliable than TCP, but performs faster because it neither establishes and de-establishes connections nor controls data flow. This protocol is often bundled with the Simple Network Management Protocol (SNMP).

user group

A group of users who meet to share tips and listen to industry experts discuss a computer or software product of common interest to the group. User group activities often include regular meetings, maintenance of a bulletin board system, or publication of a newsletter.

User login script

A NetWare login script that sets environments specific to a user and contains items not allowed in System or Profile login scripts. User login scripts, which are optional, execute after System login scripts and Profile login scripts.

username

A name assigned to a NetWare user account that the user types in to log in to the network and to gain access to network resources.

user name

A name recognized by the network, with which a user gains access to a network server.

user-network contract

An Asynchronous Transfer Mode (ATM) element specifying parameter values for Virtual Channel Connection (VCC) and Virtual Path Connection (VPC) that can be negotiated by entities involved in the connection.

Synonym: *traffic descriptor*

User object

A Novell Directory Services (NDS) leaf object that represents a person with access to the network and stores information about the person it represents.

user profile

A record that specifies a user's access and usage privileges on a network system.

user template

A NetWare file that contains default information that can be applied to new User objects to give them default property values. User templates are created in Organization and Organizational Unit objects.

User Template object

In IntranetWare, a leaf object used to create User objects in Novell Directory Systems (NDS). Through this object, a user can designate default values for User object creation (including NDS rights and file system rights). This object can only be used for setting up new users. This object replaced the older User object called User_Template found in earlier versions of NetWare 4.

User-to-Network Interface (UNI)

An interface used by a router to connect to and access frame relay network services. As defined by the ATM Forum for public and private Asynchronous Transfer Mode (ATM) access, the UNI occurs between an ATM end system (such as a router) and an ATM switch.

Synonym: *subscriber network*

utility
A program that adds functionality to a network operating system. For NetWare and IntranetWare, utilities support Windows, OS/2, DOS, and UNIX environments. These utilities are designed to work at the server console (for example, to change memory allocations, monitor server operation, and control the use of server resources), on files, and at the workstation. Appendix E provides a breakdown of common NetWare and IntranetWare utilities, along with classifications as server console, file, and workstation utilities.

Uudecode
The conversion of a file back to its original format from the uuencoded format. This encoding method is used to transfer both text and graphics files in electronic mail (e-mail) because it makes even binary files appear as strings of text characters.

Uuencode
The encoding of a file to the uuencoded format. This encoding method is used to transfer both text and graphics files in electronic mail (e-mail) because it makes even binary files appear as strings of text characters.

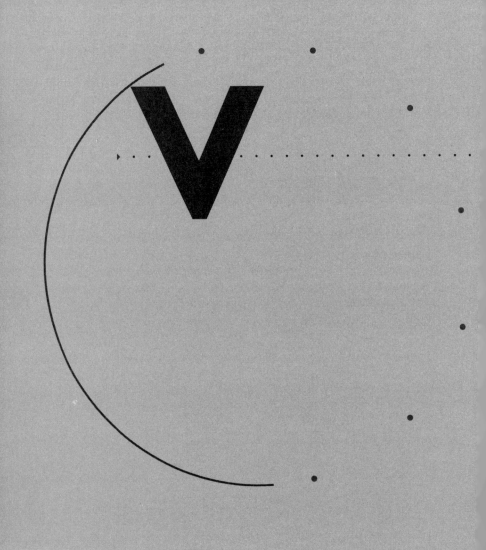

V.24

A Physical Layer (Layer 6 in the OSI Reference Model) interface used in many countries. V.24 is similar to the RS-232-C interface.

V.25bis dialing

A standard from the Consultative Committee for International Telegraphy and Telephony (CCITT) that describes in-band dialing on High-Level Data Link Control (HDLC) bit-synchronous serial lines.

V.32

A modem that transmits at a speed of 9,600 bits per second.

V.35

A standard from the Consultative Committee for International Telegraphy and Telephony (CCITT) that describes data transmission at 48 kilobits per second (Kbps) using 60 kilohertz (KHz) to 108KHz circuits.

value-added network (VAN)

A commercial network that adds services or features to an existing network.

value-added process (VAP)

A process designed to enhance the NetWare operating-system features without interfering with normal network operation. A VAP runs on top of the operating system in a manner similar to a word-processing application or spreadsheet running on top of DOS.

value-added reseller (VAR)

A company that enhances the quality of a product (for example, by improving documentation, user support, service support, or system integration), repackages the product, and resells it to the public.

value-added server

A dedicated computer, separate from the network, that fulfills a specific function for network users (such as a print server or database server).

vampire tap

A hardware clamp used to connect one cable segment to another by penetrating the insulation of the network cable segment without cutting it. A needle on the tap pierces the cable insulation to make a connection with the cable.

vaporware

A term used to describe a software product announced for release on a specific date, but still not released after that date has been passed by a significant amount of time.

Variable Bit Rate (VBR)

A connection method used in Asynchronous Transfer Mode (ATM) networks that transmits at varying rates. VBR is used for data transmissions whose contents are not time-sensitive. VBR is a *reserved bandwidth* service, but instead of generating a constant bit rate, establishes a peak rate, sustainable rate, and maximum burst size.

variable-length record

A record consisting of a variable-length portion (which may vary in size) and a fixed-length portion (which remains the same size in all records in a given file).

Variable-Length Subnet Mask (VLSM)

A capability that optimizes available address space by specifying a different subnet mask for the same network number on different subnetworks.

Variable-Tail Allocation Table (VAT)

An array that contains pointers to locations within the variable-length portion of a record.

VAX

A minicomputer manufactured by Digital Equipment Corporation.

VAX OSI Transport Service (VOTS)

A Transport Level (Level 4 of the OSI Reference Model) protocol used on Digital Equipment Corporation machines in a local area network (LAN) or wide area network (WAN).

vector

A data segment consisting of a length field, a key describing the vector type, and vector-specific data in the Systems Network Architecture (SNA) model.

vector graphics (images)

Graphical display rendered by using vector notation technology. Vector notation includes a starting point, length, and direction a line is drawn from the starting point. Vector graphics are defined mathematically rather than as a set of dots. Users may manipulate a part of the image without redrawing and may resize or rotate the image without distorting it.

Velocity of Propagation (VOP)

A value indicating the network signal speed as a proportion of the theoretical maximum possible speed. For example, VOP for electrically based local area networks (LANs) range from 60 percent to 85 percent of maximum.

Vendor-Independent Messaging (VIM)

An Application Programming Interface (API) between an application (such as an electronic-mail program or scheduling program) and a message-related service (such as a message store-and-forward service or a directory service). VIM was developed jointly by Apple Computer, Borland International, Lotus Corporation, and Novell, and is comparable to Microsoft's Messaging Application Programming Interface (MAPI).

version creep

Adding features to programs without taking care to provide compatibility with previous releases of a software product.

version number

A decimal number assigned by a developer to identify a particular hardware or software release with larger numbers indicating most recent releases. The number before the decimal point indicates a major revision to the product.

The number following the decimal point indicates a minor revision. However, a minor product revision can produce a significant difference in performance.

vertical application

An application whose functionality is limited to a narrow and specific market area of use (such as an accounting application or legal application).

Vertical Blank Interval (VBI)

A transparent component of a television signal currently only used for closed captioning, but being developed by En Technology in its Malachi product to use to download software.

very-low frequency (VLF) emission

Radiation emissions in the range of 2 kilohertz (KHz) to 400KHz from a computer monitor and from common household electrical appliances. The emissions decline as a square of the distance from the source.

vi

A standard UNIX screen-based text editor used in many dial-up, text terminal-style Internet accounts.

video adapter

An expansion board that provides text and graphics output to the monitor of a DOS computer system. This board plugs into the expansion bus in the computer.

Video Electronics Standards Association (VESA)

An association, whose members include video graphics adapter and monitor manufacturers, that sets standards for video on personal computers (particularly the standardization of Super VGA hardware).

Video Graphics Array (VGA)

A video adapter from IBM that supports several graphics standards and provides several graphics resolutions, including 256 colors in a 640×480 display.

video memory

An area of system memory used by hardware operating the computer's display or monitor.

videoconferencing

A multiparty teleconferencing technique that involves both audio and video transmissions and requires the use of a video codec (coder/decoder) to translate between video images and digital representations.

virtual

A term used to describe something conceptual, instead of something that actually exists.

virtual 8086 mode

A mode in computers equipped with the Intel 80386, 80486, or Pentium microprocessor that enables the microprocessor to emulate separate personal computer environments simultaneously; the operating system controls such external elements as interrupts and input/output (I/O). This mode is often used in OS/2 and Windows NT to multitask multiple DOS sessions.

Virtual Channel (VC)

A communications channel providing sequential, unidirectional transport of Asynchronous Transfer Mode (ATM) cells.

Virtual Channel Connection (VCC)

A logical, unidirectional connection between two entities on an Asynchronous Transfer Mode (ATM) that represents the basic switching level for ATM. A VCC may be switched or dedicated, preserves the order in which cells are transmitted, provides a quality of service (QoS), and uses performance parameters to be negotiated by the entities involved in a connection.

Virtual Channel Identifier (VCI)

A unique number identified by a 16-bit field in the header of the Asynchronous Transfer Mode (ATM) cell packet that identifies a virtual channel (VC) over which a cell packet is to travel. The VCI is used to route the cell to and from the user.

virtual circuit (VC)
A circuit providing a connection-oriented service, or in packet-switching networks, a circuit that appears to be a physical point-to-point circuit connecting two end points and reliably conveying sequenced packets. In reality, a packet-switching VC shares the underlying links and relay systems with other network users.

virtual circuit number
A 4-bit logical group number and an 8-bit logical channel number used to identify which packets belong to which virtual circuits.

Virtual Control Program Interface (VCPI)
Specifications that enable DOS programs to run in protected mode on 80386 and higher machines, as well as executing cooperatively with other operating environments (such as memory-management programs). The VCPI was the first DOS extender.

virtual disk
A designated portion of random access memory (RAM) made to act like a very fast disk drive.
Synonyms: *RAM disk*; *memory disk*

Virtual File Storage (VFS)
An intermediate transit format for File Transfer, Access, and Management (FTAM) that provides a set of common file operations all FTAM systems understand.

Virtual LAN (VLAN)
A network configuration that can span physical local area networks (LANs) and topologies, and is created by software on an as-needed basis (for example, when multiple users require interaction during a large project).

virtual link
Software used to extend the backbone area of a network by linking two partitioned areas.

Virtual Loadable Module (VLM)

A modular executable program in the NetWare DOS Requester that runs at each DOS workstation and enables communication with the NetWare server. VLMs provide backward compatibility and replace NetWare shells (NETX) used in early versions of NetWare. A *child VLM* program handles a particular implementation of a logical grouping of functionality (such as the NDS.VLM for NetWare 4 servers, BIND.VLM for bindery-based servers before NetWare 4, and PNW.VLM for NetWare desktop-based servers). Various transport protocols also have individual child VLM programs (such as IPXNCP.VLM, which handles Internetwork Packet Exchange services, and TCPNCP.VLM, which handles Transmission Control Protocol functions). A *multiplexor VLM* program routes calls to the proper child VLM to ensure that requests to child VLM programs reach the appropriate VLM module.

virtual machine

An operating system environment in which each executing application is under the illusion it has gained complete control of an independent computer and it can access all the necessary system resources.

virtual memory

A memory-management technique in which information in physical memory is swapped out to a hard disk when necessary to provide applications with more memory space than is actually available in the computer. Programs and associated data are divided into *pages*. When more memory is needed, the operating system uses an algorithm based on frequency of use, most recent use, and program priority to determine which pages to write out to disk. Memory space occupied by pages written out to the hard disk then becomes available to the remainder of the system.

Virtual Memory System (VMS)

The operating system used on the VAX minicomputer from Digital Equipment Corporation.

Virtual Networking System (VINES)

An operating system from Banyan Systems—based on a special version of the UNIX System V implementation—that provides all server functions. VINES can support up to four Network Interface Cards (NICs) per server for any topology while automatically managing protocol binding and translations required between the NICs for routing to different local area network (LAN) segments. The console includes a complete set of built-in network management tools.

Virtual Path Connection (VPC)

A cluster of logical Virtual Channel Connections (VCCs) between two entities in an Asynchronous Transfer Mode (ATM) network. All channels in a particular VPC connect the same two entities.

Virtual Path Identifier (VPI)

An 8-bit field in the header of an Asynchronous Transfer Mode (ATM) cell header. This field indicates the virtual path over which the cell should be routed.

Virtual Reality Modeling Language (VRML)

A graphics format used to construct and describe three-dimensional interactive images that requires a special VRML browser to receive the images and a special VRML server to transmit the images.

virtual route

A virtual circuit (VC) in the Systems Network Architecture (SNA) model, this logical connection between subarea nodes is a physical realization of an explicit route.

Virtual Telecommunications Access Method (VTAM)

Mainframe computer software for IBM machines running the Multiple Virtual Storage (MVS) or VM operating system that controls communications in the Systems Network Architecture (SNA) environment.

Virtual Terminal (VT)

A service on the Application Layer (Layer 7 of the OSI Reference Model) that makes it possible to emulate the behavior of a particular terminal. This capability alleviates the concern with hardware-compatibility issues when remote clients are attempting to communicate with mainframe hosts. The VT acts as a translating intermediary between the remote client and the mainframe host.

Virtual Terminal Protocol (VTP)

A Novell implementation of a Presentation Layer (Layer 6 of the OSI Reference Model) and Application Layer (Layer 7) protocol that provides a model of a general terminal for applications to use.

virus

A program designed to cause intentional damage to a computer system, obviously without the user's knowledge or permission. Some viruses may attach themselves to other programs, to the disk partition table, or to a boot track on a hard disk, so when a specific event occurs, a specific time is reached, or a specific program is executed, the virus begins to damage the system.

voice mail

A computerized, store-and-forward, voice-messaging system. Prerecorded messages route a call to the intended recipient (perhaps a person, department, or mailbox), digitize the incoming message, and store the message on disk for review by the recipient.

voice-grade cable

Unshielded, twisted-pair (UTP) telephone cable used for the transmission of voice signals, but not officially recognized as suitable for data transmissions.

volume

The highest level in the NetWare file system that represents the amount of hard-disk storage space, fixed in size. Volumes may be created on any hard disk that has a NetWare partition, with each server supporting up to 64 volumes. *Logical volumes* are divided into directories by supervisors and users with appropriate rights. *Physical volumes* are divided into volume segments, with each segment stored on one or more hard disks. Each hard disk can contain up to 8 volume segments belonging to one or more volumes and each volume can consist of up to 32 volume segments. The NetWare INSTALL program creates the first volume named SYS:, and other volumes can be defined with assigned volume names of between 2 and 15 characters. When used as part of a directory-path designation, the volume name is followed by a colon (for example, SYS:PUBLIC). When a NetWare server starts, the volume becomes visible to the operating system, the volume's File Allocation Table (FAT) is loaded into memory, and the volume's Directory Entity Table (DET) is loaded into memory; the whole process is known as *mounting a volume.*

Volume-Definition Table (VDT)

A table stored in the NetWare partition that tracks such volume information as volume name, volume size, and the location of volume segments on various network hard disks.

volume label

An assigned name used to identify a disk. Volume labels are set by the NetWare LABEL command.

Volume object

In Novell Directory Services (NDS), a leaf object that represents a physical volume on a network.

volume segment

A physical division of a NetWare or IntranetWare volume that can be stored on a hard disk. Each hard disk can contain up to 8 volume segments belonging to one or more volumes and each volume can consist of up to 32 volume segments. Disk input/output (I/O) can be sped up by placing segments of the same volume on multiple hard disks because different parts of the same volume can be read from or written to simultaneously.

volume serial number

A unique number assigned by some operating systems during the formatting process for a disk. This number often is shown at the beginning of a directory listing.

VT100

A terminal manufactured by Digital Equipment Corporation in the late 1980s that has become an emulation standard for many computers communicating over the Internet.

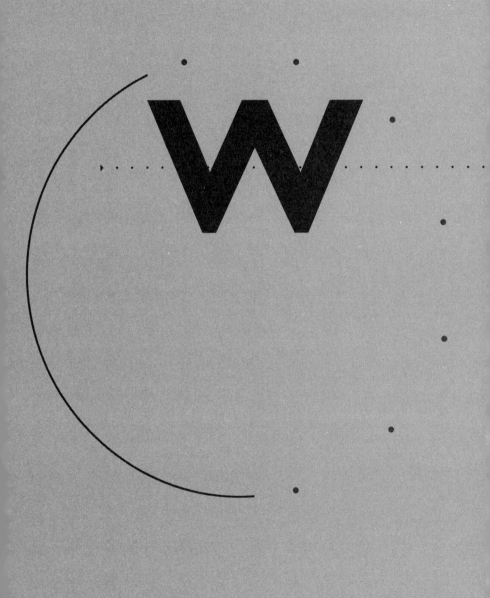

wait state

A period of time in which a processor is inactive and during which circuitry or devices operating at different speeds are synchronized.

wait time

A period of time (in seconds) designated as the amount of time to wait before signaling to the NetWare server that the normal power supply has been interrupted or shut off.

WAN call destination

A NetWare remote call configuration for a wide area network (WAN). Each call configuration equals one virtual circuit (VC) on one WAN link and contains parameters necessary for the WAN link driver to establish and maintain links to a given destination.

warm boot

Restarting a computer (without turning it off and on) after the operating system has been running for some time.

watchdog

A term used to describe packets designed to ensure all workstations are connected to the NetWare server. For example, if the server does not receive a packet from a workstation over a predetermined amount of time, a watchdog packet is sent to the workstation. If the workstation does not respond, another watchdog packet is sent. After a predetermined number of watchdog packets have been sent without acknowledgment, the server assumes the workstation is no longer connected and clears the workstation connection. The SET utility sets the period of time before the first watchdog packet, the period of time between watchdog packets, and the number of watchdog packets.

WAV (WAVE)

A Windows-based, digital, sampled sound format that uses a raw, uncompressed string of sampled recordings prefaced by a header.

waveform coding

An electrical technique that conveys binary signals.

wavelength

A measurement of the distance an electrical or light signal travels in a single cycle, used to encode particular transmissions.

Wavelength-Division Multiplexing (WDM)

A multiplexing process that involves the transmission of signals at different wavelengths along the same wire or fiber.

Wavelength-Selective Coupler

A splitter coupler that breaks an incoming signal into outgoing signals on the basis of signal wavelength.

Web browser

A client application for the World Wide Web (WWW) that enables the viewing of Hypertext Markup Language (HTML) documents on the Web. When a hypertext link of interest is located, clicking the link enables the browser to access the Internet host that holds the requested document. The browser has the capability to download information from the document or to print the document through the computer operating system. Some browsers also maintain bookmarks, which enable users to access favorite Uniform Resource Locators (URLs) easily.

Web home page

A starting point for hypertext documents on the World Wide Web (WWW) that may be sponsored and maintained by individuals, organizations, or commercial interests, and has an assigned Internet address. A Web home page can provide access to information about an organization (or individual or commercial interest), access to other Web sites of interest, and a means for contacting the Web home page host.

Web robot

An electronic program that automatically retrieves information on the World Wide Web (WWW).
Synonyms: *digital assistant*; *knowbot*; *Web crawler*

Webmaster
A person who is responsible for maintaining a World Wide Web (WWW) site.

WEBMGR
A Windows-based executable program, installed with the NetWare Web Server program that provides configuration management for the NetWare Web Server.

White Pages Directory
An Internet database that contains name and address information for users on a particular server or network. The White Pages Directory is a user-oriented database; the Yellow Pages Directory is a service-oriented database.

whiteboard
A term describing products that provide only software to enable users of a conferencing technology to work cooperatively on a document.

whois
A command used on some computer systems to generate a profile or description of a user. This command is used on the Internet to query the database at the Network Information Center (NIC) for an electronic mail (e-mail) address.

Wide Area Information Service (WAIS)
An Internet service that searches specified source locations for files that contain user-specified keyword criteria. WAIS returns a list of files that match the user-defined criteria.

wide area network (WAN)
A network encompassing a large geographical area (such as across a city or around the world). Local area networks (LANs) connect to WANs by linking with a mainframe computer, a public data network, or another LAN.

Wide Area Telecommunication Service (WATS)
A service that features unlimited use of a telephone circuit for specified periods and a fixed charge.

wideband

A communications channel capable of handling frequencies higher than the standard 3 KHz voice channel.

Wideband Channel (WBC)

A channel with a 6.144 megabits per second (Mbps) bandwidth in a Fiber Distributed Data Interface (FDDI) network. An FDDI network can support 16 WBCs. When used in a packet-switched FDDI, WBCs can be grouped together to form a packet data channel, which transmits data at a minimum bandwidth of 78 kilobits per second (Kbps) and a maximum bandwidth of about 99 Mbps. When used on a circuit-switched FDDI, the WBC may be allocated to a single connection, or broken into slower channels, each of which can be used to connect a pair of network nodes.

wildcard character

A character representing one or more unknown characters. The question mark (?) is used in many operating systems to represent a single unknown character in a filename or filename extension. The asterisk (*) is used in many operating systems to represent any number of unknown characters in a filename or filename extension.

window

A viewing area for Graphical User Interface (GUI) applications that can contain its own document or message. Window-based applications can display multiple windows simultaneously, each with its own boundaries and possibly containing a different document, message, menu, or other controls.

Windowing Korn Shell (WKSH)

A UNIX tool incorporating the MoOLIT toolkit used to develop windowing applications by providing a comprehensive prototyping facility for exercising the application early in the development cycle.

Windows 3.*x*

An operating system from Microsoft Corporation that features a multitasking Graphical User Interface (GUI) environment running on DOS based computers and a standard interface based on drop-down menus, windowed regions on the screen, and a pointing device (such as a mouse). The three main components of Windows 3.*x* are the Program Manager (the primary shell program that manages the execution of applications and task switching), the Print Manager (which coordinates printing), and the File Manager (which manages files, directories, and disks). The standard Windows package includes a Write program (word processing), Paint program (graphics), Terminal program (communications), and other utilities.

Windows 95

An operating system from Microsoft that supports preemptive multitasking (multitasking under the control of the operating system) and multithreading (the capability to run multiple parts of a program). Included with the Windows 95 package is the Microsoft Network (MSN), which is an online service package providing electronic mail support, chat forums, Internet access, and information services. In addition to MSN, Windows 95 provides built-in support for peer-to-peer networking, as well as support for Transmission-Control Protocol/Internet Protocol (TCP/IP), Internetwork Packet Exchange/Sequenced Packet Exchange (IPX/SPX), Network Basic Input/Output Service Extended User Interface (NetBEUI), Network-Driver Interface Specification (NDIS), Open Data-Link Interface (ODI), File-Transfer Protocol (FTP), Telnet, Serial-Line Internet Protocol (SLIP), and Point-to-Point Protocol (PPP). Windows 95 is the successor to Windows 3.*x*.

Windows accelerator

An expansion board or processor chip designed to speed up the performance of a personal computer's video hardware to give the impression that Microsoft Windows runs faster.

Windows client

A NetWare or IntranetWare workstation that boots DOS and gains access to the network either through the NetWare DOS Requester or the NetWare shell, and then runs Microsoft Windows.

Windows for Workgroups

A Microsoft application that is based on the Windows graphical user interface (GUI) that includes added functions for limited networking of computers to allow users to share files, exchange electronic mail (e-mail), maintain a collective calendar of events, and so on.

Windows NT

A 32-bit, multitasking, portable operating system introduced by Microsoft in 1993 and based on the Windows graphical user interface (GUI), runs Windows and DOS applications, runs OS/2 16-bit applications, and includes 32-bit programs specifically designed to run under Windows NT. This operating system supports the DOS File Allocation Table (FAT) system, the OS/2 High-Performance File System (HPFS), and its own NT File System (NTFS), as well as multiprocessing, Object Linking and Embedding (OLE), and peer-to-peer networking. Windows NT uses preemptive multitasking, with applications capable of executing multiple threads.

Windows NT Advanced Server

A version of the Windows NT operating system that features centralized network management, security functions, disk mirroring, and support for Redundant Array of Inexpensive Disks (RAID), and uninterruptible power supply (UPS).

Windows Open Services Architecture (WOSA)

An interface working at the system level that connects applications to services regardless of whether the services are provided on the network.

Winsock

A term describing the Application Programming Interface (API) that implements the Transmission Control Protocol/Internet Protocol (TCP/IP) protocol stack in a Windows environment. In order for a Windows program to access the Internet, it must have access to the TCP/IP stack. Winsock is a contraction for "Windows socket."

WinZip

A Windows program that provides the capability to compress and decompress files in TAR, gzip, UNIX compress, uuencode, BinHex, and MIME formats.

wire (solid)

An electrical wire with a central conducting element, normally a single wire of copper or other conductive material.

wire (stranded)

An electrical wire with a central conducting element, normally several strands of thin copper wire (or other conductive material) rolled tightly around each other.

wireless components

Components used in a wireless network that may include antennas or other transmitters and receivers not connected with wire or cable.

wireless LAN

A local-area network (LAN) that uses a technology other than conventional cabling to connect to a main network. Available technologies include infrared (in which high-frequency light waves transmit data at distances up to 80 feet over an unobstructed path), high-frequency radio (in which high-frequency radio signals transmit data at distances up to 130 feet), and spread-spectrum radio.

wireless modem

A modem used on a wireless network that does not transmit over telephone lines.

wireless network

A network that does not use cable or wiring as a communications medium and that uses signals covering a broad frequency range. The frequency range (which may be a few megahertz to a few terahertz) determines the type of wireless network (for example, radio wave, microwave, or infrared network). Wireless networks are used to connect machines within a building, connect portable machines to a network, and connect mobile machines to a database.

wiring (legacy)

Wiring that already exists within a building (business or residential) and may or may not be suitable for networking purposes.

wiring (premises)

Wiring that generally runs between outlets and any wiring centers or distribution frames in a house or office building. Connection to premises wiring is done with cords or cables that a user supplies.

wiring center

Components serving as a central termination point for one or more network nodes or for other wiring centers. A wiring center is designed to collect lines in a common location to continue a connection from that point on. Specific types of wiring centers include network hubs, concentrators, and Multistation Access Units (MAUs).

wiring closet

A location in which premises wiring cables are gathered (usually in one or more punch-down blocks or distribution frames) and connect to various areas of central wiring in an office or building.

wiring sequence

The order in which the wiring pairs of twisted-pair cabling are attached to pins in a connector.

word length

Either the standard data unit used in a computer (usually 8, 16, 32, or 64 bits), or the number of data bits in a communications data word.

workflow software

Any application program that is designed to describe or manage the steps required to complete a transaction or other type of task (such as flowcharting or computer-aided design programs).

workgroup

A group of two or more individuals on a local area network (LAN) who share files, databases, and other network resources.

workgroup manager

A user classification in the NetWare 3 and NetWare 4 network operating systems that grants supervisory control over any user or user group created on the network.

working directory

The host server directory that contains log and error files for each backup session. In Windows, a working directory is the default directory specified for an application.

workstation

A personal computer connected to a network and used to perform tasks through application programs or utilities.

Synonyms: *client, station*

workstation manager

A software module in the NetWare Storage Management Services (SMS) that receives ready messages from workstations available to be backed up and keeps the names of the workstations in an internal list.

Workstation Operating System (WOS)

The native operating system on a network workstation that may be different from the network server's network operating system, but is used to carry out tasks at the workstation.

workstation TSA

A NetWare Target Service Agent (TSA) in Storage Management Services (SMS) that passes commands and data between the host server and the database where data to be backed up resides.

World Wide Web Consortium (W3C)

An international industry association hosted by the Laboratory for Computer Science at Massachusetts Institute of Technology (MIT) and by INRIA and Keio University, with support from the Defense Advanced Research Projects Agency (DARPA) and the European Commission. W3C promotes standards for the Internet's World Wide Web (WWW).

World Wide Web (WWW)

An Internet protocol that enables users to search, access, and download information from a worldwide series of networked servers where information is dynamically interlinked. A Web client passes a user's request for information to a server, usually by way of a Web browser. The server and client communicate through a transfer protocol, usually the Hypertext Transfer Protocol (HTTP). The server then accesses a Web page by using a Uniform Resource Locator (URL). Search engines are available to simplify access by enabling users to enter search criteria on a topic and have several URLs returned for Web pages that pertain to the desired information. The number of available Web pages has grown from a few thousand in 1989 to several million today.

Write Once, Read Many (WORM)
An optical disc on which information can be recorded only once, but can be read and reread many times. This medium has a high-storage capacity suitable for archiving large amounts of information unlikely to change.

write-protect
To protect the information on a disk, file, or other medium against being overwritten. Methods include physically covering part of a floppy disk (or closing a notch) or issuing file commands.

Write right
A directory, file, and property access right in NetWare or IntranetWare that grants the right to open and write to files, and grants the right to add, change, or remove any values of a Novell Directory Services (NDS) property.

write-back cache
A disk-caching technique that either waits a specified length of time for a drop-in system load or waits for that drop to occur before writing information out to disk. A write-back cache improves hard-disk throughput by waiting until several disk writes can be made at the same time.

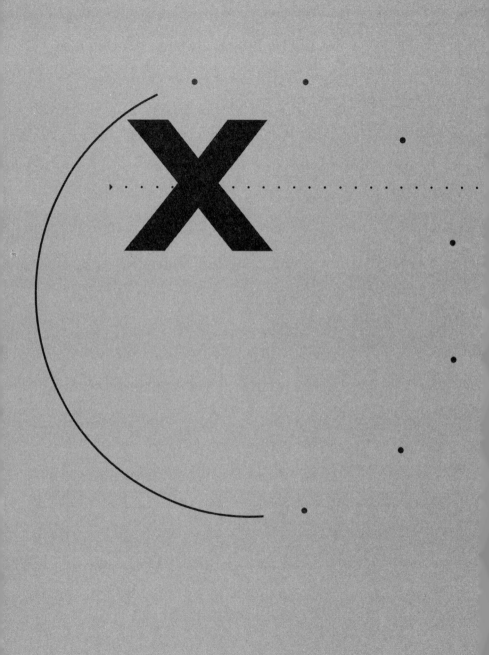

X display Manager Control Protocol (XDMCP)

A protocol used by all X terminals to communicate with workstations on a UNIX network.

X Terminal

A Graphical User Interface (GUI) that enables a user to open numerous windows and to perform multitasking operations on a UNIX system.

X Window System

A standard set of display-handling routines for UNIX workstations that enable the creation of hardware-independent Graphical User Interface (GUI) applications. The X Window System is a network-transparent, distributed system. An implementation from the Open Software Foundation (OSF) is known as *Motif*. An implementation from Sun Microsystems and Hewlett-Packard is known as *OpenLook*.

X.3

A standard from the Consultative Committee for International Telegraphy and Telephony (CCITT) that defines various parameters for a packet assembler/disassembler (PAD).

X.21

A standard from the Consultative Committee for International Telegraphy and Telephony (CCITT) that defines a protocol for communications between a circuit-switched network and user devices. This standard describes the electrical connections, the transmission protocol, error detection and correction, and other aspects of the link. The X.25 standard parallels the Physical Layer (Layer 1), the Data Link Layer (Layer 2), and the Network Layer (Layer 3) of the OSI Reference Model.

X.25

A standard from the Consultative Committee for International Telegraphy and Telephony (CCITT) that defines how messages are encoded for transmission of electronic mail (e-mail) and graphics between dissimilar computers and terminals, as well as the contents for an electronic address and how the electronic envelope should appear. Users of an X.25 network contract with common carriers to use a packet-switched network and are charged for time on the network.

X.28

A standard from the Consultative Committee for International Telegraphy and Telephony (CCITT) that defines the interface between Data Terminal Equipment (DTE) or Data Communications Equipment (DCE) and a packet assembler/disassembler (PAD) in a public data network.

X.29

A standard from the Consultative Committee for International Telegraphy and Telephony (CCITT) that defines the interface between a computer and a packet assembler/disassembler (PAD).

X.75

A standard from the Consultative Committee for International Telegraphy and Telephony (CCITT) that defines the interface between two packet-switched networks.

X.400

A standard from the Consultative Committee for International Telegraphy and Telephony (CCITT) and Open Systems Interconnection (OSI) that defines a public or private international electronic mail (e-mail) Message Handling System (MHS). This standard specifies how messages are transferred across the network or between two or more heterogeneous networks, as well as the rules to follow when converting messages between transmission types (such as text and fax). Table X.1 shows the major components that make up the Message Handling System (MHS) specified in X.400.

TABLE X.I	X.400 Components

COMPONENT	DESCRIPTION
Access Unit (AU)	A process providing a gateway between the MTS and other services.
Message Store (MS)	An archive for storing messages until they can be forwarded to their destinations.
Message Transfer Agent (MTA)	A component of the MTS providing message forwarding to other MTAs or to the destination entity (such as an MS, UA, AU, or PDAU).
Message Transfer System (MTS)	A process providing message transfer between users.
Physical Delivery Access Unit (PDAU)	A special AU providing a gateway between the MTS and services that involve physical delivery.
User Agent (UA)	An application process providing access to the MTS.

X.500

A standard from the Consultative Committee for International Telegraphy and Telephony (CCITT) and Open Systems Interconnection (OSI) that defines a means for locating electronic mail (e-mail) users. This standard is similar to a telephone book.

X/Open

An independent international organization founded in 1984 to develop an open, multivendor Common Applications Environment (CAE) on the basis of the interfaces defined by the Institute of Electrical and Electronic Engineers (IEEE) and extended to cover additional open systems requirements. Novell turned over control of the UNIX operating system to X/Open in 1995.

X3T9.5

A number assigned to the Task Group of Accredited Standards Committee for an internal working document on the Fiber Distributed Data Interface (FDDI).

xB/tB Encoding

A term used to describe data-transmission schemes that serve as a preliminary to telecommunications or network signal encoding. Common translation schemes include 4B/5B, 5B/6B, and 8B/10B.

Xerox Network Systems (XNS)

A multilayer communications protocol originally developed by Xerox that supports a distributed file system in which users can access the files on other computers and can access printers as if they were local. Novell's Internetwork Packet Exchange (IPX) is a variation of XNS, although they use different Ethernet encapsulation formats and IPX uses a proprietary Service Advertisement Protocol (SAP).

Xmodem

A file-transfer protocol that divides data into blocks consisting of a start-of-header character, a block number, 128 bytes of data, and an error-checking mechanism. An Xmodem-CRC version offers cyclical redundancy check (CRC) capabilities to detect transmission errors.

XO bit

The third bit in a Control Information (CI) byte found in an AppleTalk Transfer Protocol (ATP) packet header that, when set, indicates a request for an exactly once (XO) transaction.

XON/XOFF

An asynchronous communications flow-control protocol that prevents a sending system from transmitting data faster than a receiving system can accept it. The receiving computer sends an XOFF control character to pause the transmission of data when the buffer becomes full, and then sends an XON character when it is ready to continue with the transmission.

Xpress Transfer Protocol (XTP)

A lightweight protocol designed as an alternative for traditional routing and transport protocols on high-speed networks. The protocol is streamlined through its packet structure and transmission, error-correction, and control strategies.

XRemote

A protocol that enables serial communications for an X Window System network.

xwais

A version of the Wide Area Information Service (WAIS) designed to run under the X Window System on a UNIX computer.

Yellow Pages Directory

A term used to describe an online directory of businesses or services. Thousands of such directories exist on the Internet and range from directories categorized by geographical regions to those categorized by special interest groups.

Ymodem

A file-transfer protocol that divides data into blocks that consist of a start-of-header character, a block number, 1K of data, and an error-checking mechanism. A variation of Xmodem, Ymodem also provides the capability to send multiple files in the same session and abort file transfer during a transmission.

Your Mileage May Vary (YMMV)

A cautionary note included in some Usenet newsgroup postings or other electronic mail (e-mail) messages that indicates the reader may not get the same results as the author of the posting or message.

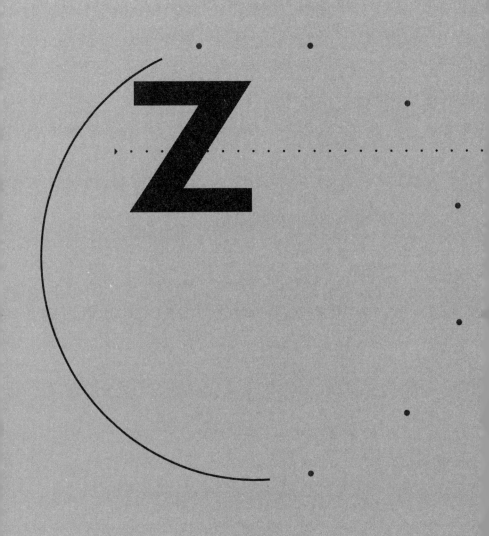

zero code suppression
A coding scheme in which a 1 is substituted in the seventh bit of a string of eight consecutive zeros.

Zero Delay Lockout (ZDL)
A technology designed to prevent beaconing stations in a Token Ring network from inserting into the ring and, thus, causing network problems.

zero-slot LAN
A local area network (LAN) that uses existing serial and parallel communications ports on computers rather than requiring Network Interface Cards (NICs). Transmissions on existing ports are inherently slower than through NICs and the maximum cable length between workstations is severely limited. Zero-slot LANs are limited to two or three network nodes.

zero-wait-state computer
A computer that processes information without going through clock cycles, during which no instructions are executed because the processor is waiting for data from a device or from memory (called *wait states*).

ZIP file
A file whose contents have been compressed using the PKZIP, WinZip, or compatible program. A ZIP file can contain one compressed file or several compressed files. Decompression requires either the PKZIP, WinZip, or compatible program, or that the file was compressed into a self-extracting archive that decompresses when its icon is double-clicked or when its name is entered at the command line.

Zmodem
A file-transfer protocol that divides data into blocks, designed to handle larger data transfers than either Xmodem or Ymodem, which also includes checkpoint restart (a feature allowing an interrupted transmission to resume at the point of interruption).

zone

An arbitrary group of nodes in an AppleTalk network that provides the capability to divide the network into smaller divisions. When a node connects to the network, it is automatically assigned to a zone. Zones are assigned names (which can be as many as 32 characters long) that are converted to addresses on the network by the Name Binding protocol (NBP) and are exchanged with the Zone Information Protocol (ZIP). All zone names and addresses are kept in a zone information table within each router.

Zone Information Protocol (ZIP)

A protocol in the AppleTalk protocol suite that enables each router to maintain and access zone information for a network and that enables nonrouter nodes on the network to obtain zone information.

Zone Information Socket (ZIS)

A socket on an AppleTalk network associated with Zone Information Protocol (ZIP) services.

Zone Information Table (ZIT)

A table in an AppleTalk network that contains the mappings of network numbers to zones, maintained by each router in the network.

zones list

A list that includes up to 255 unique zone names.

IDG BOOKS WORLDWIDE REGISTRATION CARD

Visit our
Web site at
http://www.idgbooks.com

IDG
BOOKS
WORLDWIDE
THE WORLD OF
COMPUTER

ISBN Number: 0-7645-4528-0
Title of this book: **Novell's Dictionary of Networking**

My overall rating of this book:
❑ Very good [1]   ❑ Good [2]   ❑ Satisfactory [3]   ❑ Fair [4]   ❑ Poor [5]

How I first heard about this book:
❑ Found in bookstore; name: [6]
❑ Book review: [7]
❑ Advertisement: [8]
❑ Catalog: [9]
❑ Word of mouth; heard about book from friend, co-worker, etc.: [10]
❑ Other: [11]

What I liked most about this book:

What I would change, add, delete, etc., in future editions of this book:

Other comments:

Number of computer books I purchase in a year: ❑ 1 [12] ❑ 2-5 [13] ❑ 6-10 [14] ❑ More than 10 [15]

I would characterize my computer skills as: ❑ Beginner [16] ❑ Intermediate [17] ❑ Advanced [18] ❑ Professional [19]

I use ❑ DOS [20] ❑ Windows [21] ❑ OS/2 [22] ❑ Unix [23] ❑ Macintosh [24] ❑ Other: [25]_____
                                                                    (please specify)

I would be interested in new books on the following subjects:
(please check all that apply, and use the spaces provided to identify specific software)

❑ Word processing: [26]   ❑ Spreadsheets: [27]
❑ Data bases: [28]   ❑ Desktop publishing: [29]
❑ File Utilities: [30]   ❑ Money management: [31]
❑ Networking: [32]   ❑ Programming languages: [33]
❑ Other: [34]

I use a PC at (please check all that apply): ❑ home [35] ❑ work [36] ❑ school [37] ❑ other: [38] _____
The disks I prefer to use are ❑ 5.25 [39]   ❑ 3.5 [40]   ❑ other: [41]_____

I have a CD ROM: ❑ yes [42]   ❑ no [43]

I plan to buy or upgrade computer hardware this year: ❑ yes [44]   ❑ no [45]

I plan to buy or upgrade computer software this year: ❑ yes [46]   ❑ no [47]

Name: Business title: [48]
Type of Business: [49]
Address (❑ home [50] ❑ work [51]/Company name:
Street/Suite#
City [52]/State [53]/Zip code [54]:   Country [55]

❑ **I liked this book!**
   You may quote me by name in future IDG Books Worldwide promotional materials.
   My daytime phone number is _____

❏ YES!

Please keep me informed about IDG Books Worldwide's World of Computer Knowledge. Send me your latest catalog.

BESTSELLING
BOOK SERIES
FROM IDG

Macworld®
Books

TECHNICAL BOOKS

‖‖‖‖‖

NO POSTAGE
NECESSARY
IF MAILED
IN THE
UNITED STATES

BUSINESS REPLY MAIL
FIRST CLASS MAIL   PERMIT NO. 2605   FOSTER CITY, CALIFORNIA

IDG Books Worldwide
919 E Hillsdale Blvd, Ste 400
Foster City, CA 94404-9691